THE MEN
WILL TALK
TO ME

Mayo Interviews
by Ernie O'Malley

KILCORMAC

2 8 APR 2023

WITHDRAWN

There were 4 Brigades in Mayo in 1916. You had better check on what I saw with Dick Walsh and Ned Moan. We had planned in 1913 to unite [...] about starting an Irish army. [...]

A page from the Michael Kilroy interview.
(UCDA O'Malley Notebooks P17b/101, p. 39.
Courtesy of UCD Archives)

THE MEN WILL TALK TO ME

MAYO INTERVIEWS
BY ERNIE O'MALLEY

EDITED BY
CORMAC K. H. O'MALLEY AND
VINCENT KEANE

MERCIER PRESS
IRISH PUBLISHER – IRISH STORY

Dedicated to the men and women of Mayo
who served their country

MERCIER PRESS
Cork
www.mercierpress.ie

© Original notebooks of Ernie O'Malley, UCD Archives
© Preface: Cormac K. H. O'Malley, 2014
© Introduction: Vincent Keane, 2014
© Footnotes: Cormac K. H. O'Malley and Vincent Keane, 2014

ISBN: 978 1 78117 206 3

10 9 8 7 6 5 4 3 2 1

A CIP record for this title is available from the British Library

Printed and bound in the EU.

CONTENTS

Acknowledgements — 7

Abbreviations — 11

Preface — 13

Chronology of Events Impacting Co. Mayo and
Its Brigades, 1918–24 — 19

Introduction — 29

West Mayo — 35

    Michael Kilroy — 35

    Paddy Cannon — 73

    Paddy Duffy — 96

    Tommy Heavey — 118

    Broddie Malone — 163

South Mayo — 208

    Tom Maguire — 208

North Mayo — 228

    Matt Kilcawley — 228

    P. J. Ruttledge — 264

East Mayo — 282

    Johnny Grealy — 282

    Tom Carney — 303

**Short Biographical Sketches of Men Referenced
  in Footnotes**   329

Bibliography   333

Index   335

ACKNOWLEDGEMENTS

Foremost in this endeavour to facilitate greater public access to the Ernie O'Malley Military Notebook Interviews have been Seamus Helferty, Principal Archivist, and his staff at the University College Dublin Archives, the keepers of the Ernie O'Malley Archives since 1974. This series of volumes could not have been started without their support and backing over these past few years. They shared the vision.

Many people have helped unstintingly along the journey to transcribe some of the more than 450 handwritten interviews of survivors of the War of Independence and Civil War. Special thanks should be given to Eunan O'Halpin at Trinity College Dublin's Institute for Contemporary History, who facilitated a one-day seminar on this transcription process back in 2009.

In terms of this Mayo volume, it could not have been undertaken but for the noble assistance of Dominic Price, initially, and Vincent Keane, subsequently. Dominic undertook the initial transcription of most of these Mayo interviews; those who also assisted with initial transcriptions were Frances-Mary Blake for Michael Kilroy, Roddy Ryan for his grandfather P. J. Ruttledge, and Cormac Ó Comhraí with one interview, parts of which were included in *The Men Will Talk to Me: Galway Interviews by Ernie O'Malley*, which he and I co-edited. Vincent Keane has assisted greatly with his extensive local knowledge of people and places in Mayo, which is essential to getting facts and locations accurately recorded. A project like this needs local lore, and Vincent undertook this task professionally and generously, and truly this volume could not have been completed without him.

For photographs, copyright and other permissions we are

indebted to Anthony Leonard, who provided photographs by his grandfather, J. J. Leonard; Seamus Grealy for his father, Johnny Grealy; Robert Ryan for his grandfather, P. J. Ruttledge; Micky Kilcawley for his father, Matt Kilcawley; Mary Maguire McMonagle for her father, Tom Maguire; Dr Pádraig Carney and Pádraig Walsh for Tom Carney; James Reddiough and Lew Thorne for the Swinford IRA Training Camp photograph, as well as to Mercier Press for their marvellous archive collection.

Other people have helped on specific questions: Tim Horgan, Bronach Joyce and Aidan Clarke of the Westport Historical Society, Johanna Kilcawley McGrath, Anthony Leonard, Anne McMonagle, Rosa Meehan, Eve Morrison, Cormac Ó Comhraí and Kitty O'Malley. I would also like to thank Dominic Price for his general support over many years, Kathleen Hegarty Thorne and Lew Thorne for moral support and comments on the chronology, Pádraig Walsh, and many others. I thank my family for their support in this endeavour: my wife, Moira, and children, Bergin and Conor O'Malley, and Bergin's husband, David Boyle, all of whom have been so supportive on the technical side.

Thanks must also be given to Mary Feehan of Mercier Press, along with her highly supportive staff, for agreeing to publish this volume as the third in this series of interviews.

CORMAC O'MALLEY

As this is a history with a difference and the work was already done by Ernie O'Malley back in the 1950s, it was just a case of identifying dates and strange place names, and providing short biographical notes on various individuals. My main source of information was the public libraries. The research section of the Castlebar Public Library provided me with much of what I was seeking and I extend my thanks to the staff there. Marguerite, in Westport Public Library, made some phone calls for me when I sought information regarding the North Mayo Brigade from Ballina Library. The librarians in Sligo also helped out when I was researching the Enniscrone area.

When seeking information about the Kilmeena ambush, I attended the annual ceremony at the Republican plot in Myna and was introduced to several interesting people there. I met relatives of Patrick Marley (killed accidentally at Rockfield), and Jim Browne and Pat Staunton (killed at Glenhest and Kilmeena respectively). Also in attendance was Peadar Kilroy, son of Michael, and he put me right about where Jim Moran came from. The Hughes sisters of Ballina were made known to me and told me of their father, Michael, who was injured but escaped that fateful day at Kilmeena. Hugh Feehan of Rossow was there too and had some interesting snippets of information regarding events in the Kilmeena area. Liam Ryder, always enthusiastic about national events, helped in identifying some of the townlands that were proving problematic.

In the Islandeady district I enlisted the help of Paddy Browne of Derrycourane. Paddy has an encyclopaedic mind, and he brought me around the area pointing out the Big Wall, the spot where Thomas Lally and Thomas O'Malley were killed, Driminahaha RIC Barracks, and the house where Paddy Jordan lived. Paddy knew, and was a friend of, Paddy Cannon, whose interview is included in this book. He actually got to fire some rounds from Cannon's famous Mauser rifle.

In Westport, over the months, I spoke to relations of men who were on active service in 1920–24. It was all very informal and I gleaned much information then. Ger Geraghty provided background information on his grand-uncle, Joe Ring. Patsy Staunton told me of his uncle, Michael 'Bully' Staunton, and how he emigrated to Chicago, never to return. Maureen Lambert, niece of 'Broddie' Malone, provided essential dates. Richie Joyce gave me information on his Uncle Rick, a member of the West Mayo Brigade flying column. Liamy MacNally gave me interesting facts on his grand-uncle, Willie Malone. Pádraig Kennedy was always available to tell of his uncle, Ned Sammon, quartermaster of the Westport Battalion during the Truce and Civil War. Dave Keating looked up information for me regarding the Sligo brigades. I also wish to thank Harry Hughes, who was always ready to impart relevant information for this project. A sincere thanks to all mentioned.

Lastly, I wish to thank Cormac O'Malley for inviting me to participate in this venture. It was a pleasure to be involved with the work of Ernie O'Malley.

VINCENT KEANE

Abbreviations

ASU	Active Service Unit or Flying Column
Auxie/Auxies	Auxiliary Division of the RIC
Capt.	Captain
C/S	Chief of Staff
EOM	Ernie O'Malley
GAA	Gaelic Athletic Association
GHQ	General Headquarters
IRA	Irish Republican Army
IRB	Irish Republican Brotherhood
the Joy	Mountjoy Gaol, Dublin
Lt	Lieutenant
O/C	Officer Commanding
PA	Póilíní Airm or Military Police
RIC	Royal Irish Constabulary
Tintown 1, 2	Tintown internment camps No. 1 and No. 2
UCDA	UCD Archives
V/C	Vice-Commanding Officer

Map showing counties, brigade areas and areas
of the four Western Divisions.

Preface

Introducing the Ernie O'Malley Military Interviews

Cormac K. H. O'Malley

Though born in Castlebar, Co. Mayo, in 1897, Ernie O'Malley moved to Dublin with his family in 1906 and attended CBS secondary school and university there. After the 1916 Rising he joined the Irish Volunteers while pursuing his medical studies, but in late 1917 he left home and went on the run. He rose through the ranks of the Volunteers and later the Irish Republican Army, and by the time of the Truce in July 1921 at the end of the War of Independence, or Tan War as it was known, he was a commandant-general commanding the 2nd Southern Division covering parts of three counties and with over 7,000 men under him.

O'Malley was suspicious of a compromise being made during the peace negotiations which resulted in the Anglo-Irish Treaty of December 1921 and reacted strongly against the Treaty when it was announced. As the split developed in the senior ranks of the IRA in early 1922, he was appointed director of organisation for the anti-Treaty Republicans who then took over the Four Courts in April. When the Four Courts garrison surrendered in June, he managed to escape. He was then appointed acting assistant chief of staff and officer commanding the Northern and Eastern Divisions, or half of Ireland. In early November he was captured in a dramatic shoot-out and was severely wounded. Ironically his wounds probably saved his life, as otherwise he would have been court-martialled and executed. While in Mountjoy Gaol in

1923, O'Malley was elected as a TD and later, despite his poor health, he went on a forty-one-day hunger strike. Nevertheless, he survived – a matter of mind over body!

Having been released from prison in July 1924 and still in poor health, O'Malley went abroad to the south of Europe to help recover his health. He later returned to his medical studies in 1926, but in 1928 headed for the United States. While there he began to write his much acclaimed autobiographical memoir, *On Another Man's Wound*, published in 1936 after he returned to Dublin. He had spent seven years writing that book, which he meant to be more of a generic story of the Irish struggle than of his own activities. It was deemed to be a literary success and added to his reputation among many of his former comrades.

O'Malley's memoir on the Civil War was not ready for publication, requiring more work, and over the next twenty years he sought to become more familiar with the Civil War period as a whole. What started out in the late 1930s as an effort to supplement his own lack of knowledge, had developed by 1948 into a full-blown enterprise to record the voices, mostly Republican, of the survivors of the 1916–23 struggle for independence. He interviewed more than 450 survivors, across a broad spectrum of people, by himself, covering the Tan War and the Civil War – all this at a time when the government was establishing the Bureau of Military History to record statements made by participants in the fight for freedom.

In the course of his interviews O'Malley collected a vast amount of local lore around Ireland. He wrote a series of articles for *The Kerryman*, but withdrew them. Instead he used the articles for a series of talks on Radio Éireann in 1953. Subsequently the lectures were published in a series called *Raids and Rallies* in *The Sunday Press* in 1955–56. In the meantime he used the interviews to add to his own Civil War memoir, *The Singing Flame*, published posthumously in 1978, and to write a biographical memoir of a local Longford Republican organiser, Seán Connolly, entitled *Rising Out: Seán Connolly of Longford, 1890–1921,* also published posthumously, in 2007.

O'Malley was familiar with the field of folklore and was well read in Irish and international folklore traditions, and indeed in the early 1940s had collected folklore stories from around his home area in Clew Bay, Co. Mayo. He also picked up ballads and stories about the 1916–23 period. His method for interviewing was to write rapidly in a first series of notebooks as his informant was speaking and then to rewrite those notes into a second series of more coherent notebooks. Occasionally he would include drawings of the site of an ambush or an attack on a barracks. In the rewrite process he added in his own comments in parentheses. Given his overall knowledge of the period, based on his own Tan War activities and his Civil War responsibilities, he usually commanded a high regard from his informants. He felt that his former comrades would talk to him and tell him the truth.

From an examination of his interviews, O'Malley does not appear to have used a consistent technique, but rather he allowed his informant to ramble and cover many topics. In his rewrite of an interview he often labelled sections such as Tan War, Truce, Civil War, Gaols, Treatment of Prisoners, RIC, IRB, Spies, Round-ups and the like. The tone is conversational, allowing the narrative to unfold. He wrote down the names of people and places phonetically rather than accurately. The interviews are fresh and frank and many of these men's stories may have never been told even to their children, as they did not speak openly about those times. Family members have said they could hear the voices of their relatives speaking through the O'Malley interviews, because O'Malley had been able to capture their intonations and phrasing so clearly about matters never discussed in the family before.

This present volume reveals ten O'Malley interviews that

cover activities in far-flung corners of Mayo, and neighbouring parts of Roscommon and Sligo, during the War of Independence and the Civil War. All of these Mayo men rejected the Treaty and so their interviews reflect strong Republican opinions among the Mayo Volunteers. Only three of the men interviewed here made statements to the Bureau of Military History.

In transcribing O'Malley's series of interviews some modest changes have been made to help the reader better understand the interview. To enable reference to O'Malley's original pagination, his pages are referred to in bold brackets, such as **[39R]**, the L or R representing the left or right side of his original page. Unclear words have been put in italics indicating our best attempt to decipher them. The sequence of some interviews has been changed to better reflect the historical chronology, but the original pagination has been noted and in most cases where this has been done it is also footnoted. Some interviews had two men speaking and they are clearly identified. Abbreviations have been standardised and many of them have been expanded to the full word, such as Battalion or Brigade for Bn or Bde. Extensive footnotes provide a better understanding of the people, places and incidents involved, and some are repeated in a subsequent chapter to allow each chapter to be read separately as a complete story. The text has been revised to include the correct spellings for names and places, and the original spellings, usually written phonetically by O'Malley, have been included in the footnotes at their first appearance in each interview. O'Malley regularly inserted his own comments inside parentheses, and these are reflected in the current text. Our editorial comments have been added in square brackets. Some new headings and subheadings with dates have also been included in square brackets for clarity.

Each interview has been reproduced here almost in full. Certain parts can be difficult to read as O'Malley left many blank spaces where he was missing information, and these are represented by ellipses in the text, but this sometimes means that the sentence makes little or no sense. Ellipses have also been used to indicate places where the text is indecipherable. The style of local phrasing used in the interviews has been retained, some of which is no longer in common usage and may read strangely to the modern reader. In many instances names and facts have been added in a seemingly random manner to the text and their relevance to the discussion can be difficult to ascertain. However, we felt it was important to maintain the integrity of the original text, so these problems have been left unedited.

We have relied on the integrity of O'Malley's knowledge of facts and his ability to question and ascertain the 'truth', but clearly it is possible that the details as related here to O'Malley reflect only the perceptions of the individual informant rather than the absolute historical truth, and the reader must appreciate this important aspect.

O'Malley interviewed some men several times, and thus the same incident may be recorded more than once. The duplications have been included as they illustrate clearly how a memory by the same person about the same incident may differ at different times, especially if another person is present. O'Malley made far more comments in these Mayo interviews than in the other volumes, some of them quite critical, perhaps because though he was not actually involved in any of these activities, he had heard so much about the Mayo stories over the years.

For those not familiar with military organisational structures such as the IRA during this period, it might be helpful to know that the largest unit was a division, which consisted of several brigades, each of which had several battalions, which in turn were composed of several companies at the local level. There were usually staff functions, such as intelligence and quartermaster roles, at the division, brigade and battalion level, and usually only officers at the company level.

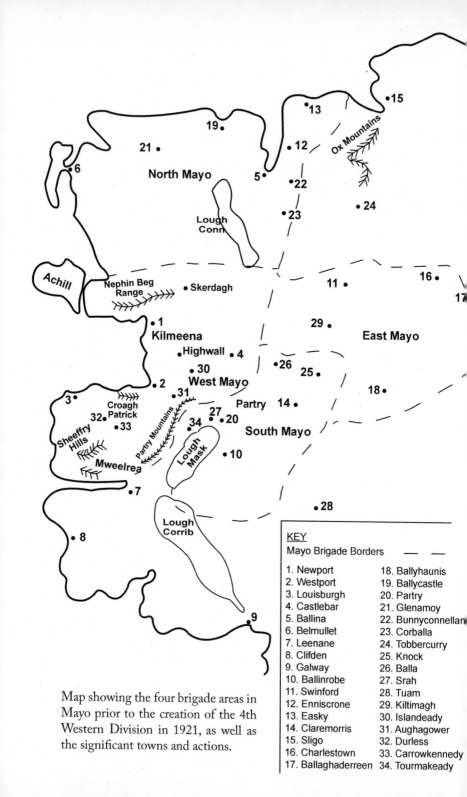

KEY

Mayo Brigade Borders — — —

1. Newport
2. Westport
3. Louisburgh
4. Castlebar
5. Ballina
6. Belmullet
7. Leenane
8. Clifden
9. Galway
10. Ballinrobe
11. Swinford
12. Enniscrone
13. Easky
14. Claremorris
15. Sligo
16. Charlestown
17. Ballaghaderreen
18. Ballyhaunis
19. Ballycastle
20. Partry
21. Glenamoy
22. Bunnyconnellan
23. Corballa
24. Tobbercurry
25. Knock
26. Balla
27. Srah
28. Tuam
29. Kiltimagh
30. Islandeady
31. Aughagower
32. Durless
33. Carrowkennedy
34. Tourmakeady

Map showing the four brigade areas in Mayo prior to the creation of the 4th Western Division in 1921, as well as the significant towns and actions.

Chronology of Events Impacting Co. Mayo and Its Brigades, 1918–24

Note: Actions in brigade areas are denoted by N=North, S=South, E=East, W=West.

1918

Apr.   Conscription Crisis – the proposal that conscription be introduced to Ireland is vigorously opposed.

May 17   Many prominent Republican leaders arrested because of the so-called 'German Plot'.

Nov. 11   Armistice Day; assault on Westport citizens by the RIC and the British Army.

Dec. 14   All four Mayo constituencies return Sinn Féin TDs in the general election. E: É. de Valera, N: Dr J. Crowley, S: W. Sears, W: J. MacBride.

1919

Mar. 29   W: Westport: John C. Milling, resident magistrate, killed.

Apr. 14   W: Sinn Féin Club in Westport closed by the RIC.

1920

Apr. 3   W: Easter burning of tax offices and RIC barracks after their evacuation around Ireland includes Deergrove/Driminahaha, Cloontumper and Carrowkennedy Hut.

Apr. 4   E: Ballyhaunis: IRA attack RIC patrol, two wounded.

Apr. 20   N: Bellacorick Barracks burned (attack led by Paddy Hegarty, Seán Corcoran).

May 12   E: Bohola Barracks burned (attack led by Seán Corcoran, M. Mooney, Tom Ruane).

June	N: Cloongee House, Foxford, raided for arms.
June	E: Ambush on two lorries of soldiers at Swinford – no casualties.
June 4	Mayo County Council local elections: Dr John Madden, Tom Maguire, Ned Moane, P. J. Ruttledge and twenty-four others win a clean sweep for Sinn Féin.
June 15	N: Belmullet RIC Constable Pierce Doogue killed.
July	At Castlebar the decision is made to create four Mayo brigades: West (O/C Tom Derrig), North (O/C Tom Ruane), East (O/C Seán Corcoran), and South (O/C Tom Maguire).
July 1	N: Culleens RIC Barracks attacked.
July 17	E: Swinford: IRA ambush 2nd Border Regiment patrol, both soldiers wounded.
July 22	N: Ballina: IRA attack RIC patrol: RIC Sgt Thomas R. Armstrong fatally wounded; Constable Regan seriously wounded.
Aug. 1	E: Near Ballyhaunis, IRA attack lorry of soldiers, three wounded.
Aug. 19	E: Swinford Railroad Relay Supply Station destroyed.
Aug. 22	E: Ballyvary Barracks attacked (led by Seán Corcoran and Seán Walsh).
Aug. 30	N: Enniscrone Coast Guard Station attacked and burned.
Aug. 30	N: Belmullet Coast Guard Station, Ballyglass, raided and destroyed.
Aug./Sep.	W: Tom Derrig arrested and M. Kilroy succeeds him as O/C West Mayo Brigade.
Nov.	P. J. Ruttledge arrested.

1921

Jan. 9	N: Beckett's Mill, Ballina, attacked by RIC; Patrick Coleman captured.
Jan. 24	Archbishop of Tuam, Dr T. P. Gilmartin, condemns the IRA.
Mar. 7	S: At Kilfaul, near Partry, a number of soldiers are

wounded (Capt. Chatfield, Corporal Bell, Privates Wade and Southworth) and one is killed by an ASU of the South Mayo Brigade.

Mar. 7 S: IRA carry out the Portroyal ambush on the Ballinrobe–Castlebar road.

Mar. 15 W: IRA attempt ambush at Gloshpatrick, near Westport.

Mar. 22 W: In the first IRA ambush at Carrowkennedy on an RIC patrol, on the Westport–Leenane road, RIC Sgt J. Coughlan is fatally wounded and Constables Maguire, Love and Creeden are wounded.

Mar. 26 W: RIC reprisal in Westport for IRA's Carrowkennedy ambush.

Mar. 29 E: IRA man James Mulrennan, wounded at Kilmovee.
E: RIC Constable William H. Stephens killed in Ballyhaunis.

Apr. N: Easky RIC Barracks attacked.

Apr. 1 E: IRA man Seán Corcoran killed at Crossard, Ballyhaunis, and Maurice Mullins arrested. IRA man Michael Coen killed at Lecarrow, Ballyhaunis.

Apr. 3 E: Charlestown bank raid.

Apr. 3 N: IRA attack a motor patrol at Bunnyconnellan, near Ballina and one RIC man is wounded.

Apr. 3 N: RIC capture IRA ammunition dump near Ballina.

Apr. 5 E: Two spies shot by the IRA at Loughglynn.

Apr. 15 N: IRA ambush RIC patrol in Bridge Street, Ballina, wounding two RIC men. This is followed by RIC/Tan reprisals.

Apr. 19 E: RIC raid in Loughglynn, where IRA men John Bergin and Stephen MacDermot are captured and executed, and Matt Kilcawley arrested.

Apr. 23 W: IRA attack RIC motor patrol at Clogher – no casualties.

May 3 S: IRA ambush RIC lorry at Tourmakeady, killing RIC Constables Christopher P. O'Regan, Herbert Oakes, William Power and John Regan, and wounding Lt

Ibberson and two others. Adjutant Michael O'Brien and Scout Pádraig Feeney, IRA, are killed and Tom Maguire wounded.

May 6   W: Big or High Wall ambush near Islandeady Dance Hall, where a high wall separates the road from the railway. Thomas O'Malley, and Thomas Lally of the IRA are killed and Frank O'Boyle and James MacNulty are wounded and captured.

May 8   W: IRA attack a patrol at the Red (Railway) Bridge, Westport, wounding five RIC men.

May 9   S: RIC Constable Thomas Hopkins on home leave is killed at Leface, Ballindine.

May 17   E: Ballaghaderreen RIC Barracks attacked from train.

May 18   W: RIC Sergeant Francis J. Butler killed in Newport and another RIC man wounded.

May 19   W: IRA ambush RIC lorries at Kilmeena. John Collins, Seamus MacEvilly, Thomas O'Donnell and John Pat Staunton of the IRA are killed and Paddy Jordan is wounded and dies shortly afterwards. John Cannon, Paddy Mulloy, Thomas Nolan, Paddy O'Malley and John Pierce are captured. Constable Harry Beckett, RIC, is killed and Head Constable Potter wounded.

May 22   E: Kilmovee RIC Barracks attacked by the IRA.

May 23   W: Skerdagh engagement after retreat from Kilmeena. Constable Joseph Maguire, RIC, is killed and DI James Munro wounded; Jim Browne, IRA, is killed.

May 23   N: Foxford Barracks attacked.

May 24   N: RIC District Inspector White attacked in Ballina. General election provides a clean sweep for Sinn Féin candidates: N/W Mayo: J. Crowley, T. Derrig, J. MacBride, P. J. Ruttledge; S. Mayo/Roscommon: T. Maguire, H. Boland, W. Sears, D. O'Rourke; E. Mayo/Sligo: F. Ferran, T. O'Donnell, A. McCabe, S. Devins and F. Carty.

May 25   N: At Bunree, near Ballina, IRA man James Howley (Enniscrone) is wounded and dies later.

May 27   E: At Aghamore, Ballyhaunis, IRA man Paddy Boland is killed.

June 1   W: Drummin RIC Barracks burned after evacuation.

June 2   W: Second Carrowkennedy ambush. The IRA attack RIC patrol lorries, killing District Inspector Edward J. Stevenson, Sgt Francis Creegan, Constables Sydney Blythe, James Browne, John Doherty, Thomas Dowling and William French, and wounding four constables. There are no IRA casualties.

June 2–July 11   W: Massive round-up by RIC/British Army after the Carrowkennedy ambush.

June 16   E: Ballyhaunis RIC Barracks attacked by the IRA.

June 22   N: Clydagh, Ballina. In an exchange of fire with the RIC Tom Nealon (Aughoose) is killed and Éamonn Gannon, O/C North Mayo IRA, Pat Bourke, Bartley Hegarty, Anthony Farrell, Tom Loftus and his father (all on the local IRA staff) are captured.

July 1   N: IRA raid on Tuffy's Post Office in Culleens. In Glenesk RIC Constables Thomas Higgins and John King are captured and killed and two other RIC men are wounded, while two IRA men are killed.

July 7   N: RIC Sgt Anthony Foody's body is found at Caralavin, near Bunnyconnellan with a note stating 'Revenge for O'Dwyer'.

July 11   Truce between the IRA and British forces comes into effect.

Aug./Sep.   Four Western Divisions are formed. O/Cs are 1st: Michael Brennan, 2nd: Tom Maguire, 3rd: Liam Pilkington and 4th: Michael Kilroy.

Sep./Oct.   IRA training camps established in Ballycarran, Belmullet, Clydagh, Enniscrone, Nephin and Swinford.

Oct. 5   W: Westport Workhouse taken over by the IRA.

Dec. 6   Anglo-Irish Treaty signed. Westport meeting for the return of the IRA internees.

1922

(terms: FSA = Free State army; IRA = anti-Treaty Republicans)

Jan. 7 Dáil Éireann approves the Treaty.

Jan. 16 IRA raid an RIC barracks in Charlestown for guns; Sgt McGovern is wounded.

Jan. 17 Swinford Barracks attacked by the IRA.

Feb. 2 Ballinrobe and Claremorris Barracks taken over by the IRA.

Feb. 14 Castlebar and Ballina Barracks taken over by the IRA.

Mar. 4 Swinford Barracks taken over by the IRA.

Mar. 8–10 Limerick stand-down: FSA troops under Michael Brennan retire, leaving the city in the hands of Ernie O'Malley's anti-Treaty troops.

Spring Michael Collins sets up a rifle-swap plan to help arm the Catholic community in the North with guns not traceable back to the new southern authorities.

Apr. 1 Castlebar pro-Treaty election rally, where Michael Collins is heckled by anti-Treaty supporters.

Apr. 13 W: Joe Ring, FSA, arrested in Westport, then released by the IRA.

Apr. 13 IRA take over the Four Courts in Dublin.

Apr. 24 FSA General Adamson killed in Athlone.

Apr. 30 FSA Comdt Simmons captured in Mayo. He is eventually released by Tom Maguire.

June 16 General election held. In Mayo N/W, Mayo S/Rosc. S, and Mayo E/Sligo eight anti-Treaty and five pro-Treaty TDs are elected. Nationally eighty-two pro-Treaty and forty-six others are elected.

June 28–30 Attack on and surrender of the Four Courts. This heralds the official start of the Civil War.

June 29 E: IRA Capt. William Moran, O/C Bohola IRA, killed; Tom Ruane, FSA, of Kiltimagh fatally wounded.

July 1 N: Boyle battle.

July 2 N: Collooney, Co. Sligo, attacked by the IRA (led by F. Carty). Michael Dockery, FSA, is killed in Boyle.

July 13   N: 'The Ballinalee', an FSA armoured car, is captured by the IRA.

July 14   N: FSA sweep of the Ox Mountains.

July 15   N: Collooney, Co. Sligo, surrendered by the IRA.

July 23   E: Claremorris Barracks burned by the IRA.

July 24   W: In Westport FSA forces led by Brigadier General Joe Ring land from the sea. Newport Barracks is destroyed by the IRA. At Glenhest, Newport, Tommy Heavey is captured.

July 25   W: Castlebar taken by the FSA.
          N: Ballina Barracks burned by the IRA.

July 29   N: The FSA takes Ballina; the IRA withdraw to the Ox Mountains.

Aug. 3   W: At Bracklagh, Newport, Sgt Lally and Pvt Deasy of the FSA are killed; Edward Hegarty, IRA, is also killed.

Aug. 4   E: Swinford Barracks captured by the IRA.

Aug. 7   E: Kiltimagh attacked.

Aug.   W: In early August Paddy Cannon is arrested.

Aug. 11   E: At Kiltimagh thirty IRA men are arrested.
          N: Near Ballina, ambush by the IRA.

Aug. 16   W: Castlebar taken by the IRA.

Aug. 21   W: IRA men Paddy Cannon, Tommy Heavey and Broddie Malone escape from Athlone Gaol.

Aug. 22   Michael Collins is killed by the IRA in Cork.

Aug. 23   S: At Brize House, Claremorris, Cannon, Heavey and Malone are recaptured.

Aug. 25   E: Tom Carney and other IRA men are captured in Ballaghaderreen.

Aug.   W: In late August IRA man Battie Cryan is captured.

Sep. 6   E: IRA James Vesey, Luke Taylor and Peter Donnelly are captured at Ballyhaunis-Kilkelly.

Sep. 12   N: The IRA launch a successful attack at Ballina.

Sep. 14   N: At Drumsheen, near Bunnyconnellan, Joe Ring, FSA, is killed and Tony Lawlor wounded.

Sep. 15–16   N: Ambushes by the IRA at Belderg/Glenamoy.

Sep. 20 N: Brian MacNeill and five others are executed by the FSA at Benbulbin, Co. Sligo.

Sep. 21 S: Tuam taken by the IRA, who then withdraw.

Sep. 22 W: Newport attacked by the IRA, who then withdraw.

Sep. 24 W: Newport evacuated by the FSA.

Oct. 2 E: In Ballaghaderreen a large IRA force of 140 men assembles.

Oct. 3 The Provisional Government offers an amnesty to the IRA.

Oct. 6 In Athlone, Patrick Mulrennan, IRA, is shot while in custody and dies of his wounds on 3 November.

Oct. 10 S: Tom Maguire, IRA, captured.

Oct. 10 The bishops' pastoral letter is issued. It is read on Sunday 22 of that month.

Oct. 14 At Ballyheane, Comdt Mitchell of the FSA is killed, as is Seamus Mulrennan, IRA.

Oct. 29 W: The IRA launch a successful attack on Clifden and Christie Macken is seriously wounded.

Oct.–Nov. E: Johnny Grealy, IRA, captured in Aghamore.

Nov. E: Tom Carney, IRA, escapes from Longford Gaol.

Nov. 14 N: Four IRA men are captured at Markree Castle, Co. Sligo.

Nov. 24 W: Newport attacked by the FSA; Michael Kilroy and other IRA men captured.

Dec. 8 Execution of R. Barrett, J. McKelvey, L. Mellows and R. O'Connor in Dublin.

Dec. 8 W: Paddy Duffy, IRA, captured in Islandeady.

1923

Jan. 17 E: IRA attacks FSA patrol at Glore, near Kiltimagh.

Feb. E: Tom Carney, IRA, wounded.

Feb. 9 Liam Deasy, then in prison, gives a statement calling for a ceasefire by the IRA.

Feb. 9–10 E: Claremorris: P. Burke (Knock), J. D. McCormack (Liskeavy), IRA, escape from imprisonment.

Feb. 15   FSA captures IRA men Joyce, Donnelly and Heneghan at Castlecarra.

Feb. 23   W: In Westport Pvt McQuaid, FSA assistant medical officer, is killed, and Capt. Togher, FSA O/C Westport, is wounded.

Mar. 6   W: Paddy Duffy, T. Ruane, C. Gavan and J. Gibbons escape from Galway Gaol.

Mar. 7   W: Joe Baker and thirteen other IRA men are captured at Shramore, Newport.

Mar. 23–6   The IRA Executive meet in the Nire Valley, but no decision is made on a possible ceasefire.

Apr. 6   W: In Dublin Tom Derrig (Westport) is wounded and arrested.

Apr. 7   N: Nicholas Corcoran, IRA, is killed in Ballina.

Apr. 8   S: Headford Barracks attacked by the IRA. FSA: McCarthy and Lyons killed; IRA: Dan McCormack is severely wounded and John Higgins killed.

Apr. 10   IRA C/S Liam Lynch is killed in Tipperary.

Apr. 11   S: Execution of six Republicans in Tuam as a reprisal for the IRA attack on the Headford Free State army post: Frank Cunnane, Martin Moylan, Seán Maguire, Michael Monaghan, John Newell and Séamus Ó Máille.

Apr. 23   W: Battie Cryan, Paddy Cannon and Broddie Malone escape from the Curragh internment camp.

Apr. 27   IRA C/S Frank Aiken calls for a ceasefire, to come into effect on 30 April.

May 24   IRA C/S Aiken calls for an end to armed resistance and a Dump Arms to be effective from 28 May.

May 24   W: In North Connemara senior staff of the 4th Western Division, including P. J. McDonnell, John Kilroy, Stephen Coyne and Jack Feehan, are captured.

June 5   N: In Ballina, IRA man Joe Healy (Ardnaree) is killed.

June 10   S: Tom Maguire and others escape from Athlone Gaol.

Aug. 25   E: Tom Carney, IRA, is captured.

Aug. 27   General election. In Mayo North and South four Sinn

Féin and five Cumann na nGaedheal TDs are elected. Nationally Cumann na nGaedheal win 39 per cent of the vote, Sinn Féin 28 per cent and other parties 23 per cent.

Sep.   N: Matt Kilcawley is captured.

Oct. 12–Nov. 23   Republican prisoners start/end a general hunger strike in jails across the country.

1924

Early   Republican prisoners are released in stages.

July 16–17   The last, senior Republicans are released from Free State internment camps.

Introduction

Vincent Keane

Those of us interested in the modern Irish revolutionary period, 1913–23, await each year the appearance of books containing new information on the topic. Too often we pick up a new publication and have to struggle through the initial sections detailing all the history that we are conversant with, such as unchanging versions of the founding of the Ulster Volunteers, the Irish Volunteers, the 1916 Rising and others. This publication is different. This is not a studious, well-structured book. Strictly speaking, this is also not a book by Ernie O'Malley. These are not his words, but he did do all the hard slog necessary for the birth of this publication, a book with a difference. A basic knowledge of Irish history from the Parnell Split of 1899 to the Sinn Féin election victory of December 1918 is necessary to understand why the IRA existed in 1918 and afterwards. What better place to get that knowledge but in Ernie O'Malley's *On Another Man's Wound*, which is a wonderful companion to this book.

We have here ten interviews with senior veterans from Mayo of the revolutionary years in Ireland. Mostly there is a narrow focus of six years of reminiscences, from 1919 and the setting-up of Dáil Éireann to 1924 and the release of the Civil War internees. Some of those interviewed go back further, taking in the local events of the 1916 Rising, but these are few.

Ernie O'Malley conducted the interviews in the early 1950s when those relating their stories were getting on in age and memories were failing. It must have taken tremendous patience on the part of O'Malley to get all this history together. Consider how he had to locate the people to interview. In those days without telephones it was difficult to track people down, but on many occasions a former interviewee accompanied him for the introduction, for though he was a respected name, with an established anti-Treaty record, he had never actually fought in the west and thus was not known personally to the men.

The Irish government decided in 1947 that it was an appropriate time in the country's history to approach the participants of the Irish revolutionary period for their personal witness statements of their involvement in the various organisations that existed in the period, e.g. Sinn Féin, the Irish Volunteers, the Irish Citizen Army, Na Fianna Éireann and Cumann na mBan. The timing was appropriate because a certain unity had been achieved in Ireland during the Emergency between 1939 and 1945. Thousands of Civil War opponents had put aside their differences and had joined the Irish Army or one of the various voluntary organisations, e.g. the Local Defence Force, the Local Security Force, Auxiliary Fire Brigades and the Red Cross. With this unity in mind, the government set up the Bureau of Military History at Westland Row in Dublin. People could go to the offices of the Bureau and make their witness statements to an army officer. If they were unable, or unwilling, they could submit a written statement to the Bureau. These statements have lately become available to the public.

However, some men, such as General Tom Barry, refused to make a statement to the Bureau. Barry's view was that the people going to the Bureau were making statements that were not verified or corroborated by their senior officers and that a person could say anything about any event, or about any person, and it was accepted by the Bureau. Due to the limitations of space, only ten of O'Malley's twenty-eight Mayo interviews are included here and only four of the men who gave them also went to the Bureau.

O'Malley's technique was quite different, so keep this in

mind as you read these interviews. He would make contact with an IRA veteran and the interview would normally take place in the person's home. His approach was dissimilar to that of the Bureau: it was all very relaxed and it was Ernie doing the writing, not taking written statements. Often, the person being interviewed would stray away from the subject in hand and that is obvious in the various narratives. But that's the nature of oral history; they were not making formal statements. So this collection is not intended to be a well-structured and complete history of the revolutionary period in Mayo.

The 1916 Rising passed by without Mayo knowing too much about it. It was wartime, newspapers were scarce and there was harsh censorship. News of the fighting in Dublin came via the railway workers whose work connected them with the capital and the west. It was a train driver who brought the news of John MacBride's execution to Westport some days after the event. The west was cut off from information and the Irish Volunteers' headquarters did not deem Mayo important enough to notify about the coming Rising. However, the RIC realised that there were determined Republicans in the county, with strong Fenian traditions, people who would eventually strike at the British establishment. This prompted them to round up and send these prospective troublemakers for internment after Easter 1916. In doing this the establishment made a huge mistake, as the interned men became more learned and determined in their efforts to work for an Ireland free of domination by its nearest neighbour.

Post-1916 a great wave of nationalism spread across the country. The various Republican organisations had a rebirth and the shackles of the Irish Parliamentary Party were loosened and finally cast aside, as witnessed in the 1918 general election. A new order was in the offing and young Republicans were no longer being cowed by the establishment, the police and the clergy. New, youthful leaders were coming to the fore and the jails were filling with those who were rejecting all the old symbols of imperialism. The heavy-handed methods of the RIC and military were to be met head-on with armed resistance, a resistance backed by the newly formed Dáil Éireann representing the majority in the country.

The old Irish Volunteer structures were revamped in 1917 and new, prison-hardened men were appointed to the headquarters staff. After the formation of the Dáil the very name Irish Volunteers was dropped, and it became the Irish Republican Army. Great strides were made and companies of the IRA sprang up all over the country. In 1920 new structures had to be organised to accommodate this new army. The old Mayo Brigade, which was inactive and functioned more as a committee that rarely met, was revamped and in 1920 four new brigades came from it. GHQ had a firm hand on the organisation and a proper chain of command and responsibility emerged in 1920.

Many in the RIC recognised what was happening and resigned. The force was much depleted and recruits, mostly battle-hardened ex-British Army men from Britain and across the Empire, including some Mayo men, were joining up. These new recruits, the 'Tans', gave the impression of ruthlessness and indiscipline, but they were members of the RIC and under the control of RIC sergeants, head constables and district inspectors, who led them on terror raids, assaulting their way across the land, as witnessed at Tiernaur, Cuilmore and countless other locations. The RIC was the front line of the Empire in Ireland, and it was creating the conditions whereby armed resistance was inevitable. Instead of being referred to as the Tan War, the conflict should be known as the RIC War.

Officially, the War of Independence was played out between 1919 and 1921. In the Mayo brigades the main actions mostly took place in the early months of 1921, in locations such as Kilmeena, Tourmakeady and Carrowkennedy. We now know that by the time of the Carrowkennedy ambush in June 1921, Truce talks were going on between Irish and British representatives. We are familiar with the numerous events across the country that forced the British government to the negotiating table in 1921. Did we win? Did the British forces win? Or, was it a stalemate, a draw? The situation was left in such an unresolved state that it was inevitable that at some future date young men would again resort to force of arms.

One thing missing from these interviews is any recognition of the tremendous work undertaken by the women of Cumann na mBan and the youth of Na Fianna Éireann. The women played an equal part in the national struggle and without their aid in carrying arms and dispatches, providing food and shelter, and generally giving full backing to the men, it would have been impossible to carry on. Armed columns of men would descend on a townland after a long night waiting to confront the enemy. Many miles would have been travelled and the column, often numbering sixty men (see Michael Kilroy's interview) would be seeking hot food and places to sleep. The women came up trumps and everyone would be catered for. While the men ate and rested, the women were on full alert.

Na Fianna Éireann, the Irish National Boy Scouts, had been in existence since 1909. When the Irish Volunteers were founded in 1913, the Fianna officers provided a cadre of young men experienced at foot drill, handling weapons, first aid, camping, etc. Boys like Liam Mellows, Seán Heuston, Con Colbert and a host of others were the nucleus of the Irish Volunteers and later the IRA. Where there was a good Sluagh (branch) of Na Fianna, a strong company of the IRA followed. All the underground departments of Dáil Éireann in Dublin had Fianna officers as clerks and dispatch riders. In the group photograph of the West Mayo Brigade ASU (flying column), at least twelve of the men started their Republican careers in Na Fianna Éireann in Westport.

After one year of relative peace, July 1921 to June 1922, the pro- and anti-Treaty sides faced each other in arms at the Four Courts in Dublin. The IRA was outgunned by a Free State army of 55,000 troops armed by the British, who also facilitated the Free State government by disbanding the Munster Fusiliers, the Dublin Fusiliers, the Leinsters and the Connaught Rangers so that they could enlist in the Free State army. It is now estimated that 16,000 Republicans were interned from 1922 to 1924. Brian O'Higgins, Sinn Féin TD, author and poet, related how at least 150 IRA men were killed on lonely country roads and city streets during this period. Can we ever forget the seventy-seven executed against prison walls?

This book is an ideal companion to the two already published on Kerry and Galway. It will give you hours of reading.

WEST MAYO

MICHAEL KILROY

(UCDA 17b/101, pp. 39–60; 136, pp. 42–44; and 138, pp. 11–14)[1]

Michael Kilroy (1884–1962) was born in Derryloughan, near Newport, but raised in Carrickaneady, also close to Newport. He attended Cuilmore and later Newport national school. He was apprenticed as a carpenter in Claremorris but became a blacksmith and started his forge in Newport in 1905. He joined the Irish Volunteers in Newport and became O/C of the Newport Company and later the Newport Battalion. Initially he was quartermaster of the West Mayo Brigade, then in August 1920 he became vice-commandant. He was later appointed commandant of the brigade's flying column or ASU. He was appointed O/C of the 4th Western Division upon its creation in August or September 1921. During the

Copyright J. J. Leonard (courtesy of Anthony Leonard)

---

1   Initial transcriptions were prepared by Frances-Mary Blake and Dominic Price, and additional corrections and footnotes have been added. This interview was carried out in three sessions and appears in three separate volumes (101, 136 and 138) of the Ernie O'Malley Military Notebooks. The three have now been integrated in chronological order with the volume number appearing before the page number, e.g. [101/39R]. Kilroy made a statement to the Bureau of Military History – WS 1162.

Civil War he was anti-Treaty, and led the Western Command in 1922 until his arrest and imprisonment in November of that year. In 1923, while in jail, he was elected a Sinn Féin TD for South Mayo and was a leader in the October–November 1923 hunger strike, before being released in 1924. He later joined Fianna Fáil and remained a TD until 1937. He married Ann 'Nan' Leonard of Crossmolina in 1914. They had eight children and lived in Newport.

This interview took place in Newport, Co. Mayo, in 1950 and September 1951.

[1913–1921 PERIOD]

[101/39R] There were four Brigades in Mayo in 1920.[2] You had better check on what I say with Dick Walsh[3] and Ned Moane.[4] We had planned in 1913 to write to the papers about starting an Irish army.[5] Seán MacDiarmada[6] once organised this place, and he said he had come across Fenian records and two of the three best organised places in Ireland for the Fenians were Tiernaur and Kilmeena.[7] Pat Moran was a famous leader from Newport, and my grandfather [was] working for him at night. My grandfather always said, 'Don't ask me any questions, and I'll tell you no lies.' Pat Moran's brother brought in the rifles to Dublin for the Fenian Rising.[8] **[101/39L]** (He always talks as if

---

2   Kilroy mistakenly said 1916 here instead of 1920 – the date has been corrected. The one brigade was divided into four brigades in July 1920.
3   Richard 'Dick' Walsh from Balla. See biographical sketches.
4   Ned Moane, not Mohane as occasionally written in the original text. See biographical sketches.
5   The Irish Volunteers were started in 1913 in Dublin and Kilroy's thought was to form a local branch of the Irish Volunteers in Mayo.
6   Seán MacDiarmada, not MacDiarmuid as in the original text.
7   Tiernaur (not Teernar as in the original text) lies north-west of Newport on the Mulranny road.
8   The Fenian Rising of 1867. The succeeding sentence in the original text has been omitted: 'Clandoolan on the South shore of the Shannon, Kilary, below Renvyle, Labesheda.'

the West had been fighting all the time whereas it was April or May 1921 before a policeman was shot in West Mayo.)[9]

[101/39R] I was quartermaster then of the Mayo Brigade but in 1920, four Brigades were formed.[10] Then Vice-Brigadier. The Brigadier, Tom Derrig, was arrested almost at once, and he had, prior to his arrest, nominated me as Brigadier.[11] The West Mayo Brigade stretched from Achill, Castlebar, Westport, Louisburgh to the head of Lough Mask and to Balla in South Mayo.

Submarines. In North Mayo Ruane was a County Councillor.[12] He ... didn't pretend [to know] anything about it, but he knew about the Portacloy area. In 1919 I was told **[101/40]** to arrange about a landing of arms from a submarine in North Mayo. These fellows around Portacloy were supposed to be in touch with submarines. They were supposed to be supplying food and petrol to the Germans. Doherty, an ex-National Teacher and ex-County Councillor, was supposed to be concerned with the exchange of food, etc.[13] Jack Munnelly, a Councillor, was supposed to fix up that meeting for me. He was a TD, and he's dead now. Our people at Irish Volunteers General Headquarters[14] knew nothing about what arrangement could be made and in case of a choice of arms, what did we want: Peters, small arms and automatics for the first run.[15]

---

9   This sentence in parentheses is a comment made by Ernie O'Malley about Michael Kilroy's views of the fighting in the west. O'Malley's comment is not entirely correct as there were at least three RIC men killed in 1920 in Mayo and two in March 1921, but in contrast to Munster, with which O'Malley was more familiar, the fighting in Mayo did start later.

10 In the original text Kilroy mentioned 1919 here instead of 1920 but he was mistaken, so the date has been corrected. Kilroy became quartermaster of the West Mayo Brigade in about August 1919.

11 Thomas 'Tom' Derrig. See biographical sketches.

12 Tom Ruane from Ballina. See biographical sketches.

13 National Teacher is abbreviated to N. T. in the original text.

14 Abbreviated to I. V, GHQ in the original text.

15 A 'Peter' or 'Peter the Painter' was a small automatic 9 mm pistol.

A Dublin man who works in Boland's. (Fintan Murphy, I said.) Yes, Fintan Murphy met Dick Walsh and I. I left Balla where I met him and I cycled on over here [to Newport] to get food. I went on to Ballycroy and at Ballyvary the bike broke, and I went down on foot to Cleary's.[16] It was a misty, foggy evening and at twilight I met two police. I fell off the bike and I was knocked out but I was all right at once. I went on to the fair in Belmullet. The doctor treated me, but I wasn't as bad in appearance as I felt. I met Jack Munnelly, and I waited in Carey's of Belmullet for a week to get a boat. I was to get a curragh to go out and get in touch, and we would have water, fresh meat and petrol. The petrol was supposed to be anchored on the ocean floor.

[101/56R][17] Tan War. Five rifles in Newport Battalion area: one for myself, one for John and one for Owney Kane, three Lee Enfields and two Mausers. Kitterick got twelve to fifteen rifles from General Headquarters for Westport.

[101/41] In August or September 1920 there was a raid in which people were arrested. Tom Derrig was arrested. Ned Lyons was on hunger strike. He was on the [Westport] quay for a week, half-dressed a week later.[18] I saw him in Dundrum lunatic asylum during the Truce.[19] He was forcibly imprisoned. Possibly they were trying to put military clothes on him; at any rate he was fighting them going through the streets of Westport.

---

16 Cleary's was a pub combined with a shop in Ballycroy on the west coast of Mayo.

17 The next two sentences have been moved here from later to appear in chronological sequence.

18 Ned Lyons was arrested and probably held in the barracks on Westport Quay, where he went on hunger strike. He was walked through Westport on the way to the train station.

19 In the original text Kilroy mistakenly says Lyons was in Dundalk lunatic asylum, whereas he was in fact in Dundrum, Dublin.

RIC. Twenty/twenty-four Tans [based] in Newport. His brothers got an awful beating …[20] A lady searcher attached to the Tans in Newport. She shot with her revolver at things in her house. Fuge, the officer, was an Inspector.[21] District Inspector Adderley who lived at the quay was a District Inspector, but a decent man.[22] Fuge was put over him.

There were once sixty-five men on my column. I went out after Tom Derrig's arrest and the lads began to join me.[23] I wasn't long out before the men joined. In the Westport area at Durless at the back of the Reek[24] or at Culleens at the back of the Reek, we intended to raid Louisburgh town and the barracks.[25] We had no explosives and but few arms. I believed then in using fire. The [Louisburgh] Battalion O/C went in who knew the place.

At Gloshpatrick,[26] at the foot of the Reek, we fixed an ambush along a ravine that sweeps to the sea at Jim **[101/42]** Fair's and at night we retired.[27] The 17th March, 1921, it was. We had about twelve rifles in the Westport district and twenty men. The rest were armed with shotguns. The people around the Reek were very friendly to us.

Westport district was very good. Ned Moane there, Joe

20 Kilroy is referring here to the brothers of Ned Lyons of Cuilmore, Newport, who were brutally assaulted by the RIC in their home. An incomplete sentence following this line has been omitted.
21 RIC District Inspector Thomas Hugh Hare Fuge (not Fudge as in the original text).
22 RIC District Inspector Albert Adderley (not Aderly as in the original text) lived on the Quay in Newport.
23 Going 'out' refers to going 'on the run' and not living at home, and this would have been in September 1920.
24 Probably Durless, not Durlough as in the original text. The 'Reek' is a local term for Croagh Patrick, the 2,510-foot mountain overlooking Clew Bay on the south side.
25 Louisburgh (not Louisberg as in the original text) is twelve miles west of Westport.
26 Gloshpatrick, not Glashpatrick as in the original text.
27 Jim Fair's, not Phaers as in the original text.

Ring,[28] Johnny Duffy[29] and John Gibbons[30] also; and a brother of Carney's, the writer.[31] We disarmed on the eve of the Truce, but circumstances threw us together when we tried to break up. **[First Carrowkennedy ambush, 22 March 1921.]** We went to Peter Máille's,[32] near Carrowkennedy, across the Owenroe at Claddy.[33] The whole village of Claddy was good.[34] I stayed with Peter, myself and Ned Moane. The following night we crossed the road on to Drummin road far from the barracks. Four RIC [men] used [to] come out from Drummin Barracks. We saw four bikes coming towards us. I told the boys to walk on the grass. Joe Ring, Captain Malone and myself.[35] The RIC got off their bicycles and we fired.

There was a dance in the village nearby and there was a melodeon going [at] the dance, but it stopped suddenly. One RIC got ahead, and I told the fellows to go after the others, and I was left blazing away with my Peter, and I saw the fellow out of the corner of my eye. I fired, and he had his revolver. The sergeant ran across the road, and then I turned on the other

28 Joe Ring was from outside Westport. See biographical sketches.
29 Johnny Duffy, brother of Paddy Duffy, came from Cloonskill, Aughagower. Both men were on the West Mayo Brigade ASU and took part in most of the activities of 1919–22. Johnny did not take an active part in the Civil War.
30 John or Johnny 'Seán' Gibbons from the Quay Road, Westport, was a prominent member of Na Fianna Éireann and the Westport IRA. He worked as a law clerk to the state solicitor in Westport. Michael Kilroy appointed him as his adjutant to the West Mayo Brigade in 1920. He was anti-Treaty and was captured at the Battle of Newport in November 1922. He had a successful law business in Dublin in later years. John Gibbons is usually referred to in this interview as Johnny or Seán Gibbons.
31 James Carney, IRA Volunteer, died of tuberculosis in 1922; his brother, Frank Carney of Mill Street, Westport, was a playwright.
32 In these interviews the speaker sometimes refers to a person by different names. For example Peter Máille could also be Peter O'Malley or Peter Ó Máille.
33 Carrowkennedy, not Carrickennedy as in the original text.
34 The word 'good' here would suggest that the village was supportive of the IRA activities in general.
35 Captain James 'Broddie' Malone (1898–1975) from Westport. See his interview.

two. The four of them surrendered with their revolvers and grenades. The sergeant was supposed **[101/43]** to be dead. This was the first action the column was in. Very lights went up, and Westport sent out British [troops].[36] We went West to *Andrey*.[37]

We went into Westport at three points to look for Tans but we did not see one of them. We heard that they had got wind of our coming, for we were very particular about keeping our counsel to ourselves. There were a lot of Tans in Westport. They were terrible and their wives also. They were very anxious to meet Broddie Malone and Charlie Gavan.[38] They went in to meet this Tan who was to have met them, but he didn't turn up.

At the first fight we decided to fight in the open. We had several attempts at ambushes. At Glenisland we spent a whole day there. There was another ambush on the Islandeady road. Local fellows were taken out to cut the road. The Tans next came out, went past and came back again. Two boys were killed.[39]

Joe Ring had the lads on Leenane road but nothing happened. **[136/44L] [Round-up after Tourmakeady.]**[40] The military[41] came in across the hill from Tourmakeady, [from] Galway, from Castlebar and from Westport, Kilmeena.

---

36 Very lights were used by the military in the evening to illuminate the sky to view the surrounding locality, but were also used to signal to other troops that assistance was needed.

37 The 'Andrey' location cannot be identified.

38 Charlie Gavan (not Gavin as in the original text) was from Mill Street, Westport. He became a member of Westport Na Fianna Éireann and IRA company. He was arrested early in 1921 at Loughloon, Owenwee, and interned. He had been mentioned in a secret RIC report in 1919 as one of the people seen in the locality of the home of the assassinated resident magistrate J. C. Milling. Gavan was anti-Treaty and became O/C of the Westport Company after Broddie Malone in 1922. He was captured with Paddy Duffy in Castlebar in December 1922 and interned. He escaped from Galway Gaol. In later years he was the rate collector for the Urban District Council in Westport.

39 The two cousins, Thomas O'Malley and Thomas Lally, were killed at Big Wall.

40 There was a round-up by the British forces, including the RIC, immediately after Tourmakeady on 3 May.

41 O'Malley mistakenly says here '(after this attack in Carrowkennedy)' which has been omitted.

I had Newport column mobilised at the Leap Furnace[42] and only after being mobilised, when we got the word, I told them that we had come out for active service and I put it up to them to go. We had got word from Galway that Tom Maguire's men were in trouble so I had decided to go.[43] We started at nightfall (Why at nightfall? The word had come in hours before this), and we were at the Partry Mountains at dawn. I think there were very nearly fifteen Newport boys, and they had rifles. I had control of three rifles myself. (About Maguire's men, Michael Kilroy does not like Tom Maguire for he stood out against Fianna Fáil.)[44] I heard that Tom Maguire's men took off their shoes and they ran.[45] There was a place called Headstone, which had a wood on the left, where we left the road. The officer, who was wounded in Tourmakeady, this fellow was a great boast who was after him and when he was coming up the last hillock Tom shouted.

[101/43] Kilmeena [ambush, 19 May 1921].[46] We thought we would cut every road but leave the Newport–Westport road open. We were down from the priest's house in Myna.[47] We lay down at dawn, but it was bright before we lay down. Most of the men were near the Dance Hall and on a hill each side of us. At 12 [p.m.] they came **[101/44]** along – lorries

---

42 The salmon leap at Lough Furnace, just west of Newport.
43 Kilroy had heard about the attempt by the British troops to round up Tom Maguire's men in the hills just north and west of Tourmakeady after the ambush on 3 May 1921.
44 O'Malley might be referring to Maguire not having joined Fianna Fáil in 1926 and having stayed with Sinn Féin.
45 This allegation by Kilroy has not been corroborated elsewhere and may reflect Kilroy's personal attitude towards Maguire.
46 Kilmeena, not Killmeena as in the original text. The Kilmeena ambush was on the Westport–Newport road. At a point there the road crosses over the railroad, and this bridge was close to the ambush site and not too far from the local dance hall at a crossroads.
47 Myna (not Minagh as in the original text) is halfway between Newport and Westport.

and two cars. I passed down, then took up a position around O'Flynn's.[48] The military came out from Westport. There was a fight for two hours, and one of our lads, Seamus MacEvilly, was wounded almost at once.[49] Staunton of Kilmeena was killed and Collins was killed.[50] We had three wounded, Paddy Mulloy of Tiernaur and Nolan ...[51] We had about forty men, most of them armed with shotguns. The military used rifle grenades and two machine guns. John Madden was by himself along a bank, and a rifle grenade dropped right where he was.[52] Commandant Paddy Jordan was wounded.[53] We covered the boys' retreat. I told him to come out as I thought he was hurt by briars. He died of wounds afterwards as did MacEvilly. All the British got were the four wounded. They were said to have had several men wounded.[54]

One of the men waited behind with the two fellows, Nolan and O'Malley, and MacEvilly. He was said to be a spy for the British for he was said to have come around with the Tans later: Pierce, an Artane boy who worked in Westport.[55] He disappeared afterwards.

[136/44R] At Kilmeena there were whip-cracks from explosive bullets. Paddy O'Malley, my cousin, had his leg broken

---

48 John O'Flynn (sometimes Flynn in the original text) was a tailor whose house was near the Kilmeena site. See his interview, UCDA P17b/136.

49 Seamus/Jim MacEvilly (not McEvilly as in the original text) was a brother to Tom MacEvilly who was active in Sligo. Although the original text says he was killed almost at once, this must be a mistake, as it says only a few lines later that he died of his wounds afterwards.

50 John Pat Staunton of the Castlebar Company, IRA; Tom Collins of the Westport Company, IRA.

51 Thomas Nolan.

52 Dr John A. Madden from Ballycastle. See biographical sketches.

53 Paddy Jordan from Letter, Islandeady, died from his wounds on 23 May 1921, at King George V Military Hospital, Montpelier Hill, Dublin.

54 RIC Constable Harry Beckett, referred to as a Tan, was killed there.

55 John Pierce (not Pearse as in the original text) had attended the Artane Industrial School for orphans in Dublin and worked at the tailoring business in Westport (not Castlebar as in the original text).

in Kilmeena, and he was brought in a prisoner to Westport, where he could see the treatment of the wounded who were slung out of the lorry.

[138/13L][56] Paddy O'Malley (who was wounded and then captured in Kilmeena) was a great shot, and he could make allowance for it. (The bad rifle which he had, I expect.) I was using his rifle at 200 yards [138/14R] distance from the back of O'Flynn's and I got him, the man I was firing at. O'Flynn's house (the tailor's) would shield Madden from the machine gun which was close to O'Flynn's. We examined it first (P. O'Malley's rifle) but it was not suitable. We had not many rifles in Kilmeena. At Fr Conroy's house the Tans knelt down on the road, and they were exposed to us. We got several rounds into them before they ran across to the other bank. Jim Kelly was then in Cummins' house, and he (or they) were cooking eight hens, and he was in his aunt's house helping, with a few more men (now he is dead).[57] The first man who was hit was hit from O'Flynn's, and he was then inside the second fence (behind the ambush position) and about then Paddy O'Malley was wounded and some of the RIC emptied rifles into his flesh when he was captured. There was an order issued to occupy the second fence but Staunton and MacEvilly were knocked out there.[58]

Jordan rolled himself in under briars.[59] I told him to come

---

56 O'Malley included a folk saying in the original text that does not tie in with the interview and it has been omitted here: 'Shandrum. As wise as the red-arsed bees are the Kanes of Shandrum.'

57 Jim Kelly later went to work in England and it is said died during an air raid. Tom Cummins was a neighbour of O'Flynn, also just above the Kilmeena ambush site. See Cummins' interview, UCDA P17b/136.

58 Pat Staunton and Seamus/Jim MacEvilly were referred to as 'S and McE' in the original text.

59 Paddy Jordan was living at Letter, Islandeady, where his father was the national schoolteacher. He joined the IRA Islandeady Company and became its O/C. He was badly wounded at Kilmeena, was mistreated with other prisoners when captured, and died of his wounds a few days later in the King George V Military Hospital, Dublin.

out, and then he did come out, and he lay himself beside me quietly until I had to retreat. Jordan and I were together, and we were moving …, when he discovered a gap lower down in a field which was between him and the road.[60] I went down to Paddy O'Malley then. There was a Balla man there who was working in Kilroy's in Castlebar, Tommy Nolan. Pierce was there and Pierce said that he would not leave.[61] There was Tommy Nolan there and someone else, four or five of them were there. There **[138/14L]** was not good cover in which to come away. I got to Browne then who was a cool man and he was there with his old shotgun and at that distance he was too far away from the enemy to fire at any of them with result. Tom Nolan had his leg broken on him. I heard the RIC as they were coming along the road towards the wounded men. They shouted when they came up to our wounded but they did not kill them.

[138/11R][62] [Skerdagh engagement, 23 May 1921.] The three of us, Captain Jim Moran, Seán Connolly[63] and myself, came to Upper Skerdagh and we were at the back of Dyra's house. (This happened after the Kilmeena ambush. The wounded with the Column had gone as far as Skerdagh at the foot of the mountains. Kilroy, who had not long been married, went off to

---

60 O'Malley drew a diagram of the area in the original text but it is not included here.

61 John Pierce of Dublin had been confined to the Artane Industrial School for orphans in Dublin where he learned tailoring. He came to Westport in 1919 and worked for a local tailor on the Fairgreen. When captured at Kilmeena he made a complete statement to the RIC relating how he and John Collins, another Artane pupil, had come upon the IRA men training near Corrig in 1920 and they eventually joined up with the Westport ASU. See Tuam Diocese Archives, b/4/08-11/04 1920-21, statement of John Pierce to District Commissioner R. F. Cruise. There is still a question as to whether he was working for the RIC at the time. In any case he was court-martialled and given a five-year sentence which he served in England until being released after December 1921.

62 This third segment of the interview is transcribed from UCDA P17b/138, pp. 11–14.

63 Seán Connolly was also known as John or Jack Connolly.

see his wife with two of his men.)[64] We did not like to awaken the people of the house for it was now probably 3 o'clock and soon the sun was rising in front of our eyes. The MacDonald's house was in the same yard as Dyra's and Lenehan's house was nearby. There were men in MacDonald's house, the wounded, and there were men also in every house in Lower Skerdagh. There were two or three in Dyra's, Madden and myself, but Connolly and Jim Moran were in Lower Skerdagh. They came up to us on Sunday for on that day the boys heard a rumour that they were dead and they wanted, the two of them, to show themselves in their haunts. They went back by the Gap then. Connolly was a Commandant. Stepping stones led into it from the old road.

Browne from Kilmeena was in another [house], Dyra's, who were relatives of mine in Skerdagh. He was Michael Dyra, my cousin. The river has a gully out at *Alt Buida*. Browne got a wound later across his stomach, and it let out his intestines. We went to Jimmy Kane's that evening, and we were urged to get out.[65] Poor Jimmy was an old man, and the last thing he said was, 'If you're careful now it's not likely that there will be any more fighting', but I had the urge to leave and so we left the place in the darkness. (I think it was here that Mrs Kilroy was.) Some people said later that the Tans and the RIC went straight on [138/11L] the road behind us, but that information is not definite. It was dark when we left Kane's house and over the stepping stones: and at the back of two houses, right at them, we were discussing what a fine retreat we could make from Skerdagh when [an IRA] guard in Lower Skerdagh fired for they (the RIC) were so close. We were then three-quarters of a mile away up the hill. Then the RIC replied with several shots.

---

64 O'Malley is not accurate here as Kilroy had actually married Ann 'Nan' Leonard of Crossmolina in 1914.
65 Meaning to leave the area.

Jim Moran had no rifle with him on that morning, and then we suggested that he could help John Madden to get out the wounded men. (Moran was the best shot they had in that column, and I do not know what kind of a shot Connolly was.) Jim then went in to Madden, and Jack Connolly and I went down the hill together. It was dawning now, nice and bright. The others (RIC) were within 150 yards of us. I suspected that what I saw were their caps (with the sharp edges), and they were over us for they were coming in and we were in the hollow. They were forty or fifty feet higher, and then I saw the edges of their caps. I told Jack to be careful for I thought that they were the enemy. I flopped down at once and I spread out my hands so as to save me the shock of the fall and I gathered my rifle so that the policemen would not see any movement on the grass. It had been a very severe winter and at the time on the mountain sides everything was yet grey. I gathered in the rifle slowly, then I got it up so that I could sight [my target] and each of us got his two or three rounds, before the RIC took cover … 'What's that?' I heard one of them say at the first shot. '[It] struck the peak of my cap. Take cover, take cover. You should take cover in a way like that.' (There had been twenty-four in the barracks **[138/12R]** of Newport at the time.) After about thirty minutes Madden came out, and he was higher than the enemy and he was firing down, but he could not see anyone, and he would not trust himself to going further. 'Michael, where are you?' he shouted. But we did not reply to him for we were under their rifles.

Jack had no cover and he was lying beside a stone.[66] We were 200 yards from the RIC, but it is hard to judge distance when you are lying down. Madden was by a mound which is used on the mountains to catch a hawk and they would set a trap on that morning on a shooting range. We backed up one at a time, but

---

66 An account of the MacMenamin folk story has been omitted from here as it is also related on page 101/47, transcribed later in this chapter.

I couldn't move for the rifle was sticking in my side; we moved one leg after the other backwards up the hill. But very shortly the other four came on to our assistance, Johnny Gibbons, Tom Kitterick, Paddy Cannon, MacDonagh, the slater's son from Westport, in Upper Skerdagh.[67] We then divided the ammunition amongst us. The three wounded men went up Glenlara. We went behind the houses in Upper Skerdagh, but there was not a move out of the RIC and when we were under cover they would put up a rifle to see where we were and we would fire at it from 600 to 700 yards away. They could not stir then, the RIC.

We only retired when we saw that the British were coming in from Newport to the Crossmolina road … down by Skerdagh School in view (of us) but the RIC did not know, and we fell back for several hundred yards, and we rested in a **[138/12L]** mountain stream for a few minutes, but it was a dried-up stream at that time. The military went on up by the old bridle path. There was an old trench by the road, but it was filled in and we walked on that into Glenlara and where we went out of the side we crossed to Chambers' to the right. We were first walking on the left to the nearest house. The weight of them (the men who were with us) went in on our trench, only an odd man went on one side. We went across to the house where we got a can of milk and bread from Mrs Chambers, and when we were at the gable of the house we saw RIC on the crest of the hill from which we had come from [sic]. Then they saw us going away 300 to 400 feet high from Chambers'. We moved in the valley diagonally up the hill.

The RIC in the Buckoogh side opened bursts of fire from machine guns on us, only bursts in every direction they were.[68]

---

67 John MacDonagh of Monument Street, Westport, was in the Westport Company. His father, also John, was the Centre for the IRB in Westport.
68 Buckoogh Mountain (not Buccagh as in the original text) lies just north of

We went straight up Birreen through what had been a landstrip, thirty or forty feet, [which was] mossy and more rushy, [and] chosen for its colour by us.[69] Several shots tore up the earth around us. We were then extended in breadth and in length. Then we saw this RIC man, and I shouted 'Halt.' The lads halted, and I told them I thought we should wait until we saw if he was looking across his sights, but I heard another burst from another direction and we lay down. We had brought the milk can with us from the gable of the house and when it had been emptied, it had been thrown to one side. The milk can was brought up diagonally. The RIC passed below in the valley. They were extended on Buckoogh to this man whom we thought had noticed the gleaming tin can. All the officers passed on by the river.

[138/13R] I had a telescope, but we did not use it then, but we did make use of it when we were on the Turf Bank on top. There the bog had been washed away deep to the stones underneath. They were all RIC as far as I know that day who passed up the valley. Munro was a District Inspector who would not allow the RIC to burn houses in Skerdagh.[70] He himself was wounded there that day. I heard later that loads of [RIC] wounded were sent over to Foxford where Paddy O'Malley [was, who] was wounded in Kilmeena. I found that the sight on his rifle was crooked for I took it from him before I left him. Madden and I put it into the fire in MacDonald's, and we hammered it, and we went up on *Alt* to test it there, and we found that it was firing all right now.

The officers halted under us, and they moved on in, and we moved up the hill to the top until twilight came down. The RIC

Newport.
69 Birreen, not Bereen as in the original text. What is meant by the term landstrip is not known.
70 RIC District Inspector James Munro, promoted to temporary county inspector in November 1920, was stationed at Newport.

all went in to Shramore. They saw that our men were going out the Keenagh way and they turned in the Shramore direction. The military also went down to Shramore, but they went on down by the roadway to *Turclear* to Tiernaur.[71] (Liam Willy Chambers lives and is married in the valley Shramore, between the old and the new river. I think he is now in Glenlara.) From the turf banks on top of that rise we saw their ambulances and transport in close to Jack Mularky, one of these houses on the Skerdagh old road at the foot of the mountains of Birreen. We thought we saw them two or three times moving in objects through the telescope and we thought then that the objects were their wounded.

We came down later to MacDonald's where we had a feed of salmon, for Connolly and Moran had brought this salmon back with them when they had gone away to show their friends that they were still alive. When poor Dyra was getting **[138/13L]** out of his bed a bullet flattened itself on the wall beside him.

Then we surmised that this area would be quickly surrounded so we made for a crossing which was out Jack *Duffer's* where there were stepping stones. We crossed by the bridge and this was thought to be a risk. We were at the end of it, and it was a dark mid-summer night and the time, 12 o'clock, and as we looked across the lake on the level of the river we saw that the opposite side was filled with headlights of cars. We began to run, a mile up it was, and when we were at the road we had to run to get out of the headlights. We ran and we jumped, and all of us got across the road except John Madden. The cars pulled up and then sent out outposts to the bridge. We ran all that whole mile, and we were able to run it too, for none of us were overweight then.

At first Jack Connolly and I, when we were lying on the hill at Skerdagh, had fifty rounds. That was gone when Paddy came,

---

71 Turclear is unclear and not known. Tiernaur, not Tirnar as in the original text.

and he had fifty rounds and 200 rounds of explosive bullets which belonged to Jim Moran who had managed to get [them] when he raided Rossmore Lodge. We had dumped that stuff, but after the action in Kilmeena we felt that what was being fired at us had a whiplash and crack, and it came high over our heads like the sound of a good whip. We used up all that stuff (which was dum-dum ammunition). We slept in Glenisland. The hares turn back on their tracks when they are not caught.

[101/44] No spies shot in our area. We never gave people much chance of getting information.

Our Intelligence was very poor in this Brigade area.

[Skerdagh, 19 May.][72] [101/45] The Kilmeena area was surrounded locally so we got to Skerdagh.[73] The people were very good there. We got there on the Thursday night of the fight. On Sunday I came in with Jim Moran and Jack Connolly to meet my wife to Carrickaneady to John Kane's about one and a half miles from Newport.[74] We were chatting away. Jim Kane was our outpost, and we had two rifles. At that time we had two wounded men, Jimmy Swift was one of them; he had lost a toe and he was in Upper Skerdagh. When we started to go Jim Kane came in from outpost. I was very anxious to go along to Upper Skerdagh with two rifles. We got there at 3 or 4 a.m. and we thought it too early, and as we were talking, the outpost fired and the Column got out from their billets. There was an ambush at Skerdagh and the lads retreated to … and two houses in Upper Skerdagh, and we went from there to Jack …

This was the 23rd of May. I saw the edges of caps in the mist, and I saw a rifle raised 150 yards away at me in the dawn and I flopped down as I thought his hand was on the trigger,

72 This is mistakenly recorded as Carrowkennedy in the original text.
73 Meaning the area was surrounded by British troops and the RIC. Skerdagh is about three miles north-east of Newport.
74 Ann Leonard Kilroy. Probably Carrickaneady (not Carrig as abbreviated in the original text) as Kilroy was reared there as a boy.

and I heard him say, 'Wasn't that a good shot so early in the morning.'[75] I hit the peak of his cap between me and the eastern sky. 'What was that?' I heard him ask. 'It struck the peak of my cap.' 'In that case,' said another voice, 'you'd **[101/46]** better take cover.' Jack Connolly and I kept the twenty-four of them there.

[The] Tans, they were under Munro, the officer.[76] There was only one man left in the barracks in Newport. We kept them there until Madden got out, and he shouted, 'I cannot see them.' He [Connolly] and I were in a bare bog on a downward slope, and they were up over us and the sun was in our eyes. We had on two gabardine coats which saved us (by neutralising our colours with the bog).[77] They were in perfect cover above and the gun was a great trouble to us. We had to back up the hill. We got up. Kitterick and three others came to us and there were seven in all.[78] The bullets were falling out of the sky on us; and we divided our ammunition. At 12 noon we saw lines of lorries coming down by Skerdagh school. We moved off, and they seen us, but we went on at our leisure. We were taking food at the gable of a house when we saw the RIC coming in at Creggans' [house], and we left the tins we were drinking out of behind us. There's a hollow in Glenlara along the eastern side, a mossy hollow and the gabardine coats and the rushes were the same colour.[79]

The police were into our heels, but we didn't run at any period. The soldiers brought the machine gun on to the other side of Buckoogh and the machine gunner sprayed a burst and then halted to rise us.[80] Then another **[101/47]** burst would come

---

75 In the original text O'Malley used the symbol 'x' which probably stood for yards which has been used here.
76 RIC District Inspector James Munro was based in Newport.
77 The gabardine coats would have been like trench coats.
78 Tom Kitterick from Westport. See biographical sketches.
79 Glenlara, not Glenlaura as in the original text.
80 Buckoogh mountain (not Buccagh as in the original text) lies just north of Newport.

away up the valley. He sprayed us once. We took cover, and a Tan moved near us. The rest were above going for Skerdagh and looking to catch us on the side of Buckoogh. Jim Browne of Kilmeena was wounded, and he died later. The can we had left behind us was in the Tan's way and he passed within a stare of us. We got higher up the mountain, and when we looked down we could see them. They wanted to burn Skerdagh village, but Munro, the District Inspector, wouldn't allow them.

There was a prophecy known as Brian Roche's prophecy, and I often heard the Skerdagh fight talked about before it came off. There was to be a fight in Skerdagh and a red-haired man would jump on a horse and unless help was sent out immediately, they'd all be killed. The red-haired man was MacMenamin, and he rode in barebacked to Newport for help on a Skerdagh horse.[81] One of the police said that he seen St Patrick going around amongst us all that day.

We must have been spied on, for our fellows went to a wake on Sunday, and the Tans, acting on information perhaps, came out on foot.

Jim Browne had only a shotgun on the bare mountainside, but he wasn't a bit afraid.

Kitterick wanted us to surround them with seven men, two of ours whose ammunition had all gone. The Tans **[101/48]** said they couldn't put a rifle up that day, but they would be fired on. We moved then across up by Islandeady to Aughagower and a very good place it was. We hadn't been there for six weeks, but a woman said to me, 'I was expecting you to-night.'

Carrowkennedy [second ambush, 2 June 1921].[82] We got

---

81 See also Ernie O'Malley, *Raids and Rallies* (Mercier Press, Cork 2011), pp. 234–5.

82 Carrowkennedy, not Carrigkennedy as in the original text. This ambush was on a fairly level stretch of the road halfway between Leenane and Westport, and just before a turn in the road. There was a schoolhouse on the west side of the road.

twenty rifles, one machine gun and plenty of ammunition. Ned Moane is in Carrowbawn, beyond Ryan's the vet.

We were moving around, and we came back again to Claddy to Peter O'Malley when a scout brought in word that two lorries of Tans and a car had gone out the road to Leenane, and they have to come back for the Leenane–Louisburgh road was blocked.[83] We rushed out and collected the men. Ring and I went off towards Westport for a better place, but the men whistled us back. Joe Ring asked us to allow him to go across to a hillock where he could enfilade them. The Tans opened up on Ring, on their left flank. Our lads then opened up, and the lorry driver was killed. This delighted Erris and Belmullet for the driver was a terror there.[84]

I told our men to concentrate on the machine gun always. There were three of them killed at the machine gun, and they couldn't get the machine gun into action successfully.[85] Some say they shot the ring out of his grenade as he was trying to fettle up his grenade in a lorry, and he was killed. There was a **[101/49]** sergeant who had his legs out of the back of a lorry, but our fellows when they had nothing to do shot at his legs, and they shot the calves off his legs. A Tan was killed at a bridge and a bunch of them ran into a house and refused to surrender, and they wouldn't let the people of the house out. So we told them we'd put the house on fire if they didn't come out, so they came out and surrendered. That fight put the heart across them in Mayo.

[136/42L][86] On the road south of the Nevins, near the old schoolhouse, there was a trench in the road and the RIC rooted out the people who were working on the bog to fill in the road

---

83 This Peter O'Malley of Claddy should not be confused with Peter O'Malley or Pádraic Ó Máille of Kilmilkin, Co. Galway.
84 The driver was the RIC District Inspector Edward Stevenson.
85 O'Malley sometimes abbreviated 'machine gun' to M/G in the original text.
86 This segment of the Kilroy interview is transcribed from UCDA P17b/136, pp. 42–4, and is inserted here as it relates to the Carrowkennedy ambush.

and during this operation our fellows noticed them. When I went out they were just leaving the road. We had issued orders [that ...] be destroyed at the crossroads on the right going out beside the old schoolteacher.[87] Some of our scouts said that the RIC could not go out by the Leenane road for this road was cut. When the order was sent out for everyone to get out and follow us over, the boys were mobbed under Commandant Malone to get them to such a place.[88] Dr Madden and I went off on the Westport road to get a better position, and on our return we were whistled at to say that the enemy were coming. Commandant Malone was ordered to get them into position first, and he had his men in position then. The position was all on one side (it was not) but we thought we could find a better position at a bend nearer to Westport about a half a mile or three-quarters of a mile away, and then we would have been over them all the time.

The last line [of men] was right over the road, was close to the road and it was elevated, and I believed in getting in to close quarters with the British. There was a good lot of cover there really. On the left as you got out from here, about eighty yards roughly, Jack Leonard [took] a photo of this [scene] and he united the photos (to form a panorama; maybe he means that the position which Malone's men occupied above the road was eighty yards long.) North-east of the barracks and not 200 yards away and the barracks is beside the house (I expect he means that the new Garda barracks is beside the widow's house where the second lorry halted). Canon MacDonald had talked so much of shooting from behind hedges that in the first patrol encounter I said to Tom Kitterick if there is grass on the side of the road let us keep to it.[89]

[136/42R] Most of them (the group near the widow's house)

---

87 Michael Keane was the schoolteacher at Carrowkennedy national school.
88 'Mobbed' would mean mobilised. Commandant Broddie Malone.
89 Canon MacDonald was in Newport.

were along a fence. Captain Jim Moran was in a hollow south of the road and there was someone with him to prevent a flanking movement, and to give protection. There was a road between us which shielded us from the RIC. There was a particular arrangement so as to get the machine gunner. South-west of us and west of the road was Commandant Connolly and the Newport men on a height eighty feet in height and steep, just at the gable of the (new) barracks and south of the barracks between the two roads between the school and Nevins', or over the school. There were six to eight men there, and they were all nearly Westport men. They had a few rifles. I brought a 7 mm Mauser personally, and Jack Connolly had it. In '15 or '16 I bought it. We were to open fire and to let the lorries in.[90]

The first lorry was guided into the best place (for us) for the driver was hit in the forehead dead centre. He halted it at a little thicket between the road and us, and the RIC now slipped in (to that position) and the RIC fired out of that until the end of the black sally which was cropped by the cattle so that you could not see him. They could not move. The first lorry had the machine gun, but they pitched it out, and they tumbled out of it. They made efforts continuously to use it, but they could not put up their heads, above all to keep their eyes on the machine gun and let it be used. They got up bursts but not aimed bursts. There were three or four killed. We had a fine shot, James Keane from Carnaclay outside of Westport on the Lodge Road.[91] Jim Moran and Jack Connolly commented that Joe Ring had said wouldn't it be a good thing **[136/43L]** to have someone on the

90 O'Malley had included a rough diagram indicating the three lorries in a row, but it is not included here. The three sentences following this have also been left out as they related to Kilmeena not Carrowkennedy and were not significant.

91 Carnaclay, not Carrinaglee or Carnacleigh as sometimes in the original text. It was on the Lodge Road near Westport, not the Buckoogh Road (near Newport) as in the original text. James Keane lived at the Lodge Road, Gortaroe, two miles north-east of Westport.

hillock across the road (opposite to Broddie Malone's position) to enfilade the RIC, and the men let Ring go, and as he went across they [RIC] saw his haversack and they shot at it from under a fence. The axle of the lorry was getting it, for he [it] was being sniped at by Joe Ring from the hillock to the east out in the bog. [To the] East was a double hump with a hole in the centre. South of them (RIC) were Moran and Connolly, and Moran got in on them when they got into Keane's house.[92]

It was Johnny Duffy who had burned the RIC hut, and we went from this hut to the north.[93] There was an old bohereen coming up to the position and on through it. There I was to the south-east of the RIC hut, and I was trying to fire through the foliage, but the weight of the fellows were to the north of the hut and north of the gravel quarry. I went down to the bohereen to find Joe Baker down there.[94] He was wonderful on active service, very cool and clear by himself. He congratulated me then. The first lorry had the rifle grenades and one of them exploded in the lorry and the boys said that they had shot the ring out of the grenade. In my opinion the down side of the lorry was all little bits of steel slobbered up, and low canvas in between them.[95] The side of the lorry was shallow and he probably dropped the grenade when he was trying to put it in position in the cup. It tore the head out of him, as big as an egg the hole in his head was. There was only one sound man from the first lorry who remained unwounded who was in that thicket. Two hours it lasted, between two and two and three-quarters hours about. They were damned tough. Gerald Bartley's brother, who was in the RIC, knew him.[96]

---

92 This house belonged to the schoolmaster, Michael Keane.
93 The Carrowkennedy RIC hut was burned over Easter in April 1920.
94 Joe Baker was from Co. Tyrone. See biographical sketches.
95 Slobbered is rural Mayo jargon, indicating something poorly done or sloppy.
96 Gerald Bartley, then of Clifden. His father had been in the RIC and his brother was then. See O'Malley, E., *The Men Will Talk to Me: Galway Interviews* (Mercier Press, 2013), p. 78.

Poor Delahunty was caught under his own lorry, and he had only the spokes of the wheel to protect him.[97] They brought the wounded to the **[136/43R]** house (above them). Ring wanted to shoot some of them. I saw a poor fellow standing in line, an RIC man who had been wounded, and I gave out to them for not looking after him, after their own. (I suppose he was an Irishman, and Michael had pity instead of contempt, also there was another aspect of him. Once he said to me that the Irish RIC had always fought better than the Tans. He had very little experience of warfare so that he could not qualify this desire of his, but in Munster we always felt that the Tans fought well in difficult circumstances. They had been trained in warfare.)

The first fellows (in the first lorry) came out and surrendered. Johnny Duffy was then given charge to go on to take the surrender. They would not surrender. They were in the Keanes' house, and we threatened them to set the house on fire. Johnny Duffy went up to the door of Keanes', and he made his own man, the RIC who went up with him, an interpreter. It was a thatched house, and we said that if the family inside were injured we would then deal with them inside. There had been four killed at the machine gun from the first lorry, and there had been a few wounded; and in addition poor Creegan had the calves of his legs shot out, and he bled away. Our lads brought him up on a door to the house, but he bled to death. His comrades, however, did not bother about him.[98]

There were none of the IRA wounded. We captured: machine gun, pans of ammunition, rifle grenades, not many of them, and rifles. The Special District Inspector, who had given the people in Erris hell, was killed, and he came up to Max Green and gave him

---

97 Gus Delahunty worked for the Railway Hotel in Westport and was ordered by the RIC to drive one of the vehicles involved in the Carrowkennedy ambush. He survived by crawling into a culvert by the road.

98 Three following sentences have been omitted as they appear to relate to Glenamoy in 1922, are not significant and are out of chronological order.

... He was a Catholic and he, I was told, slighted him, and they were in the Lodge up **[136/44L]** there, Shrawmannough Lodge in Ballycroy, for someone belonging to him lived in that Lodge. This District Inspector, who was driving the first car, was killed.[99] The RIC were allowed to send a cyclist into Westport. We went back to the same house we had been in in the morning, and then we went to Joyce's in Durless, to the south-west of the Reek.

Drummin Barracks was destroyed in May.[100] They [RIC] arrested Harney,[101] who is now the garage man in Louisburgh, that was the nearest they were to us, but they didn't come to Durless.[102]

Willie Malone lives in Breaffy.[103]

Inishbee.[104] There was a dug-out found there which had been made for the arms of the submarine. There were boats on top of it for when a raid was made, but the dug-out was found (in the Civil War).

[101/49] There was a kind of fight at the Red Bridge in Westport[105] and a fight at Clogher Crossroads on a very dark night.[106] We had no loss in either scrap.

After this scrap we went into East Mayo, and we dumped our arms at the back of the Reek (caves there), after we had gone to Nephin, Castlebar, Bohola,[107] Balla,[108] out on the

---

99 RIC District Inspector Edward Stevenson.

100 Actually on 1 June 1920.

101 Andy Harney.

102 A section of this page following this sentence, on Tourmakeady, has been moved to place it earlier so that it is in chronological order.

103 Breaffy, not Breffney as in the original text.

104 Inishbee is one of the outer islands in Clew Bay, beside Inishoo, and a dug-out was maintained there.

105 The Red Bridge incident occurred on the night of 8 May 1921.

106 The Westport ASU, under Joe Ring, was in the Clogher area on the night of 22 April 1921 when two RIC Crossley tenders caught up with it. Both sides exchanged fire at the Clogher Crossroads but no injuries were reported.

107 Bohola, not Bohoola as in the original text.

108 Balla, not Ball as in the original text.

Partry road near the Partry Mountains[109] … to Owenwee.[110]
There was a round-up by about 5,000 troops. They seemed to
guess where we were. We dumped our arms in Owenwee where
they were also pitching a camp. There were four to five of us,
Jim Rushe, Dr Madden, Kitterick, Ned Moane and I.[111] We
went up the mountains. I am always interested in minerals so
I thought I'd have a good look.[112] We saw lights in a house
and what were they but lights of the Protestant women there
who were cooking for the British outposts. **[101/50]** And I was
marching around, as you can well imagine, [looking] for the
mine and three of the lads got sick of me, and they went up the
road.[113] Kitterick and Moane were with me when we saw lights
coming in under us in the hollow. The lads above saw them
also, and they sent down a man who did not get in touch with
me. All our arms were dumped at this time. We were looking
for the others then, but we couldn't find them. We went into a
glen beside Gibbons, the herd. It was a cul-de-sac, and I sent
up a lad to a breach for a good place to get out, so we followed
him up. There were huge boulders there which would give us
cover. An aeroplane would come up every few hours to search
the valley. We could see troops moving around, and at 2 or 3
o'clock the RIC came in and searched for footprints, and they
went up the cliff, and at 4 [o'clock] we saw some rifles coming
from behind the hills. Ten Auxies or Tans came down by the
rock I had got under. Gibbons brought us up tea on the evening
of that first day.

Second day. We were in a shelf overlooking the lake. We had
heather in our caps and belts so as to be less easy to see. The

109 Not the Sheefrey Mountains as in the original text.
110 Owenwee, not Owenbride as in the original text.
111 Rushe, not Roche as in the original text.
112 Kilroy had an interest in mineral ores and rock formations.
113 Kilroy's reference to 'for the mine' might refer to his interest in minerals and to
    the fact that there were old mines in the mountains.

plane was on a level with us, and if we had our rifles we could have shot them off so they got in to bathe in the lake, 300–400 yards away.[114] Then we got away out to Petie McDonnell's area.[115]

[101/51] IRB. Only a few [IRB] in Newport. Westport was the strongest group. Diarmuid Lynch came to a Connaught Convention in 1915 at which I was to represent West Mayo, but he had to leave. Alec McCabe of Kesh was there.[116] There was no IRB meeting during the Truce.

At a Sinn Féin Convention in 41 Parnell Square, we were called in a bunch irregularly for men were going in and out and we were told who to vote for.[117] At the time I thought it was all right. This was IRB influence at work.

[TRUCE]

The Split. Joe Ring was a Liaison Officer in Galway.[118] He was a bit vain. Johnny Gibbons had been there before him, but Johnny couldn't stick it. Ring was the only officer we lost.[119] Tom Maguire lost a good few men.[120] O'Grady, a quartermaster, was imposed on Tom Maguire by General Headquarters. He went as engineer.

The 4th [Western] Division was formed during the Truce by Eoin O'Duffy at about late harvest time: West and North

---

114 Plane, not plain as in the original text. O'Malley also included an 'x' after 300–400 in the original text, probably referring to yards.
115 Probably Petie Joe McDonnell, not MacDonald as in the original text.
116 Kesh, Co. Sligo.
117 The Irish National Forester's Hall, now the Kevin Barry Memorial Hall, where the Gaelic Athletic Association and the IRB often met in Dublin.
118 Liaison officers were appointed by the IRA in various areas to coordinate or liaise with the British about the taking over of their barracks and other practical matters.
119 Kilroy's reference to 'lost' refers to the number of his officers who joined the Free State army.
120 Tom Maguire (1892–1993) of Cross. See his interview.

Mayo Brigades, Connemara.[121] [The] 2nd Western [Division]: South Roscommon, South Mayo, Galway city area. There wasn't a man there who didn't see through O'Duffy who talked about his finger which he had lost in action. We felt he was very vain, and it was evident in his speech.

[TREATY]

[101/52] Westport people held a public meeting there on before 6th December, and they called upon the Government to accept the Treaty being offered. No one mentioned war, but then no country ever does want war. That meeting in Westport was organised by Dr Moran, and he was responsible for that motion on December 6th. (Westport also passed a motion in 1916 approving of Maxwell.)[122] In Castlebar twenty-six turned out as special constables. Moclair captured sixteen Balla rifles, but Dick Walsh, with a rusty revolver, recaptured the rifles.[123] (Tom Quinn of Castlebar, my uncle, was one of the special constables.)[124]

West Mayo was very firm with us. Very few of the men's relations turned against us. Newport town was never any good. I heard it said that a man could be shot in the streets of Newport and no one could hear of it. There were terrible raids on the Fenians there, and nothing could be made out of it. (No one arrested?) A man swore on the Fenians there but it was all personal enmity and even the magistrates suspected it.

The Castlebar Meeting.[125] We were in the barracks there.

---

121 Eoin, not Owen as in the original text. The western brigades were consolidated into divisions in August–September 1921: 4th Western Division (O/C, M. Kilroy) had: West Mayo, North Mayo and West Connemara Brigades; 2nd Western Division (O/C, T. Maguire) had: South Mayo, South Roscommon Brigades and Galway city.

122 General Sir John Maxwell was O/C British forces in Ireland at the time.

123 Moclair of Castlebar, not Manclair as in the original text.

124 O'Malley's mother's sister from Castlerea had married RIC Constable Tom Quinn of Castlebar.

125 The meeting was held on 1 April 1922, just two weeks before the IRA took

There was a big demonstration for Collins to speak at.[126] He left it all on Dickeen Walsh, and Collins got through the barricades, north of Castlebar.[127] I was in barracks, but our lads were all on edge. Our fellows were crazy for a scrap, and Collins had a bunch of really cocky **[101/53]** Dublin men with him. Our lads chased them up streets like autumn leaves. They pitched their guns up on top of presses, and our lads got them afterwards.[128] We had a chap in barracks as a prisoner, maybe it was Joe Ring, and he was on hunger strike. Afterwards Collins wanted to know if he could see him. I met Collins at the gate and the detention is at the gate also.

We were asking GHQ at this time to pay the debt we owed shopkeepers for clothing and for feeding our men. 'Can you have a little patience?'[129]

We were filled up with the thought of this debt at the time. I said to Collins, 'We can't forget that you hold the purse strings, and you're too close to them.'

'Well,' said Collins, 'that's the meanest thing a man ever said to another.' Collins saw Joe Ring, then Harry Coyle, **[101/54R]** a Scotch helper whom we were very fond of, but we locked him up.

We took £22,000 out of the Bank for our area, and I paid our debts with it.[130] We sent £2,000 up to Dublin to the Quartermaster General, Liam Mellows.

I was close in correspondence with General Headquarters on account of the post. 'You've got your money now, and you don't pay anyone.'

over the Four Courts in Dublin.
126 Collins spoke at an open-air venue on the Castlebar Mall.
127 Dickeen Walsh was probably Dick Walsh of Balla.
128 Press meaning a cupboard for storage.
129 The next four paragraphs were included in the original out of chronological order and have been moved here to correct this problem.
130 This refers to a bank raid rather than a withdrawal from their own account at the bank.

[**Limerick.**] I came down to Limerick with a column from Pilkington and Tom Maguire.[131] I went down there for an HQ Staff meeting, Tom Maguire and I. We crossed the Shannon near Ardnacrusha at Ballina, and we went to one of the barracks.[132] I remember [meeting] Seán MacCarthy about either engineering or supplies, and we brought cylinders of guns back with us.[133] We had to go across the fields in the 2nd Western Division for all roads were blocked there and there were trees across them.

[**101/54L**] **Swap of rifles.**[134] Our men had very strict instructions not to swap rifles. Captain Broddie Gibbons, Battalion O/C there, was one of the officers concerned and there were some of Tom's (Maguire's) officers also. There were about forty rifles or so and they were ordered to be sure that the other rifles were placed in their hands before they would part with their own rifles. They didn't get the new Lee-Enfield rifles so the Free State didn't observe our conditions and they came back again with their old rifles.

The West got no German Mauser rifles (Free State). We sent up a team to Birr Barracks for rifles and they brought them back. They penetrated five-eighths-inch steel plate.

CIVIL WAR

[**101/53**] Seán Lehane came on to Paul Bofin and his men and himself were in rags.[135] They asked Bofin if he could do anything

131 In March 1922 William/Billy/Liam Pilkington was O/C 3rd Western Division and Tom Maguire was O/C 2nd Western Division. This meeting took place at the time that O'Malley, then O/C 2nd Southern Division, had taken over Limerick city from Michael Brennan, O/C 1st Western, who was pro-Treaty.

132 Ballina village straddles the River Shannon between Counties Clare and Tipperary.

133 Seán McCarthy was anti-Treaty and the O/C East Limerick Brigade.

134 In the spring of 1922 Michael Collins had a plan to have new British arms issued to the anti-Treaty IRA and their old, untraceable arms sent to defend the Catholics fighting in the North.

135 Seán Lehane had been O/C No. 3 Brigade, Cork, and was assigned to be O/C

for them. 'No trouble whatever,' said Paul. 'Have a good rest and we'll get lots of clothes for you.' Paul Bofin sent in his order to a shop and on a certain day when the clothes were due, he held up the train and took off the clothes. Wasn't that an easy way of getting supplies without hurting the shopkeeper?

[101/55R] Poor Devins captured 'the Ballinalee'.[136] Pilkington and I were very good. To train our men I wanted a loan of the armoured car for I wanted to show them what it was possible to do for our fellows were crazy for fighting.[137] We used double-steel shutters with our car 'The Queen of the West', to show men how they could go up under the enemy when covered by fire. Our fellows came out of the armoured car and were snatching mines from one another in Clifden where they wanted to set the mines at the barracks. The ex-soldiers captured said they had never seen such fighting in all their lives like that. The others there, Free State under O'Malley, fought there until the roof came down on top of them.[138] The double-steel shutters in Clifden were put in ... four men. They took out the windows of the houses opposite to the Staters and silenced them by firing through their loopholes. O'Malley in charge of them was afraid he'd be executed by us. Their barracks was blown asunder.

We made hundreds of mines in Castlebar during the Truce, hundreds of them; and we made 200 grenades every second day. We moulded and cast necks for Headquarters. This went on for ... We sent a big amount of grenades to Sligo free and to Tom Maguire also. All we sent away were good but we used

---

1st Northern Division in spring 1922.

136 The Free State armoured car 'Ballinalee' was captured by the IRA and renamed.

137 Armoured car was written as a/car in the original text.

138 Commandant Patrick O'Malley, an ex-RIC man, had been involved with the West Connemara Brigade flying column in 1921 but had taken the pro-Treaty side. He was from the Clifden area and was involved in unsuccessfully defending Clifden from the Republican attack on 29 October 1922. See Jack Feehan interview, O'Malley, *The Men Will Talk to Me: Galway Interviews*, p. 166.

vertiginous cartridges for our own grenades and most of them didn't work. [55L] We used very strong white metal which held the explosive force longer and made it stronger.

Dr Madden went in to start a fight. They placed a mine at the old gaol, at the gate where I was captured. It exploded but it had not been sufficiently tamped.

[101/56R] In Tipperary in MacCarthy's of Cahir, Lynch had me appointed to take charge of the Western Command.[139]

It ['The Ballinalee'] had been sent up and captured with Éamon Enright at Kinvara and there was Michael MacNulty who had married a MacCarthy.[140] We stayed a couple of days there. I had expected that Clifden would be captured before I got back.[141]

'The Ballinalee' was brought to Ballina. The Free State were very frightened of us. Before we left ... all men with arms were to move down to meet us and we were to take Ballina, then Westport and next Castlebar, and so clear the county of the Free State. Then we were to seize a train and land at Athlone. I heard that MacEoin was boasting how impregnable his barracks was there.[142] Petrol in cans up a ladder would take it, we thought.

In the Ox Mountains Carty had his Headquarters.[143] He insisted on raiding Tobbercurry in daylight.[144] He had no respect much [sic] for Pilkington. He raided it and just shouted at the Free State in Tobbercurry. A contractor ... in gaol told

139 Liam Lynch was chief of staff of the anti-Treaty forces from June 1922 until he was killed on 10 April 1923. This meeting took place in mid-October 1922 and Ernie O'Malley, then assistant chief of staff, attended.
140 The Free State 'Ballinalee' armoured car was captured by Seamus Devins.
141 A plan had been established for the Republican forces to approach Clifden from Mulranny and attack it.
142 Seán MacEoin (not MacKeown as in the original text) was born in Ballinalee, Co. Longford, and at this time was a brigadier general, O/C Western Command of the Free State army, with his headquarters in Athlone.
143 Frank Carty from Sligo. See biographical sketches.
144 Tobbercurry, not Tubbercurry as in the original text.

me the plan of rolling a mine from a plank from an armoured car. Instead, Frank Carty brought back a load of bicycle tyres ...

We left the Ox Mountains in the night when the armoured car came along. Two of our ASUs were **[101/56L]** captured in that area and their rifles were taken as well. The 3rd Western gave us twelve rifles for that. The armoured car began to sink [into the mud] and we shifted it. We could do nothing then for that night and the Free State landed at Westport next day.[145] We were in Ballina at 11.30 a.m. We ran right into a drove of sheep which the women drove out to block our way, but we drove over the sheep. The Free State officer in Ballina said, 'We were waiting up for you all night, Michael, but we didn't expect you at 11.30 in the morning.' Tom Ruane got the officers in the hotel, and he made them put up their hands.

I was impatient to get away then but one of our officers said, 'It's good enough to see it in the papers to-morrow', so I knew that the higher officers didn't want [a] fight, so I went back to Newport. The weather got bad then. We meant to go around by Ballycroy to tackle Newport.

[101/57R] At Glenlossera[146] beyond Ballycastle the armoured car began to sink in the road ... it reached Sligo.[147]

I had sent over to England for a lathe. It came to a photographer in Ballina, and we captured it in the Workhouse yard in Ballina. It was for finishing grenades. I took it apart and put it in a lorry, and we hid the parts in various places.

Beyond Glenlossera Lodge we heard a shot, and I doubled the guards. We took a prisoner, and we found that the Free State were there to rush us at the Lodge. We captured them next day, twenty of them. I sent Tom Ruane, Senator, Ballina. His wife

145 The Republicans recaptured Ballina on 12 September 1922, though two civilians were killed in the crossfire.

146 Glenlossera, not Glenlassaragh as in the original text.

147 The words 'it reached Sligo' do not make sense since the car was going west not east.

has a draper's shop, no pretensions, a good soldier he was. I sent him with twelve men to attack the twenty, and they came out and lay down their arms.

At Belderg, O'Malley,[148] a fine lad, now in the Guards, captured a rifle: fifteen rifles captured and we had twenty to twenty-four revolvers from Ballina.[149] We went to Glenamoy, west of Belderg, to a shooting lodge to Diarmuid O'Donoghue, a cousin of Dr Madden. We found it emptied of Free State for they had left a short time before. I was so tired I fell asleep on the floor, and I was awakened by …[150] 'I didn't know it was you,' I said, 'I thought you were Staters.'

'You're surrounded,' he said. He crept out west of us, firing. Joe Bourke also was surrounded and he was isolated. He wouldn't surrender in his house. He kept the Staters back in the pitch dark and in **[101/57L]** the grey dawn of the morning a bunch of fellows came up the road. They were Staters. We flattened them out in an hour. We got forty-five or fifty rifles that day. We had to let the Staters go for we couldn't bring them with us, nor could we give them food. These men were in a state of rebellion at their treatment. Afterwards they'd do anything for us. We fed them well and they were very hungry. They cheered me in Athlone Barracks when I was a prisoner. Later we had to lie down on the floor, heads and points, for there was little room. We got the people to kill a sheep for us, and after a few days we came in to Shramore. Lots of courage, confidence and ability our men had.

Family bitterness made splits in a few families, but not in many. There was a food boat captured in Newport. Then I got word to go to an Executive Meeting, and I told Petie McDonnell

148 Belderg, not Bellderrig as in the original text. This O'Malley could not be identified.
149 Ernie O'Malley from time to time uses R(1) and R(2) in his notes to refer to rifles and revolvers.
150 The name 'Michael' has been omitted here as the man could not be identified.

to have Clifden taken when I got back.[151] Petie had good fights with the Tans. You had best see him.

[Capture and imprisonment.] [101/58L] I was wounded in the middle of the back.[152] The wound came out at the side of the ribs. I was brought to Athlone. We were to be executed at the time of the Bagenal arrests, and MacEoin made a special journey to Dublin to save me, and he said to me, 'I don't know the result but I did my best.' Mulrennan was shot sitting beside Paddy Hegarty in Athlone.[153] Lawlor fired a few shots at him, then Lawlor and MacEoin were going around making sport of the prisoners, hitting them with sticks. MacEoin would say when Lawlor fired, 'You missed him.' Ask Peter Hegarty about this.[154] He'd know.

I was brought to the Joy to be executed.[155] When in Athlone I was under Dr Maguire, a decent man, who holds an appointment in Wicklow. Mulcahy boasted that he had so many of the higher officers that he would execute three of them.[156]

The Detention [barracks] in Athlone was very cold and was filled with prisoners. I was court-martialled in the Joy. I got Conor Maguire to defend me.[157] They wouldn't let him plead

151 Petie Joe McDonnell. Clifden was captured on 29 October 1922. See O'Malley, *The Men Will Talk to Me: Galway Interviews*, pp. 65–98.

152 Kilroy was wounded and captured at Kilbride, Newport, on 24 November 1922.

153 Captain Patrick Mulrennan of Lisacul, Ballaghaderreen, a prisoner in Athlone internment camp, was killed by Brigadier General Lawlor (not Lalor as in the original text) on 6 October 1922. Paddy Hegarty, of Laherdane, also a prisoner there, was a witness. Later that year the IRA in Dublin intercepted a letter from Lawlor to his mother wherein he boasted about how good a shot he was when he killed Mulrennan. This letter was published in *Éire*, the Republican newspaper, January 1923. Mulcahy Papers, UCDA P7/B/87.

154 For Paddy and Peter Hegarty in North Mayo see their interviews, O'Malley Notebooks UCDA P17b/109, 137.

155 Mountjoy Prison was commonly referred to as the 'Joy'.

156 Richard Mulcahy, former chief of staff of IRA, had become the chief of staff of the Free State army.

157 A barrister with Republican sympathies, who later became a minister in the Fianna Fáil government.

so he had to withdraw. There was no sentence promulgated. The court-martial didn't last long. I was never told my sentence.

Larry Houlihan was in charge of 'D' Wing.[158]

Tommy Reidy from Kilmeena used to live in a tunnel in the Joy.[159] There was opposition between two parties. Our fellows were in favour of bursting the doors, the other crowd under Matty Connolly were for shouting 'Socko. Put a sock in it', and it **[101/58R]** kept a soreness going. Doors were burst with books at hinges.

Paddy Coughlan, O/C of ... Wing, was on the run. He was hidden amongst our fellows and the Staters didn't know him.

[101/59] I began to shake the railings and I found I could near shake them loose and with other fellows shaking we had in a few minutes flattened the ring railings which were set in a concrete base. We knocked over a whole section of railings on its granite base whilst the lights of the lorries were switched off.

Nineteen of us were taken to Arbour Hill and put in solitary confinement.[160] I never felt the days passing by for I was interested in things I had to work out in my mind. Michael Burke of Wingate was also planning new types of engines for new types of aeroplanes (jet propulsed). A thing like that goes through men like pickle and nobody is accountable for it.

I had made a blackboard. The tunnellers wanted it to hide a place so they took it from me. There is a black box in every cell in which a heated pipe came through to make a hole for a man's shoulders. They dug out bricks to get to the basement; and when the man went down there was a Stater below, staring up at him.

The chimney tunnel reached close to the wall.

---

158 To be 'in charge' refers to the commander or O/C of the prisoners who was elected by the prisoners from their ranks.
159 Tommy Reidy, not Reedy as in the original text.
160 Arbour Hill was another prison in Dublin used by the British and Free State armies.

Hunger strike.[161] Billy Pilkington was opposed to it. It was hard he thought to get a strike to succeed when there was a big number of men on strike. A hunger strike should consist of picked men only. **[101/60]** The decision was hanging fire. I wasn't one way or the other. I didn't like it and I wouldn't oppose it.[162]

Con Moloney signed the form in a day or two. At least he got out of jail.

Kilmainham. The eyes were rolling in the heads of some of them. Paul Bofin took a feed of dry bread, and he had to lie across the table with the pain. Jack Keogh, he was only a short time on hunger strike. Ned Bofin: there was a queer streak in him. Pilkington didn't like him.

Jack Feehan, Divisional Quartermaster.[163] At an election in North Mayo we published a list of bills paid by us when the banks were raided in North Mayo. Feehan yet holds these stamped receipts.[164] He is building houses somewhere now.

At GHQ I was against the raids on the banks for money. I said we would burn our fingers that way.[165]

Executions. No men were executed [by the Free State] in the 4th Western Division. O'Malley from Oughterard was executed

---

161 O'Malley often uses h/s as an abbreviation for hunger strike. It began in Mountjoy Prison on 12 October 1923 and spread rapidly so that at one point over 12,000 prisoners were on strike, but it started to collapse as the days went on. After several men became seriously ill and one died, the strike was called off on 22 November. The Free State offered an incentive to release prisoners if they signed a form in effect stating that they would not take up arms again against the Free State.

162 The next sentence suggested that Pilkington thought that going on a hunger strike might be a way to get released from internment, but the sentence is confusing and has been omitted.

163 See his complete interview in O'Malley, *The Men Will Talk to Me: Galway Interviews*, pp. 99–186.

164 Some of the details of these accounts as well as a list of their equipment are included in the Jack Feehan interview in *Galway Interviews*, pp. 136–37.

165 The sentence following, which did not make sense, has been omitted.

in our area in Tuam in the Workhouse.[166] The Battalion Section who look after unmarried mothers there, take care of his grave.

[138/14L] The Men of the West. (Liam Willy has this song.)

Hurrah for the bold Michael Kilroy, boys,
Who of bullets was never afraid.
He was always the last in the fighting
While leading West Mayo Brigade.

The Moanes in Castlebar had songs as well about the Column. Carrowkennedy soon told a story.

It was a vicious circle whenever there were raids on or small round-ups of the population. Men ran away as soon as they saw either the military or the police, for they were afraid of being beaten and questioned. Then whenever they were seen as they ran away they were fired on. The Tans, the RIC, the military and the Auxiliaries took anyone whom they met with (outside of those who had stringent Anglo-Irish voices), as the enemy, and they certainly behaved towards them as if these men and women before them were their enemies whom they were armed against.

166 James O'Malley from Oughterard, Co. Galway, was executed at Tuam on 6 April 1923, shortly before the ceasefire was called.

PADDY CANNON

(UCDA P17b/136, pp. 49–58)[1]

Patrick 'Paddy' Cannon (1899–1970)
was born in Cornacushlan, Islandeady,
which is between Castlebar and
Westport. He was a well-known
athlete in his youth. He joined the Irish
Volunteers in 1917 in the Islandeady
Company of the Castlebar Battalion
and became the adjutant there. He had
the reputation of being a crack shot with
his Mauser rifle. He joined the West
Mayo Brigade flying column or ASU

*Copyright J. J. Leonard
(courtesy of Anthony
Leonard)*

in May 1921 and was soon involved in its actions in Kilmeena
and Carrowkennedy. He went anti-Treaty and was captured at
Castlebar in August 1922 and interned at several locations.[2] He
was part of the mass breakout by tunnel in April 1923 from
Tintown internment camp, the Curragh. When Fianna Fáil
came to power in 1932, Cannon got a job in the Mayo Health
Board and worked his way up in this organisation, eventually
becoming secretary to the board. He married Miss Heffernan,
and they lived at Mountain View, Castlebar.

This interview took place in Islandeady in the early 1950s.

---

1   The initial transcription and some of the footnotes for this interview were
    prepared by Dominic Price. Cannon made his statement to the Bureau of
    Military History – WS 830.
2   In his interview, Tommy Heavey says that Paddy Cannon, himself and six
    others escaped from Athlone on 21 August and were recaptured, but Cannon
    does not mention this episode.

[1917–1921 PERIOD]

[49L] I joined the Irish Volunteers in 1917 in Islandeady, and I was the Adjutant between 1917 and 1920. On the 10 October 1920 there were 107 men on the roll. There had been sixty to seventy men there before Conscription.[3] We had two German Mausers.[4] I had a long German all through and Paddy Jordan had a short Mauser.[5] They had been brought down from GHQ by Tom Kitterick about the middle of 1920 with between 300 to 400 rounds of ammunition.[6] The long Mauser held one in the breech and five in the magazine and the short Mauser held ten cartridges. It had a flat trajectory up to 600 yards. It was a sniping Mauser (the short) and it was deadly accurate for I tested it after the Truce at 500 yards. (One of the great drawbacks was that men in many areas had had no practice with .22 ammo nor had they fired any shot out of a rifle before they had gone into action; hence a rifle was a mystery to them.) We had a big number of single-barrelled shotguns. We had two dozen shotguns but we were short of single-barrelled shot cartridges. Our area went to two miles of Westport road to Sheeaune Hill and less than two miles on the Newport road and within five miles then of Newport (this doesn't make sense).[7] Near Kilmeena our territory ran down in an angle close to Newport.

RIC. Deergrove was burned in April 1920, and the RIC

---

3 The threat of enforcing conscription in Ireland in early 1918 was never imple-mented as the proposal faced overwhelming opposition from the population.

4 German Mauser rifles were long-barrelled guns and in the original text were occasionally referred to as a 'German'. It was a favoured rifle for sniping.

5 Cannon's 'all through' expression refers to all through the fighting period. Paddy Jordan (1896–1921) was born in Derrycreeve but lived in Letter village, where his father was the schoolmaster. He joined the Irish Volunteers and was a founding member of the Islandeady Company IRA and its O/C, and later V/C of the Castlebar Battalion.

6 Tom Kitterick. See biographical sketches.

7 Sheeaune Hill, not Sheehan as in the original text. It is difficult now to be accurate about the boundary lines of companies, battalions and brigades, as the lines changed frequently.

went into Castlebar.[8] They came in before any trouble began. This barracks was closed on the grounds of economy. Glenisland had a Company.[9] It was a half parish of Islandeady, and it was not so strong. We were in the Castlebar Battalion, and the Castlebar Company was the nearest Company to us.[10] Paddy Jordan was on the run for about a year. He was the O/C of Islandeady Company, then he was the Vice-Commandant of Castlebar Battalion. In about November or December 1920,[11] Dr Madden, Jordan I think, more or less organised a column, and the column went out under Jordan who was the [49R] Vice-Commandant and Chambers, O/C the [Castlebar] Battalion, who was not on the run.[12] He remained in Castlebar. There were troops in the military barracks, a few hundred of them, between 300 to 400. The Munsters were in it for a while, and then came the Border Regiment.[13] Generally, the soldiers were all right. The Tans and the RIC did the dirty work.

I joined the column in May of 1921. In January it started really. There were about fourteen or fifteen men in it. They stayed mostly in Islandeady and Glenisland where they laid in ambush for a car, for the RIC went out on patrol every Tuesday.[14] The car did not turn up when they lay for it. Staunton was on the run for a while.[15] His house was close to Cloggernagh school

8 Deergrove RIC Barracks, burned on 3 April 1920, was known as Driminahaha Barracks, as it was situated in that townland. It was built by a landlord, Palmer, who financed the manning of it during the Land War of the 1880s.
9 Company here refers to an Irish Volunteer company.
10 Castlebar Battalion had several local companies including Ballyheane, Ballyvary, Castlebar itself, Glenisland, Islandeady, Parke and Turlough.
11 O'Malley mistakenly wrote 1930 in the original text.
12 James Chambers.
13 The official regimental names were The Royal Munster Fusiliers and The Border Regiment, based in Northern England.
14 Probably Glenisland (not Gleneady as in the original text), as it is the half parish of Islandeady.
15 Michael Staunton, whose blacksmith's shop was the local meeting place at Cloggernagh.

house, just beside it on this side, and this car load of Tans and RIC went out to raid his home.[16] He was on the run on the 6th of May 1921.

[Big Wall, 6 May.][17] There was a point picked for the blocking of a road at a bridge this side of the Cross. There were no trees and no bridge to cut, so the fellows decided that they would knock wall stones out on the road when the car passed on from there towards Westport. (He is describing the ambush at the Big Wall.)

The [RIC] lorry passed and they blocked the road. They raided the house 200 yards away, and they came back again. Lally, O'Malley, F. O'Boyle and MacNulty were captured.[18] They beat them up badly in the gaol, which was the Headquarters for the RIC. There were close on 100 RIC there then. There was a fourteen foot wall and in place there were two walls around it. They would keep prisoners there for a few days. They threw a slop bucket on his head and they kicked it on to his head. The road was trenched at the ambush point, and they brought my father who was at Islandeady chapel doing the Nine Fridays, and the [RIC] took him to Westport, but the ambush party had then left the position, [50L] and he knew about this ambush position at the Big Wall (why did he know about it?), but the men had left it.[19] After some hours they (the IRA men), who were at the Big Wall, learned of the shooting at Cloonkeen.[20]

16 Cloggernagh, not Cloggera as in the original text.
17 The Big Wall is often referred to by others as the High Wall. It was a wall about nine feet high located beside Islandeady Dance Hall on the Castlebar–Westport road, separating the road from the railroad.
18 F. O'Boyle, not N. Boyle as in the original text. Volunteers Thomas O'Malley and Thomas Lally, who were cousins, were caught in the act of blocking the road and were shot on the spot on 6 May 1921. A memorial to them was put up in Cloonkeen, where a lady donated a site for the memorial though they were actually executed in Cloggernagh.
19 The Nine Fridays refers to the local tradition of visiting the same church on nine consecutive Fridays to gain an indulgence.
20 Cloonkeen, not Clocheen as in the original text.

They had been there from 5 to 6 a.m. until 11 a.m. There were twenty to twenty-five men at the Big Wall waiting for anything that would come. They didn't go on by road then, so you had to ambush between the principal towns, and on the principal roads. There were about eight of us there in the position throwing down the stones. When the lorry passed it was assumed that it was heading for Westport. They followed down after us for some distance across country, and then they gave it up. I rejoined the Castlebar Column two days later. We were in Aille and there were three columns.[21] The fellows were sent in to the various towns, and there were three towns, to bomb street patrols. That operation didn't come off until the Wednesday night before Kilmeena. The three columns separated. We came through Islandeady. We sent in three or four Castlebar men to bomb any of the patrols. The Newport men went in to Newport where a Sergeant Butler was killed.[22] The Castlebar men returned to Islandeady on Wednesday. Four or five joined us, and we went towards Ballinacarriga[23] close to Sheeaune in the half parish of Kilmeena.[24] The Castlebar Column had eight rifles and a few Martinis, four Lee-Enfields, a few single shots, and a few shotguns.[25]

[**Kilmeena ambush, 19 May 1921.**] We got into the village of Ballinacarriga, and we did not know that Michael Kilroy and his column were there. We got in there at 1 a.m., and his sections did not spot us as we went in there not by the orthodox

---

21 Aille (not Aill as in the original text) is on the Westport–Ballinrobe road near Aughagower.
22 Sgt Francis J. Butler, RIC, was fatally shot in Newport on 18 May 1921 by Jim Moran and Jim Browne.
23 Ballinacarriga, also known as Ballynacarriga, is a townland close to Islandeady about three miles from Westport to the north side of the Westport–Castlebar road and was known for being a safe place for those men 'on the run'.
24 Sheeaune, not Sheehane as in the original text.
25 O'Malley wrote these armaments twice and they have been consolidated to avoid repetition.

way. Kilroy got the surprise of his life. The village is near the D on the Westport road, near to Clogher Lake. It was a friendly village, and the people would go out of their way to **[50R]** help a column. On one side the place was fairly well protected by lakes on the eastern side. Kilroy recovered from his shock at our entry. He had got word that the Newport men had shot an RIC man, Butler in Newport, and he expected that there would be an influx of RIC into Westport on the next morning, so he decided to set an ambush on the road at Kilmeena. What discussions he had with Dr Madden, I do not know.[26] We headed out to Rossow Bridge by the by-road to the tailors at 5 a.m., just at day light in the morning.[27] There was a survey then made at a few points as a kind of a commune. There was a point picked close to the bridge which crossed the railway and it was practically on it, but the railway overlooked it as they passed. You could fire straight into a lorry coming from Westport, but there was not a complete cover from lorries which were on their way from Newport, for to deal with them we would have to go to the west of the road. On Cummins' side the cover was too small for our men, and as a result later on, after three-quarters of an hour we went to the back of the Dance Hall. Old Cummins amused me.[28] We held a fence about thirty to thirty-five yards from the road. We had heavy GHQ bombs, about a dozen in all.

We took up our position. One fellow was sent back to the Parish Priest's house as a left wing flanker to protect us.[29] He had no rifle but he had a Peter the Painter.[30] There was a party on the hill over [the] tailor's, and there were four or five in that group.[31] Dr

26 Dr John A. Madden. See biographical sketches.
27 Rossow Bridge is north of Kilmeena, and south of Newport.
28 Tom Cummins was a close neighbour to John O'Flynn near the Kilmeena ambush site.
29 Parish Priest is written as P.P. in the original text.
30 A German 9 mm automatic pistol.
31 John O'Flynn was a tailor (not taylor as in the original text) and is sometimes referred to as 'Flynn, the tailor.'

Madden was halfway between us and Moran's flank, in a quarry.[32] He was just behind the tailor's (Flynn). It would be half 5 or 6 [a.m.] now. Later the flanking parties were sent out.

The Reverend Mother in Westport was dead, and as she was being buried, two or three carloads of priests and nuns came from the Newport direction. We had calculated that cars would **[51L]** be coming on from Newport. The British, we thought, would have come in to Newport during the night, and they would have been going out during the day as a result of the killing of the sergeant. There did come cars, but they were two or three carloads of nuns principally and they were damn near shot up. I had the first pressure taken when someone who was near shouted, 'They're clergy.'[33]

I was at the end of the fence near Cummins' house. We … our … so that we could line that fence which was at [right angles] from the Newport cars.[34] There was no signalling arrangements, and there was no arrangement for a blockade. The Newport lads who had been on the shooting in Newport, Jimmy Moran and … were sent back to a village which was a mile up to the north -east to rest.[35] There were four or five of them; nearly six, and there were old barracks near Fr Hurley.[36] The lads waited and they saw a policeman turning up from Newport and they shot him when he was in the barrack's yard. These two men went to rest and they were to turn up later. We stuck it out. We were just preparing to go …[37]

Old Cummins was there in the morning, and we were there

---

32 James/Jim Moran of Shraloggy, a townland north-west of Newport.

33 Cannon's reference to 'pressure' refers to his pressure on the trigger preparing to fire. The line following this explaining the casualties at Kilmeena has been excluded as they are better explained elsewhere.

34 O'Malley included a diagram in the original text, which is not included here, and it reflects a right angle at the crossroads.

35 Referring to the killing of Sgt Francis J. Butler by Moran and Browne.

36 The former RIC barracks was in Brockagh village.

37 An incomplete sentence in the original text following this has been omitted.

a long time when Cummins saw us. He paraded up and down in front of the ambush position, and Michael Kilroy sent me down, as I was a stranger, to threaten him, and then he cleared back to his house. Jim Kelly had gone to C[ummins'] and there was a feed cooking, and Kelly was in Cummins' when the fight started. About 10 [a.m.] the nuns passed by at 10.15 for … 11 o'clock.[38] No other cars passed until 3 or 4 [p.m.] that day save horse cars. There was a wind up station in [51R] Kilmeena.[39] Canon MacDonald's (the Parish Priest in Newport) car came out and was outside of the priest's house at the bridge. I put a few bullets through it for some of the RIC got behind it. Newport Column had five or six rifles then, and there were a few Westport men. Tom Kitterick was not there.[40] We were getting tired. The first lorry came through. We were getting tired and had concluded that nothing could happen. I was falling asleep. It was a warm fine drowsy day. Jim MacEvilly was practically asleep, and I didn't know that a lorry was coming, and we were looking forward to a feed just then. The lorry was in front of the ambush position before we saw it. We jumped up and blazed[41] but it had gone past me at the Dance Hall when I fired and I got in two shots (or I fired two shots) before it disappeared. It went on at a shocking bloody pace across the bridge. Fire started from the flanking party on the Newport road out of view from us. The lorry party which had gone past us halted a half a mile away and then walked back, and there were from nine to ten RIC in it.

The flanking party fired on the Tans. They came along back

38 There was an 11 a.m. service in Westport for the mother superior.
39 A 'wind up station' is the last mass station or house where mass is to be said in the course of the stations in a townland.
40 O'Malley writes the name Butch Lambert here in the original text but there is no context and the name has been omitted.
41 A repetitive section about looking forward to a feed has been omitted from this sentence.

to the railway bridge, the Tans. We thought that our firing party had been able to occupy that lorry of RIC. The second lorry came on and we saw it in the distance behind the Canon's car over the railway bridge at … and a Crossley pulled up beside it on the other side of the bridge. They could not see us. We lined the fence at right angles to them on the far side of the road. One of the RIC went up the field on our side of the road, maybe to draw fire, and some went behind the Canon's car. Then a machine gun opened from the bridge near the Parish Priest's house. It opened up indiscriminately as we had perfect fire and it [52L] practically peppered Dr Madden who was in the sandpit, for he was in the direct line of fire. For five to ten minutes firing we were ducking from machine-gun fire. The next thing I knew of was that fire came from behind us. The Tans had come back to the railway bridge and had opened up on our rear from not 200 yards away. (Why is it always Tans for there was a mixture of them, Tans and RIC! Does Tans make the status more important for they were more desperate men?) We rushed away. Collins was right in front of me as we crossed the gap, and he fell right across my feet. Down on the road Jordan, O/C Castlebar Battalion, had been with a few men, and he was wounded then and completely exposed to the RIC on the bridge.

… Hughes was shot through the arm … and was lying on the ground.[42] Swift was wounded in the foot. Both … were exposed to fire. Kilroy got out to [Hughes' position], and he lay down and the RIC moved up on the road until Madden began to fire on them. The RIC chucked rifle grenades, some at Madden, and we had pot shots up at them (the flanking party had then left their

---

42 James Swift and Michael Hughes were from Castlebar. O'Malley includes a diagram in the original text, which is not included here, with numbers and letters indicating six locations of individuals, the dance hall and actions, and the text has been modified slightly to remove those references.

position) and Madden crossed over the road to us. We were an hour there in that position. We were very much exposed to them [RIC] there. We were exposed to the machine-gun fire from the bridge (near the priest's house) at intervals. I rushed across that field and they cut the ground all around me, and it was a long bloody **[52R]** field to cross. Jim MacEvilly was badly wounded in the guts at the back of that fence behind where Madden was, for we came across him later. Then I found Madden … I fired twenty-eight cartridges, I was firing at a target at the time, and I would say that the action lasted an hour. I had 100 rounds in the morning and I had seventy-two in the night time. We retired singly covered by the RIC. Swift got back with Hughes who could walk. Swift limped badly for the bullet had shattered one of his toes. We had cover behind a big hedge.

(How long did Johnny Gibbons continue to fire at the RIC?) He fired, I know. Fifty percent of the main body were wiped out. We had the following casualties: wounded P. O'Malley; Jordan, wounded then died; Swift wounded; Hughes wounded; Collins killed; MacEvilly killed; Staunton killed; O'Donnell killed. And then there was Pierce.[43] No one ever knew what happened to him. He vanished completely. (This makes a list of five to six wounded.)

[Post-Kilmeena Skerdagh engagement, 23 May 1921.] We got back to Ballinacarriga at 10 o'clock when it was dark. Moran and Company met us on our way back. We found them in the next village. They came back with us. We headed that night for Skerdagh at 12 o'clock. There were stepping stones at Derryloughan.[44] It was a very fine year, and there was no rain

---

43 O'Malley's numbering of three people in the original text has been omitted here. The full names for this list are Paddy O'Malley, Paddy Jordan, James Swift, Michael Hughes, Seán Collins, Jim MacEvilly, Pat Staunton, Tom O'Donnell and John Pierce (not Pearse as in the original text).

44 Derryloughan, not Derryboyhan as in the original text.

from May until the Truce.[45] It is a ford there.[46] Even in the darkness we could see the tops of the stones. I remember that in East Mayo it rained that year one night. We were then in the Lower and in Upper Skerdagh, and we went into bed and we stopped there until Monday morning. This was Friday morning. On Friday, Saturday and Sunday night we stopped there. The people were good there, very good. Madden took a toe off Swift, who later on a horse got away up the Skerdagh River and down Glenlara.

[53L] At about dark when it was starting to break dawn, Michael Kilroy and Seán Connolly were out doing a round. Kilroy became nervous, and he did a round of the sentries that night. He ran into RIC who were coming up on foot. I was in a house away from the firing in Lower Skerdagh. We were between a quarter to a half a mile to the east of the firing. I was in bed, and there was Jim Kelly from the Newport Column from the half parish and another chap, MacDonagh of Westport.[47] Mulchrone, the man of the house, got us out. There was the sound of Mills Grenades bursting and of rifle shots. We didn't know it but we saw Tans' heads. Kelly had a pair of opera glasses. We saw the black uniform but we couldn't be sure of it. They were 600 yards away from us. We met Swift who was going up on horseback up the river, and Hughes who was walking with the Castlebar men, and then I met Kitterick,[48] and we headed down towards the firing. Kitterick and I went down, I think, with Johnny Gibbons. We got down then. Kilroy, Madden, Seán Connolly and MacDonagh, the four of them lining the brow of

---

45 The Truce was effective as of 11 July 1921.

46 O'Malley's original text referred to 'here' but this has been changed to 'there' for clarity.

47 John MacDonagh of Monument Street, Westport, was in the Westport Company. His father, also John, was Centre for the IRB in Westport.

48 O'Malley includes a list of six men he called the rearguard: John Madden, Tom Kitterick, Seán /John/Jack Connolly of Tiernaur, Johnny Gibbons, Paddy Cannon and Michael Kilroy.

a hill and firing very occasionally. The RIC were from 700 to 800 yards away.

I understand from Michael Kilroy that he was only thirty yards from them at first. We could see the glint of the sun on their caps. They were well under cover and they were on a rise then. They had our position and we heard the bullet[s] crack, and it is close to you there when you can hear it. We stuck there until 11 a.m. and in all there were seven of us. At one time Kilroy thought of rushing the RIC, but there was no cover for us and we thought that it was madness. They had rifles above. The RIC used rifle grenades **[53R]** or hand grenades earlier in the morning during the close fighting. At around 11 o'clock we saw lorries, at least two of them, on the Newport–Castlebar road about two miles away. We saw RIC who got out and then Kilroy decided to leave the place. We crossed back over a slope which was completely exposed, but they never spotted us. This was a few hundred feet higher up than the position we had held all the morning and we crossed the river.

There was a house at the entrance to Glenlara and very close to it, on the right of the river. We were very thirsty, and Michael Kilroy sent me in. The people were up for they were listening to the firing, and I got a good cake from them and milk and water. We sat down there (I suppose to eat the food) when Kilroy told us of his encounter in the morning with the RIC. We sat on the back of the river there. Madden and I got uneasy for we were delaying too long. I went back with the can, and I left it in the house. (No you did not.)

Glenlara was a long valley deep down between hills. We then decided that we would go up the hill on the right at the back of the house. We heard firing when the reinforcements arrived and we were going up a very steep hill up 200 to 300 feet when we heard the crack of a bullet right in on us and we dropped down at once but there was no cover. We had our trench coats on us

and we lay there. They were chucking bombs into bushes on the
river and there were bursts of machine-gun fire. But within a
few minutes we saw an RIC man pass 150 yards on our flank,
and they passed on up the river, forty of them. There were two
on either side strung out as they advanced. The chaps on our
sides and we were exposed, so we lay down for an hour until
they passed up. **[54L]** We moved up to the top of the hill where
the earth had slipped and had left cracks five to six feet high. It
was bog solid and dry, and we stopped the day there. Then we
heard an aeroplane come over, but we stopped there until it was
dark. In the evening we came down to Jack MacDonald's house
(where the wounded had been). There was a pig hanging up and
also a poached, boiled salmon. There we heard that Jim Browne
had been killed.[49] Jordan died in King George 5th Hospital in
Dublin.

Then we went off unfed with cold salmon in two jam jars
and we came along across the village of Muckanagh at the back
of Glenisland Mountain and we came along the road between
Skerdagh and Muckanagh.[50] A road runs to Glenisland from
Castlebar through Glenisland and a bye-road, and as we came
along we saw lights dim at 3 a.m. We thought them to be enemy,
and one of them came around a turn close to us, and we were
on the road. Kilroy knew this country, and we had to travel on
the road for some distance. The lights came towards us from the
Glenisland direction, not more than 200 to 300 yards away, and
then shone on us. There were dim lights then on cars and that
is why the light had come so close. We leaped in off the road,
down across a drain to the bog on the right.

There was a rise with a rock about the size of a clump of turf
100 yards away, and we got behind it. The lorry pulled up at
the place where we had got off the road and we were in doubt

49 Jim Browne, from Drumgarve, Kilmeena, was known as the 'General'.
50 Muckanagh, not Mucknagh as in the original text.

as to whether they had seen us or not. But it was still dark. We found that Dr Madden was missing, and there were only six of us now. The lorry started off again. Kilroy said we may have to fight if Madden does not turn up. A couple of lights **[54R]** passed on. Madden came around the hill after ten minutes all wet. The lorry had pulled up over him and had let off either troops or RIC, who headed across country towards Skerdagh. We came into Muckanagh then. There was one house. Michael Kilroy, MacDonagh and I and we went to it. It was a good slated house, but the man wouldn't put us up. Then we went back, all of us, to Broddy O'Toole's house. MacDonagh and I went out on sentry then. Kitterick and Gibbons were there (or on sentry). That night we went to Letter in Islandeady where we spent a night.[51]

That day that Skerdagh was rounded up there was a big round-up starting from Ballina and Crossmolina. They did Nephin partly also.[52] Then we went on towards Aughagower close to Aille, close to Rockfield village, and on the next night we contacted the Louisburgh men at Curvey village.[53] The Westport and Newport Columns were there. Then on to Owenwee, and I think that we stopped two nights there. Then to Drummin to Claddy,[54] above Carrowkennedy, and when we were on our way in Michael Kilroy and Broddie Malone showed us where the first Carrowkennedy encounter had taken place.[55]

[Carrowkennedy, second ambush, 2 June 1921.] I was out on sentry with MacDonagh and we went to bed at 8 in the morning and when I wakened at 4 o'clock, I was told that

---

51 The original text says 'The night', but O'Malley probably meant 'That night'.
52 Meaning the area around Nephin Mountain. This would be about 23–24 May 1921.
53 Probably Curvey, not Curry as in the original text, which has been a strong IRA area.
54 Claddy, not Clady as in the original text.
55 Broddie Malone (1898–1975) from Westport. See his interview.

lorries had passed through and that there was possibly a round-up. Two Crossleys, they said, and a Model-T Ford had gone through towards Leenane. Johnny Duffy said that the lorries could not go out that way for Sheeffry Bridge was destroyed.[56] (It was half destroyed only.) When Kilroy heard that, we moved into the ambush position. We came down the road and we cut across the scrub. We were divided up into firing parties. We put the Louisburgh Column on the hill at the back of the school. There were between five or six of them there. There was one section of five-six-seven for the first lorry or the [55L] extreme lorry. Then there were five or six for the second lorry, Jimmy Flaherty, Rick Joyce, MacDonagh, Staunton of Westport. We were just in positions, about 100 yards from the other section. We let the first lorry through and we were to take the second lorry. The trees hid them from us. They were stunted trees, hazel or blackthorn, on our left between us and the lorries. We could hear them, but only in front of us we saw them. We were about 120 yards from the road then. The second lorry never came into our view because the space was widened. (They were cut off by the nature of the ground.) The Ford was being towed by the second lorry. Firing was opened on the first lorry before the second lorry had come into the field of fire. The driver and the passenger were shot in the first lorry and the machine gun in it was the gun which had been used against our lads in Kilmeena. We had to move down to the left about fifty yards. There are hillocks there heading into the house. The Louisburgh section had opened fire on them. They were heading into a thatched house, and we opened fire on them, on the last two or three as they went in.[57] Then they shut the door and we saw no more of them.

---

56 Sheeffry, not Sheefry as in the original text.
57 The RIC from the second lorry ran into a thatched (not tatched as in the original text) cottage.

Meantime, I moved back. Joyce, Flaherty remained in front 150 to 200 yards away, and I went back to the first lorry, and I joined the others. They had got the RIC out on to the road and they had fired a few volleys but they had no cover. We stuck on to them. This was a semi-armoured lorry. It was well perforated when we went down. It was one-eighth of an inch thick, the steel; one stretch of metal, but not good at close range. We stuck there. A few rifle grenades were thrown up at us but they were about forty yards short of our position. Joe Walsh of Westport was with us and there was a mark like a full moon with a white circle in the middle. A grenade would come out **[55R]** every now and then. Michael Kilroy decided to send down fellows who would bomb it. Johnny Duffy and another man went down, but in the meantime Joe Walsh had a pot shot at the white spot on the side of the lorry. Off goes the bomb inside. Then up went the white flag and Johnny Duffy was there just within bomb throwing distance of the lorry.

We sent the surrendered RIC man from the first lorry back to the cottage where the second lorry men were, and then the RIC came out, and they surrendered. We got twenty-one rifles, a machine gun[58] and several boxes of bombs.[59] Gus Delahunty's Model-T Ford had been commandeered, and he had been towing the car. He remained in the drain on the side of the road when the firing opened, and there he stayed until the fight was over.

[Round-ups, June.] The British rounded up the entire country towards Tourmakeady on the next day. The lads picked out some of the new rifles but I kept to my old rifle. We had used a great deal of ammunition in Carrowkennedy. We were only a few hundred rounds to our credit but we had twenty-one rifles, thirty–forty Mills bombs, revolvers and revolver ammunition. We dumped the machine gun and all the spare old rifles in

58 The machine gun would have been a Lewis machine gun.
59 The bombs would probably have been nothing more than grenades.

Durless.[60] Then we went on to Durras, Boras, Killeen, round towards Drummin, again to Kinuary,[61] near Tourmakeady, down to Ballinacarriga and to Buckoogh again,[62] Derrymartin, Largain below Castlebar, then to Greenaun's.

Twenty-five Auxiliaries came into that village. It's a poteen centre, and our fellows had got some the night before, and it is still a poteen country. Paddy Duffy and Rick Joyce and two other fellows …[63] In the village of Largain, there were only four houses in it, but these lads went on to a house in the next village, and we got word that the Auxiliaries [56L] were seen coming in, and we got to the mountain at the back, and we found that the four of them were missing. They, all of them, had stopped in the one house which was in a side boreen and every house in that village, and the village really consisted of scattered houses, was rounded up except the house in which the four men stopped.[64] The people were all rounded up and they were brought up to a hall which was between the two villages. At 11 o'clock the four boys had their breakfast and a neighbour told them that the place had been rounded up. The Auxiliaries were a flying column from Foxford who were heading for Castlebar, and they used to camp for a night when they were travelling through the villages. They had been a few days on the go at the time. They were taken up by lorry to Foxford, and then they'd make their way back across country. This crowd also camped out for a night on the shores of the lake at Islandeady. They would put out sentries and they would search the byroads.

In the case of Skerdagh I heard that someone from Glenhest

60 Durless (not Durlus as in the original text) was in the Louisburgh Battalion area.
61 Kinuary, not Kinury as in the original text.
62 Buckoogh (not Buckagh as in the original text) is north of Newport along the side of Lough Furnace.
63 Paddy Duffy of Aughagower. See his interview.
64 A 'boreen' refers to a small road, perhaps only a laneway.

had come into Newport Barracks to give information about the column, which was quartered in the two villages. I think that the fellow concerned went to England, but that he never returned from there after the Truce. Telephones did not come west of Athlone until 1927 or 1928.

Ballinacarriga was never raided more than any other village we frequented, but we used that place always when we were passing through from Aughagower to the Newport side.[65] Greenaun's poteen made it hard for fellows to be made to get up when the raid by the Auxiliaries that was on that morning.

There was a Gun Boat inside of Clare Island.

We went from Owenwee to [56R] Glenmask, and we got word that a round-up was to start from Ballyheane. The Castlebar Column, who were over forty, went to Glenmask. We dumped our arms in a dug-out which had been built there by the local lads. We handed our arms over and we went home on foot singly.[66] We must have passed through a column … in the dark. I … was the O/C of the column and we heard voices and stones being knocked and we lay low. The British did not round up Glenmask that day. They came in and they passed out at the end of the village which is a cul-de-sac. There are scattered houses, Congested [District] Board houses of fifty-six families in it. Out the country, villages are scattered.

CIVIL WAR[67]

[Internment and escape.] Paddy Grace was handcuffed to Peadar O'Donnell, who had a box of books tied to him by a bit

---

65 Aughagower lies just south-east of Westport but is sometimes known locally as Aghagower.
66 The words following this in the original text, 'we came back', have been omitted as they make no sense here.
67 Cannon was captured in August 1922 in Castlebar by Jennings, an ex-British soldier who was then a Free State army officer and had previously drilled the Islandeady Company.

of cable.[68] 17th of March,[69] Peadar was changed from Tintown Camp up to Finner Camp, and on the 22nd April, we escaped from the camp in Tintown 1.[70] I came out with Jim Browne, who was a relation of 'General' Browne who had been killed in Skerdagh, and Hughes.[71] We went on towards Kilcullen, and we got into the roof of a vacant house, a two-storeyed house in the village, owned by a brother of Brennan, who had been the Hut Commandant of our hut in Tintown.[72] Tom Mullins was with us and Paddy Kelly, who was married in Athlone on the Connaught side, and both of them had been prisoners in Hare Park (then it was known as the Rath Camp) under the Black and Tans. We stayed in the garret on Sunday, and a brother of Brennan, who knew we were there, brought us to his own house. We went to Brennan's father's house. We were in the rafters of that house. We went to Brennan's house where we had a wash up. We had decided **[57L]** to head up towards Cavan on our way home. Old Brennan brought us out, showed us the North Star, and off we went. We avoided houses and we were heading north, but at daybreak Tom Mullins, who was in charge of us, thought that he heard a sentry shout. The men who were in front halted and so did the other lads, but it was dark. Tom Mullins told them to divide into twos and threes and I went to the right,

---

68 Peadar O'Donnell was on the Army Executive of the IRA and had been a divisional officer in Donegal. He was captured in the Four Courts in June 1922 and imprisoned in Mountjoy. He was transferred to Finner Camp in Donegal and held there as a hostage and under sentence of death. He eventually escaped from prison. He was a well-known Republican/socialist and was an advocate of a socialist policy within the IRA. He was the author of two books on the revolutionary period.

69 1923.

70 There were three internment camps in Tintown, at the Curragh, Co. Kildare. Its official name was Hare Park.

71 Gus Hughes.

72 The Brennan brothers were probably Jim of the Kilteevan Company and John 'Jack' who was O/C South Roscommon Brigade and who was arrested in August 1922 and interned in Athlone.

and I headed away. I was with Heneghan of Ballyheane and a quarter of a mile further on we crossed a main road and got into a bunch of whins.[73] We were cold and we lay back to back and we fell asleep. It was daylight and we didn't know whether it was morning or evening.

We were in *Sonnadle* village. We saw the end of a house a half a mile away, the only house we could see. Then an old fellow came in down the road. He had a white flannel coat on him, and he drove sheep around. He came out across the fence up along it, and as the dog and the man passed the fence, the dog leaped in on top of us and out again, and the old fellow moved away. We called him back and we asked him his name, and we said that we would hold him responsible. He told us not to move, and we were more doubtful then, but after an hour he came back with a basket and can of tea and cooked rashers and two eggs each, and we ate them all. He asked us were there any more men and told us that we could move up to his house in the evening.

'Yer a nice pair of boys,' he said, 'you wouldn't tell me Tom Mullins and Paddy Kelly were with you, but I came across them on the far side of the road. I met them in Hare Park last year.' Seán Scanlon from Sligo, Paddy Hegarty of Lahardaun, there were four of them.[74] Joe Doyle, this old fellow, had a big farm of land, and Mullins [57R] being ravenous and Kelly cocked up his head. 'That's like Tippety Cat.' 'Who's that?' said Mullins. Do you remember the old fellow who used to play 'Tippety Cat' in Hare Park? He was a prisoner in Hare Park in the Civil War. Paddy Kelly married into a business. Nolan, he has a very good memory, and he is on the Athlone side of the Shannon.

They called him back, and they met him and he told them about the other two lads in the whins. He was to bring them

---

73 Heneghan, not Henehan as in the original text. A whin is a type of wild gorse bush.
74 Lahardaun, not Laradane as in the original text.

to his house, Scanlon, Hegarty, Gus Hughes, Browne, Mullins, myself and Heneghan. He brought us to his hayshed. At dark we went to his house and we wrote our names in an autograph album which he had from Hare Park (Rath Camp) in the British times. He came damn near to Kelly and Dunne on the run in Kildare near Celbridge, and he brought us to Dunne's house. And we came to Cardwells of Celbridge;[75] we went into it in the darkness. I walked away in my sleep along the canal there. Miss Carrols was there, and there was a little boy or nephew of hers who was out on sentry. We were having a meal in the kitchen at 7 or 8 o'clock in the morning, and it was dark then, about to make day. There were four of us in it.[76] Four of the lads had a feed, including myself, and we waited till they were finished. They went out and they had a sleep in the hay barn. We were sitting down with the sun out and I was ravenously hungry.

I got up from the table to wash my hands which were dirty from the rafters. The young lad shouted the military are coming in, and he pointed to the way they were coming. We went out, and we ran across an open field with the two lads who were on the run in Kildare. The military opened fire, but they didn't hit any of us. They cut the ground. There was a very low [58L] fence of sods. Scanlon and the two local lads got away for they had a rifle and a revolver and they fired back.[77]

[Recapture.] We were brought back to Naas Barracks for a week. We would have been out of the camp three days in all. Then we tunnelled in Keogh Barracks, and we were brought on to Gormanstown Camp.[78] Johnny Pidgeon was court-martialled also that day. He had lost his glasses and we hardly knew him.

---

75 Cardwells, not Cardrells as in the original text.
76 At this point there were only four men moving together as the others had split off.
77 Cannon was recaptured by the Free State troops.
78 In Inchicore, Dublin. Formerly Richmond Barracks under the British.

We were charged with having taken part in an engagement with Free State troops.

Pump Square, Athlone Barracks. We were in 'O' Block. How to keep the tunnel in a straight line. Hold the light at the far end and sight on it for if you went to the left or the right you would go in a circle. We went crooked when we were making that tunnel. There was a steam roller working over us on the road around Pump Square. We came up. We were thirteen to fourteen feet under the Coffee Bar in the British times. Then it was used for holding court-martials on Free Staters, and we often listened in to these court-martials. Then we headed for the wall, and we came up but we found that we were inside the wall. The Staters found the tunnel before this, however, and they were digging holes in the tunnel. They put down wire and they said that they had put in bombs. We went around these obstructions. Our tunnels were two feet high and came up the end two feet inside the outer wall on a Saturday night. The Free Staters saw the opening on the following morning and they thought that the old tunnel was caving in and we began again and all we needed was one day in which to finish the work. But it was between two to three days before we started again. We had been six months on that but we were moved to the Joy.

[58R] In Tintown 1, Scanlon from Co. Sligo looked after the electric light in the tunnel. He grooved a pole and we put down the light. When you were below and the electric light was put out and you were not to move; and when it went on again you were to move.

The Tunnel. On the 12th of January we went into the hut.[79] Peadar O'Donnell who was then in charge of the camp in Tintown was in our hut. The tunnel began on 19 January. There were squares for horses (as in horse stables) on the floors, for

79 In 1924.

these huts were originally for horses. And the squares were nine inches square so we cut out nine squares with large nails and we sat them up on a piece of timber that exactly fitted the space and we used soap to keep it in position securely.

PADDY DUFFY

(UCDA P17b/113, pp. 1–10)[1]

Patrick 'Paddy' Duffy (1897–1975) was born in Corveagh, Aughagower Lower, eight miles from Westport. He joined the Irish Volunteers in 1919 and was in the Westport Battalion area before he joined the Westport flying column in March 1921. He participated in several of the column actions. He went anti-Treaty, was vice-commandant of No. 1 Brigade, 4th Western Division, and was captured and imprisoned in Galway in December 1922, but managed to escape in March 1923.

Copyright J. J. Leonard (courtesy of Anthony Leonard)

This interview took place in Cloonskill, near Aughagower in May 1951.

[1916–1921 PERIOD]

[2L] I joined the Irish Volunteers in Aughagower in 1919.[2] It comprised the area of the Westport–Castlebar road to Tonlegee and Westport–Leenane road. This was a very staunch area and it was the best in the county. Cushlough[3] was formed in 1916

---

1 The original transcription and some footnotes were done by Dominic Price. Pages 8R–10L of this interview, which relate to Galway, were reviewed by Cormac Ó Comhraí and are also found in O'Malley, *The Men Will Talk to Me: Galway Interviews*, pp. 201–8. Some Mayo-related pages and notes have been added. It appears that Ned Moane was present during this interview and made some comments but they are not included here.

2 Aughagower is used for consistency throughout the book rather than the local spelling of Aghagower which sometimes appears in the original text.

3 The village of Cushlough (not Cuslough as in the original text) is near Derryherbert.

to 1917 as far as Aasleagh, it ran during the Conscription time.[4] All of it was in the Westport Battalion area. There were two rifles in the Aughagower Company area, a .45 automatic from the American Army left by a Martin Malone who had been an American soldier.

[2R] [Glosh.] The column was an organised effort on the 15th March 1921. There was an attempted ambush at Gloshpatrick (near the Reek).[5] We waited there for two days. They went into Louisburgh, about twenty-five men, but they never came back our way.[6]

We remained on as a Unit then.[7] There were probably ten men and Joe Ring was in charge [3L] of the (Westport) column.[8] Derrykillew is outside of Carrowkennedy going on towards Drummin. Ring, Kilroy and Broddie Malone were there. That was the first time that we ever formed up as a Brigade [ASU] Unit. I met John Madden (Dr) in Corveagh, and it was the first time I saw the Newport men. For a month we trained. We were at disc practice.[9] We went around the [Westport] Battalion area through practically all of Aughagower and Cushlough areas. We took possession of Westport, and we spent the night there. This was used as a training exercise and also to drive off the enemy. We spent four to six hours inside the town from 10 [p.m.] to 4 [a.m.], but no one came out of the barracks, and we moved out of the town.

---

4   Aasleagh, not Ashleigh as in the original text. The Conscription Crisis occurred in April 1918 when the British government, after defeats on the Western Front, decided to extend conscription into the British Army to Ireland. When most sections of the Irish community objected strenuously, the British decided not to enforce conscription in Ireland.
5   Gloshpatrick, not Gluish Patrick as in the original text. The Reek is a local name for Croagh Patrick.
6   Louisburgh, not Louisburg as in the original text.
7   Unit meaning an Active Service Unit or flying column.
8   Joe Ring. See biographical sketches.
9   Rifle practice for the IRA was conducted by firing at paper discs (not disk as in the original).

There were many reprisals [by RIC] in Westport so we wanted to show that we could occupy the town if we wished to do so. Michael Kilroy then went back to Newport, and we were ten men again. We lay out at the High Wall in Islandeady for a few times and at Brackloon, the wood four miles out from Westport.[10]

[**Tourmakeady, 3 May 1921.**] One morning word was sent out that Tom Maguire[11] and his column was in trouble in Tourmakeady,[12] and then we moved out to Derrycraff. We left at 10 in the night, and we arrived there at 4 o'clock. We found a wounded man there, Bourke, wounded in Tunney's of Derrycraff. We left Brackloon at 10 in the morning so that it must not have been on the day of the ambush. Ask Tommy Tunney of Derrycraff, miles out from here. It is beside Derryraven near the Constabulary Hut. When we left Brackloon six lorries, 600 yards apart, came in from Leenane.[13] They were spaced very far apart that day.[14] That would be the Westport military coming back from their round-up operations in the mountains.

The High Wall [6 May]. I was beside Paddy Jordan, who was later killed [3R] in Kilmeena, and the Castlebar men who were thoroughly untrained. He was in charge of them but he actually was standing up on top of the hill. I was right beside him then. Someone shouted that there was a lorry coming, and he made a sudden movement, made a dive (for cover), and then the lorry pulled up, turned around and went back (towards Castlebar where the RIC killed [two] men). Jordan and MacEvilly from

---

10 The High Wall (sometimes referred to as the Big Wall, c.f. Michael Kilroy's interview) was a high wall, about nine feet high, at the Islandeady Dance Hall on the Castlebar–Westport road, separating the road from the railroad.

11 Tom Maguire. See his interview.

12 Tourmakeady, not Turmakeedy or Toormeadeady as sometimes in the original text.

13 Leenane, not Leenaun as in the original text.

14 O'Malley included a diagram of the lorries here which is not included.

Castlebar were killed in Kilmeena.[15] 'You lie down and I'll stand up,' was their attitude. In the Kilmeena ambush there was a car of nuns in front, and the men who were lying in ambush mistook the carload of RIC in the second load for another collection of nuns and they let it through. (This is not correct I understand. For anyhow Gibbons would have fired a shot on the hill near the priest's house, but why the British were warned of this means before they came into the line of fire 450 to 500 yards further down the hill has always been very strange to me.)

On the evening before Kilmeena we were at the High Wall and nothing happened. There were Westport and Castlebar men, and Michael Kilroy was in charge. Broddie Malone[16] was sent in to Westport to attack a patrol for we were getting no fight out in the country, and I understood that Broddie with eight men was to go into the town and attack a patrol if possible, and Jim Moran was sent in to Newport to attack RIC. As a result of this activity if anything happened there would be a movement in either direction by the British. Then it would be safe for Michael Kilroy to pick a point on the Newport road. Before we went into Westport a patrol of ten men, we were told, had gone out towards the station. We came out at Tim Hastings' and we waited for this patrol to return.[17] Apparently they had scouts out also, the RIC. They went into the Roche's house. Maybe they had [4L] seen us moving in that evening. We came in at 10 o'clock at night, between 10 to 11 [p.m.] at dusk, and we remained there until 3 or 4 o'clock in the morning until daybreak, and we decided that we would come back the next night. We were to report back to Westport. Ring wasn't with us. (It seems to me that Paddy Duffy's facts are somewhat distorted and that he should have been seen together with

15 Seamus/Jim/James MacEvilly (not McEvilly as in the original text).
16 Broddie, not Broddy, as in the original text.
17 Tim Hastings had a garage.

Broddie Malone and a few men of the Westport Column who were looking for a fight at the time.)

We had eight rifles, and they (the RIC) should have reported back like the Newport men. We didn't know (the next morning) what the Newport patrol had done. Johnny Collins had a Martini-Enfield. He was from Artane and he was killed.[18] There was a spy story about the other Artane boy.[19] Collins and Pierce from the Westport unit were there at the fight.[20] Hogan, Maurteen Naughton were only kids then, and they were badly armed also.[21] Our best armed and our most experienced men were not there. He wanted Kilroy to do something by himself. We were in Corrig between Ned Moane's house and Westport (less than one and a half miles from Westport) when we heard the shooting between 3 and 4 o'clock.[22] We passed across the railway and at Carnaclay, halfway between Westport and Kilmeena, he told us that the column, nearly all of them [were] killed and that it was a wipe out.[23] He had a very miserable story to tell. The Castlebar fellows disappeared after that. They had lost rifles. That's my story anyhow.

We went as far as Rockfield which is outside of Doon in Aughagower, and that same night Willie Malone and Joe Walsh got off a train at Islandeady with Johnny Berry. They had come back from England to join a column, and it was the day of the Skerdagh ambush. That day of Skerdagh we were in the neighbourhood of Cushin,[24] but we heard about it a day or two afterwards and we heard the way **[4R]** in which the RIC and Tans had abused the prisoners in Kilmeena. We thought that

---

18 The Artane Industrial School for orphans and delinquents in Dublin.
19 John Pierce.
20 Pierce, not Pearse as in the original text.
21 Naughton, not Hochtor as in the original text.
22 Corrig, not Corr as in the original text.
23 Carnaclay (not Carnacleigh as in the original text) lies north-east of Westport.
24 Cushin, not Cushen as in the original text.

there would be an escort on the train that our wounded would be in it. We got word at Cushin, on the night of Skerdagh, so we decided (Joe Ring being in charge) to go into action against the train on the following day. So we blocked the line outside of Westport and we flagged the train down. We took off the mails and we censored them. That showed that we were not depressed by what had happened on the Newport side.

[Red Bridge, 8 May.] There was a dance held here in this house (his own house) on the night of the Red Bridge, for the column. Three of the lads left the dance. Broddie Malone, Joe Baker, Tommy Kitterick, and they went into Westport. They bombed the patrol, and they came back at 2 o'clock in the morning.[25] Nobody else at the dance knew where they had gone or why they had gone and when they came back to this house the dance was still on so they danced away again. They told us then so we remained that night billeted in the country.

After March of 1921 there was no night work on the part of the RIC and the Tans, so that meant no raids in the countryside. During Christmas of 1920–1921 there was the worst raiding and the RIC were then at their most abusive. The military at the Quay were rough on the street but the Tans were tough. So that Christmas of 1920 was really a bad time here.[26]

The Newport men rejoined us here in this area with Michael Kilroy. They were aggressive and we were. We went into Westport several nights on patrol work. We had a curfew for the RIC and the RIC had a curfew for the town's people. The RIC had a good intelligence system even out into the country but their intelligence system was not intelligent enough. We ourselves did not know when we were going out or when or where we were next [5R] moving to. Michael Kilroy knew about this and generally word was sent ahead to the local company so

---

25 The RIC patrol was bombed from the Railway Bridge in Westport.
26 O'Malley mistakenly wrote 1921 in the original text.

that there would be scouts on guard and houses prepared for the men to sleep in. The Post Office was not organised here.[27]

In December 1920, before the column was formed, my father, who had been in the USA, was pulled out of bed Christmas night by the Tans. They raided Aughagower with three lorries and a car at the Chapel during the first Mass on Christmas morning for men. They stood at the door while Mass was going on. Brigie O'Malley was staying here, and she said that they raided my house. I was not at home but then they said, 'We'll get him at the Chapel in the morning.' And so I heard about it. She knew where I was staying then and she came across to tell me. Several people saw me going to Mass and when the raid took place they all assumed that I was inside the Chapel. An old man named Paddy Nancy (McGing) in Tonlegee, he thought that I was in there in the Chapel, so he asked my father how did I get away from the RIC, and my father says, 'He has great power, he waved his hands and then Paddy went through the roof.'[28] And some time [later] in his own house, he said 'Were you the boy that went through the roof?'

My brother was in Belfast doing Engineering, and during the Pogroms he had to leave the University.[29] Whenever there had been a raid on or when my mother knew it was safe, she used to hang a white apron up on a bush. That was the 'All Clear' signal. You could see it from Corveagh, and on St Stephen's Night 1920 the Black and Tans raided Corveagh,[30] and they pulled me out of bed then, and they said, 'Mrs Duffy used to

---

27 Post Office written as P/O in the original text. This might mean the IRA had not been able to receive solid information from the local post office.

28 In a community where there were many families of the same name, it was custom to append the name of a man's mother or father to help distinguish him, thus Paddy McGing, son of Nancy.

29 His brother in Queen's University, Belfast, is not identified. Duffy had three brothers in 1921: Johnny (on the ASU), Owen (aged 22) and Edward (aged 25).

30 26 December 1920.

put out a white apron as a signal'. So there was spying going on locally. Probably the [5L] loose talk in Corveagh village was to blame for that.

I was a good shot as a result of practice with the disc. We got plenty of that. Michael Kilroy impressed this on us, and trigger practice. We spent two hours of time on it every day for months. (Johnny and Paddy are good shots.)[31] (Intelligence reports of course depend upon writing and country people do not like to write.)

John Keane was a natural shot.[32] He went Free State and now he is dead.

(At Kilmeena were there two machine guns in action?) The one on the side of the road did the real damage. On the hill at the back of the Dance Hall the two men were killed.

[Carrowkennedy: second ambush.] [1R] The fellows who were working on the bog had to bring out both their carts and turf so that the road could be filled in for the passage of the lorries.

We got two cans of milk at sunset at O'Malley's house. So we sat in 'the Street' and we drank and ate bread. After the first Carrowkennedy[33] we went eastwards to Arderry[34] on that night and we were in position over the Bohaun[35] road when the British raided the village of Sraheen[36] while we were in Arderry. We crossed the road to Darby Hasting's pub and then (this is after the second Carrowkennedy) we went out by Derryherbert through Drummin Chapel to Durless, and then when it was daylight we saw an aeroplane over Carrowkennedy

31 It is hard to tell who is making this statement, Ned Moane or Ernie O'Malley.
32 John 'Jack' Keane, not Kane as in the original text.
33 The first Carrowkennedy ambush was on Sergeant John Coughlan's patrol on 22 March 1921 at Derrykillew, Carrowkennedy.
34 Arderry, not Arderagh as in the original text.
35 Bohaun not Bohan as in the original text.
36 Sraheen, not Shreaheen as in the original text.

in the distance when it must have been about 5 or 6 o'clock in the morning.[37] A peeler had cycled in to Westport on a bicycle that late evening, but reinforcements with troops had not come out until that morning afterwards. (This was a policeman called Potter, killed in the Skerdagh fight.)[38]

We stayed two nights in Durless, and we left at 12 o'clock at night. And from that on every village we went into was raided two hours later after we had left, and from East Mayo (by their information about our movements) they drove us back into the round-up which they had been preparing for us. We burned all three of the vehicles, the two lorries and the Ford Car. From above when we lay on the hill waiting for the RIC we could see all of the houses which the RIC had burned the night following the first Carrowkennedy.

[2L] The Widow Sammon[39] had been evicted over sixty years ago before Sligo had sold the land.[40] A [RIC] hut[41] had been built to protect Francis Mulholland and Peter Scahill was put in instead.[42] There were RIC in Aille and they were watching him [Scahill].[43] She herself fought with Peter Scahill in Cushlough and in the Chapel.[44] 'God blast you, you old buffalo,' she said to the magistrate when she was in court. She got hold of Scahill by the whiskers within the Chapel and hardly could the priest part

---

37 Durless, not Durlus as in the original text.
38 O'Malley is mistaken here on Potter. RIC Constable Joseph Maguire was killed, not Potter, and RIC District Inspector James Munro was wounded at Lower Skerdagh on 23 May 1921.
39 Bridget Sammon, not Salmon as in the original text and O'Malley's *Raids and Rallies*.
40 Lord Sligo.
41 The Carrowkennedy RIC Hut.
42 Scahill (not Skahill as in the original text) and Mulholland were the new tenants.
43 The Aille RIC Barracks was not too far from the Mulholland and Scahill lands. Aille is used throughout this interview instead of Aill, which was the spelling used in the original text.
44 'She' refers to Mrs William O'Brien, who was a 'do-gooder' towards poor people.

them. She was half cracked. She was William O'Brien's widow. William O'Brien (who lived in the cottage where afterwards [2R] Joseph MacBride used to live) fed half the people around him there. Drummin and Aille and, I suppose, Westport men came in it then.[45] She, the widow, got the place back, and she was reinstated by the IRA in 1920. Fr Corcoran, who was a curate in Aughagower, told her to go into a house, but Canon Flatley tried to put her out.[46] Fr John he'd get anything for you, but indeed she wouldn't let Fr Flatley do that to her.

We put in a couple of hard nights in it [the widow's house]. The door [to the house] was bolted; Gavan was in it, one shoe was off and the other was left up on the hob and the door had to be put in on the first drive.[47] Gavan left. Murphy, a pensioner policeman took over. He and all his family were armed, and they used to fire out the window [of the hut] at us. But they were better armed than we were. Some of the RIC were good. The Sergeant would not tell them [RIC Constables] what was going to happen before they went out on a raid until half an hour before they went out. But one of them gave the word that night, and he went away as hard as he could to give the warning.[48] They were raiding for guns then.

There were RIC barracks at Aille, Kinuary, Drummin, Carrowkennedy Hut on the lands between the two Brigade areas.[49] Then we had none. The [Carrowkennedy RIC] Hut was burned at Easter 1920. Aille was evacuated two nights after Kinuary which was a bit north of the ... in Kiltarsaghaun. There were four or five arrests in the area of the two companies. Mick Tunney was arrested there.

45 Referring to the Irish Volunteers.
46 Rev Fr John Flatley, not Flattly as in the original text.
47 Meaning the door had to be given a hard shove to open it.
48 It is unclear what night this happened.
49 Kinuary, not Kinnurey as in the original text. Drummin and Carrowkennedy were burned on 3 April 1920.

[5L] After Carrowkennedy we went on to Joyce's of Durless and to the other neighbours. Then on to Cregganbaun ... [and] to Aillemore and then to Rarrigal near Durless, then to Glenummera village and Doo Lough Lodge. Then through Errily to Derrinbohan below Newport, about twenty miles, but we never saw a sight of anything then. Then [on] to Coolnabinna village below and in[to] Derrymartin village in Glenlara below Skerdagh.[50] The next day we got our photograph taken.[51] I was on sentry duty. Jack Leonard of Lahardaun took it, and Mrs Walsh of Westport has it. Then I do not know where was the next place we went to. It was a village between Lahardaun and the Windy Gap.[52] We spent a night in Shanbally on the summit of it and then we went on through the Gap to Crumlin in Falladaun and four villages or the next day two miles away and that was the night of the raid.[53] And we slept through that raid in the only house, Rowland's, that was not raided. Mr and Mrs Rowland were married either that week or that day.[54] In the house next door, Lanagan's, apparently the fellow who lived next door was on sentry duty, and he ran down. Johnny Duffy and Battie Cryan got out at the back door as the military were at the [6R] front door.[55] The Black Watch, who were Scotch, and then he ran to open the front door for them. 'How did you get your pants and shoes on so quick?' he was asked at once. His answer, 'I was up with a cow,' he said. They took him out and

---

50 Coolnabinna, not Coolnabinnia as in the original text.
51 This photograph of the West Mayo Brigade flying column is included in the photographic section.
52 Also known as Barnageehy.
53 Crumlin, not Cerinlin as in the original text.
54 Harry Rowland, not Roland as in the original text.
55 Battie Cryan (1897–1974), not Batty as in the original text. He was from Sligo, learned his drapery trade in Mohill, Co. Leitrim, and came to Westport to work for Charles Hughes' drapery. He joined the Irish Volunteers in 1914, was interned in 1916 and went on the run in 1920. A member of the West Mayo Brigade Flying Column, he was anti-Treaty and was captured in 1922.

they put him up against the gable of the house we were staying in, and they fired shots over him and that is why they did not raid our house, for we slept through it and we never heard a sound/peep. It was 11 o'clock in the day then when we woke up. The column thought that we had been taken prisoners so they sent in a girl to find out, but when she came in to our house no one knew of the raid for we were at our breakfast. That was the poteen area. Shunnagh, the next village, was near Park, and it was in the East Mayo Brigade, and it was also another poteen area.

Then we went to Ballycastle near Bohola, to Prizon[56] near Balla, and from that to Teevinish on the border of Aughagower.[57] At Cloonsonvagh, near Errew, then to Teevinish beyond Tonlegee.[58] (Why all this wandering? They must have been followed up but if so, there was a weak link somewhere.) On a Saturday night we were in Tonlegee when we got wind that there was a military camp at Kilawullaun which was going to sweep that area, and we left Tonlegee and we came to Cloonskill and Lanmore intending to billet there, but we got word that a camp was being established at the Ballinrobe road two miles from here.[59] So we left here for Owenwee, and we occupied defensive positions.

We were on the alert all day. The British established a camp which was two miles away. They had actually their tents down, and they had both infantry and cavalry. Probably Michael Kilroy knew about the British intentions as we [6L] were disbanded and divided into groups of twos. I was with Joe Baker, Tommy Heavey. Dan Gavan (who had been at Carrowkennedy),

56 Prizon, not Pregon as in the original text.
57 Teevinish, not Develish as in the original text.
58 Tonlegee is used throughout this interview instead of Toonlegee, which was the spelling used in the original text.
59 Kilawullaun not Cullawallun, and Cloonskill not Clashhill, as in the original text.

Joe Walsh, Willie Malone and I. We went to McGoverns of Derryulra[60] near Carrowkennedy towards Drummin when we got a great welcome.[61] We had three men in each house, and we were the two nights without sleep. We heard the hum of the lorries at 3 a.m. on Monday morning, and one of the girls ran out to look, and she came back to say that there were cavalry coming up the bohereen. We heard them. We went off through to Lettermaglinskin[62] through a bog on to the Sheeffry[63] mines, and when it broke day in Sheeffry all we could see was MacPherson's garden occupied by about 200 camps, and a fleet of lorries about 100 yards away from where we were sleeping. Then someone noticed a fire. That's a lime kiln, says Joe Baker. I went over and I looked, but it was a military camp. Joe Baker wanted to sleep. Then we decided to move, but as we moved an aeroplane came down, and they must have spotted me in it getting into a bunch of ferns for they went up the hill, and I went down the hill in full daylight. Cavalry must have spotted us in the morning.

Down the river I called into Pat Cox's, which was burnt, and they were now sleeping in hay along by the river.[64] I went down the bed and banks of the river in spots to Paddy Cox's of Cuilmore.[65] In a barn he was, and we had breakfast together, and we went on again. I could see them [British Military] all over the place, and I went on by the Erriff River to Flynn's of Cushlough near Derrymore close to Derby Hastings', across one mile from it.[66] When I got to Flynn's they saw no movement, but after ten minutes the old man Flynn came out to say that there were a

---

60 Derryulra, not Derryilla as in the original text.
61 Carrowkennedy, not Carrick as in the original text.
62 Lettermaglinskin, not Letakernaghiskineen as in the original text.
63 Sheeffry, not Sheffry as in the original text.
64 Pat or Paddy Cox's, not Corr's as in the original text.
65 Cuilmore, not Coylemore as in the original text.
66 Erriff, not Errif, and Derrymore, not Derryboe, as in the original text.

million RIC coming in towards us from Lackderg. **[7R]** They rounded up all Sraheen from Kilawullaun.[67] Every man whom they [British Military] met they forced to walk to the camp at Carrowkennedy which was at the centre of the operations now where the Garda barracks is. The people whom Flynn actually had seen were the people who had been rounded up, and there were between 200 and 300 of them. I crossed to Hoban's of Erriff where I met the five other lads who had been with me. Then we went to the hill over the house, but the people were awful nervous, so we went to Kerrin's of Derrymaher where we saw the soldiers and the horse coming towards that place, so we cleared out again. The road in looked so bad to them that they turned back, and they went on to Carrick by another road. We had our rifles with us. We had been told to dump them, but we could not. The British did not capture any one of us. Andy Harney, who was 'on the run' was the only one whom they captured on that day.[68]

On Wednesday we were in Aille and on Thursday we were here. On Thursday morning we saw the army moving from Cushlough towards Castlebar, about two miles long was their length then [of their column], and on Friday morning we read about the Truce in the [*Irish*] *Independent*. At night, while they encamped, they fired Very lights every three minutes from the mountain tops.[69] When we were leaving on the first night at Derrymaher we walked into the Very lights. That was at Slievenangh Mountain and we had to go back. The lights had a terrorising effect on us for we were untrained.

---

67 Kilawullaun, not Cullayawalla as in the original text.
68 Andy Harney (not Andie Hernan as in the original text) of Louisburgh Battalion – around early July.
69 Very lights are a type of flare used by the military to illuminate the sky so that movement on the ground can be seen.

THE TRUCE

The Exchange of Rifles.[70] In January or February of 1922, 150 rifles from the Division were sent into Castlebar. Every rifle which we had was to have been sent in. That gathering up of rifles included the following Brigades: 1. West Mayo, 2. North Mayo, 3. North-East Mayo, 4. East Connemara. **[7L]** I was sent two lorries, and there was an escort with us in the lorries, and it was snowing. We went on to Markree Castle in Sligo.[71] When we got there I had been told by Michael Kilroy or rather by Petie Joe that we could get rifle for rifle in the exchange.[72] Before we unloaded our rifles I asked for the rifles which were to be given in exchange for them. Frank Carty was in charge of the troops there.[73] I was told to bring in the rifles, but these Sligo men meant it in good faith. I said that I would put them in a room with my own escort on them until we were given other rifles for them. We brought in our 150 rifles and I put Jimmy Flaherty in charge of them. He was from Westport. I discussed this matter of exchange with the Sligo men and they agreed with me. They said that they would go with me to Dublin to see Michael Kilroy and they let me go. I told Michael Kilroy that I did not turn over the rifles when he asked me what had happened. He then went to Beggar's Bush Barracks to arrange for the exchange, but he returned to me to the Exchange Hotel where I was an hour later and he told me to go back to Sligo and then to take the rifles back to Castlebar.

Mally Flaherty, who was a Connemara man, and who had been serving in the Free State Transport, either stole or begged or borrowed a Crossley [tender] to get me down to Markree

---

70 The exchange of rifles is often referred to in other interviews as the Arms Swap. This heading is taken from the top of 7L.
71 Markree, not Mackre or Marker as in the original text.
72 Petie Joe McDonnell, then O/C West Connemara Brigade. See his interview in O'Malley, *The Men Will Talk to Me: Galway Interviews*, pp. 65–98.
73 Frank Carty. See biographical sketches.

Castle and we were back there that night, and we took back the rifles to Castlebar that night. We went down at sixty miles an hour. Michael Kilroy told me to get back hurriedly for there were people ahead of me and they were on the train, the Free State officers. Outside of Boyle we saw the train although we did not know that they were on it. And as we left Markree Castle with the rifles, we met a car [8R] of Free State officers who were coming up the driveway. When I was leaving Castlebar with the rifles I was not given any particulars or any careful instructions.

(Who were IRB? Moane and Ring?) ... John F. Kilcoyne, Ned Moane, Captain of 'Ring's Own', Derrygorman Company, all of which went Free State.[74]

[CIVIL WAR]

[Capture.] I was Brigade Vice-Commandant when I was captured in Islandeady on the 8th of December.[75] Charlie Gavan was captured with me, and I had spent two months there. We had two scraps the night before this, and we were asleep. The column had been in Kilmilkin, and I was then trying to create a diversion as I had a wound, a ricochet bullet, in the side of my leg. I attacked a lorry on the 7th of December, at Liscarney on the Leenane road.[76] We didn't know that there was a raid on that morning. She [a girl] saw a Free State soldier as she was going to Mass, and they followed her, and they caught us asleep in our beds.

Captain Curtain in the Tan War escaped from the Rath Camp in a tunnel.

[Internment.] We had cut the bars in the Garrison Detention cells in Athlone. Mick Kilroy, Dick Walsh, Tom Maguire, Dr Mick Mullins, Johnny Gibbons of Westport,

---

74 Derrygorman, not Derrygormack as in the original text.
75 Islandeady, between Castlebar and Westport, Co. Mayo, in 1922.
76 At the Liscarney crossroads by Anne Keane's home.

were there in five cells, more or less condemned cells they were. And also there was Michael Mellett of Claremorris. There were twelve cells and there were forty men as prisoners. These five lads who were to have been executed were there with us. They didn't know until the night before. They put those in the one cell. Tom Hughes though, he told me it was for execution purposes.[77] I saw him as he came upstairs that morning. He asked me for a brush and polish and it was ten minutes to 8 [a.m.]. He was to have been shot at 8 o'clock. Neat and tidy Tom Hughes, who lived at the Hill of Berries, south of Athlone was near his … He [8L] was in a cell with me one time. There were Joyce, Burke and three others to be shot.[78] A fortnight later, at the end of February, we were transferred to Galway Gaol. We cut the bars with knives. We stuck them into our leggings as we left (Athlone). We meant to waylay the sentries, disarm the first sentry and then disarm the change of guard [at Athlone]. There was a square block patrolled on the outside with one on the inside and one outside the prison. We intended that when he passed our window to pass down and wait on the corner with our stockings filled with sand, then disarm the fellow in the hall. We got fistfuls of sand in the yard. We had a revolver and a bomb also. Then we had intended to wait for a change of guard. 3+5+5 rifles and the keys of the guardroom which was on the outside of one wall. Go back as the guard and then surprise the guardroom where we would get twelve rifles. Then we would be thirty yards from the Water Gate on which there was a sentry. Then we would storm that and get over the wall which was ten to twelve feet in height. We were to go on Saturday night but we were moved on Saturday morning. Dick Walsh told us that Saturday night would be the best for it was pay night, and then the soldiers would be drunk.

---

77 Referring to the condemned men who were isolated.
78 Stephen Joyce, Martin Burke and three others.

Galway [Gaol]. Johnny Gibbons, Charlie Gavan, Dick Walsh, Tommy Ruane from Ballina.[79] A number, 150 to 200, went to Galway from the Gymnasium and from Claremorris. Ten to twelve from the Garrison Detention and the rest went to Dublin. It was bad there. It couldn't be worse. The prison in itself was bad. The authorities were not too bad, but they made no sanitary arrangements. On the way, as we were going down by train, we decided that the 4th Western Division would appoint the Camp Commandant and the Staff of the Gaol so that **[9R]** an escape could be arrange[d] for without a leakage.[80] There were 150 prisoners removed from Galway to make room there for us and they were sent on to the Curragh and to its camps.

[Escape.] The following morning we appointed John Gibbons as the Camp Commandant.[81] Tom Ruane was the Deputy O/C, and I was the Quartermaster. We made contact through the Galway lads for there were ten of them in the reception who were awaiting execution. We had blade knives, and we thought that in two weeks time we would be able to cut through the bars. When we were in Athlone we were cutting in the daytime. We had notches created for we were under the sentry's nose.[82] The outside Galway men made contacts for us, and a priest or a Free State soldier[83] slipped in hacksaw blades to my cell one morning and he was in touch with the Widow

---

79 Gavan, not Gavin as in the original text.
80 A camp commandant would more usually be referred to as officer commanding or O/C prisoners and his deputy would be deputy O/C prisoners, as elected from among the prisoners.
81 John Gibbons, 4th Western Division.
82 Notches presumably refers to notches cut in the window bars of the prison.
83 After the escape it was reported that '15 of the Jail Garrison are at present under arrest', clearly showing the lack of trust that the prison authorities felt in their own soldiers: Operations Report, 6 March 1923, CW/OPS/03/1, Military Archives.

Walsh[84] of the Old Malt (House). They arranged also to throw over ropes from the outside. There was a locked grill between us and the reception room. We could talk to them through the grill. We cut the bars of the cell, and we bored a hole through to the next cell so that eight men could go through the one window. And we went [that] night through three windows, six plus twelve plus eight in ours. We had decided to let out the men who might be executed and the rest of the prisoners were completely unaware of all this work.

There was a difficulty in our boring. A trial hole brought us to a big block of cement and after a night we pulled Dick Walsh of Balla through with a great deal of pulling, but we took off a chunk of cement, which made it a bit bigger.

The signal for our escape was a man who would whistle at one o'clock, 'The Wearing of the Green', which meant that the rope had then been thrown over the wall.[85] We had our bars cut and the bars were again **[9L]** in position kept upright with soap. And we had our blankets cut then into strips. There was an eighteen foot drop. We pulled out the bars. Charlie Gavan was the second last to be down. The blanket broke but he was near the ground. Dick Walsh slipped and he didn't know (the rope was broken) and he was shook. He was *linked* over to the wall by Charlie Gavan.

Gerald Bartley was the first to get over the wall.[86] He was going up the rope but the top of the wall was wide and it was curved at the top but he could not get a grip on it to drop on to the outside, so he slid back into the yard. I tried then and I could not get over the wall, so I got my feet up and I went up

---

84 Agnes Walsh. Her husband, Michael Walsh was a Sinn Féin councillor. He was taken from this public house and shot, and his body dumped into the River Corrib at the Long Walk, in October 1920.

85 The Republican escape from Galway Gaol was on 6 March 1923, starting at 1 a.m.

86 Gerald Bartley born in Co. Mayo but from Clifden.

feet first. I went out and down on the far side. And I was about an hour outside when twelve came out.[87] I explained that there were no loops or knots and we tried to throw it over again and I climbed back again. I met Charlie Gavan on the top of the wall and I dropped the rope inside.

But the man on the inside allowed the rope to drop as he saw the rope with loops and out I slid, and I was badly shook. I have always had a sore hip ever since that fall. The County Council Offices which are across from the Gaol were occupied by troops. There were boys inside or the guards outside spotted something and fire was opened. The last man who came down broke his leg and was recaptured.[88] Gerald Bartley and Dick Walsh and six men inside who were executed three days later.[89]

The 6th [of] March 1923 was the day of the escape.[90] We scattered and broke up into groups under machine-gun fire. We had made a map inside of the county and of the route which we intended to follow. We were told to go on to the street until we met a railway. Then after three [10R] miles on the railway we would meet a stile, then we would meet a house and then we were to go on up to the mountain. We went on to a railway which reached a quarry on Salthill. Then we went on to Barna where we met a man on the road and it was still dark. We had

87 Fourteen men altogether escaped: seven from Co. Galway, one from Co. Tipperary, and certainly five and maybe a sixth from Co. Mayo. The men were: Paddy Duffy (Aughagower), Thomas Ruane (Ballina), John Connelly (Mayo), Johnny Gibbons (Westport), Charles Gavan, John Walshe (Derryullinane, Mayo), Paul Conneely, John King, Joseph Corbett, John Burke (all four from the Clifden area), John Herwood (Cornamona), Matty Fahey (Peterswell) and Tim Duggan (Galway). The Tipperary man was John Gargan (Clonmel).

88 Paddy Duffy's interview seems to be contradicted on this point by Jack Feehan in his O'Malley interview. See O'Malley, *The Men Will Talk to Me: Galway Interviews*, p. 175

89 Among those who almost escaped was Séamus Ó Máille of Oughterard who was one of those later executed; Roll of Honour East Connemara Brigade, UCDA P69/165 (Twomey Papers UCDA). The executions were on 11 April, not 7 April as implied in the original text.

90 Duffy mistakenly says in the text that the date of the escape was 4 March.

bits of shirts on us but we had no boots. We decided that we would tell him who we were and we did tell him. He asked me, 'Do you know a fellow inside named — ' and when we said we did, 'That's my brother,' he replied. He took us to his brother-in-law's house and there we were given new milk and poteen. It had been pouring rain from the time we had started out from the Gaol. We stayed all day there, but on the next morning he drove us on. Johnny Gibbons, Tom Ruane, Paul Conneely[91] of the Clifden Battalion and I together to Spiddal[92] to Dr Charles Gullin (Macken's house), a school teacher and guide, then on to Rosmuck, to Maam, to Leenane, fifty-six hours from Galway to Louisburgh town.[93] The town was not occupied by the Staters and it was good then. We got arms again and we rejoined our units.

In March or in May we snipped Westport a few times. There were between ten and fifteen of the lads together. We had plans then for Galway Gaol. Christie Macken was O/C of the 2nd Western then, and he planned to take the Gaol so that we could release the prisoners.[94] We could mobilise fifty well-armed men with land mines and they were well trained also. Mrs Walsh had a boat on the Corrib[95] which used to call in Finny or Clonbur over twice a week.[96] It was a trading boat. I never saw it. We knew of no active men in Galway City within twenty miles of Galway Gaol.[97] We could be in Tourmakeady today in two and

---

91 Conneely, not Kineely as in the original text.
92 Spiddal, not Spiddle as in the original text.
93 The schoolteacher reference is probably to Christie Macken's family.
94 Christie Macken (1898–1972) from Inverin attended University College Galway and moved to Dublin where he was in the IRA. During the Truce he was sent to organise Galway and Mayo and went anti-Treaty. He became O/C of the 2nd Western Division.
95 Lough Corrib.
96 Finny (not Femey as in the original text) on the shore of Lough Mask, near Clonbur.
97 Duffy's analysis of the IRA in and around Galway city is largely accurate. The IRA had always been weak and poorly armed in that city. After the Treaty

a half or three hours, board the boat, blow a breach in the wall and take out the prisoners, [10L] put them on board, or take the County Council Office.[98] Then on came the 'Cease Fire' order …[99] There was a built-up gateway there for the old gateway had been built up again and we felt that would blow it in.

Tom Maguire got out after the 'Cease Fire'. There was an old lavatory which had a brick wall, but someone discovered [that] if a brick was taken out [we could get out] and twenty minutes later there were five of them who got into the Transport Sheds and as civilians walked in front towards the hospital where there was only a six foot wall to cross. Mick Mullins was with them and when they got that far they got over the wall and away with them. This was on a Sunday evening.

split much of the IRA leadership supported the Free State. Anti-Treaty IRA men from the city tended to serve with Republican columns outside the city. Several of these columns were captured within the opening two months of the Civil War and the areas close to Galway city saw little Republican activity for the rest of the conflict.

98 Reference as to how long it would take to get from Galway across Lough Corrib, then across Lough Mask to Tourmakeady, Co. Mayo.

99 With the death of Chief of Staff Liam Lynch on 10 April 1923, Frank Aiken, as the succeeding Republican chief of staff, issued 'Cease Fire' and Dump Arms orders in April and May 1923. The second part of this sentence has been omitted as it is incomplete.

TOMMY HEAVEY

(UCDA P17b/120, pp. 44-62)[1]

Thomas 'Tommy' Heavey (1904– 1995) was born in Enniscorthy, Co. Wexford. His family moved to Westport in 1912 where his father, Pat, was employed by the Livingston's Brewery and was a friend of Major John MacBride. When the brewery closed in 1916 Heavey's family moved to Holyhead, Wales, and he was sent to Belcamp College, Balgriffin, North Dublin. When he graduated he joined his family in Dundalk where his father then worked for Macardle's Brewery.

Copyright J. J. Leonard (courtesy of Anthony Leonard)

Heavey joined the IRA in Dundalk in 1919, just before the family moved back to Carrowbawn later that year, where their neighbour was Ned Moane. Heavey joined the Westport Company of the IRA and worked closely with Moane, later becoming active with the Westport No. 3 Battalion of the West Mayo Brigade ASU, which became part of the 4th Western Division in August or September 1921. He was anti-Treaty and was captured in Glenhest on 24 July 1922 and interned, but escaped with Broddie Malone before being recaptured at Brize House, Claremorris, and sent to Mountjoy and later Tintown in the Curragh. He managed to escape again and after leaving Neill 'Plunkett' O'Boyle's unit in Wicklow, he was recaptured in Valleymount. However, neither Mountjoy or Kilmainham could

---

1 The original transcription of this interview and some footnotes were made by Dominic Price.

hold him, and he escaped a third time in December 1923. In later years he married, and raised his family in Ballina.

This interview took place in Ballina in October 1951.

[1920–1921 PERIOD]

[44L] I was one of the first actually. I was touring with Ned Moane.[2] I was in the Westport Battalion (Bn 3), and I was about sixteen at the time.[3] We did the Louisburgh area.[4] Ned believed in keeping in touch with the key men: Paddy Kelly and Andy Harney in the area.[5] It was always a kind of a safe area to retreat to afterwards. He visited Company after Company. Louisburgh, Tallaghbawn, Murrisk was in the Westport Battalion area. Bradley was the [Murrisk] Company Captain.[6] We were both on the run. There was a message from the District Inspector Maguire who had sent in, about the 1st November 1920, that some of the murder gang were arriving secretly; and that they would probably be flogging people and shooting.[7] So Ned pulled me out with him for I lived at the time beside Ned. Through the clergy we would send out word then.

Stevenson and Donnellan came along then as District

2 Edward 'Ned' Moane, not Moyhane or Mohane as sometimes in the original text. See biographical sketches.

3 This would have been Battalion No. 3 of the West Mayo Brigade in which there were four battalions: 1. Castlebar, 2. Newport, 3. Westport and 4. Louisburgh. The companies in the Westport Battalion included: Aughagower, Belclare, Cushlough, Derrygorman, Drummin, Murrisk, Owenwee, Westport and Westport Quay. Heavey is mistaken below when he says Louisburgh and Tallaghbawn were in the Westport Battalion, as they were in the Louisburgh Battalion.

4 Louisburgh, not Louisbourgh or Louisburg as sometimes in the original text.

5 Paddy Kelly was more commonly known as P. J. Kelly. Andy Harney, not Andie as in the original text.

6 John Bradley (not Bradly as sometimes in the original text) was O/C of the Murrisk Company.

7 RIC District Inspector Maguire of Westport Barracks was friendly to the cause. He later became a Superintendent of An Garda Síochána in Limerick and died in 1926.

Inspectors when things got hot.[8] I think that Maguire was living in Waterford. This murder gang consisted of three plain clothes men for we had expected armoured cars and lorries, but actually only the three men came then. It was a kind of bombastic show off around the town. They were swinging guns. They brought the [44R] military from the Quay.[9] (I took a tin hat from off one of them who was hanging around the Castlebar road to meet a girl. They wore green tin hats then.) The three of them raided with the military then, and there were quite a number of raids. Their attitude in Westport was to kind of make us look foolish. But these three were not violent. It was really a bit of swashbuckling more than anything else. From Westport there were Tom Kitterick,[10] Broddie Malone,[11] Joe Ring,[12] the two Duffys,[13] Hoban,[14] myself, John Dick Gibbons,[15] Johnny Gibbons,[16] Charlie Gavan.[17] Outside of our people[18] were Myles Hawkshaw[19] and Charlie Hughes,[20] and then the Sligo's and the Livingston's dependants.

8   RIC District Inspectors Edward James Stevenson and Peter Donnellan from Mohill, Co. Leitrim. Donnellan was involved in the Kilmeena ambush.
9   There was a British Army camp on Westport Quay.
10 Tom Kitterick of Westport. See biographical sketches.
11 Broddie Malone (not Brodie as in the original text) from Westport. See his interview.
12 Joe Ring of Westport. See biographical sketches.
13 The Duffy brothers, Johnny and Paddy, lived at Cloonskill, Aughagower. Johnny was O/C of the Aughagower Company. Having left secondary school Paddy joined the West Mayo Brigade ASU. Both were involved in most of the ASU engagements and were anti-Treaty. Johnny, however, refused to take up arms against the Free State and stayed neutral during the Civil War.
14 This could have been Thomas Hoban, a rate collector and a neighbour of Heavey, but he was not a member of the IRA. His home in Carrowbawn was burned down after the first Carrowkennedy engagement by the RIC.
15 John Dick Gibbons lived in Mill Street, Westport, and was transport officer for the Westport Battalion.
16 Johnny 'Seán' Gibbons was a law clerk who lived on the Quay Road, Westport, and was adjutant of the West Mayo Brigade and later the 4th Western Division.
17 Charlie Gavan from Westport.
18 People who were not in the IRA but were supportive.
19 Myles, not Miles as in the original text.
20 Charlie Hughes from Lankill, Aughagower, came from a Republican family. He was interned in 1916. He worked in Lennon's drapery in Westport and

When the scare died down some of the lads went back to work, but they used to sleep away from home, but Moane and I and Ring were permanently out, and Charlie Gavan. None of the other lads were caught except Charlie Gavan, who was arrested in Brackloon near Murrisk in what he thought was a safe house, but he was obviously given away.[21] Derrig then worked in Ballina, and he only paid Westport a flying visit on a Sunday.[22] He was arrested, and then Michael Kilroy took over. Then Kilroy, in about two months was in charge and Kilroy joined us.[23] The Brigade headquarters was set up in Ballinacarriga, near Islandeady, and convenient it was for it was across our main lines.[24] This went on until the middle of February when the column started. We varied in the way we kept together. Ned Moane and I, or Michael Kilroy or Kitterick, if he was back from Dublin, and Johnny Gibbons. We carried revolvers or automatics. There was an odd rifle here and there in the Westport Battalion. The British raided the Workhouse while Charlie Gavan and Tom Kitterick were in it. They raided the ward where they were, but a nurse, Satchwell, put them under patients' beds. Then she bluffed the British who turned out of the ward into another, [45L] and then she slipped them out of the ward they were in, into a house which they had searched. Termon, Roscommon, was her parents' home, and he was supposed to be one of the lads.[25] They found a cap of either Tom Kitterick or Gavan's after they had left the place that day.

There was a dangerous and vicious RIC Sergeant, Hanlon,

eventually became the owner of the business. He employed many of the young IRA in the town, including Battie Cryan and Tommy Kitterick. He was anti-Treaty, but kept a neutral stance in the Civil War. His store supplied boots, breeches, leggings and trench coats to the ASU.

21 Brackloon is a townland on the southern slopes of Croagh Patrick.
22 Tom Derrig from Westport. See biographical sketches.
23 Michael Kilroy from Newport. See his interview.
24 Ballinacarriga or Ballinacorrigan, not Ballinacoriga as in the original text.
25 The 'he' refers to Ms Satchwell's father from Termon.

who was promoted to a Head Constable. He would have been in command after Stevenson that morning in Carrowkennedy. Sergeant Creegan was looked upon as officious, and he was a Head Constable also.[26] Ring asked him at Carrowkennedy. 'How do you get promoted?' 'By long service,' was the answer. French, who was a Tan, was a wild madman.[27] I brought him a drink, but he wouldn't take it from me.

I can remember the night of the formation ... of the column as we were marching on towards Owenwee at the back of Croagh Patrick. We had about fifteen there with shotguns, rifles and revolvers. Broddie Malone was in charge of us. There were the two Naughton brothers,[28] the two Duffys, Baker (a solid man).[29] We were to meet Ned Moane, the Brigade Adjutant. Michael Kilroy was in Teevenacroaghy School which is on the foothills of Croagh Patrick.[30] It was a very wet night and we were drenched when we arrived there, but no one turned up. We became very mutinous.

I know someone had said, 'We won't recognise this bloody Brigade.' Kilroy had taken off his moustache and Moane had decided to grow one. 'You can't,' said Baker dryly 'for Moane has taken Kilroy's moustache.' We left them and we circled the Drummin side. Red Pat has the halfway house now between Westport and Castlebar.[31] We arrived in a village, Furgill, and we hung around for a couple of days, and some of the lads went home.[32] Eventually both Kilroy and Moane did turn up, and we

---

26 The ranking RIC head constable in Westport at the time of Carrowkennedy was Head Constable Hanlon, not Sergeant Francis Creegan.
27 RIC Constable William French, who was killed in the Carrowkennedy ambush.
28 Martin and Paddy Naughton (not Nocton as in the original text).
29 The brothers Johnny and Paddy Duffy and Joe Baker.
30 Teevenacroaghy, not Teevena Croagh as in the original text.
31 Red Pat Joyce of Durless, near Louisburgh.
32 Probably Furgill (not Forragaill as in the original text), a townland, not a village, near Cartoor, west of Drummin West.

trained. We had a bit of snap shooting with a rifle.[33] We had no hand grenades, but we had a hand-made thing which [45R] was made out of a gas pipe. A good safe area this was.

The next thing I recollect [is] being marched to between Lecanvey and Murrisk to attack a lorry.[34] I think it was Patrick's Day or the eve of it. We stayed all day. It was wet the night before, and there were awful hailstones nearly all day. Broddie Carney was there that night. (He was a brother of Frank Carney, the playwright.)

Glosh.[35] Certain of the fellows disbanded, and the Brigade Staff left us there. Joe Ring was the O/C of the Westport Battalion, and he was in charge of the column when Kilroy was not there. We moved around from place to place, around Islandeady, but principally in the Westport Battalion area for we were nearly all Westport men. Castlebar had then formed its own column. Some of us got fed up as we were doing nothing; and we were constantly urging Joe Ring to have a crack at something. There were constant lorry patrols between Westport and Castlebar. Then Joe was a hard man to understand. He was a great man for the limelight. This evening we were billeted around Aughagower.[36] The local Parish Priest was in touch with The Castle.[37] (He was a friend of MacMahon.)[38] I think they [IRA] captured one of his letters.

A few of us mutinied for we wanted to get away on our own. Bully Staunton, Mill Street, Westport, and John MacDonagh, Butch Lambert of the Quay.[39] Us four broke away, and we went

---

33 This possibly should read snipe or sharpshooting.
34 Lecanvey (not Lecanvy as in the original text) lies just west of Murrisk.
35 Glosh, not Gloush as in the original text.
36 Aughagower, not Aghagower as in the original text.
37 Referring to Dublin Castle, the seat of British administration in Ireland.
38 This sentence appears to be a comment by O'Malley who placed the question mark, and it has been placed in parentheses.
39 Michael 'Bully' Staunton was a member of the West Mayo Brigade ASU. This would have been about 6 April 1921.

into Westport to attack the RIC. When we got in there we found that the RIC patrol had gone back to the barracks. We fired a few shots, and we hung around, but they didn't come out again. And the next day we met up with the column. Joe Ring was furious and that night he sat astride on the Castlebar road to await reinforcements. He disarmed us. He took our rifles from us and he left us our revolvers. And I think a day or two later Jim Duffy from Prospect was killed. My gun I gave to [46L] Jimmy Flaherty who was an ex-British Army man.[40] He pulled the trigger. Jimmy had cleaned my Parabellum and I stuck back the magazine.[41] There was another empty gun on the table, and Jimmy picked up mine, pulled up the bolt action and pulled the trigger, and poor Duffy died within a quarter of an hour. We buried him at night, and we made a coffin at night near Islandeady. We buried him somewhere near that place.[42]

Just after that Kilroy, Dr Madden and Moane joined up with us permanently.[43] We were out towards Drummin. Sometime after the Duffy accident we had a clash with a patrol near Clogher which is in the half-parish.[44] We were on the road spread out when a tender and a touring road car came along from Westport, so we got behind ditches. I was with Ring, and I was talking about mutiny. Joe Ring opened fire, and some lads behind were not under fire. Broddie Malone was out in the open. They put out their lights for this was at night, then they ran on a little, and they stopped, dismounted and opened fire for a while. All we saw was the lorry, and we fired into that. They started off the engines and they got away. They said we were seen carrying away dead and wounded.

---

40 Flaherty, not Flah as in the original text.
41 A Parabellum is an automatic 9 mm pistol of German origin.
42 Jim Duffy of Prospect was buried at Cushin on the night of 7 April 1921. He was not related to the Duffys of Cloonskill.
43 Dr John A. Madden from Ballycastle. See biographical sketches.
44 23 April 1921.

[First Carrowkennedy ambush][45] The Brigade Staff went on to Drummin, and they billeted in Claddy.[46] This was on the 22nd of March. Kilroy and Moane asked me to go to John Hastings,[47] who was the Company Captain of Cushlough, bank porter, discussing the possibility of an ambush.[48] I stayed a long time with him, more time than I should have spent, and as I reached the main road near Cushlough Chapel a woman stepped out of the shadows in the bright moonlight and told me to be careful, that four police had gone up the hill and they were wheeling their bikes. They had gone up towards Westport. I went on carefully but just then I heard the **[46R]** shooting, and I doubled up towards the Drummin branch road, and just as I reached it, I met Kilroy, Ring and Broddie Malone, and as they moved off towards Claddy, Kilroy said to me on the way up, 'It's terrible hard to kill a man.' They had met the four RIC men. The Sergeant, Coughlan, had been killed;[49] Constables Maguire, Love and Creedon had been wounded. We fell back at once to Aughagower. We had carbines, revolvers and their egg-bombs.[50] From that on patrols moved out and they kept us on the go. In the daytime we left the houses and we went to a remote spot. Cuilmore, Westport.[51]

Clogher really came next on 23 April for Carrowkennedy was in March.[52] The [RIC] ran away from us again.[53]

---

45 'First' refers to the ambush on 22 March 1921 and 'second' refers to the one on 2 June 1921.

46 Claddy is used throughout this interview instead of Clady, which was the spelling used in the original text. Claddy is near Carrowkennedy.

47 Hastings (not Hasting as in the original text) was a porter in a local bank.

48 Cushlough, not Couslough as in the original text.

49 Sergeant John Coughlan.

50 The British Mills grenades were referred to as 'egg-bombs'.

51 This refers to the Cuilmore (not Colmore as in the original text) near Drummin, not the Cuilmore near Newport.

52 The first Carrowkennedy (not Carrick as in the original text) ambush was on 22 March.

53 Referring to the RIC running away at Clogher. Clogher was a stand-off with

[Tourmakeady ambush, 1921] May 3rd. We were in the next townland to Claddy, and we marched on the main Tourmakeady road to Sraheen or I think we came to Derrycraff school before we were stopped.[54] I was at the tail of the column. There were up to fifteen of us, Malone and Ring and the Westport crowd. This would be in the early afternoon, and it took us a couple of hours to get there. We saw no military that day and we came back. I don't know where to. We went across the Castlebar–Westport road, and we hung around for a few days. We had Willie Malone, Joe Walsh from England [who] had come from Liverpool, and a third, Johnny Gallagher, merchant in Cullane, who was told to go home until he was needed. We hung around at the Big Wall (which is on the railway edge about three miles out on a Westport–Castlebar road) about March 20, and we had still eighteen–twenty men, who were nearly exclusively Westport men.[55] They [RIC] obviously knew we were there. (Why?) We would clear off for a bit, and then we would come back again.

[Big Wall ambush, 6 May.] The idea was that a lorry ran from Castlebar to Westport and back again, probably on communications, and we were after this. (Did a lorry run in such a manner in other areas because communication by **[47L]** wire or by phone was becoming difficult or unreliable?) The 5th of May it was.[56] It was a military lorry. We loopholed the Big Wall, and then we had more rifles for Kitterick was with us now (and I expect he had brought rifles down from Dublin). We had arranged to have the road cut between us and Castlebar

no injuries on either side.

54 Sraheen is used throughout this interview instead of Shreaheen, which was the spelling used in the original text.

55 The Big Wall is a nine foot wall that separates the road from the railroad beside the old Islandeady Dance Hall.

56 Heavey relates this as 7 May but many others have reported 6 May and so the date has been changed here. Perhaps there was confusion between the start of the action on one evening and its ending in the following morning.

as soon as the lorry had passed a certain place. I think that the lorry passed by the cutting party who were concealed, and that it then came into the view of our Scouts who were on a hill. They must have seen something suspicious for they turned back, but they came upon our fellows who were cutting the road, and they opened fire on them. Two were killed and two more wounded and captured.[57] This was the 6th of May, and we retired on to Owenwee that night.

Charlie Hughes was in the town and some of the houses around Drummin, two of them anyhow, were burned and other people were pulled out of their houses and beaten.[58] Malone's father was taken out. Ned Haran of Bridge Street, a publican: they forced spirits down his throat and they poured drink in through a tin dish and they nearly suffocated him. They tied old Malone to a trap, and they made him drag it. Willie Reilly was useless but an Irish Volunteer was beaten by them as he [Reilly] pulled the trap.[59] 'Don't whip me sir,' he shouted. 'I can go faster if you like', was the yarn told about Willie Reilly.

[Red Bridge, Westport] The 8th of May. The [RIC] patrol was attacked at 8.30 p.m. at the Railway Bridge.[60] Joe Baker, Broddie Malone and Tommy Kitterick were on this job. The Red Bridge it was known as. The patrol was bombed. 'A bomb attack on a large RIC patrol several of whom were wounded', was the newspaper report.

[Kilmeena ambush, 19 May.] There was some undercurrent whatever it was between Kilroy and Ring. Kilroy kept strictly aloof from Ring. One was jealous of the other. (Why were men left a

---

57 The two killed were Thomas Lally and Thomas O'Malley. The wounded were Frank O'Boyle and Jim McNulty.
58 A heading before this paragraph in the original text, 'The First Carrowkennedy' was moved to earlier to fit the chronological sequence.
59 Willie Reilly, not Riley as in the original text.
60 Red Bridge was in Altamount Street, Westport, and carried the railroad extension on to Achill.

couple **[47R]** of miles from Kilmeena on the day of the ambush there?) Michael Kilroy stayed with the Castlebar crowd, and he left Ring and his men alone. We were still separated from the Brigade. We moved in from Owenwee to Corrig in the Westport Parish, and we thought that we would go into Westport again.[61]

18th May. The Newport RIC Barracks was sniped by 'little' Jim Moran, and Sergeant Butler was killed on the Castlebar road.[62] And on the 19th of May, Kilmeena took place.[63] We heard the firing from where we were in Corrig and we sat there all day. For quite a while this firing went on. It was a very still summer's day and I think that the firing went on for some hours. There were between fifteen to eighteen of us there. Broddie Malone was with us, but Moane was with the Castlebar Column. We heard there had been a disaster and we heard about our fellows being brought in prisoners. Then on a day or two afterwards a report came in when we were a bit away from Westport that there was fighting down below in Newport near Skerdagh, and that a troop train had gone down and we were told that the whole column had been captured. After that the Castlebar Column was disbanded, or it was sent off to rest. Josie Doherty of Newport came along with the Brigade Staff and joined us, [as did] Jim Kelly of Ballintleva, which is in between Clogher and Islandeady, in the Clogher half-parish.[64]

We returned towards Tallaghbawn or in that direction of the Kilmeena Ambush:[65] [killed: James/Seamus MacEvilly, Patrick

---

61 There is an area two miles from Westport known as Corrig (not Carrig as in the original text) where the IRA used to rendezvous and it is likely that from there they could hear the shots fired at Kilmeena.

62 Jim Moran and Jim Browne killed RIC Sergeant Francis J. Butler on 18 May 1921, not 19 May as in the original text.

63 This took place on 19 May, not 21 May as in the original text.

64 Ballintleva, not Ballincleera or Ballinasleer as in the original text.

65 Heavey's list of killed and wounded was not accurate and was confusing; in order to bring clarity his list has been entirely replaced by a list of those killed, wounded, captured and escaped.

Staunton, Johnny Collins, Thomas O'Connell, Paddy Jordan
died later; captured: John Cannon, Paddy Mulloy, Thomas Nolan,
Thomas O'Donnell. Paddy O'Malley was wounded, captured
and died a few days later; Swift and Hughes were wounded but
escaped. Total]: five killed, four wounded. It is said that Lord
Sligo, who saw some of the RIC hauling round their prisoners,
objected. There was a young fellow Pierce who was a tailor.[66]
He [48L] also had been captured unwounded, and he was taken
around in the lorries with them afterwards. He disappeared
later. He was a young Dublin fellow. (An Artane boy, I think,
but nobody else heard about him later; it is surmised that he
gave some information.) The British had a Constable Beckett
killed and a Head Constable Potter wounded (in Skerdagh).[67]
Kilroy was waiting for a lorry, but if the Sergeant in Newport
had not been killed I expect there would have been a lorry, but
on account of the shooting more lorries came on. There was talk
of a train having passed up first along the line[68] while the lads
were in position in Kilmeena (?).[69] Big Paddy Cannon of the
Board of Health, he was in it, I think.[70] And Mark Killilea got
a slight wound there (?).[71] There were rifles lost that day as well.
Ten men lost between captured, wounded and killed.

[Drummin Barracks, 1 June 1921.] The Westport Column
had fifteen good rifles then. We went back to Drummin and we
billeted around Oughty. The Joyce house was in Durless, and

---

66 John Pierce, not Pearse as in the original text.
67 Constable Harry Beckett (not Beckets as in the original text) was killed in
     Kilmeena. O'Malley is mistaken here, as it was Constable Joseph Maguire who
     was killed at Skerdagh on 23 May, and Head Constable Potter was wounded
     there.
68 The line refers to the railroad line from Westport to Newport.
69 O'Malley adds a question mark here as if to question the statement.
70 Paddy Cannon. See his interview. The mention of the Board of Health refers
     to the period of the interview.
71 Heavey may have been mistaken regarding Mark Killilea as there is no record
     of his being wounded or even of his participation. O'Malley adds a question
     mark here as if to question the statement.

they were a very unassuming family, nothing was a trouble to them as far as we were concerned and they were all butchers.[72] And on the night of the 1st of June, it was excellent weather, we went to Drummin for the barracks had been evacuated. We entered it; but GHQ had already warned us about the booby traps which might be used against us by the enemy in unoccupied barracks or maybe it had been mentioned in *An T-Óglach* (or maybe it was time that officers, especially senior officers, would use their common sense to protect their men).[73] They went in by the back window and there was a bomb slung across the back door. Johnny Duffy and Michael Kilroy went in and they cut the string which was attached to the bomb, and they took the bomb. It was a Mills Grenade. And then they had found a good grenade. (In the police grenades I heard that the **[48R]** explosion was too powerful because it powdered the metal shell or was this what happened in this unprimed explosion. This I heard anyhow.) We set fire to the barracks then, and we went back on this Wednesday the first of June to Claddy. That night I was up all the night on sentry duty. Bully Staunton was an inveterate smoker, and I had trouble with him that night. Very often we used the local lads at night, except when there was special danger, when some of us would be left up to stiffen the others.

[Second Carrowkennedy ambush, 2 June 1921.] I was in bed next day until 6 o'clock when I was suddenly pulled out of bed. I was told to get out, that a convoy had gone out towards Leenane. It was close to 6 o'clock. It was known that a bridge had been cut further out along the road. Erriff Bridge maybe. I didn't then know that the bridge had been cut. We expected something to come as a result of the burning of the barracks

---

72 Durless, not Durlus as in the original text.
73 *An t-Óglach* was the internal training newsletter of the IRA, first edited by Dick McKee and later by Piaras Béaslaí.

of Drummin. I jumped out of bed, and we took up positions close to the road. I was with the crowd. Broddie Malone was in charge of our section. There was Paddy and Johnny Duffy, Battie Cryan, Jack MacDonagh, Joe Baker. I think Tommy Kitterick was further down with another party. Joe Baker was on my left and Jack MacDonagh was on my right.

There was a wall there which was very heavy at the base: and you could be up against it and you could make a post hole in the wall (the wall was of big boulders and smaller stones as it climbed up). We had time to do that, for the lorry stopped at Darby Hastings' pub for I heard someone say, 'They're at the pub.' The wall slanted down and behind the boulders were men who had a clear view. I heard the whine of the engine then. I never saw the other two vehicles until the fight was over. I think Johnny Madden (Dr) was ahead between us and Westport. It was understood that the lorry would be allowed to a certain point before we fired. The field was a bit narrow, **[49L]** and we were cut off from the Leenane view.[74]

The lorry came along at a moderate speed. Fire was opened, and everyone concentrated on the driver. Jack Keane was with us and he was a splendid shot.[75] He afterwards died of tuberculosis.[76] The lorry kind of jerked a bit and stopped dead in the middle of the road. The RIC jumped out over the sides and out of the back very rapidly in all directions. They got the Lewis gun out for they didn't go back again for it. Yet I didn't see it in any of their arms when they got out. The Lewis opened up on us after a very short interval of time. The rifle grenade fire was heavy, but it fell short of us. 150 yards about, we moved away from them.

74 The 'narrow view' might refer to there being a limited field of view from their firing position.

75 Jack Keane (not Kane as in the original text) from Gortaroe, The Lodge Road. He went pro-Treaty and served in An Garda Síochána. He died in 1924 in Monaghan.

76 Tuberculosis is written as T.B. in the original text.

They were firing upwards as well as they could not possibly hit us. Now and then you'd see them; and they were behind the road wall. A little ditch was there, I think. They all didn't get out of the lorry. After a few bursts the machine gun was put out of action. I don't think the machine [gun] was on the road close to [the] lane. Then after a quarter of an hour the machine gun started again, and it got in a few more bursts which were longer this time. They [RIC] got off a couple of pans, and it was silenced again, but they let off more stuff this time.[77] I think that finished the second gunner. Three times it opened up and three times it was silenced. We didn't pay any attention to it.[78]

[56L] Donnellan, the RIC District Inspector, told me that the accelerator of the lorry had been hit.[79] The driver, the District Inspector Stevenson was killed, and another man in front, who was beside him, was killed, so I suppose the spare driver was gone then.[80] This he told me after the demobilisation.

[49L] I was told later that Joe Ring was across the road. He got into this position himself. Moane would have been second in charge after Kilroy. I heard him say that he (Ring, I think) could spot everything through his glasses, and I heard Tom Kitterick say to him when the fight was over: 'You must have been a long way away, Joe, if you had to use your glasses.' Then it became dull. We tried to make our bullets ricochet around the lorry. We could see a [49R] rifle slanting up out of the lorry and I expect this was the rifle which was being used to throw the grenades, but we could not see a figure in the lorry. For about two and a half to three hours the action lasted and our ammunition was running out. I started off with

---

77 A pan is a magazine to hold rounds or bullets of ammunition for the Lewis gun.
78 The next three sentences relate to Carrowkennedy and have been moved from p. 56L to here.
79 RIC District Inspector Peter Donnellan (not Donnelan as in the original text).
80 RIC District Inspector Edward Stevenson (not Stephenson as in the original text).

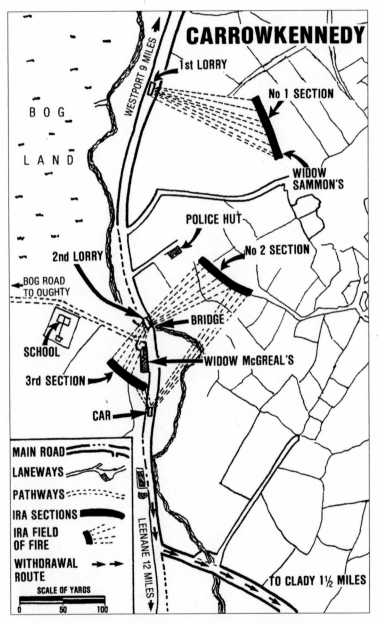

Plan of the second Carrowkennedy ambush, taken from Ernie
O'Malley, *Raids and Rallies* (Mercier Press, 2011), names amended.

thirty rounds, and I was now down to seven. We would shout down to them. They defied us to stand up and fight. Insults were being bandied between the two sides. You would watch for a puff.[81]

Kilroy came along and he was very worried about the ammunition. 'If the ammunition goes it will have to come to bayonets', and I was very worried for only two or three of us had bayonets. I had one and Jack MacDonagh of Westport had one, and Paddy Duffy, for we used to do a bit of sparring with the bayonets. But then Kilroy told Baker to take me and MacDonagh and to get down that laneway to outflank the lorry. It may have been a dried-up river bed. We reached the laneway and we stooped down for a view of the lorry, so Joe [Baker] told me to go forward to see could I get a crack at the back of the lorry. I had to crawl at this time. I stopped when I could see into the open back of the lorry, and I could see a rifle moving up slowly. It fired in the direction of the positions which we had left. I would say that there was a burst of firing from those positions on top, and then I fired two shots into the back of the lorry, and almost at once there was an explosion in the lorry and practically at once the white handkerchief went up. We hadn't our bayonets fixed then. A story went around then that it was I who had bombed the lorry.

Someone came down to take the surrender. I stood up until I was told to come out. I suppose I thought it was a trap. I was told by Broddie Malone to stay on guard over the prisoners. There was only one of them unwounded. (Was it Collins?) He was a constable **[50L]** and an Irishman. There was an Englishman who was limping and who had been wounded in the ankle, but not badly. On a doorway Sergeant Creegan was carried up.[82] He

---

81 The puff of smoke that would come from firing a rifle.
82 Doorway probably refers to the actual door itself. RIC Sergeant Francis Creegan from Westport Barracks.

was very badly wounded, and I brought my two fellows up there too. Two who [were] in the front of the lorry were dead. Willie Malone, I think, actually took the machine gun. I brought the two prisoners up close to the house. Joe Ring, who was swinging a short Webley [revolver], came along and this Cullen [RIC] rather turned his back and he was tearing up something, and both Ring and I tried to stop him. Ring poked the revolver into his stomach, and told him that he would have to tell what was in the contents or he would shoot him. Cullen said that it was just a routine report or something. But the pieces were pieced together and there were addresses in Westport on it. Poor old Creegan was dying there, and the rest of the [flying column] party went down [to] the other position which was along by the road.

Jack Keane brought the slightly wounded man along with him as a shield, and Jack was sent to make this man call on the others [RIC] who were inside in a house to surrender. I saw Kitterick floating up and down; that's all I can say. Then Cullen went away on a bicycle for Westport to get help for the wounded, and the town was eight miles away.[83] The lorry was ablaze then. The armour plating was low. I saw Kilroy firing two rounds of ammunition at it at close quarters, but I do not know if they did penetrate the steel. I believe old Darby of the pub is there still.[84]

The widow's house.[85] The RIC were asked at first to let out the women and the children, but this they refused to do. This slightly wounded Black and Tan was told that if they did not surrender, the prisoners would be shot; and they surrendered.

83 Cullen, an RIC man, was not wounded and apparently cycled into Westport for help, although Paddy Duffy says it was Potter.
84 'Darby' Hastings of Cushlough, who owned the Halfway Pub near the Carrowkennedy ambush site.
85 The widow, Mrs McGreal, not Mrs McGrale as in the original text nor as noted on the map in *Raids and Rallies* (Mercier Press, 2011), p. 251.

There were about twenty-five rifles and a Lewis [50R] gun and a Lewis pan and revolvers. There were quite a few grenades. A box of ammunition for the Lewis guns and a box of drums.[86] Some of the RIC had hardly fired a shot and each of them had two cloth bandoliers of ammunition.

Broddie Malone wanted to shoot [Head Constable] Hanlon as I think there was some scene between some of our fellows and Michael [Kilroy].[87]

We went back to Claddy. I had two rifles; my pockets were loaded with Mills Grenades. Four lads and I also helped to carry the Lewis gun between Flaherty and myself that night in relays.[88] We hung around Claddy till it was dark. We got the first alarm at 6 o'clock, and it started between that and 7 o'clock (at 7 p.m. on Thursday the 2nd of June a large party of RIC men were attacked at Carrowkennedy, six of whom were killed and four wounded. All arms and equipment were captured. It is described in the official report as 'the largest scale attack so far in the West'.) We went down into the bog, crossed the road to the west on the Westport side of Cushlough Church, very silently in twos we went. We had warned the people in Claddy to tell them that we had gone towards the east, and this confirmed the impression that we had given the prisoners. O'Malley [IRA] was congratulated by the officer who questioned him later.[89]

We came to the back of the Reek, I think to Furgill, for the split up definitely.[90] M. Kilroy had part of the crowd, and Ring and the Westport men were together. The next night when we

86 Drums or pans of ammunition for the Lewis gun.
87 Broddie, not Broddy, and Hanlon, not Hogan as in the original text.
88 Flaherty, not Flagherty as in the original text.
89 This O'Malley (not O'Mally as in the original text) was a local IRA Volunteer who sent the reinforcements to the east of the ambush site.
90 Furgill, not Forragil as in the original text. Heavey is mistaken here for the ASU then went on a four-week trek around the county avoiding the pursuing British forces.

fell in, Ring called for a marching song. So some of the boys obliged, and the song proceeded until we heard Kilroy shouting 'Stop that row'.[91] We had been told that the British had swept the other direction. M. Kilroy, in front of us all, took Joe Ring to task, but Joe chipped back at Michael in an impertinent way. Kilroy demanded his rifle, but Joe refused to give it up. Then [51L] Michael Kilroy grabbed it and asked for volunteers to step forward to disarm him, and at least two men made a move: Rick Joyce from Westport and I, and when Joe saw the move, he handed up his rifle. We felt that area was safe, and we got up to Bofeenaun area near Crossmolina which was a hopeless district belonging to North Mayo.[92] In the Tan War it was a purely neutral area. We came out through the Punchman's Gap, the Windy Gap. We were not mobilised until we came to Crumlin close to Castlebar.

[Round-up.] Next day very early the Tans came along in lorries along the main road, by chance, apparently coming in to raid.[93] We got out of the houses. They saw us. The range was too great. They were on the main Pontoon road, and the road into Crumlin was three-quarters of a mile (long or away?) or then they would have been further in.

'The night of the long bottles.' If these fellows had not been up drinking they would not have seen the RIC. They [RIC] came in, and they searched some of the houses. The hill at the back of Crumlin we were on that day. The RIC did not want to come in. The capture of the Lewis gun by us shook them considerably. [District Inspector] Donnellan told me this afterwards and it made them cautious. The following night they [RIC] left picquets out around the area for we came back

91 'To fall in' in the military sense means to line up.
92 Bofeenaun, not Baufinnane as in the original text. 'Hopeless' would refer to their not being supportive of the IRA.
93 The Black and Tans were fully sworn-in constables in the RIC organisation, and they reported to the local head constables or sergeants.

down the hill, and we were very cautious crossing the Pontoon road, and we moved on towards Bellavary.[94]

Ring had gone home on leave now, and when he got home he took all the credit for Carrowkennedy when he met his cronies to talk about it. We billeted in Bellavary and Turlough. There was a rumour about that a big round-up had started so we must have had some Intelligence that worked (I think Intelligence in the West was bad). We skipped next night and made a long march to Westport by the Leenane road, **[51R]** and we went to Bohea,[95] and we were hardly in bed when some more information arrived, and we were told to break up into small groups; and we were recommended to dump our rifles and to hold on to our short arms. I went off to the mines, more from curiosity than anything else, to Sheeffry to see the silver mines there.[96] Johnny Gibbons was with me and Paddy Duffy. At Sheeffry we dumped our rifles. The round-up took place. We saw the cavalry. We spent two or three nights out altogether. They rounded up all the males in the villages. We were on the qui vive all the time.[97] They used star shells at night from the Bay.[98] Madden got pneumonia. After 'the night of the long bottles' Kilroy made all the men take the pledge, and we were ready to march off when one of the scouts just then came up to Kitterick with poteen, and he put it in his pocket.

Kilroy sent out small columns. (Paddy Duffy was in charge of that operation during the time, the smashing up of stills.) The round-up went on for a week or ten days.

---

94 Bellavary, not Ballyvary as in the original text.
95 Bohea is a townland on the Westport–Leenane road between Knappagh and Liscarney.
96 Sheeffry, not Shefry as in the original text.
97 Qui vive meaning on the alert.
98 The star shells were fired by the British navy ships probably in Killary Harbour and not Clew Bay, and they lit up the mountains around Killary Harbour during the round-up.

TRUCE [PERIOD]

The military in Westport were a small body at the Quay who moved out shortly afterwards to Castlebar. There was a Colonel Packington there in charge when I took over the barracks. There was only a Battalion there, but actually there were between 300 to 400 men. And there were a lot of Tans in the Gaol, about 200 of them.[99] The Tans were shoved in when things got hot in Co. Mayo. (But surely not 200. This was due, I expect to a concentration before demobilisation.) There were about forty Auxiliaries in the Railway Hotel in Westport, but we never ran into them! I was acting for Johnny Gibbons who was with Staines and Ring on liaison work (Ring and Michael Staines were then in Galway). I was the Assistant Brigade Adjutant then. Ring was his Deputy (Staines was the Brigade Adjutant in October of 1921). When the Division was formed [52L] Moane was O/C, the Brigade, Johnny Gibbons, the Vice-O/C, Paddy Duffy, the Quartermaster, and myself, the Adjutant.[100] Tommy Kitterick was cashiered by Michael Kilroy for not being able to explain how he had given out his funds. The area was very solidly Republican. When the Division was formed Joe Ring had no military position. Ring brought [Jack] Keane, Joe Walsh from the column, 'Ladeen' Hogan,[101] the brothers Naughton, and Joe took the Carnaclay Company or Sheeaune Headquarters, his native spot (into the Free State Army).[102]

Some fellows were chained to the Chapel Gates in Westport.

---

99 The Tans were using the gaol for their accommodation.

100 Referring to formation of the 4th Western Division in August or September 1921.

101 A ladeen usually refers to a young man. In this case Hogan was a small man and was on the ASU but went pro-Treaty and became a lieutenant in the Free State army.

102 Carnaclay is a townland two miles east of Westport where the volunteers controlled by Joe Ring met. Sheeaune (not Sheehan as in the original text) is a townland two miles east of Westport on the Castlebar road, in the centre of the pro-Treaty Derrygorman Company.

Geraghty (or he ordered Geraghty to be chained to the Chapel Gates for not turning up for guard duty), and Fr John Gibbons released him. I wrote to Fr Gibbons and I told him that he had no right to do that, and I said that when civilians in Westport were being maltreated by the Black and Tans, I did not see you interfere for them. 'I'll have to see the Bishop,' he said, and he saw Michael Kilroy and the Bishop, and the Bishop denounced me at the last Mass. 'I had an interview with the Divisional Commandant who is a Catholic, a gentleman and a soldier, and the officer has been censored.' So said the Bishop.[103] 'They don't know whether you are a commandant or a private,' I said. The newspaper stated that I had been arrested. This was after the ratification of the Treaty. O'Duffy took my side[104] and he had the *Freeman* representative arrested.[105] Tobin was his name, and he was sent under escort to Beggar's Bush.[106] I think Tom Derrig told me that O'Duffy jumped at Tobin, and when Michael Kilroy came back from Dublin he said, 'I'm told to ask you to withdraw your resignation.' (Kilroy should have backed the Brigade Adjutant as any good soldier against this pronouncement of the Bishop.) Micky Wynne, who was on evacuation, wanted to take over Castlebar Barracks, and I was with him. We seized, **[52R]** on behalf of the Provisional Government, and I put into the barracks a guard from the Castlebar Company. Michael Kilroy ate the head off me over this.

Paddy Duffy went down to Finner Camp with arms for the North, and he brought them back again for the other material which was to have been exchanged for them had not turned up.[107]

103 Dr Thomas P. Gilmartin, Archbishop of Tuam from 1918 to 1939.
104 Eoin O'Duffy, assistant chief of staff, IRA.
105 Referring to the journalist, Tobin, of *The Freeman's Journal* newspaper.
106 Beggar's Bush Barracks in Dublin became the pro-Treaty army headquarters.
107 Finner Camp in Ballyshannon, Co. Donegal.

Johnny Barrett was from Crossmolina and Broddie Malone were in charge of the men who went down to Limerick the time of the occupation. (They came down in March to help me for I was the O/C 2nd Southern Division.)[108]

Castlebar [meeting, 1 April 1922.] [Charlie] Byrne came, Alec McCabe from Sligo, Anita (?) McMahon from Achill, a strong Sinn Féiner, and some Sligo lads with him. Alec pulled a gun on the platform for we [IRA] were making noise; and at once there was twenty guns trained on the [FSA] lorry. Alec passed the gun to Byrne, and Byrne jumped off and tried to get away, but Willie Malone, Paddy Duffy and I chased him but I lost him. Willie got close to him, and he ran to Fogarty's (in Spencer Street) and in the shooting inside in this hotel, Mrs Fogarty was wounded in the shoulder.[109] He was captured, Byrne, and he was taken to the military barracks. Mick Collins was shouting, and he was trying to talk; but he lost his temper. You could not hear what he said. Kilroy tackled him at the door of the hotel, the Imperial (in the Mall). 'I want to see you, Mick,' he said. 'Have you your hands on the money bags, Mick?' And Collins replied, 'That's the greatest insult you ever say to any man.' And this Kilroy told me afterwards.

There was a foundry in the barracks in Castlebar then. It was working full-time.

Michael Kilroy was an amazing shot. In Skerdagh he saw an RIC man who was training his rifle, and he kept waiting until the RIC man had taken the first pressure.[110] Then he [53L] dropped, took aim and got the man.

---

108 This incident occurred in early March 1922 when Ernie O'Malley took Limerick back from Michael Brennan, O/C of the 1st Western Division, who was pro-Treaty and had taken over Limerick from the departing British military.

109 Fogarty's and Mrs Fogarty, not Geraghty as in the original text.

110 Meaning the finger pressure on the trigger of the rifle.

[CIVIL WAR PERIOD]

Evacuation of Castlebar [24 July 1922].[111] For months before this we had talked about a landing at Westport Quay, and also we had talked about the taking of the stores, but Kilroy was too occupied with the bomb factory. Joe Ring (now with Free State Army) came in to Westport Quay on the [24 July]. He had an armoured car on the boat, a whippet. Willie Malone was then in charge of Westport. I was out to see that mines were put on the bridges. I saw that the Bellavary Bridge was done, but when I got back to the barracks I found that it was on fire.[112] The Rev. Jeffrey Prendergast was a Catholic Curate in Castlebar, and he was with the people who were seething around the Post Office which we had attempted to burn.[113] I pulled my gun on Fr Jeffrey, fired a shot or two, but then I found that the other lads had gone.

[**Capture and escape.**] Near Glenhest, Kilroy told me to go up the road, when I was ambushed by poor Joe Walsh, who was now in charge of the Free Staters who were coming in.[114] This was later in July. I was brought to Athlone. I escaped from Athlone with Harry Brehony and Broddie Malone. I was with Joe McDevitt and Jack Jordan from Ballina in a cell. Frank O'Beirne and Brehony had an escape planned and I was included.[115] We were all in the Garrison Detention in Athlone.

---

111 The evacuation of Castlebar by the anti-Treaty forces was on 24 July as Free State troops landed in Westport.

112 Bellavary, not Bellyvary as in the original text. 'Done' meaning the mines were set.

113 Catholic curate is written as C.C. in the original text.

114 Joe Walsh of Mill Street was a former member of Fianna Éireann and son of Thady Walsh, a publican. He returned from England to join the ASU. He had no rank in the Westport Company but was under the influence of Joe Ring, who promised him a commission in the Free State army in 1922, where he became a captain. He was at the attack on Newport on 24 November 1922 when Michael Kilroy was injured and captured. Joe Walsh was mortally wounded and died at Castlebar Hospital later.

115 O'Beirne, not O'Byrne as in the original text.

The bolts ... of nails on the wooden doors. We cut out the keyhole square, and we pushed it back with soap to hold it for the padlocks which were on the bolts. Each cell had to be done like this. I think it was three cells we did, only one got out of my cell and nine in all got out. We lifted a huge flag in the vestibule when we came out.[116] It had been prepared by removing some stuff but it had not yet been lifted. We lifted it, and there was a cavity down to a boiler below to a big engine room. The door of the engine room had never been locked or closed. This **[53R]** was on the ground level then. We were out into a passageway that ran around the big square block. It was a very wet night, and there was a sentry in the yard outside and Dominick Benson, a Sligo man, had a bar taken out from a cell window, and he stood at one corner waiting for the sentry, and we had a ladder made out of bed boards. That night we put it together quickly; and we put it up against the perimeter wall for the sentry had not come around on that night. The first man up took a rope made out of blankets and we held the rope. He got into the garage yard, a huge big garage yard and [all] the lads did this. Frank Burke was the last man. He pulled up the ladder and then he put it down and he came down himself. We were all in our stocking feet and it was very wet. We crossed the garage yard, and we came to the other wall which we crossed in the same way.

Seamus Fox, an Athlone man or a Mullingar lad, was the guide. We crossed the main road near the boathouse; and we waded on and we got a boat from its moorings. We brought back a boat then, and we paddled across the Shannon with our hands. We landed in a factory yard on the far side. It was pretty dark, very dark, indeed. Each bridge was held by the Staters. Fox led us to the Southern Station, but a shot was fired at us there, and then we went to Corissins on the lake on the Connaught

116 A flag is a flat stone.

side, and a fellow in a Free State Army uniform brought us out in a motor boat. We lay all day in Corissins in a hazel thicket and in desperation we went to a house. Seamus Maguire of Mullingar also went with us, but then he went off with Fox. Eight of us escaped. We went to this house. Frank O'Beirne approached it first and he said, 'I know you don't agree with us, but can [54L] we get in to dry ourselves?'

'Come in,' she said. 'Ye the fellows who have escaped and ye have the welcome of the world.'

They were very friendly. These people got in touch with someone who had a boat and who was also a businessman in Athlone, and he turned up with his cabin cruiser after nightfall, and we went on board in the dark. We saw that his companion was in uniform, and when a motor boat chugged behind us, I heard him cocking his automatic in the darkness. They brought us to Cove Island on the north-west of the lough. Broddie Malone would know about this man. We stayed for a day and a night in Cove Island, and the people there were good. They dumped us on the Roscommon shore (under the aegis of) Volunteers, and we arrived up in Dan O'Rourke's house. And he got a horse and trap ready for us (he had been a TD who voted for the Treaty: as a Brigadier he had been hopeless) and it was then he told us about the house that was burned in his area. That pony and trap left us in Loughglynn,[117] and then the three Sligo fellows, Dominick Brehony (who was murdered afterwards on the sides of Benbulbin by …), Frank O'Beirne, and Dominick Benson, left us.[118]

Then Broddie Malone and Paddy Cannon and I went on together. We went to *Bull Knockca* to a teacher named King

---

117 Loughglynn (not Loughlynn as in the original text) is near the Co. Mayo border of Co. Roscommon.

118 On 20 September 1922 Brehony, Brian MacNeill and four other Republicans were executed in Co. Sligo.

there,[119] and on [to] Bohola way next evening, and near Bohola walking up a field on rising ground we saw an armoured car on the road and who was visiting the place but Michael Collins' sister, who was married in Bohola, to inform her of Michael Collins' death.[120] Mrs Sheridan, sister of Michael Collins, is a teacher in Bohola. We met someone who told us that there was a South Mayo Column near Balla, and Dolan was in charge of it and Kit McKeown (from Longford). We contacted them at Brize House where McEllin used to live.[121] There was Kit McKeown, Dolan, [54R] and about fifteen men in all with rifles (Four Court Mauser rifles).

[Recapture, 23 August.] We were just ready to leave at nightfall on the next evening when a scout dashed in shouting 'They're coming, they're coming.' The bullets began to fly. It was a large two-storeyed house with a basement. Malone and I made a dash for one window to jump out of it, but a burst of machine-gun fire came through us. We tried to open the window then but Broddie Malone was hit in the left arm and the left thigh. I dragged him away from the window. The front door was closed. I brought him to the basement. The column returned the fire from the upper windows. An armoured car plastered the windows from the outside. It was pitch dark now for we were waiting for the darkness to start (out to get away). After an hour and a half we surrendered. They came to a window which was over our heads in the basement, and they threatened to bomb us. Malone did not want to surrender. Our outposts got away.

The Staters were in a vile temper. There was a Sergeant Ellis who was very bad who was pushing us around. I told them that there was a man who was severely wounded. An officer

119 Possibly Knock though it appears to be Bull Knockca in the original text.
120 Collins was killed on 22 August 1922.
121 Brize House was near Balla.

came out of the armoured car and announced to us that Mick Collins was killed. They took us into Claremorris to a bare room in a house. They threw us all in together then. We had no sanitary arrangements, no beds. Next morning they drove us all to Athlone. Cannon had a letter on him addressed to himself in Athlone. Cannon and I were put in a cell at once then, and for a week we were allowed out for a quarter of an hour each evening. We were then allowed to mix with the other prisoners. It was beginning to get crowded. There were thirty-six in that little block, and there were others outside. Then we were shifted to Pump Square, where there were no bedclothes and no mattresses. [55L] Some of the earlier arrivals had had mattresses.

We made an effort at a tunnel in the big barracks room. There must have been 300 in the block. There were about thirty men and they all were Westerners whom we knew. Poor old Dr Ferran ('Poor old' means that he is dead) was there and Jim Rushe also.[122] He lifted up the boards[123] and we found that there was plenty of space for dumping. We sunk a shaft. It was not propped.[124] Tommy Reidy had been a miner in Wales, and if it would be a Λ in shape it would hold down (?) old earth.[125] He worked at the face and just as we reached the [outside] wall, it was captured.[126] We had gone at least 120 yards. The prisoners were left in during the day and there was a count in the room in the morning. Then after breakfast the lads went down, and at dinner we went in for mugs, and we went to a big Mess Hall, and then we cleared out again. Then we went down for tea and

---

122 Dr Francis P. Ferran. Rushe, not Rush as in the original text.
123 Meaning the floor boards.
124 O'Malley refers to another account here, but omits the name, so the note has been left out.
125 Reidy, not Ready as in the original text.
126 Meaning they had just reached the outside wall when the tunnel was discovered.

then came Roll Call in the room when the lads came up. I don't think there was any night work. I shared a blanket with Tom Mullins from Breaffy, Castlebar.[127] He was with the Offaly Brigade in the Tan War. He teaches in Denmark Street and he lives in Howth.[128]

A bit of earth could be pushed along the joists near the shaft, so it had not to be brought up at all. Sometime after Christmas, this was found out in 1923. Tom Mullins had experience of a tunnel in Hare Park in the Tan Time.[129]

Poteen in the Joy. A whiff of the wash was as if you were passing Guinness's Brewery.[130] (This also we were accustomed to get for we came home from school at the back of Richmond Street across the Canal Bridge on Jones Road where there was a Distillery, and there we used to get that smell of stewed tea, which showed that whiskey was brewing.)[131]

[55R] MacEoin, Seán.[132] Fellows slipped in to rooms in the daytime, but it was strictly forbidden. (I expect the Staters wished to let the lads out of the huts for they were afraid of tunnels.) This day Tony Lawlor and MacEoin arrived in the compound.[133] Mulrennan, who lived near Ballyhaunis, was sitting down hammering a ring on the floor outside the door. (Then why floor?) Some fellows, who were in the room, cleared out when they saw MacEoin and Tony Lawlor. MacEoin said something to Tony Lawlor, and Lawlor fired at Mulrennan. MacEoin is alleged to have said, 'That was a bad shot,' and

---

127 Breaffy, not Breffey as in the original text.
128 Denmark Street and Howth in Dublin.
129 Hare Park (not Harepark as in the original) was part of the Curragh internment camp.
130 Wash referred to the mix for making poteen.
131 Jones Road was located beside Croke Park, Dublin.
132 Seán MacEoin, not McKeown, McKeoin or MacKeon as sometimes in the original text.
133 General Anthony 'Tony' Lawlor, not Lalor as in the original text. See biographical sketches.

Lawlor said, 'I won't miss this time,' and he hit Mulrennan in the thigh.[134] It was neglected, the wound, and he died.

Jack Keogh got a uniform, a Free State uniform; and he went in the uniform where the sentry was. An officer was approaching from the other side, and there was a narrow alleyway. Then the Free State missed him on the count. I was missed specifically that evening.[135]

Mountjoy [Gaol] was a relief after Athlone. About fifty of us went to the Joy (when the tunnel was discovered). I was thrown into 'D' Wing. Tom Mullins was my cellmate. Peadar O'Donnell was there and Jim Ryan. The whole Wing was cleared [out] to Tintown 1 after a very short time. I was in bed for ten days on the first of the month.

We were the first prisoners who came in to Tintown 1. There were 120 prisoners in a hut and four huts made 480 [men]. Peadar O'Donnell was the Camp O/C, and Mick O'Hanlon was the Hut O/C.[136] The possibility of a tunnel seemed very remote then. There was a mixture of Mayo and Kerry in the hut. James Fran, who had a bad leg, was there, Jimmy Donnelly, Paddy Cannon, and Tommy Reidy from Athlone, who was killed in the [United] States, a fancy tunneller he was. For the way in which the floor of the hut was camouflaged, small Paddy Cannon, [56L] Reidy and Tommy Mallon, were mainly responsible. They had to cut out eight stable squares, which they tapped with a maul, and they broke out in one piece. There was a wooden base made for the support of this weight of concrete. And this was so that it could be pulled up and down. There was a hook at the top of it to allow you to get a finger in to it: and it

---

134 Patrick Mulrennan from Lisacul, Ballaghaderreen, was deliberately shot by Tony Lawlor on 6 October 1922 for no apparent reason.

135 It is not clear why Heavey would also be intentionally missed during the evening count of prisoners.

136 Michael O'Hanlon of Armagh. See his interview in O'Malley Notebooks UCDA P17b/106.

was all camouflaged with soap and dirt and you would pull the whole thing up at one go. This was near the entrance door just against one of the supporting posts so that no one was likely to walk on it; and a five foot shaft was sunk, and there was forty yards of tunnelling. The heavy Curragh earth had some sand in it, and there were fairly heavy stones, which went (further on) into big stones. The dumping of the earth was a bit of a problem. The corrugated hut had wooden sheeting and the corrugations outside were short of the ground, some had to pack the grooves of the corrugations from the outside to keep the earth from slipping down: and there were tell tale bits at the end and an odd bit doubled down. Football was played outside [the hut] and we had to help the lads (who knew nothing about the [tunnel], or some of them anyhow) to catch the ball and when it was not caught at times there was a dull sound. That depended on how well the packing was done [in the tunnel].[137]

[56R] **Tintown 1 Camp.** The hut was open so that we put our 'spotters' on to the outside in the compound, and as well there was a 'lounger' at the hut door. Then in a short time the lid was lifted up and a fellow dropped down the shaft. He had to stay down. One man was at the face of the tunnel and another brought back stuff in a small bag which was scuffled back from the head and was brought to the shaft. The small bags in which the earth was carried were made out of blankets. At night all this earth was brought up. There was an Intelligence service in the hut, and Peadar issued a warning about loose talk and said that our duty was to get out of imprisonment.[138] Only certain men in other huts had been told. Most of the miners, were in our hut (the professional miners) and they were Mayo men.

---

137 If the ball dropped on the ground and made a dull sound and the guards heard it, they might suspect that there was tunnel activity. Five lines of biographical notes at the bottom of 56L and the top of 56R relating to this period have been omitted here.

138 Peadar O'Donnell, the prisoners' O/C.

Mick O'Hanlon was the Hut O/C. He was a gentle kind of a man and his transparent innocence impressed the Staters (but who does not like him: Jerry Davis?).

Hughes, from Dundalk, we had most to do with. He was a fussy man, and he was continually worried about us. He was afraid for himself that anything would happen. He would come in at night or on an odd surprise visit. At night when we dumped,[139] we had a fellow at the main door, for the view was quite good, to give us warning. The only light was reflected lights from the ark lights. At night the excavated earth was dumped between the corrugated tin and the sheeting. Football, Chess, Physical Fitness, a run around the camp for a quarter of an hour: maybe twenty would start off to see who would last the longest, but that run could be made to keep **[57L]** us fit for an escape, some ten or twelve of us. We had boxing gloves there. Kelly from Sligo was a good boxer and a tough little merchant he was. An effort was made to start classes, but they were not successful in our hut. The tunnel occupied our minds. How long did we remain down at a time below? About an hour for it was hot and clammy. Seán Scanlon got the electric light brought down there. He was a Sligo man and he is now in the USA. One night Peadar O'Donnell was up long after lights out. He had a board removed for dumping stuff at the end of the hut, the far end of it from the door when suddenly the door opened and the lights went on. He was only half dressed at the time: in his trousers and fortunately he got the board back into place. Hughes came in, and he came up along to the bed where Peadar was, and he saw him moving. 'What are you doing out of bed?' he asked, and Peadar said, 'I have a touch of diarrhoea', as he put his hands to his stomach. There were two men below at night.

---

139 Meaning dumped the earth from the tunnel excavation.

[Escape.] In the end in a race against time we worked at night for the tunnel had to come up in the compound of the new Camp Tintown 2, which was shortly to be occupied. Hence the hurry in our work. When we thought we had gone in far enough a screwdriver was stuck up, and we were just inside Tintown 2, and we could see that we were thirty-five yards about from the shaft. That was just the distance from the shaft to our wire, and there was a sentry outside the wire. One sentry met another sentry at night, and they called out 'No. 1 Post and all's well,' and they kept it up vigorously that routine. On the night of the escape it was a dark night and just ten days before the Cease Fire.[140] Peadar O'Donnell had been taken away in the meanwhile up to Drumboe Castle in Donegal. A wire cutters had been [57R] got hold of. Tom Mullins got his hands on it and he, with Tommy Reidy the miner, who had been a shop assistant in McGreeveys of Westport before he went off to England. These two and another broke the ground, and they came out into Tintown 2. They went ahead and we were told to go in parties of six at a time with one man in charge of each party, and there was to be an interval of ten minutes between each six. The fellows had picked out the landmarks they would make for when they got out of the camp. Instructions were issued as the sentry passed up and down, and you waited until you heard his steps retreating, then you dashed to the washhouse of Tintown 2 Camp which was about twelve to fifteen yards away, and there you waited for your six men. Then you made for the far lower corner of the wire where we had been warned that there was surgical adhesive plaster which was set to mark the spot where Tom Mullins had cut his way through. Then when we got through we crawled under the wire and we waited for our six, and off we started to make our way.

140 The ceasefire was effective as of 30 April 1923. Battie Cryan refers to 23 April as the escape date.

I was in the fourth section. Tracey from Ballygar was one of the University Teaching College students in St Patrick's College.[141] He had not finished his work there and he never did finish as a teacher; and a Flannigan from Lahardane, Battie Cryan of Westport who was a column man in the Tan War and is now in Ballinamore, Co. Leitrim, and two others.[142] I was in charge of this section. We travelled in what we thought was the best way. We ran for quite a while. The escape began at 10 or 10.30 p.m., and it was now midnight, and we went along blindly for there was nothing to guide us. We reached a thicket in which there were holly bushes when it was breaking day. We saw no landmarks. At first we saw the old Water Tower (high up on the plain of the Curragh in the Curragh Camp), but then we lost it. I thought **[58L]** that it would be a guide, but we could not see it. It was in some estate that we pulled up and we dumped ourselves down in the thicket.

We remained hidden until midday when a couple of red setters found us out and they barked at us. They were followed by a Scotsman in plus fours who at once emptied his pocket of money (when he was asked to). He was told to keep his mouth shut and he was very nervous. He gave us some directions all right. After a discussion I decided to head for the Wicklow Mountains in the Kilcullen direction which had been pointed out to us. Tracey and Flannigan agreed to come with us. I had some sweets but we had no food with us. (Why?) We remained hidden all that day in the undergrowth; and in the night we kept on again. We saw houses, but we were afraid to go in to them for fear that we would be given away. There is a blank in my mind of what happened until Sunday when we took a chance, and we went into a house, and it was friendly. They were very good to

141 Tracey, not Tracy as in the original text. University Teaching College is written as UTC in the original text.
142 Battie Cryan, not Batty Cryne as in the original text.

us. There were children in the place. They gave us food, and they put us on the way towards Blessington, and we went to a village beyond Lackan where they said that we would probably get the Plunkett Column, for it was said to be around Lackan.[143] Next day we went on across country.

We had no guide, and we arrived to the house of a schoolmaster named Lambert. The other people whom we met previously must have sent ... Lambert to us. They were very much all right, the family, and they sent for Neill Boyle at once. His ... father or his grandfather had been connected with the Prison Van escape in the Fenian times in Manchester when men were hanged as a result of it.[144] He had been a native of Malahide.[145] They brought us to the [Plunkett's] Column. I asked Peadar O'Donnell about this Northern chap (Neill Boyle who was [58R] now known as Plunkett) but he could not trace him. There were then about twelve men on the column. They had twelve rifles. Boyle's deputy was McFree. One lad was from Blackrock, a typical Dublin man.

We stayed six weeks with them. I eventually left to get into Dublin thinking that I could get down west. We went to Richardson's Hotel, Granabeg [near] Glendalough to collect supplies.[146] We commandeered a car in Valleymount from a Major Horridge,[147] an Overland it was,[148] and we went in to Glendalough in it, and we were welcomed enthusiastically there, and we got back again. I think that there had been a Free State post in the Royal Hotel there, and it had now been evacuated. At

143 Lackan, Co. Wicklow, not Lacken as in the original text. Neill 'Plunkett' [O']Boyle, sometimes referred to as O'Boyle, led the column called here the 'Plunkett Column.'

144 This refers to the execution of three IRB men in Manchester on 23 November 1867, generally known as the Manchester Martyrs.

145 North County Dublin.

146 The place names in this sentence were rearranged to make more sense.

147 Valleymount, Co. Wicklow, between Granabeg and Blessington.

148 A Willys Overland 4 Touring or Model 90.

Ballyknockan we were attacked by a large party.[149] We were in bed at dawn taking it easy, no sentries. Then there was firing and they (or we) had two Thompsons. A party of between seventy to eighty came charging over the level ground. We did not fire, but we kept retiring, and as we reached cover of the wall on a hill they fired; and then they ceased when the two Thompsons of ours opened up, and they withdrew there.

We had been in several houses then, and the people were very good. At another place in which we were on the Dublin border we came across a party on the road. They saw us before we saw them, near Glenasmole it was, and they opened fire on us and we returned it. I was in Naas when the Plunkett Column was captured. We came back towards Valleymount. Fr Maurice Browne who was there was good, and he was the Catholic Curate in *Bragnor*. Then I decided I would go to see Paddy Ruttledge in Dublin (he was some kind of a Republican Minister at the time) so that he would be able to help me to get home.[150] I left the column with a local lad, Riley, who was to guide me away from the column. Riley had a rifle.

[Recapture] We were crossing a field near Valleymount towards the shop there when we heard voices on the road calling on us to surrender, and we saw rifles across the road 100 yards [59L] away. We surrendered. Riley dropped the rifle, but they went back and they got it. We were brought to Blessington, and we spent the night there. Next day we were brought to Naas. McCorley was the O/C of Naas.[151] We were court-martialled there by two officers and by McCorley. They tried to find out which of the two of us had been carrying the rifle, and we were threatened with

149 Ballyknockan, Co. Wicklow, not Ballynockan as in the original text.
150 P. J. Ruttledge, then Minister of Home Affairs on the Republican side. See his interview.
151 Felix McCorley, from Belfast, had been a high-ranking officer in the Belfast Brigade. Both he and his brother, Roger, went pro-Treaty and joined the Free State army.

shooting if we did not say who owned that rifle. Then we were thrown into a huge cell in which there was a huge bed which held the two of us but in which six to eight of us … could lie on. That evening news came in that Plunkett had been shot.[152]

The following morning the remainder of the Plunkett Column came in as prisoners. They had their tale. They had had a sentry out on duty, and apparently he fell asleep or he came into the house (where the rest of the column were). The column were all in the one house. The alarm was given. It was a small three-roomed house, and the door was banged. Fire was opened on the house from both sides. The gable was at one point, and the ground was nearly as high as the roof, and the attackers got on to the roof. There was a mother and a daughter in that house also. The Staters announced that they would throw bombs down the chimney so the lads inside asked the Staters to allow the women to go out from the house, and this the Staters refused. Apparently Plunkett said that he would go out to surrender to save the women, and then the firing stopped when he said so. He opened the door, and he went out with his hands up above his head, and at a stile in the wall that surrounded the house, he was shot through the head twice. He had announced that he was Plunkett. (Had anyone else left the house before Plunkett had left it?) There was supposed to be a conversation on the outside 'Are you Plunkett?' McCorley **[59R]** asked. 'I am.' 'You're not coming in alive,' and he fired twice.

There was a tradition that one of Michael Dwyer's[153] men was shot there in the same yard in Knocknadroose trying to escape, near Granabeg, a back road from Valleymount to Glendalough, and it's up on the height.[154]

---

152 Neill 'Plunkett' O'Boyle was shot by Felix McCorley after he had surrendered.
153 Michael Dwyer, the United Irishman of the 1798 Revolution who fought in Wicklow and Wexford.
154 Knocknadroose, Co. Wicklow, not Knocknaduise as in the original text.

They didn't beat up that column, the Staters. We heard odd shots outside. The column were brought out to be tried, one by one. I never got my sentence, but I was told that I would get it in due course. The chaplain told us to repent. He asked us would we sign the form.[155] 'It's only asking you to give loyalty to your own Government.' I didn't.

I used to parade the fellows in the morning; and when a party went anywhere I also put a man in charge. And one day he said, 'No bloody murderers are going to give orders to my men,'[156] and this annoyed me, so I had then to get rations myself for his soldiers used to jump to attention when I gave an order, 'Right turn.' Then they would move off. I was shifted on my own to the Joy when it was pushing on in the year.

I was sent into 'B' Wing, Mountjoy. Seán MacBride, who had been taken up from Newbridge, and Tom Kitterick, as spruce as if he had walked in from O'Connell Street.[157] We were joined by Tom Derrig, who had been recuperating in the hospital.[158] It filled up gradually with fellows from Newbridge. Art O'Connor, Éamon Donnelly came in beaten up during the election.[159] His head was all bandaged. Tom Derrig was in my cell, and in the next door were Kitterick and Tom Burke of Dublin. There was a tunnel started from the roof. I used to whip pyjamas out of parcels (in 'the office') for the workers were in the tunnel. It was all soot. You had to go down the big flu and a climax came about the pyjamas, for one of D. L. Robinson's disappeared for which he had paid six guineas somewhere in London. I **[60L]** was the O/C Parcels.

---

155 Referring to the Free State army form indicating that the signee would not attack the Free State again.

156 The 'he' probably refers to Felix McCorley, O/C of Naas where Heavey was being held.

157 Seán MacBride, the son of Major John MacBride, and nephew of Joe MacBride of Westport.

158 Tom Derrig had been wounded in the eye during his attempt to escape after his capture. See biographical sketches.

159 The general election was held on 27 August 1923.

There were two of us. Seán MacBride went with me for a bit. I was permanent, and I could take on another fellow. There was a Poilíní Airm, a fellow in civvies, who was a kind of a smart alec and who was also fond of smutty stories.[160] When the laundry would come in we would whip a parcel, either it was whipped coming in or going in (to the Wing). I would close my eyes to the whipping. All our own pyjamas were sent to the tunnel to the workers there, for I was sleeping in a green shirt. Silk pyjamas, they were (D. L. Robinson's). He kicked up a fuss. Paudeen was gone at the time, but he got no satisfaction.[161]

Poteen. We found the urn and the stuff up in the dump in 'B' Wing in the loft. We did not bring the urn down. It was made of black piping, its container alone. We brought down a big Dixie [pot]. We used flaked meal which we got through a convict with sugar and yeast which a Military Police brought in to us.[162] It was allowed to ferment for a fortnight in one cell. Then we tried to boil it for distillation, but we could not then use the gas for long enough to make up the heat. It [the gas] was only turned on for meals, and bribing the guards would not work then for they could not do anything about it. We drank the wash and quite potent it was, but a bit too sweet. There was almost five gallons of it. One night there was a raid on the Wing. The Dixie [pot] was covered with a basin in which a shirt was steeping, and Paudeen came in and he searched our pockets, and he made us get out of bed. Paudeen remarked about the dirty bastards who had their clothes steeping in their cell. He told one of his men to lift off the basin and he scooped around in the Dixie [pot] looking for something which he thought might be dumped in it. 'Shagging' MacBride he used to call Seán.

160 The Poilíní Airm, or 'P/A' as in the original text, were Military Police who helped guard the prisoners.
161 Paudeen (Pádraig) O'Keefe from Cork was deputy governor of Mountjoy Jail during the Civil War.
162 Military Police is written as M.P. in the original text.

[60R] Life in the Wing followed the usual routine: card-playing, bridge principally and some solo, a few lectures. MacBride and I made a ladder out of the protective wires on the landing which had been placed there to prevent prisoners from throwing themselves over on to the ground floor. We made quite a stout ladder. We cut out the frame of a window by making a hacksaw out of a knife. We cut away the metal frame, and Mark Killilea we had to call in at the end.[163] We did that from the nearest cell to the circle on/from the first landing. We removed the window which was camouflaged with some soap, and after lights out we prowled around. We left it swinging out of the cell. Seán and I went into the bakehouse several nights, or yard, and we wandered freely, but we never ran into anybody. Our problem was how to get over the outer wall for we needed a rigid ladder, but then Gilmore jumped the wall one day.[164] He went up the ladder then over the wall and away. Seán and I had been watching that ladder this day and we were wondering if it would be left there that night, but George saw it first.

MacManus, who was the new governor, came along and he started new rules about lights out and things we would need to [change].[165] I was off the parcels by this time, and Barney Mellows was on them then.[166] MacManus wanted us to exercise at fixed hours, and generally he intended to reduce our status to that of a convict. We became mutinous at once. We had refused to carry out the new routine and he came in by himself to settle matters. He was having an argument with Kitterick, was it, and a crowd of us around him, and there were a few Military Police. He was standing apart arguing, when one of [61L] those heavy iron balls used for playing bowls in County Cork was dropped

163 Mark Killilea was from Galway.
164 George Gilmore.
165 Dermot MacManus, the new governor of Mountjoy Jail.
166 Two sentences from the original text have been omitted here as they were not in context and relate to Petie Joe McDonnell.

off the top landing and nearly missed his shoulders. He lost his nerve straight away and he retired with his friends to the Circle. The following day infantry were called in to remove us forcibly. They were unarmed. They used a hose. MacManus issued batons to the Military Police, and this we objected to; the Military Police themselves also objected to their carrying the batons. Some of the lads were battered, pushed out and were thrown down stairs. Others were fortunate in the men who handled them, but the hose was turned on to the most of us. We shifted from this cell where MacBride was, where we had cut out the windows, and we were now on the top landing, waiting.

Roger McCorley of Naas came along, and I jeered at him, and he fired a shot which passed between MacBride and I as we stood in the doorway, and he fired from the ground floor.[167] So he then shouted to the troops who then dropped what they were at and they came on towards us. They grabbed Seán first, and they dragged him out, and they fired him out into the yard, and they did the same with me, but I was bumped off the iron stairs as I came down. And we were all locked out in our misery. There was a fine four-wheeled wooden cart near the bakehouse. Some lads set fire to it, and they made a good fire out of it, and we used it to dry ourselves. Then Mark Killilea, to keep himself warm, began to shake the railings; and when he found that there was one of them coming out, he got other men and they lifted up a good stretch of railing. Then their double turreted armoured car and riflemen were brought up on the outside of the gap. Now it was dark.

Men on the Run. First I was in 'D' Wing, then I was in Tintown 1 Camp, and then I was back in 'C' Wing. I think Paddy White was **[61R]** the Adjutant of it. Seán Lemass was

---

167 Roger McCorley (not MacCurly as in the original text) from Belfast had been a high-ranking officer in the Belfast Brigade, but went pro-Treaty and joined the Free State army. His brother was Felix.

there until he was released. Art O'Connor, Malachi Sweetman, a mother's boy kind of thing, and D. L. Robinson. I think that the hunger strike was spontaneous. Kitterick and the others had been taken from every one of the Wings to Arbour Hill, and then they had been let back again. Art O'Connor was against the hunger strike. Tom Kitterick and Seán MacBride were for it. Johnny Buckley from Cork was there. Though ill, he went on hunger strike. We went on hunger strike then.[168] After a few days many were called out; we were told to get up, and we dressed. I dressed but Seán said that he was too sick, and I saw him being carried out on a stretcher, and I packed his stuff and mine into a big box. He was brought out into an ambulance in the yard, and there I sat beside him, but an officer came along, and he said that the ambulance was for stretcher cases only so I was taken off in a tender, and I was dumped into 'B' Wing Kilmainham [Gaol].[169]

On the next day I asked for my box, but I was told that it had not yet arrived and when I looked for Seán MacBride, he could not be found either. Frank Casey was there. Miss Duffy in Bricin's was on duty in Kilmainham, and she told me that the water we got was all doped with glucose, the hot water which we used with salt and with pepper.[170] I have tried glucose in the water, but when salt is used at the same time you would not know the taste. Seán MacBride said that Kilroy called off that hunger strike on his own, that if he had told the people outside that they could have got better terms for the prisoners. (Is this correct?) Kilroy was then the O/C of the prisoners. (Did he act on his own?) Seán thinks that then the Free State were hard pressed. Grady, who was a chemist assistant from Clare was

168 The hunger strike lasting forty-one days started on 12 October and ended on 22 November 1923.
169 23 October 1923.
170 St Bricin's Military Hospital, Dublin.

West Mayo Brigade Flying Column, photograph taken 20 June 1920, Nephin Mountain.

Back row, l. to r.: Comdt Michael Kilroy, quartermaster Tom Kitterick, Comdt Ned Moane, Capt. John Gibbons, Joe Walsh, Paddy Cannon, Pat Lambert, J. Kelly, Comdt Josie Doherty, Comdt Broddie Malone, Jim Rushe, Comdt Joe Ring.

Middle row, l. to r.: M. Naughton, J. Hogan, J. Harney, Dan Sammon, Jack Keane, Jack Connolly, Rick Joyce, Pat McNamara, Willie Malone.

Front row, l. to r.: Dan Gavan, Tommy Heavey, Johnny Duffy, John MacDonagh, Comdt Paddy Kelly, Jim Moran, Jimmy Flaherty, Battie Cryan, Michael Staunton.

Lying in front: Dr John Madden, medical officer.

Insert, top l. to r.: Comdt Paddy Duffy, Joe Baker; *bottom l. to r.:* Michael Gallagher, Tom Ainsworth.

(*Copyright J. J. Leonard, courtesy of Anthony Leonard*)

South Mayo Brigade Flying Column.

Back row, l. to r.: Tom Maguire, Martin Flannery, unknown, unknown, Jim Duffy, unknown, Terry O'Brien, John Collins, Tom Lally.

Front row, sitting, l. to r.: John McGing, Tom Cavanagh, Séamus Burke, Michael Shaughnessy, Michael Corliss, Michael O'Brien, Tom Carney, Patrick Gibbons, ? Murphy, Paddy Maye (standing).

Front row, on ground, l. to r.: Michael Costello, John Ferguson.

(*Courtesy of Mary Maguire McMonagle*)

Austin Stack, Éamon de Valera and P. J. Ruttledge, 1924.

(*Courtesy of Mrs Emer Ryan (née Ruttledge)*)

Wedding of P. J. Ruttledge and Helena Roddy, 1928.

Standing, l. to r.: M. J. Walsh; Dr Frank Roddy; Dr Patrick Roddy; P. J. Ruttledge TD; Helena Ruttledge (née Roddy); Éamon de Valera TD (best man); Dr Michael Roddy.

Seated, l. to r.: Margaret Walsh (née Roddy); Frank Aiken TD; Alice Boland (bridesmaid); unknown.

(Courtesy of Mrs Emer Ryan (née Ruttledge))

Michael Kilroy's family and in-laws.

Back row, l. to r.: Andrew McNeely, Sal Leonard, unknown, unknown, unknown, Ann 'Nan' Kilroy (Mrs Michael Kilroy), unknown.

Front row, l. to r.: Nora McCarthy, May Kilroy (Mrs John Kilroy), John Kilroy, Michael Kilroy, Nancy Mulderrig.

(Copyright J. J. Leonard, courtesy of Anthony Leonard)

Michael Kilroy and firing party, 1921.

Left to right: Michael Kilroy, Captain Willie Malone with a Lewis machine gun and Dr John Madden with the first Thompson gun to reach the West.

(*Copyright J. J. Leonard, courtesy of Anthony Leonard*)

Swinford Training Camp.

Back row, l. to r.: Brigadier Tom Carney (Kiltimagh), Seamus MacEvilly (Kiltimagh), Captain John Carroll (Ballinamore), Bill Moran (Charlestown), J. B. Lavan, Captain Mick Brown (Ballaghaderreen), Thomas Campell (Kilkelly), Captain Murtagh (Kiltimagh), Harry McNichols (QM and O/C Treengaleeragh Company).

Front row, l. to r.: Paddy Greenan (Kilkelly), Mick McDonagh (Kiltimagh), Matt Durcan (Bohola), Michael McNicholas, Captain Pat Hyland (Kiltimagh).

(*Photograph and identification courtesy of James Reddiough, Pádraig Meer, Joe Mulhern, Micksie Clarke and Joe Byrne; photograph restoration by Lew Thorne*)

Tom Carney's wedding photograph, Swinford, 1934.

Back row, l. to r.: Mary Carney (Tom's sister), Tom Campbell (IRA Captain, Kilkelly), Mary Quinn (Swinford), unknown, Jim Groarke (IRA Volunteer, Swinford).

Front row, l. to r.: Mrs Tom Campbell, Tom Carney, Con Campbell, Evelyn Groarke Carney (Mrs Tom Carney).

(Courtesy of Dr Pádraig Carney)

Tom Maguire recuperating after Tourmakeady, about June 1921.

(Courtesy of Mary Maguire McMonagle)

Free State army soldiers who arrived in Westport, 24 July 1922.
(*Courtesy of the Wynne Collection*)

Car captured at Louisburgh RIC Barracks during the Truce, 1921, with
(*left to right*) Petie Joe McDonnell (O/C West Connemara Brigade),
P. J. Kelly, Stephen Reilly and Jim Harney, all from the Louisburgh
IRA Battalion. Also in the picture are Mrs Petie McDonnell and two
unidentified children. (*Courtesy of Harry Hughes*)

E Company, Auxiliary Division, RIC, at Westport.
(*Courtesy of Vincent Keane*)

Commandant
Matt Kilcawley
(O/C North
Mayo Brigade),
1922, and Bridget
McEvilly on their
wedding day,
1933. (*Courtesy of
Micky Kilcawley*)

Some of the West Mayo Brigade, Westport House Demesne, on the occasion of the funeral and re-interment of James Duffy, 15 February 1922, who had been killed accidentally on 7 April 1921 near Westport and buried secretly in Cushin, Aughagower.

(*Copyright J. J. Leonard, courtesy of Anthony Leonard and Harry Hughes*)

Close-up of the West Mayo Brigade, Westport House Demesne, on the occasion of the re-interment of James Duffy, 15 February 1922, including (*front, left to right*) Tommy Heavey, adjutant; Ned Moane, O/C brigade; unknown; unknown; Johnny Gibbons, vice-O/C; Rick Joyce, engineers; unknown; possibly Willie Malone, signals; Jimmy Flaherty, training; Paddy Duffy, quartermaster; and possibly James Chambers of Castlebar.

(*Copyright J. J. Leonard, courtesy of Anthony Leonard and Harry Hughes*)

there, and there was a medical officer [62L] Fitzpatrick who was attending us. I got pneumonia, and I was given injections for the first time. I was dumped into the Royal Exchange Hotel,[171] and MacBride said to me that if I had only got in touch with them the whole situation could have been saved, and Seán was cursing Kilroy at the time. I think that my feeling about a hunger strike at that time [was] that it had died as a weapon.

(Who put the Camps on to the hunger strike? Was it our GHQ?) Frank Aiken: 'It is Frank all right, but I'm doing the bloody aching.' This is what a Kerryman said who was on hunger strike, and who had just read out a dispatch from the Chief of Staff. 'Stick it out lads, and I'm with you', was supposed to be the dispatch.

Westport was fantastic in its Christian Brothers for they taught Irish history. In the Land League days Westport was very good.

In Cushlough, which is beside Carrowkennedy, a brother of James Tunney, the senator, wrote poems in the Ballina *Western People* and in the *Mayo News*. He wrote a history of the West Mayo Column in the *Western People*.[172]

The North-West Mayo Brigade comprised the following: Erris, Ballycastle, Ballycroy and Erris generally. Tony Farrell, was a travel agent in New York, O/C of the 5th Battalion,[173] Martin Ring of Lackan near Kilcommon, *Frohels*, his brother.[174]

Pat Madden, who was Free State, was a Commandant. He used to send us out word, and when he was on a raid he would walk through the house.

---

171 Hotel in Dublin.
172 Pat Tunney from Derrykillew, near Carrowkennedy. RIC Sergeant Coughlan was killed at their gateway in the first Carrowkennedy patrol ambush.
173 O'Malley placed '(Bde?)' here after battalion, questioning whether it was a battalion or a brigade. There have been a few references to there being a North-West Mayo Brigade and so this is quite possible, though Michael Kilroy in his interview does not mention there being one in that area.
174 O'Malley wrote Martin King first, then Ring.

When the lads were captured at Headford, Maguire, O'Malley, [and] Cunnane,[175] and the Archbishop left Tuam, my brother was the senior curate there, and he said that if *Healy* stayed there[176] that he would be executed. They were brought into Ballinrobe and Canon Dalton came to Pat Madden, and he said, 'You should bring in no prisoners. I'll report you.' Pat Madden said that he was stuck to **[62R]** the ground by that remark of the Canon's. Dr Healy of Tuam and the Canon went to sympathise with ...

Fr Conroy in Kilmeena.[177] (I think these are Republican priests.) Fr Michael O'Hara of Swinford. Fr Tom Byrne [from] below Ballina, on the Sligo road. He was a great character. Fr Heuston of Lower Bangor was a great priest; he is now dead.[178] Fr MacHugh was the Catholic Curate in Aughagower.[179] He denounced the Carrowkennedy Ambush as murder ...

175 Seán Maguire, Séamus Ó Máille and Frank Cunnane (not Culhane as in the original text).

176 This sentence is confusing in the original text as clearly Dr Healy would not have been executed. Six Republicans were executed at the Free State Workhouse Barracks in Tuam, Co. Galway on 11 April 1923: Frank Cunnane (Kilcoona, Headford), Seán Maguire (Ballinrobe, brother of Tom Maguire), Michael Monaghan (Clooneed, Headford), Martin Moylan (Farmerstown, Annaghdown), John Newell (Winefort, Headford) and James O'Malley (Oughterard).

177 Fr Conroy, not Conway as in the original text.

178 Bangor Erris.

179 Fr MacHugh, not McHugh as in the original text.

BRODDIE MALONE

(UCDA P17b/109, pp. 65–82 and 120, pp. 63–68)[1]

James 'Broddie' Malone (1898–1975)
was from Westport. He joined Na Fianna
Éireann in 1915 and was inducted into
the IRB before Easter 1916. By trade he
worked with his father as a blacksmith.
He joined the Irish Volunteers and was
made captain of the Westport Company
in 1918 and then later vice-commandant
of the Westport Battalion. He took over
command of the Westport Battalion

*Copyright J. J. Leonard
(courtesy of Anthony
Leonard)*

when Joe Ring went Free State. Malone was anti-Treaty and
was captured, wounded, then escaped, but was captured again in
August 1922. Malone came back to Westport after internment
in 1924. The IRA financed some hospital treatment for him in
1926. He was still being harassed by the Garda Special Branch
up to 1930 when he had become a member of de Valera's Fianna
Fáil party. In 1932 Fianna Fáil created a new Volunteer Reserve
force to the National Army and Malone was appointed area
organiser for Mayo and set up several branches of this new force.
This organisation was set up to draw young men away from a

---

1 The initial transcription and some of the notes were done by Dominic Price.
This interview was made in several sessions and appears in two separate
volumes of the Ernie O'Malley Military Notebooks (109 and 120). They
have now been integrated in chronological order with the volume number
appearing before the page number. In the second interview it appears that Ned
Moane and a Broddy Molloy participated with Malone, and O'Malley placed
the name of the speaker in parentheses. However, on occasion it is not clear
who is actually speaking. There is some duplication in the narrative, but it was
deemed important to leave both versions in to show that a narrative by the
same person might vary slightly.

resurgent IRA and the newly formed Blueshirt organisation. Malone eventually became a captain in the Irish Army in 1939 and saw out his career there in the Military Police. He married Freda Courtney of Castlebar in 1935 and they lived in Castlebar.

This interview took place in Castlebar in sessions in 1950, October 1951 and May 1952.

[1915–1921 PERIOD]

[**109/65R**][2] I was born in 1898.[3] I joined the Fianna in Westport in 1915 and we had about twenty-five Fianna in the town area.[4] Derrig had formed the branch and been O/C of it in 1915.[5] In 1916 we were mobbed and we formed up on Farnaught Hill, a half a mile outside [Westport] on the Leenane side.[6] Ould Joe MacBride[7] was in charge.[8] We waited for a message to come to us on that Easter Sunday, and we were armed with a few rifles and shotguns; then, when no message came, we went home. Derrig said to a few of us that we, the Fianna, might have to march to Galway and that we should have a few days rations

2   The first two sentences of this interview are being placed in this footnote as they do not seem relevant to Malone's story. 'Maurice Sweeney, Division Engineer, Assistant Brigade Engineer, lives in Oughterard [Co. Galway]. Lee's wife was very pretty and was the toast of the Tans.'

3   1898, not 1798 as in the original text. This sentence has been moved from the start of the next paragraph to here to facilitate the flow of the narrative.

4   Na Fianna (not just Fianna as in the original text) or the Irish National Boy Scouts, was co-founded by Countess Markievicz in Dublin in August 1909. Many of its members joined the IRA on reaching eighteen years of age.

5   Tom Derrig from Westport. See biographical sketches.

6   'Mobbed' refers to being mobilised or called out for duty.

7   Joseph MacBride (1860–1938) was born at his family home at Westport Quay. He was highly thought of by the young men of the Westport area and was a link back to the Fenian Movement. His brother John was executed in 1916. Word of the insurrection failed to reach Westport in time for him to partake in it, but MacBride marched the Volunteers and Fianna out to Farnaught Hill (not Fornock Hill as in the original text) in defiance of the RIC. He and a large group of Westport Republicans were interned until Christmas 1916. MacBride was elected as TD for the area in 1918 and held this position up to the 1930s. He voted for the Treaty.

8   In charge is written as 'i/c' in the original text here and elsewhere.

ready. Derrig was arrested with Moane and with a lot of people who were not in the movement at all.[9]

I was in the Fianna all through 1917, but I went into the IRB before 1916. Broddie Reilly swore me in, and Joe MacBride was in charge of us.[10] Every Friday night he came in to Westport, and he lectured to us, on First Aid, and we went on route marches to Kilmeena to Fr Conroy (dead), and to Islandeady.[11] Tom O'Brien of Moyhastin, a great old scout, was in the IRB, Charlie Gavan and Tom Derrig.[12] There were a lot of ould fellows such as Tom Navin and Nealis's in the West, and Broddie and Ownie Reilly, Martin Geraghty, whom we were amazed to see as members.[13]

I never attended an IRB meeting after the Tan War. Before 1916 Joe MacBride had us subscribe five shillings to the Arms Fund.[14] We got no arms nor did we know that 1916 was to come off. There was no meeting of the IRB held to vote on the Treaty. Joe Ring was in charge of the [Westport] Battalion in about 1917. He was never in the IRB for he talked too **[109/66R]** much.

In 1918 I was made a Company Captain, and I was in charge of over 100 men. We had no rifles, but one rifle was captured in Westport by Tom Derrig and Kitterick[15] from a Tommy for which they got six months each.[16] When Moane was brought back for trial in Westport, the Cushlough Band turned out to

---

9 Edward/Éamonn 'Ned' Moane, not Mohane or Mohan as sometimes in the original text. See biographical sketches.
10 Broddie Reilly, not Broady as in the original text.
11 Fr Conroy was the parish priest of Kilmeena and supported the national movement at the time. The '(dead)' means the man was dead by the time of this interview.
12 Charlie Gavan, not Garvin as in the original text.
13 These names are Navin, Nealis and Ownie, not Neavin, Neallis and Owney as in the original text.
14 Five shillings was written as 5/ in the original text.
15 Tom Kitterick. See biographical sketches.
16 A Tommy was a British solider.

give him a welcome, and the RIC and military turned out.[17] The RIC stood behind the band and the procession. Then the RIC charged and clogged hell out of the lads in Castlebar Street, but the lads fought back and a lot of the police were hurted.[18] Ring told the lads to get pick handles[19] from outside the shops and he got a plant on him under the ear which knocked him out, and Ring got six months for this.[20] Willie Malone, who was in the burnings in England in Liverpool and is now in Breaffy,[21] was captured for that row also, and Joe Walsh, who was afterwards killed, and another fellow. The baton charges went on from Thursday.[22] The lads from Cushlough defended themselves with [bag]pipes, but the big drummer they couldn't get at for he was a big, powerful man, and he defended himself with his drum. In the Courthouse we were shouting for Ned to give him heart.[23] Then we tore up the paving to get ammunition for the fight, and you could see the spikes being knocked off the padded helmets of the RIC. All shuts (shutters) were put up on the shops in the town, and at night we'd draw the RIC to where other of our lads were lying in wait with stones. The lads were then in genuine hostility to the RIC for their arms and heads got hit by their batons. Extra RIC had been drafted in, and soldiers with fixed bayonets were waiting at the **[109/66L]** back of the distillery.

On Armistice Night, 1918, there was more hostility. You know where the Cosy Wear factory is at the back of Lorcan Gills'. Halls Mill it was then and the British took it over. They lighted a large fire to enjoy the 11th November, and they got

17 Cushlough, not Cuslagh or Caslagh as in the original text in places. Moane, not Mohane as in the original text
18 The word 'hurted' is an old form of 'hurt'.
19 The words '(from a cutter)' were included here in a parenthesis but have been omitted.
20 Ring was sentenced to six months in jail for attacking an RIC man.
21 Breaffy, not Brea as in the original text.
22 Charges by the RIC.
23 Ned Moane.

drunk and decided to play hell in the town. The crowd in town became hostile to them. The military took off their belts and they made for the people. There were a few soldiers hurted and I took small pieces of metal from the forge, one and a half inches or so, and threw it at them (Broddie was a Blacksmith). That made for hostility again for the British didn't care or know where they struck. I made a baton a foot and a half long of a wide piece of lead bound with a flat head, but I never used it.

The AOH[24] was very strong in Westport once, but the American Alliance[25] was strongest in Kilmeena. There was a John Molloy there who was in everything, and who has a great memory. Kilmeena was marvellous. Derry, a half a mile on the Aughagower side, was good. Derrygorman, that was the best also and Drummindoo.[26] There were a lot of them AOH who became Irish Volunteers and who were later with the columns where we slept who fed us and encouraged us.

[109/67R] Liam Mellows came down to us from Leenane once and Seán MacMahon came down once to us.[27] (There was a Northern Adjutant in Portobello[28] who has a shop in the Curragh, and there was a Mayo man, Dr Meenaghan from

---

24 The Ancient Order of Hibernians (AOH) was a Catholic fraternal organisation founded in New York in 1836 which in due course established branches in Ireland. It supported the Irish Parliamentary Party and their constitutional approach.

25 The American Alliance was a branch of the AOH more intent on seeking the complete freedom of Ireland, as distinct from the AOH Board of Erin that was dedicated to the policies of John Redmond. The younger people were followers of the American Alliance and were against the recruiting of Irish men to the British Army.

26 Drummindoo, not Druimduagh as in the original text.

27 Liam Mellows led the nationalist activities in Galway during the 1916 Rising and managed to evade capture and went to New York for several years. He was later on the headquarters staff of the IRA, went anti-Treaty and was quartermaster general of the anti-Treaty forces. He was captured in the Four Courts on its surrender in June 1922 and was executed on 8 December 1922 without trial.

28 Portobello Barracks, Dublin.

Ballindine, who found a Military Police fast asleep on my bed once and who nearly went on fire about it.)[29] Moane came home from gaol and he started off on a vigorous training scheme. Charlie Gavan, who had been Captain of the [Westport] Company, was shifted to the battalion before me. He used to have myself parade a mile and a half outside of the town in McGing's shed on the Leenane road, I think.

Dáil Fund. Kitterick was working on this, and bloody well the people responded in Westport area. Fr Conroy was the head man on that, and he brought the money to Dublin. He had all the books with the names but he was tipped off about a raid so he buried the books.[30] Later when he was searching for the papers-books, the local lads tried to locate them, but they couldn't. He went to Galway after that burial, and he was very ashamed when he couldn't find the books, for he was a terrible accurate man. I think what happened was [that] the papers were in a dump with the ammunition, and at night some of the young lads came to get the ammunition and they threw the papers away, I expect.

Kitterick was released from gaol and he came back here. He went on a hunger strike in Belfast and in Dundalk, and he was released at the time of Conscription.[31] The priests all the time were friendly and even Frank Molloy of Westport joined up as an Irish Volunteer. The RIC were quieter then for they had a **[109/67L]** healthy respect for us, and the elections of 1918 left us stronger.

1920. My father was pulled out from the house [by the RIC].[32] At night they'd raid the house, police from the Westport

---

29 Probably Dr Meenaghan, not Meenihan as in the original text.
30 The names of the contributors, which would have been incriminating.
31 The Conscription Crisis occurred in April 1918 when the British government was considering imposing conscription in Ireland to bolster the European war effort.
32 Michael Malone was a blacksmith and lived at the Fairgreen, Westport.

Barracks or the Quay disguised, and they'd raid the town, the military and the Tans. They were always disguised, and they always wore masks and that was just before our column was formed. They pulled out Reilly on the Fairgreen, Stephen Reilly, and they made him paint the old monument to Dr Johnson on the Fairgreen red, white and blue, and they made him sing 'God Save the King'.[33] They put a funnel (tin dish) in Ned Haran's throat down which they poured drinks of all sorts. They put my father under Ned Healy's cart, who was a jarvey on the street, and they beat him with a revolver over the head. Then they put him under the car, and he was trying to think of the shackles if it was short so that he could fire the cart over on top of them. Four of them got on top of the cart, and he pulled them 100 yards or so, then he upended the cart, and they were scattered and he got away from them.

We had a few rifles, and we had a party standing by to watch for a crowd of the enemy who were to come in to the town but they never came on, so we never met them. I used to go to the forge **[109/68R]** to work, but I knew I would get no mercy from the RIC if they got me, so I carried a Peter[34] and a long Parabellum,[35] and if the people saw any one coming they would tell me, and I'd hop out the back. The RIC man used to look into the forge, Fagan, every day, to see if I was there. There were fifteen to twenty RIC there under a Head.[36]

The District Inspector here, Molloy,[37] was very good, and he sent word to us whenever he could but through a priest. No

33 Dr Johnson had been the Westport Dispensary medical officer during the famine years and the people of Westport had erected a statue in his honour at the Fairgreen. Fairgreen, not Fair Green as in the original text.

34 A Peter the Painter or sometimes 'Peter' was a German C96 Mauser pistol named for Peter Pinklow and using 9 mm rounds.

35 A Parabellum was a German pistol using 9 mm rounds.

36 Meaning the head constable of the RIC.

37 RIC District Inspector Molloy. District inspector is written as D/I in the original text.

information ever came out to us from the RIC themselves. There were a lot of Mayo fellows in the RIC in other places who gave information. John Staunton of Westport Quay handed over a barracks in Donegal as an RIC man, and Thomas King, who had been in the Irish Guards and was then in the Tans, flattened a District Inspector before the Truce. (This must have been the King who came up to me in Westport and wanted to drink with me for I had been very decent to him, he said, when he was slightly wounded in Drangan RIC Barracks when I captured it.[38] He was dressed in khaki as I remember.) Leyden, now in Lecanvey, resigned from the RIC, Thorn Hill, Lecanvey. Dan Sammon, an ex-column man, would show you his house.[39]

We made pikes for Conscription. Tim Horgan and I had a portable forge and in cart houses we would make springs of carts into pikes, with bags around doors and windows to hide the light of our forge inside.[40] Canon Reidy in Balla had recovered some cannon, which had been on the Armada, and he had some of it there. Also he had forty-eight pikes, and he said he'd give me one, but he died and his pikes were not at the auction. Powers Distillery helped him when he was trying to reroof **[109/68L]** Ballintubber Abbey, which had been once burnt when the attackers were trying to get a chief, who was in occupation of it or maybe in sanctuary, out of it.

Our column was then between eight and ten [men]. Michael [Kilroy], Ned [Moane] and John Gibbons were on the run. First of all Tom Kitterick brought us down some Parabellums, Peters and rifles from Dublin. The column then had some Lee-Enfields and shotguns.[41] As soon as we had the extra stuff we made a large column, and we headed for Teevenacroaghy at the back of

---

38 Referring to O'Malley's capture of the Drangan Barracks in Tipperary. See Ernie O'Malley, *Raids and Rallies* (Mercier Press, 2011), p. 57.

39 Sammon, not Salmon as in the original text.

40 A cart house is where carts are stored.

41 The Lee-Enfields were English-made bolt action rifles using .303-inch rounds.

Croagh Patrick.[42] Ned Moane, the Brigade Vice-O/C, was with us, Michael [Kilroy] and Johnny Gibbons and company captains and officers were present at a meeting where we decided to go on to Culleen near Louisburgh above Lecanvey.[43] Martin Dawson, an ex-soldier, a Westport man, who is a melodeon player and was wounded in Portobello, is now in the Asylum in Castlebar, and he is a ballad singer.

We were all talking about an ambush, and we wanted to have one on the Louisburgh–Westport road, and when we were there in the area we heard that a lorry had gone over with RIC. We took up a position at a flank, and we waited for them when they would be on their return journey from Louisburgh. It rained all that **[109/69R]** day while we were lying out, but the police never turned up. We believed that they had got word. One of our fellows went to Confession in the middle of the day in Louisburgh and was that information, which was extracted or given in Confession, passed on to the RIC? The Louisburgh men were to fire on the RIC barracks there so as to bring out the RIC from Westport, but they didn't fire.

In Capermacloughlin we went up for tea, and then we decided to hold a position quickly on spec, and while we were there we heard of a police car.[44] We remained there all day, but nobody came along our road. There was an old legend which we remembered that no blood would be spilt beyond Belclare Bridge, and none was spilt. We went on to Pat Duffy's of Prospect for we had more than twenty-five men and five Louisburgh men making thirty, about ten or twelve rifles or shotguns to shoot drivers of lorries or cars. Johnny Duffy was picked for that job. I had a Martin Henry, and a useful article it was.[45]

---

42 Teevenacroaghy, not Tiene na Croghan as in the original text.
43 Culleen, not Cealleen as in the original text; Louisburgh, not Louisburg as in the original text.
44 Spec refers to speculation.
45 A Martin Henry is a rifle.

[120/65R] Michael Kilroy went to a conference [in East Mayo] to Seán Corcoran and Paddy Mullins.[46] We had from eight to ten rifles in the Westport Battalion, really in the Westport Company area. Kilroy sent on an order that four rifles be sent on to East Mayo. Ring, the Battalion O/C, sent on the order, but I, who was the Company Captain of Westport, refused to send on the order. I **[120/66L]** was then marched down to a court-martial, and Kilroy asked what was my explanation. I said that we were prepared to use these rifles and to fight with them. This was before the ASU was formed.[47]

[109/69R] Prospect. On the brow of Croagh Patrick on the way to Owenwee to Cougala by Clogher Cross, we slept in Cougala Lake.[48] In the morning as we were coming on the Clogher road we came on two lorries at Lack and I was caught between two fires. They pulled up and we wounded a few but they got away to Newport on an old road. I had said to Ring we won't engage them, but when he was on the road he fired and the column acted well. We went to Corrig for a rest, first to Walsh's of Derry, [then] to Corrig.[49] Then with the help of the Castlebar Battalion we decided on an ambush at Islandeady near the Big Wall where we could use bombs.[50] We got into position early in the morning, and we remained there for **[109/69L]** about six hours, about thirty [of] us or more. Further on Cloonkeen culvert was to have been torn up.[51] The enemy came to within 300 yards of us and turned back from our position at Joyce's.

---

46 Probably early 1921 as Seán Corcoran was killed in April.
47 The next five lines of the original text have been moved in part to the Carrowkennedy action later in the chapter (see p. 175).
48 Probably Cougala, not Curragh as in the original text. O'Malley corrected the place name to Owenwee from Owenbuidhe.
49 Probably Corrig (nor Curragh as in the original text) which lies on the south side of Westport. The date was about 23 April 1921.
50 In some interviews the Big Wall event on 6 May 1921 is referred to as High Wall. Here Malone mentions it out of chronological order.
51 Possibly Cloonkeen, not Cliskeen as in the original text.

Then they fired at the lads who were tearing up the culvert and killed two of them, O'Malley and ... two first cousins, but the rest got away.[52] We were to have lifted the culvert on one side also so that the [RIC] would have had to stop. We had to hop it quickly as we headed for the mountains above Aughagower.

[Carrowkennedy: first attack, 22 March 1921.] We went on to Lanmore to Claddy, looking down on the Leenane road beyond Cushlough for an ambush position.[53] Michael [Kilroy] called Ring and I so that we would have a look at the position just before dark. We chose a position on a bye-road from Cushlough to Drummin, and we walked along the road for Michael wanted to have a bog, and then right over his shoulder I spotted four RIC cycling a good distance away. I pulled my Peter. 'Here, they're coming,' I said, and on we walked, and they came on behind us. Then the sergeant jumped off and we let them have it.[54] We got four revolvers off them. One was wounded as he was lying on his back on the ditch. The RIC fired as Michael had a flash lamp. **[109/70R]** He shone it on him, then Michael fired.[55] Then the RIC fired hoping to get Michael in the head for Michael had flashed his lamp into the ditch. They were badly wounded and the sergeant was killed.

The column was ready at Claddy[56] waiting for reinforcements, and we were afraid of their bloodhounds, but fellows took us on their backs and they carried us across streams.[57] The enemy then played hell about this area for they came out from Westport. We had then up to forty men and about fifteen rifles and the rest of the men had shotguns, revolvers and automatics. We moved from place to place without achieving any result, lying in

---

52 First cousins Thomas Lally and Thomas O'Malley.
53 Lanmore (not Lammore as in the original text) is in Aughagower.
54 RIC Sergeant John Coughlan.
55 Probably RIC Sergeant John Coughlan.
56 Claddy, not Clady as in the original text.
57 This was to avoid having the bloodhounds follow their tracks.

positions for a whole day at a time – on the Leenane road.

[120/68R][58] The column … was at Claddy. Broddie Malone, [Michael] Kilroy and Joe Ring walked along the road towards Drummin having an ambush position in their minds. Broddie was in the middle of the road … Suddenly out of the tail of his eye Malone saw RIC cycling behind him. 'Police are coming, Michael, on bikes,' he said. He pulled his Peter [the Painter] and placed it in the flap of his coat. The three of them walked on confident enough that they would hear the RIC get off their bikes for otherwise the distance would be too great for accurate firing. They heard the noise of the bikes halting. Then they turned as they found the police with their revolvers in their hands. It was dark when the action was over.

[109/70R] Baker, Kitterick and I were to get the Westport patrol, but we had to run for it.[59] We fired grenades and wounded a number of them, but they were too spread out. (This was I think at the Red Bridge, close to Westport Railway Station.) They terrorised the town then, and I think they must have burned some houses there.

Then we decided that each battalion would do a stint in its own area, so I went into Westport. The same was to have been done in Newport and in Castlebar; then we were to meet near Kilmeena with eight men. I had to shoot up a patrol. We went to Westport, but we had no luck. I do not know whether they got word of it or not. Our Intelligence Officers were out on the town, but we got no information from them.[60] The rest of the column was in Kilmeena, when they saw lorries passing, and

58 This is a second version of the same first Carrowkennedy attack told in the second interview. It appears that someone other than Malone is speaking here.

59 Joe Baker of Omagh, Co. Tyrone, where he had been in the IRA, came to Westport in 1920 to work in the jewellery trade and joined the Westport Company and its ASU. He was anti-Treaty and was leading the last fighting column when captured at Shramore in March 1923. He was sentenced to death while in Galway Gaol but not executed.

60 Intelligence officers is written as I.Os in the original text.

they engaged them. We were in Corrig at the other side, the Newport side of the town, but we couldn't contact the column. (Even though it was only three miles away from there.)

[109/70L] One night we were in John Dick Gibbons' in Mill Street, Westport, sitting there quietly. Tim Hastings' pub is now where the place was. Mrs Gibbons got the teapot, but it fell out of her hands and I got up at once feeling that something was to happen. 'Something is surely going to happen,' I said, 'we'd better be going,' and it wasn't ten minutes later when the [RIC] crowd came to the front door. 'Here they are,' I said. We had a ladder previously put up which ran across to John Gibbons'. They took a cousin of that house who had just come back from Galway.[61] The night before I was shot in the Civil War I dreamt about being shot even to the men who were on the party that shot me.[62]

We tried different roads so that we could get a patrol in Westport, then we decided on a complete attack to occupy the town and capture one patrol. We held up the people who were out walking one evening, but a policeman's wife spotted us, and she flew away down for the patrol was out (and she must have got in touch with them) for they went into Dr O'Rourke's (where Dr Gill's house now is), and they remained there, but we didn't know where they had gone at the time. The lads were damn good then, and they'd be sore [109/71R] with you if you didn't pick them for action, and all of them felt like that.

[120/66L][63] The British were in Derrycraff at 5 in the morning. Tom Tunney lives there, and they came in there from Tourmakeady and from Ballinrobe, and they took the old

---

61 O'Malley inserted '(Book 9)' after Galway in the original text but it is omitted here and probably refers to the number of another interview notebook where he heard the same incident.

62 Civil War is written as C/W in the original text.

63 This is where most of the second interview has been inserted in part in chronological order.

Tourmakeady road over to the Ballinrobe road and the British formed a square.

The relief (attempt) of Tom Maguire's Column. We were lying in an ambush position in above Knappagh, the Westport Battalion and some of the Castlebar men.[64]

(B. Malone).[65] A dispatch rider came, some of the Shraheen dispatch riders, at 4 [p.m.] in Shramore we got word. Ned Moane and we came in to Newport just after darkish, and we held up the town, and we got clothes and food, and we brought them with us up through Islandeady through Carnaclay through Derrygunan out to Ardagommon across Westport to the Ballinrobe road crossed over the Cordarragh Mountain.[66] The local fellows were out from our Companies. At 6 or 7 the next morning we were there, but we found it was over.[67]

(B. Molloy) In Knappagh we had a good crowd of the Castlebar men and the Westport ASU, twenty men anyhow. We went on through Bohea, [120/66R] Lanmore, straight out through [to] Jimmy Kildea, [of] Roigh Cordarragh,[68] and then to Tom Tunney's of Derrycraff where we got word two hours later at about 6 o'clock [p.m.] that it was all over, the round-up of Maguire's men. We met Michael Costello in Derrycraff, a ginger fellow there, who told us that it was all over.

Kilmeena [19 May 1921]. We were ashamed then of the activity of the battalions and fellows from each battalion were sent back to have a crack at patrols. We went into Westport

---

64 A line has been omitted following this as it was incomplete.
65 O'Malley writes the name (B. Molloy) here in the original text which suggests that there was another man, Broddie Molloy, present in addition to Malone and Moane. There is some confusion as to who is speaking.
66 Carnaclay, not Carnacleagh as in the original text. Malone is probably mistaken here and it should be Cordarragh Mountain (not Curra Mountain as in the original text) as is mentioned below. It is actually a mere hill of 200 metres.
67 The 'it' here refers to the action of Tom Maguire's column in the hills above Tourmakeady on 3 May.
68 Cordarragh, not Curdaragh as in the original text.

about eight or nine of us, down through Morrin's Wood, now cut down, opposite the Railway Station and by Tim Hastings' (where the garage is, I expect, on the Fairgreen), and our scouts told us that there were no RIC out on patrol.

They, the Tans, had some system of Intelligence by which they knew that we were looking for them. At Forrigle we stayed a night, and Forrigle was raided next morning. That was two nights after Carrowkennedy, and so on, night after night, until they drove us into the round-up below Castlebar. [RIC] Patrols were out in the morning, and they had forces stationed all round and they wanted to lure us on to attack them. There were only myself [Molloy] and Madden and Broddie Malone. Ned Moane, would know [about this]; and we didn't know where we were going to go until the last minute, and then we would go straight across country.

[B. Malone][69] The guys who beat my father, and who beat hell out of him, we believe that they were officers who were stationed at Halls Mill, Westport Quay, before the column was formed.[70] A fine young tall fellow clattered him with the revolver and tried to put it back [in] his throat; and he died at fifty-seven. They put him under a trap, and they made him pull it along the street. He was thinking of getting at the shackles so that he could upset them [Tans]. He ran then and he went out through the house, and out he went out the back; and they came back again soon afterwards at once [120/67L] looking for him. The lads who were just on sentry duty, Butch Lambert and his father and his brother, Bull, were taken out at the Quay alive, and they put matches between his fingers. That night on Fairgreen they asked for our house at a pub and she [a girl] gave them the wrong house, and they broke in the windows

69 The reference here to the beating up of the speaker's father suggests that this is now Broddie Malone speaking.
70 Broddie Malone's father, Michael.

with stones. Our two brothers and one of the sisters got out the back. Tom Johnny [Malone] is alive, but Nelly [Malone] Kane is dead. They pulled out the O'Reillys of the Fairgreen. Willie O'Reilly is in Pole's place at the shore, and Stephen and Ownie [O'Reilly], and they bet hell out of them; and they painted them red, white and blue.[71] They shoved drink back their throats and they made them sing 'God Save the King'. They had to teach them the song. In early March of 1921 this was. Lamberts: they [Tans] took them out, and they lighted matches between their fingers. They were Sinn Féin. Paddy [Lambert] particularly would(n't) say what he was.

Ned Haran had a bakery below Charlie Hughes in Bridge Street, Westport.[72] There were a couple of gangs out, at least three gangs with cars. (From the Quay it was said they went out the Ballinrobe road, crossed down by Sandy Hill to the Quay.) They put a funnel in his mouth, poured down porter and they made him drink a few pounds of ling.[73] Then they made him drink more of his own porter and they took him out and they fired shots at him. He was a Sinn Féiner. After that we put two scouts on the town every night, and we kept this up until the column was formed. And in McGing's shed in Sandy Hill, outside of the town on the Leenane road, due south-west from the Station, we had men with rifles and ammunition. We had our sentries out and we slept on hay in the shed where we could lie down; and we would be disbanded before the daylight, and that was a fearful period.

[120/67R] The poor lads who did our sentry work had a hard time of it. They could go on the run, but they couldn't work. I was in John Dick Gibbons' house on Mill Street when we heard

---

71 Pole's place might refer to Pollexfens grain importers on Westport Quay. Earlier in the story Malone calls this family by the name Reilly. 'Bet' spelled phonetically probably means the past tense of 'beat'.
72 Haran, not Harin as in the original text.
73 Ling is a variety of fish eaten in Mayo.

the knocking. They were then getting in to Hearns, and we decided to shift. After 12 o'clock [on] a moonlight night; and we chased back and then did we meet Baker. And we headed for our house, and when I arrived there I was told about my father, and I seen Kane's window broken, and we cleared [away] up the back, towards the railway. Then I came back to the forge. I had a [Peter the] Painter and I could see a light in the car. I was going to let fly, but Baker said 'don't fire', so I didn't. In the morning we went back, Baker and I, and we met *Murnim.*

We were there (Ned Moane's) at daylight and at 1 o'clock when they came on. The fellows were tired and sleepy; and we had mostly shotguns. Mostly Newport and Castlebar men and the Westport men had the rifles. There were about between twenty-two and twenty-three [rifles]. Johnny Gibbons was with a rifle to fire above the bridge near Fr Conroy's house on the right hand side going to Newport, and the men inside were two fields from the road. Two lorries went down the road and one remained behind and it had a machine gun on the bridge and from there the damage was done. We didn't expect that many. It was dark when we moved in and we couldn't leave it. The machine gun cleared the fence behind which the fellows were. I was on the back of the hill below Johnny [O']Flynn's, the tailor's cottage. There is another railway bridge there.

[120/63L] [Carrowkennedy: second ambush, 2 June 1921.]
Broddie Malone, Ned Moane.[74]

[Moane][75] We moved out at 3 to 4 o'clock, a good while after dinner. M. ... had been cleaning his ammunition when a scout came in to say that the enemy had gone out the road.[76] We went out then. We did not expect them to come out so soon.

---

74 Both names appear here indicating that both were present and the probable speaker is noted in square brackets.

75 There is a reference in the paragraph to Malone which suggests that Moane is speaking.

76 The M. could refer to Michael Kilroy or Malone.

(The bridge at Glenacally[77] had been blown up by Petie Joe McDonnell.)[78] The RIC got men out of the bog, and they made them fill in the broken gullet on the roadway with turf. This was a culvert which had been broken down the night before because that breaking down was then continual work. The repair of the road took the RIC then about a half an hour. Then we doubled and we were murdered coming but then we eased off.[79] Michael [Kilroy] told me and Broddie Molloy to take the men to hold that position.

[Malone] Moane,[80] Joe Ring, [John] Madden and Michael Kilroy went to the bend in the road so as that they might pick a better place. Ring was sent across the road and he was told when we were below that if you come over to the shoulder of the hill on that far side of the road you will give the RIC the idea that we have more men there and that will prevent them from lying on the road and from making use of cover.

B. Malone. Ladeen Hogan (dead), Willie Malone of Breaffy,[81] Joe Baker, Joe Walsh (dead), Johnny and Paddy Duffy, Rick Joyce, who was with Moane, Battie Cryan who has a shop in Ballinamore, a bloody good fellow who was elderly, shocking moody, and he felt that he was being exposed on the flank when I told him to move over. [Tommy] Heavey, Butch Lambert, (Tom Nigger Ainsworth, Johnny Gibbons, Rick Joyce USA, Ned Moane, Johnny Berry, Lanmore, in USA), Jimmy Flaherty, Jim Moran.

Then across the far side of the road further down beside the house were Larry McGovern, Paddy Kelly, Dan Scanlon, Jim Henry, a bloody good lad, now he works with Jack Connolly....[82]

---

77 Glenacally, not Glen-a-cailin as in the original text.
78 Petie Joe McDonnell (not MacDonnell as in the original text) was O/C of the West Connemara Brigade. See O'Malley, *The Men Will Talk to Me: Galway Interviews*, p. 65.
79 Meaning exhausted from the fast pace of their march.
80 Moane, not Maughan as in the original text.
81 Breaffy or Breaghwy, near Castlebar (not Breify as in the original text).
82 A section has been omitted here as what is said cannot be corroborated. At

[120/66L] Some of the [men] on the next morning walked into the round-up and they had to go back again to the mountains. **[120/63R]** Eleven plus Broddy equals twelve … equals twenty-seven men.[83] Madden was in the green patch below in the first position. (He was on the right of the Westport road from Broddy Molloy's section: and evidently he readied them.)

Two of the enemy tried to get up on a flank (whose flank?), but they were driven back by Ned's men. Michael Kilroy sniped from my position at the wheels and then while he was there the bomb exploded. Sergeant Creegan may have put up the handkerchief.[84] The timber of the rifle was blown (into) across the two legs. 'Why didn't you surrender sooner?' I asked him.

'How could I with Hanlon blowing the whistle?'[85]

There was a good deal of timber between Moane's position and the widow's house. The RIC got into (in through) the widow's house on the right of the Leenane road. There were three or four with the Head Constable Hanlon, but the rest of them were under the bridge on the road.

Ned Moane. We were in the old police hut when we saw them coming around the corner. The little car was being towed

one point during the Carrowkennedy fight some men who were positioned at the old schoolhouse were thought to have moved from that position. O'Malley records **[120/66L]** 'They satisfied Michael Kilroy afterwards as to why they had moved back', and **[120/63R]** 'Michael Kilroy took a poor view of it but he knew that Connolly would not shirk a fight.' O'Malley questions why he is not being told the truth and states that this is the third time that he has heard of men moving from their assigned place, but no other interview included here confirms his views. Afterwards an inquiry was held but no action appears to have been taken as the men continued in their active positions. On this point see P. J. Kelly BMH WS 1735, pp. 21–2; Tommy Heavey BMH WS 1162, pp. 62–3; Jack Connolly, UCDA P17b, p. 33.

83 Several lines which have been omitted here recite the number of men at the ambush, but the original text is confusing so has been reduced to one sentence in the text.

84 RIC Sergeant Francis Creegan who lived at John's Row, Westport, and was originally from Fermanagh.

85 RIC Head Constable Hanlon was next in command to the district inspector.

by the last lorry. Delahunty was brought out to drive the car.[86] He was commandeered by the RIC, and he drove from the railway hotel.

(Broddie M[alone].) I found French on the road flat, in near the drain, and he could put his handkerchief into the drain to wet his mouth.[87] A week before I had had his name to say he had been bad at our house. Only from the gable of the widow's [house] was there any firing then. **[120/64L]** She was there with her boy. Constable Hanlon went inside the bed.[88] The woman lay down in the bed, and the constable, who now runs a restaurant in Cavan town, went in behind her.

I was first to the lorry. 'You won't shoot us,' they said. We took the rifles and the ammunition and we made for the Lewis gun which was in the first stoppage position, and Jimmy [Flaherty] fixed it. The first lorry was armour plated. The District Inspector and another RIC man were in front.[89] The driver was not killed at all. They fired themselves out of the lorry. The machine gun was slung down to them, and the gunner used it at the fellows who were behind what is now the Guards' barracks. He put in a pan, and we opened fire, and we got him. The second fellow serving up the [machine] gun, and the bullets came up to the wall. They were firing grenades with copper rods bound at the top and a cup there, but the grenades fell short of our position. They fired from under the fence as well as from the lorry. The second gunner was knocked out. The third man took the gun, and he was using it when he was wounded.

---

86 Gus Delahunty who worked for the Railroad Hotel in Westport.
87 RIC Constable William French was twenty-five years old, was a Tan and came from Gloucester, England.
88 Hanlon was a head constable, not a sergeant as in the original text here and elsewhere.
89 District Inspector Edward James Stevenson; six other RIC killed were Sergeant Francis Creegan and Constables William French, James Browne, John Doherty, Thomas Dowling and Sydney Blythe.

Sergeant Creegan had his legs badly wounded.[90] One RIC man was killed in the lorry. One was wounded in the heel. There were two unwounded whom we let into town later. There were three machine gunners killed or wounded; District Inspector killed; driver killed; sergeant killed; dead in lorry killed; [Constable] French further up the road was wounded.[91] He drew his revolver on my mother and he threatened to shoot her if she did not get in off the street a few minutes before it was Curfew. They broke up our house pictures and our furniture.[92] The fellows at the school [house] and Madden and was it Kitterick [who] swept the place from below, and Ring from across the road.

Moane. The machine gun moved up to the corner where the fellows above were and let [shots] in bursts towards the windows of the house. A fellow was sent up; an unwounded man, a Tan, was sent. Johnny **[120/64R]** Duffy, who fixed bayonets, [was sent] to take the surrender then.[93] Broddie [Malone] had a helmet and an American uniform and I had a bayonet also. (But was it fixed?) I had a breeches and buttoned gaiters, the colour of the … We had fine trench coats which were fleece lined inside and they never let in rain.

The wounded were carried up to the house and they were left outside. We gave them lemons and cigarettes … Jimmy F[laherty] rushed in with the Lewis gun from the fence off the road, the concealed bohereen; and he opened [fire] up on the house.[94] He got three or two bursts in, [after] when they surrendered. The fire had been stopped. French was here under this new quarry on the road.

---

90 Creegan was a sergeant, not a head constable as in the original text.
91 O'Malley uses some abbreviations here in the original text: K for killed and W for wounded.
92 In the original this sentence follows the next, but it has been moved here as it makes more sense coming before it.
93 In the original notebook O'Malley includes here a diagram of the position.
94 Bohereen meaning a small road or track.

[**Malone**] There were one or two of them under the bridge. Browne was killed on the bridge and French who died nearly at once.[95] 'I have you at my mercy at last', and I seen them coming out and he, Hanlon, the Head Constable, came towards me and then he spotted Tom Kitterick.[96] 'Can I have a priest Tommy', he asked for he had spotted Kitterick's Peter the Painter.[97] 'I'll priest you,' said Tom.

When we carried up the wounded, I said to Michael [Kilroy], 'I suppose we'll shoot the lot of them.' 'Oh no, Broddie,' said Kilroy. 'Our nature **[120/65L]** is not hard enough.' Ring must have heard this remark and repeated it for he had the name of sparing the Tans that day. Michael Kilroy said to the RIC that we wanted none of our houses or any more terrorism from the RIC and he told the RIC to resign from their force. I knew Creegan as a young lad. He called me 'Willie' at first and then 'Broddie', and I felt sorry for him. 'Why the hell didn't you surrender?' I asked of him. Doherty was a big, stoutish man.[98] He was shot at the gate and he was leaning against it. He was shot down through the spine and we didn't know that he was dead. He wasn't long in the town then.[99]

Head Constable Hanlon was a big blustering bully who did terrorise our people, and to them he would say what he would do to us. We used to get letters from home about him threatening to shoot Mammy; the [RIC] man Finnegan who was out of Altamont Street was not there that day. They were told that if anything happened to our families and people or to their houses, or to the town, or to the village of Claddy, that their families

95 RIC Constable James Browne.
96 RIC Head Constable Hanlon, not Halloran as here and elsewhere in the original text.
97 Automatic pistol.
98 RIC John Doherty.
99 Referring to Westport town.

would be shot and that we would burn out their people.[100] When Hanlon went back to Westport he was not offensive any more. There were seven killed, four wounded.[101] Now every man of us had an extra rifle, and we had the Lewis gun and the pans for it to carry; ammunition; two boxes of bombs (one of egg bombs and one of Mills grenades) and we distributed the booty. We had grenades that day when we were going into action, a special grenade loaded with TNT (perhaps he means War Flour) in a jam jar cut in rings of metal in squares.[102] We worked these grenades on the Red Bridge (near the Railway Station in Westport), and they made a shocking blast. Kitterick got these bombs so he should know about them.

[120/65R] The RIC had both cloth and leather bandoliers, but mostly they had cloth. Some of the rifles which we captured had the timber blown off the barrel. We allowed two of them [RIC] to go into the town (of Westport) on foot. The others were moved up beyond the bend from the bridge. The ambush lasted about [several hours], and it was 9 or 10 o'clock [p.m.] when it was over. We got cans of milk or bread and butter, and it was dark night when we were going to Derryherbert near Drummin, and not a dog barked at us. We went down a half a mile where there is an old passage, and we crossed at the back of the church (on the main road to Leenane and to the left of it). We went east first, and then we switched to the west. We went to Durless, breaking daylight it was when we went into Black Pat and Red Pat's houses. They had two wethers killed in the house that morning.[103] Red Pat now lives in the Half Way House on the Westport–Castlebar road. A man in

---

100 Claddy, not Clady as in the original text.
101 The nine in the original text has been changed to match what actually happened.
102 War Flour is an expression used by the IRA to refer to homemade explosive materials.
103 Wethers, not weathers as in the original text. A wether is a ram.

each of the houses did the cooking. James and Pat are now left in Durless. There were four brothers in the two houses. Pat and James [are] in Islandeady now. For the meal we had two sheep, four to five ducks and a piece of home-cured bacon.

[109/71R] [Carrowkennedy.] The next position we got into then was Carrowkennedy.[104] We occupied Claddy, and grand people they were, and we always loved to come back there to them.[105] We had a good look over the ground, and we fixed everything and then we went back and we had tea. The position was near to where we were billeted on the Leenane road. A scout came in and he said that the enemy had passed on, so we occupied our position and Michael [Kilroy] told me to place the men. He had a good sense of ground, and he knew when any position was covered by fire. We had forty-two men at the school, now the new Garda barracks. The main body was on one side, and on the other flank there was a party to cut off the enemy retreat towards Leenane, and a party to cut them off from Westport. The scout who was on a rise, signalled with his hand and a shout or a little *schola* ... and all the column could see it. We were to let them in to a position, those in the first lorry, so that they would face us and then we would open fire on them [RIC] when they got in. There was a District Inspector Stevenson driving the first lorry and as somehow he realised something he turned his head towards the rise, and he got a bullet through his head.[106] The machine gunners jumped out of the lorry, and they got a machine gun into action. They turned it on us, but we killed the machine gunner. The next one of them turned it on the school, and he was put out of action, and the third gunner was grazed across the body, and then there was no other gunner to handle the gun.

---

104 Carrowkennedy, not Carrickkennedy as in the original text. This is a second version of the ambush.

105 Claddy, not Clady as in the original text.

106 RIC District Inspector Edward J. Stevenson (not Stephenson as in the original text) was the son of an RIC officer.

The last lorry [men] went into a house, the widow **[109/71L]** McGreal's.[107] They were firing rifle grenades which fell twenty yards short of us for we were only 130 yards away. We decided to send down two bombers to bomb the first lorry and to make the men surrender. We opened fire on a sniper and we shot him as he was using a grenade, and he fell backwards and the grenade blew the timber off of a Lee-Enfield across an RIC man, and it knocked out some RIC and Tans. The two lorries surrendered then. We took away our prisoners and we carried up the wounded. Jim Flaherty we gave the machine gun to then. He cleared the jam and he turned it on the house where the RIC were, and after he had used a few pans, they surrendered.[108]

There was one Head Constable Hanlon, who was a bit of a terror in Westport, and who had threatened to burn my house and others, and to do us in when we were captured. 'I have got you at my mercy at last,' I said to him. 'I know you have Broddie,' said he. 'Can I have a priest Tommy?' said Hanlon for he saw Kitterick running towards him, and he (I suppose expected that he would have given us in the reversed circumstances, a speedy death) was afraid.[109] 'I'll priest you,' said Kitterick, and then Kitterick and I began to laugh.

[109/72R] We had lemons and some cigarettes, and we gave them to the Tans, and we laid out their wounded. 'I suppose we'll shoot the lot of them,' I said. 'Ah,' said Michael [Kilroy], 'our nature isn't hard enough.' (The Tans should have been shot anyhow for that was a General Headquarters order.) They thought they were going to be shot, but Ring went around making himself a big fellow, and he repeated Michael's words, and afterwards he was praised by the RIC as if he had prevented

---

107 Mrs McGreal, not McGraile as in the original text.
108 A pan refers to a round-shaped flat container with rounds of ammunition which then feeds into the gun.
109 Tom Kitterick.

them from being shot.[110] I lifted up a badly wounded Tan out of a drain, and I asked him his name. He had terrorised my house and always he had threatened to shoot me when he caught me, and I had just then got a letter from home about him. 'I'm fucking cold,' he said when I asked him how he felt. French was his name and he was an Englishman.[111] There were eight to ten of them killed and a big lot wounded. There were three lorries and they had an awful lot of grenades and ammunition. Each of us was loaded down with rifles. We learned to call the Lewis 'Mrs Murphy', and her pans were known as 'her wardrobe', which the lads had to hump around. Jimmy Flaherty, the gunner, lives just above the Fairgreen in Westport. Creegan was wounded badly across the legs.[112]

[Post-Carrowkennedy.] We moved off then through Claddy heading as if we were going towards [east] but we doubled back then towards Erriff–Leenane, but I am not sure of this.[113] We lay low there for a week. There was a great house, Pat Joyce's of Durless at the back of Croagh Patrick in Drummin,[114] and they'd kill a sheep each, the Joyces, and a few ducks whenever we came, for there [were] **[109/72L]** no women in the house. Kitterick was in bed one morning, and he walked to the door 'It's a great house,' he said. 'You can have a piss from the door.'

Kitterick went through hell getting stuff for us, and Duffy said he wasn't sorry that Kitterick wouldn't go forward for a position for he was one of the best quartermasters in Ireland.[115]

Tom Kitterick came back to Westport, and we were in Tom Lydon's of Cordarragh who was a marvellous character.[116] 'Our

---

110 Joe Ring of Westport. See biographical sketches.
111 RIC Constable William French.
112 RIC Sergeant Francis Creegan.
113 Erriff, not Errif as in the original text.
114 Durless, not Durlis as in the original text.
115 Paddy Duffy from near Aughagower. See biographical sketches.
116 Possibly Tom Lydon (not Laddon as in the original text) of Cordarragh (not Curragh as in the original text).

silent quartermaster', we called him for he kept clothes and other supplies and he had also a dump for them. Paddy Duffy came running in one night to say that there were lights coming up the road. He had just got out of his house as they were trying to surround it and the column had gone across the mountain, and Tom Lydon wouldn't tell him where we were.[117] It was Kitterick who had come up the road in a car. We were all out on Cordarragh Mountain lying on wet grass when we heard a shout 'It's Kitterick.' Tom had just come back from Dublin, and he got a great lift out of the fright he gave us.

Then we got word that the enemy was in Cloonskill, two and a half miles away and that they were heading our way. So we decided we would cross the mountain **[109/73R]** into *Tourmadora* at the back of Cordarragh in a hollow, to Duffys, so we started off up the mountain in heavy mist, soaked to the skin in an hour. We had to have several halts as we were jaded out. Ring and I were at the rear, and we got a sniff of good spirits as the column moved off, and I knew then that there was a bottle of brandy going around, and when we got in to Duffys wet to the skin and were taking off our stockings, ... said, 'Everyone here will have to take a drop of brandy', and he turned to the man who had the brandy bottle. 'The cork fell out of the bottle,' he said, 'when I was coming across the mountain.' So there was no brandy for us. There were a lot of beds in that house, and Kitterick went to bed with the man who had carried the brandy, and he began to moan when he was in bed that he had awful bad pains, but he was ignored, and then he said to his companion 'I've shocking bad pains,' and the man said, 'I have a little drop left here,' and so Kitterick finished it.

[120/68L] **[Malone]** I had an ambush prepared on the Leenane road at Knappagh at the entrance to Owenwee above

117 The RIC search parties.

the church in Owenwee, a mile on the Leenane road.[118] We were above Knappagh waiting for lorries, and we were between 100 and 150 yards away from the road. We had about twenty-two men with rifles and shotguns, and of the arms ten were rifles. We waited there all day for lorries went from Westport to Castlebar, and they returned on this road but not while we were there. But a cyclist came heading into the road and he spoiled us for the ambush for he came to us for reinforcements. He brought us word that Tom Maguire's men had been surrounded on the far slopes of the mountain over Tourmakeady. We marched out the Leenane road, we crossed the Lankill–Derrycraff road, a silent village road, and then on to Tom Tunney's of Derrycraff.[119] There one of the fellows who had been in the fight told us that it was finished, and we had best go back as the round-up was on and that we would be in it. Johnny Duffy is your man for that information.

We were tired. We had done about six miles. Then that **[120/68R]** night we cleared out towards Tonlegee which was a great village. Ask Ned Moane about it. There was an O'Malley family in it and the girls are still there. The Máilles are second cousins of mine.[120] I stayed in their house, and Ring stayed there also. After the first Carrowkennedy we went that way. At the time of the second Carrowkennedy both Tom Kitterick and I had got letters from home about Constable Hanlon and our minds were made up as to what we would do to him if we ever came across him.[121] I had a Peter. 'Hanlon,' I said, 'I have you at my mercy at last,' and when Kitterick saw Hanlon he came up the road with his Peter in his hand, but when Hanlon saw Kitterick, he said at once, 'Tommy can I have a priest?'

118 Owenwee, not Owenbride as in the original text. This was just before 8 May 1921.
119 Probably the Lankill-Derrycraff road (not Landen as in the original text).
120 Máille is the Irish form of O'Malleys.
121 Head Constable Hanlon, not Sergeant Hallinan or Halloran as in the original text.

[109/73R] Poteen. We were in a village in East Mayo where they were making poteen, and when we got up there were from six to eight bottles of it. The man was working at a lime kiln, and he'd walk in to the house, take a bottle, empty a glass of it and this was on a hot summer's day. Time after time I saw him drinking from the bottle, and when I asked what it was, I was told it was poteen.

[Round-up, June 1921.] We were in Owenwee village when 3,000 Lancers and Troops who had come as far as from Sligo, tried to surround a complete area in which we were. There were Auxiliaries from Leenane, Lancers from Ballinrobe **[109/73L]** and from Castlebar.[122] We had got word that there was to be a round-up so we decided to dump our rifles, to break up the columns into twos and threes, allow the men to carry side arms and whoever was left alive could reorganise the column. We started off, each had his own route. The Ballinrobe crowd were close to Cordarragh.[123]

[Joe] Ring, Battie Cryan, Johnny Duffy and I were to head towards the enemy and get by him in the darkness. I was in *Karein* village, in Flynns, when a plane came over the house at the crack of dawn. I woke up out of my sleep for I thought it was a lorry. We hurried on our clothes and then we headed towards Cordarragh Mountain and Shraheen, a mountainy area. The plane would circle and pass over us and then drop down, and it would circle repeatedly as if it had spotted our men. We ran for an hour and a half as hard as we could. We went to Jimmy *Geldens*, where there was a teacher, a girl, and she got tea for us. Then up we went for Cordarragh, and we were just on top of a hollow when we heard the plane again, and we folded ourselves up in our coats, but by peeping out we could see his face. Then we **[109/74R]** worked our

---

122 Ballinrobe, not Ballinerta as in the original text.
123 Cordarragh, not Curragh as in the original text.

way across Cordarragh, away from Shraheen to Derrycraff.[124] We had no dugout in the Tan War.[125] Away in the distance we saw a funeral coming along, and we watched it. It was the Lancers. They came to a position right in front of us, and they halted, and we thought they had seen us. We divided our ammunition, and we waited an hour for them. Then we decided to crawl like sheep with our coats over our shoes into a little hollow. A good mile away the Lancers were. Johnny Duffy would know for he lives in near Crosagha on the Ballinrobe road on the right beyond a school on the left two and a half miles from Westport. We could see the enemy on the top of *Colick* Hill, so we decided then to take a lower route 500 yards from us. We slipped through to Tonlegee whose manpower had been rounded up by the British.[126] That was the procession which we had seen and had thought to be a funeral for they took with them every man who was able to walk. We came back into Morans of the Deerpark on the Aughagower side. Battie Cryan, Ballinamore, Co. Leitrim, a shopboy in Charlie Hughes' and an awful doubting Thomas.[127] Ring and I went out and got food and went to bed. Cryan dreamt of Finnegan, an RIC man in Westport, and he dreamt that he [Finnegan] had taken him prisoner, and he woke up, and he rushed out in his shirt to us outside.

There were a few other round-ups. In Drumneen, near Islandeady between the two lakes, Ring was waiting for me with part of the column.[128] I came to McHales and I didn't like the house.[129] I was uneasy so Joe Baker and I went in to Muldoons. I was still uneasy so I asked the boy of the house to go out on

---

124 Derrycraff, not Derracraff as in the original text.
125 This line has been added here – it is written as a note in the blank space at the top of the original notebook on page 74R.
126 Tonlegee, not Tounlegue as in the original text.
127 Battie Cryan, not 'Paddy' Cryan as in the original text.
128 Drumneen, not Drimaneen as in the original text.
129 McHales, not MacHales as in the original text.

the rise **[109/74L]** and to tell me if he heard a lorry noise, and in five minutes he came back, and Joe Baker wouldn't move – he hopped when he saw my bandolier. I tapped on Ring's window, but Ring said it was all imagination. He came to the door, and Jack Kane had gone fifty yards when he heard English voices in the fog. We moved into a little wood between the lakes, and I sat down in the wood. We had two sections posted, and we moved towards the lake when Baker said he had left his rifle bolt behind him, and then we got into Ballinacarriga and to Cuiltrean. The Auxiliaries from Westport were to have been in Ballinacarriga to hold the pass and we would have been caught between the two lakes.

We shot no spies but there were a few suspects.[130] Dr O'Rourke was the enemy intelligence officer in Westport or should have been for he cleared out at the Truce. Mostly the RIC here were from the Midlands or they were Clare men.[131]

Jack Leonard lives in Bofeenaun near Lahardaun.[132] He was an Intelligence Officer, but he is feeble now.

[TRUCE PERIOD]
Mick Staines took Ring as Liaison Officer for Galway.[133] The McCanns, near Burrishoole, are cousins of the Staines. Ring was a good type but a vain type. **[109/75R]** Staines, it is said, had offered him the Chief Commissionership of the Guards. He came to see me when I was wounded, and I implored him not to

---

130 In many of his interviews O'Malley asked about whether spies had been shot locally.
131 Referring to the Westport area.
132 Bofeenaun and Lahardaun, not Boofeenaun and Lardahan as in the original text.
133 This is in early 1922. Michael Staines was a staff officer from the general headquarters of the Irish Volunteers and later the IRA, a member of the IRB, and was elected a TD. He was arrested, and then released in July 1921 at the start of the Truce. He was pro-Treaty. Liaison officers were appointed to all the divisional areas.

fight against our men. 'I can't,' he said, 'Collins has ordered me to go.' Ring was [Westport] Battalion O/C, and I was Battalion Vice-Commandant. Kitterick told us that the [Republican] position was lost when the Treaty was signed in London. He was brought up to Beggar's Bush [Barracks] by O'Duffy as a quartermaster.[134]

Eoin O'Duffy. He talked like a mad chieftain at that meeting when the Divisions were formed. Christie Macken was Adjutant.[135] Brian MacNeill, Adjutant in Sligo,[136] O'Gorman Adjutant for Tom Maguire. Martin Brennan, ex-TD in Tobbercurry. Frank O'Beirne, Joe Duncan, Tobbercurry, Bassy McGlynn, the driver of 'the Ballinalee'.[137]

Split. A couple of country lads from Derrygorman Company went Free State.[138] Theirs was a fine Company, and this was due to Joe Ring who was from that area. Jack Kane from the column and Joe Walsh from it went Free State. Ladeen Hogan also left us.[139] No senior officers went Free State. One Battalion O/C, Joe Ring.[140] I was then Battalion O/C in his place when Ring became Liaison Officer for Galway. I was in Dublin on a Thompson gun course, and when I came back I saw two soldiers outside Haran's house, and they told me that Ring was a prisoner inside. There was a crowd booing and cheering outside. Ring

---

134 Eoin O'Duffy (not 'Duffy' as in the original text) was assistant chief of staff of the IRA since 1917.

135 Christie Macken was then adjutant of the 4th Western Division.

136 Brian MacNeill. See biographical sketches.

137 The 'Ballinalee' armoured car fell into the hands of the IRA after a battle at Rockwood, Sligo town, on 13 July 1922. The IRA used it to great effect for two months. One of the drivers, Tom Langan, actually painted the car two different colours, green on one side and black on the other, to give the impression that there were two armoured cars operating when people were reporting sighting it. It was captured again by the Free State army in a burned-out condition but was put back in working order.

138 Derrygorman, not Derry as in the original text.

139 Ladeen, not Laddon Hogan as in the original text.

140 Malone is referring to the West Mayo Brigade and its officers and noting that Joe Ring went Free State.

wouldn't submit to arrest. He was upstairs and Willie Malone had been Acting Battalion O/C whilst I had been away. Ring was recruiting for the Gardaí. Fr John Gibbons, Catholic Curate in Westport, had been very good in the Tan War.[141] 'This is terrible that you have to take Joe and he won't go.'

'The Brigade has issued an order to me to arrest him', and when Joe saw **[109/75L]** me, he said, 'I'll go with you Broddie.' So I brought him to Castlebar from which he was released after a few days. In order to work up the area around Westport the Staters made a unit, 'Ring's Own', and they bought a special *cape* from Charlie Hughes in Westport. They were trying to make a battalion out of it, but they couldn't recruit enough of fellows from the area.

When Collins held his meeting in Castlebar, we were in Westport, but we went over to hear him speak opposite the Imperial Hotel.[142] Kitterick knew Collins very well. Michael [Kilroy] said that anyone who wished could go to the meeting, but there were to be no interruptions. Alec McCabe got up to speak, and I was there when he spoke.[143] Someone asked would he [Collins] pay for the troops (in barracks). Paddy Duffy would know about this. Alec was stomached at the question, and he was threatened.[144] He had his gun in his hand and our fellows pulled them then. There was a fellow Charlie or Christie Byrne on the platform with Collins, but he hopped off it, and he ran up the street. There was an order issued that he would have to be taken prisoner for he pulled a gun. He came as far as Spencer Street to Geraghty's Hotel. He fired at me, and I fired at him,

---

141 Catholic curate is written as C.C. in the original text.
142 1 April 1922.
143 McCabe, not MacCabe as in the original text.
144 'Stomached' is an Irish way of saying that he was bemused or flabbergasted. The question related to Volunteers being brought into barracks and being trained. Only one allocation of money had come from GHQ towards expenses. This led to the banks being raided the following month.

and I missed. Then he dived upstairs, and he planked his gun on top of a wardrobe, and then he got under the bed. **[109/76R]** It seems that he had lost his nerve at the meeting, and he opened fire. Paddy Higgins, who was Training Officer for the Division got up and proclaimed the meeting. Michael [Collins] had remained in the [Castlebar] military barracks. Later in the barracks a trial was held on [for] Byrne. Alec McCabe had also been arrested and Collins was brought along also to the barracks. Michael McHugh defended the culprits. He had been in charge once of the old Mayo Brigade.

Exchange of Arms.[145] In Ben *Ban* Paddy Duffy went down about the arms to Sligo so he should know what happened there. At the time the Brigade had fifty rifles or more and at least thirty rounds a man. Nearly all of us carried 150 rounds at the beginning. At the Mill, Westport, two scouts of mine, Broddie Duffy and Patrick Blaney, watched their chances, and they grabbed a … with equipment of ammunition and then went up through our forge and out on the railway. The belt had 150 rounds in it. This was well before the Tan War.

I volunteered for Active Service in the North. There was a Divisional ASU. We were to wear a Boer Hat.[146] Jack Feehan was to go to Dublin to get the hats. I was equipped for service in the North and there were fifty or more men in it from the Fourth Northern Division. Baker proved that this unit was there.

Limerick Occupation.[147] We occupied the Courts on the

---

145 The nationalist community was under siege in Northern Ireland and has asked Michael Collins for arms, to which he agreed. Since he could not give them weapons that the British Army had supplied, he made an arrangement with the IRA GHQ to swap new British arms for their old arms. After some subterfuge on behalf of the Free State army, the IRA pulled out of this 'exchange of arms'.
146 A Boer (not Bold as in the original text) hat was a slouched hat.
147 In March 1922 Ernie O'Malley had surrounded Limerick which was then held by the pro-Treaty 1st Western Division from Clare, commanded by Michael Brennan.

Shannon with fifty men or more and we had a Lewis gun. We stayed there until the occupation came to an end with yourself (EOM) there. We had trouble ourselves then with some officers from the Second Western [Division], Maguire's area, who were organising the Free State army in his division. We took them **[109/76L]** prisoners in a priest's house and MacEoin was expected to come on there.[148] Christie Macken and I went up there with the ASU, and we mined the road along which MacEoin would come. We held a little wood and opposite was a rocky peak of ... slate which would ricochet our bullets. Martin Hare from South Mayo was in charge of the mine which was in the centre of the road and was not well concealed. He went up on the shrubbery up on to the hill to peep out. 'Do you think it will go off?' I asked.

'If it doesn't you will find yourself in a bad way,' he said.

Conventions. At the last Convention Cathal Brugha stood up.[149] 'We want no politicians here,' said Seán O'Hegarty, so Cathal Brugha turned and left the room and as he did he said, 'I'll be there,' he said, 'when you want me.' (Frank Busteed, who is a tough man, told me that at the height of the Tan trouble the Cork people would have hung the IRA in the streets.) Cohalan was to have been shot, but wasn't shot by the IRA. One battalion in the West voted against Tom Barry's motion.[150] This was the Louisburgh Battalion.[151] Paddy (P. J.) Kelly of Louisburgh, who

---

148 Seán MacEoin (1893–1973) (not McKeown as in the original text) was born in Granard, Co. Longford and worked with his blacksmith father. He joined Clonbroney Company of the Irish Volunteers and went on to command a local IRA flying column, one of the few in the Midlands. He was captured in 1921 and released after the Truce. He was pro-Treaty, joined the Free State army in 1922 and commanded its Western Command based in Athlone.

149 IRA Army Convention held in Dublin in June 1922.

150 Tom Barry had made a motion to the effect that both the pro-Treaty and anti-Treaty sides should unite and attack the British forces that were still in Ireland, and that action would help bring both sides back together again.

151 A section of this sentence has been omitted as it relates to the movement of men referred to in footnote 82 of this chapter.

now has a shop in Westport, **[109/77R]** was in charge of that [Louisburgh] battalion. After Barry's motion to give the British seventy-two hours notice of an impending attack, he adjourned to the Four Courts, and we were very annoyed for we felt that the other fellows from the First Southern Division had let us down. Tom Harney[152] from that battalion was a good man.[153]

[120/65R][154] Éamonn Corbett in East Mayo had terrorised the people. ... Corbett was in East Mayo when Fr Michael O'Hara asked us down there. He [Corbett] was playing hell then. Kiltimagh Battalion was split in two over the splitting of a barrel of petrol which was captured from the Station, but the Ruanes gave it out to their friends.

[CIVIL WAR]

[109/77R] Attack on the Four Courts [28 June 1922]. We got word that the attack was on, from the Division who were in the [Castlebar] Barracks. I was in Castlebar with the ASU. There was word of fighting in Sligo so it was decided to send the unit [ASU] to Sligo. Everyone was then mad for action. I met Frank Carty[155] in Tobbercurry and I thought him a nice type of fellow, and whilst I was there the Staters came in to Collooney[156] from Ma[rkree] Castle.[157] Carty decided to attack Collooney for there was a shop in the town in which the Staters were, and a fellow named McCann was in charge. We crept in, put a charge of **[109/77L]** gelignite underneath the place and it went up. They came out very shaken as prisoners; so we had the town by

---

152 Tom Harney (not Hearney as in the original text) of the Louisburgh Battalion.

153 A paragraph of twelve lines has been omitted here involving men escaping from a kitchen during the Tan War where they thought there was a *cailleach* (a witch), but the text and context are not at all clear.

154 These two sentences are from the second interview but probably related to the late Truce or Civil War period and thus have been placed here.

155 Frank Carty of Sligo. See biographical sketches.

156 Collooney, Co. Sligo, not Coolney as in the original text.

157 Probably Markree Castle; written as Ma … Castle in the original text.

Saturday evening. On Sunday we were at the old RIC barracks and our lads were in it, when down from the [Markree] Castle comes an armoured car which opened fire on us. The roads or bridges had not been blown up, and we hadn't even sandbags to protect us, but the car backed out and went away. We saw a big lorry with soldiers in it heading down towards the bridge. We chased them, but they put up no fight. They were from Athlone. I was grabbing rifles for my men from these fellows, but afterwards Carty said that the rifles should belong to the Division, but he cleared me to take two of them.

I had to go back to a conference in Castlebar which was to decide whether we should go to South Mayo or not. After a few days or maybe a week, I went back to Collooney to Sims' house in the town. I didn't like it for the hills were all around, and I had a premonition about something for I wanted to get out.

Next morning, there was a report that we were being surrounded on all the hills, but no one could see the Staters, but I made out for a hill on the road home. I went up it under a hedge, but the Staters were holding the hill above **[109/78R]** us, so we had to lie down under machine-gun fire, but we rolled down the hill, crossed the railway line in spurts and then lay down on a road dominated by the hill. I spotted a cottage, and we said we'd get into it and hold out there until night. We came across the road safely, then on we went on our bellies in a drain from a pig sty and as far as a labourer's cottage. Dominick Benson and Frank [O']Beirne were with us. The owner of the cottage had already cut sleepers into lengths to protect his family.[158] The Staters didn't know where we had gone. I got a feather bed and I planked it in the window. I found a box with lime in it, a butter box, so I planked it up and I made a loophole of it. Now we had six fellows holding three positions.

158 Wooden railway sleepers.

[**Capture.**] Out of Collooney comes a Republican, running and the Free State were firing at him, and he headed in towards us. The Staters came down, and they ringed us round, but we let them have it whenever we saw them and so the fight went on. The Staters had fresh men, the disbanded British Army men. The gable end where I was had a stack of turf ten yards from it, and from behind the turf a Stater used to hurl a bomb at my window. I waited for him with a revolver. When I went in I put all my ammunition on a table. Their tracer bullets came right in …[159] It was a bright night, and we fought on. The following morning at 9 [a.m.], we buried sixteen rifles underneath the floor but the Staters never checked on the rifles captured. We were brought out up the road to Collooney. Tony Lawlor wanted to blow in the cottage with an eighteen pounder, but Seán [**109/78L**] MacEoin wouldn't let him use the gun on us, for he'd known of us through Ring.[160]

There was a fellow called Farrelly, who when we were going up the road, a big fellow he was, accused us of shooting Callaghan, a man who had his hands up, in the ambush. MacEoin tried us on the side of the road, and he heard Farrelly out. Benson and Frank O'Beirne had been in this ambush, but I couldn't say I wasn't in it, so I said nothing. Louis Connolly had been captured in Dooney Rock, and he was a young fellow. 'That's not so,' said Louis, 'he was killed behind a machine gun fighting.' Callaghan had a wife and nine children, and he had been a good man in the Tan War.

Then they brought us into Athlone, and they put us into the Detention,[161] and they gave us officers' food for a few days, but then the good food ceased. I was in charge of the prisoners in the Detention, and in charge for the Staters was Walsh, an old

---

159 The words 'and it … was on an altar' have been omitted.
160 Brigadier General Anthony 'Tony' Lawlor. See biographical sketches.
161 Detention Barracks.

British sergeant major. We couldn't get parcels from home, and he wouldn't give them to us.[162]

At Mass we found that we could seize the guard at the same time as we were coming back from Mass, and we made plans for the next Sunday, but on that day we weren't allowed go to Mass at all. **[109/79R]** Mass used to be held in the gymnasium. There were a good few of us there in Athlone. Seamus Maguire, the Brigadier of Westmeath, [now] in Gaeltacht home spun industry. Frank O'Beirne was a good lad. Farrelly had a guard set on me. Drunk one night, he came in and he threatened me with a revolver, and the lads on each side of the cell kept close to the wall to avoid the bullets which they thought would come in.

We decided to escape, and I used to talk about it with Harry Brehony, who was Vice-Brigadier of Sligo and a very good man who was killed later. The cells were on the bottom floor, and there was a staircase which led to the cells on top. There were three or four men in each cell, and there were thirty cells. We worked it out that if we made a few ladders we could escape. There was a boiler house with a wall and the Military Police housed up another side. In the yard outside there was a sentry and the wash up was there and a dining shed. Underneath the cells there was a … range and a boiler which were out of use, and if we lifted a flag we could get out to the yard. We had two fellows from each corner who were to get the sentry. I got a hack-saw blade from the 'Sandy Row General', a Belfast Protestant named Henderson, who passed it on to me. I sawed a six foot by nine inch bed board into two, and with a fork I pulled the nails out of the dining-room shed, galvanised wire nails they were. Each of us had two bed boards and the fellows made rings to drown out the noise. I slept on one ladder and Paddy Cannon slept on another.

162 Malone might have meant that parcels were sent in but Walsh would not deliver them.

[Escape.] We waited for a dark and stormy night so that we would be able to cross, first into Leinster [109/79L] as we knew we'd no chance in Connaught.[163] There were nine men to escape – three Mayo, three Sligo, three Westmeath. We got out to the yard, and we had set one man to tackle the sentry, but the rain poured down, and there was a breeze but the sentry was in under the dining-room shed, and he stayed there. We had a rope made of strips out of a blanket, but the two bed boards when tied together were two feet short. He … brought the rope, but he fell down into a garage in the barracks. Up I went, whipped up, slid down the rope and all the fellows came across. Dominick Benson lifted the ladder and came down over with us. We had thought of getting out near the water gate, and we waited [there] for the water gate was between the two posts. We didn't bring the rope, but we went up the ladder and slung down in our stockinged feet with our shoes tied around our necks. O'Beirne had to go without his shoes.[164] Tommy Heavey didn't bring the ladder. We rushed across the road to the boat house, but there were no oars. We loosened two boards for there were four [boards] in one [boat] and five [boards] in another, and we rowed across with them heading for the Gas House on the Leinster side.[165] We got up to the [109/80R] Gas House for Fox knew the runs and he led us up and out of Athlone.[166] We had to link hands in the dark to guide each other. We had to cross the railway line and when crossing it someone stumbled against a wire which made a bell ring and a sentry blazed at the sound.[167] We ran into a potato field and buried ourselves in the

163 'To cross' meaning to cross the River Shannon. The escape was on 23 August 1922.
164 Malone refers to him sometimes as Beirne or Byrne and sometimes as O'Beirne. This has been standardised to O'Beirne.
165 They rowed across the Shannon River to the Leinster side.
166 Runs refers to streets, lanes, etc., within the community.
167 Blazed refers to opening fire with a gun, blazing away.

shucks and moved along them to the open fields. We were going all right, running and walking when we reached a building at Coosan, two miles from Athlone where we lay in a *neat* wood.[168] We were to have been brought food, then we would get across to the Connaught side.

Maguire and Fox left Paddy Cannon and I. O'Beirne was cribbing about food so we tried to buy food and who was in the house we called to but a Mrs O'Connor, a Republican, and we got into it and were given a great reception, and O'Beirne got shoes. They took us to Lough Ree in a motor boat that night – a draper in Athlone (did that).[169] We landed in Quaker Island. We rowed to the Roscommon side to Dan O'Rourke's house. We quickly reached Ballaghaderreen, from which we went to Kilkelly, Bohola. Then we knew that everyone would know us for we were going to Colgan's house, and we crossed the field when up comes the Free State with an armoured car and a lorry, but we walked on straight and they didn't spot us. We got through a fence and we ran like hell. The Colgans told us there was a column near Brize outside Claremorris.[170]

[Recapture.] We didn't get a rifle. Kit McKeown was in charge of that column there, and we slept upstairs with a blanket over us. [109/80L] This was an empty house that the column was in, and Kit went off next evening, and we were left there with the column. There was a sentry at a tree, but the Free State came up in force, opened up on the sentry, who ran for the house, and then the Free State ran for the house. I was downstairs, and I dashed upstairs for two rifles which had been left by McKeown, but here were the Staters running for the main door when I shut the door. I fought from a window, but I was hit in the arm.

---

168 Coosan, not Couishin as in the original text.

169 Lough Ree, not Reagh as in the original text.

170 Brize House (not Broys as in the original text) where B. Malone, P. Cannon and T. Heavey were recaptured on 25 August.

They brought in the armoured car, and I was hit in the thigh and the left arm. I was the only one who was wounded. I was bleeding for two and a half hours, and I knew that if I fainted I would not get any attention. The Red Cross man who was with them [Free Staters] bound me up when I came out, and Cleary, a tinker who was serving with them, recognised me. He was put in charge of me and I decided to hop it.

I was taken to Claremorris and there I met a Red Cross man, Stack, who checked my wounds thoroughly and who took me straight off to hospital. Up comes an order from General Frank Simons to take me back to the barracks, but Stack said no, he would not allow me back, and Simons said, 'Take him back by force.' They had intended to shoot us as we came out of Brize **[109/81R]** House. That I heard later. Simons is now an Income Tax Collector in Roscommon. Joe Fennelly, the Divisional Engineer, from Roscommon, was the decentest Stater of them all in Claremorris, and he came in every day to see me. Nurse O'Reilly, who is now in Ballaghaderreen, would know a lot about the [National] Army officers in Claremorris. She is now a Matron. She was from Roscommon. She also was in Dublin Castle with the British.

In Brize my blood could not be washed from off the floor.[171] I was kept in the workhouse for a month.[172] Dr Harrison tried two operations to remove bits of bone, but he was not a doctor at all. He had been in Turkey as a Captain in the British Army, and he was a nephew of Charles Lever. He had escaped from the Turks. Seán MacEoin accepted him as a doctor for Harrison said that he would later on send on his credentials. I had £2 or £3 on me, and Nurse O'Reilly put it around my neck inside my

---

171 The following line in parentheses has been omitted here as it can't be deciphered completely, although it does mention that 'this was written up in the *Irish Press*'.
172 Claremorris Workhouse.

shirt. After a month I was taken to Athlone to the Military Hospital. Dr Cooney, a brother-in-law of Seán MacEoin, was in charge of it. 'There's no bullet in your arm,' he told me, but I said there was. 'Do you know more than I do?' he said. 'If I lose my arm,' I said, 'you'll hear about it.' Then the lads kicked up a row.

I was sent to Mountjoy and from there to Portobello.[173] I was upstairs when you [EOM] were lying wounded there and I used to come down to see you.[174] When I was wounded my mind was clear, and I knew where I was. A priest came into Claremorris, but I couldn't speak at the time.[175] 'Will you go to Confession?' he'd say to me. 'I don't want to [109/81L] go to Confession,' I answered. Then he'd walk around my bed again. Then he left me alone.

There was an officer, Louis O'Doherty, B.L.[176] He came in, and he was a friend of Higgins.[177] He was landed into the guard room, and he got sent up to the hospital by Kevin O'Higgins, and he was there when I came in. And he'd talk about … every evening, about … 'I was out with O'Dea,' and O'Doherty said, 'I know that chap', and he came over and he handed him a fiver.[178] We went out to the canteen. I went to the hospital at … O'Doherty went back again to the Non Commissioned Officers's Mess with a sheepskin coat. He was offering the coat and O'Doherty bought it and a … was trying to buy it. They

---

173 Portobello Hospital Barracks is now Cathal Brugha Barracks.
174 When O'Malley was wounded during his capture in Ailesbury Road on 4 November 1922, he was first taken to Portobello Hospital Barracks.
175 This refers to the time Malone was first taken to the Claremorris Barracks after his capture.
176 O'Doherty received a Bachelor of Laws degree afterwards, and thus Malone refers to him as 'B.L.' He is sometimes referred to as Doherty in the original text.
177 Probably Kevin O'Higgins, then the Free State Minister for Home Affairs.
178 This was more than a week's wages in those days.

bundled O'Doherty out of Portobello to Wellington.[179] He was a foreign-looking guy, very black.

I used to slip down to see you [EOM] for the Military Policeman was fairly friendly; Captain Bayou, we used to call him later. Then I was sent on to the Curragh Hospital. James Grace from Dublin was there with us, and he would try to fight. Morrin from Blessington was very bad also. He was a doctor. 'I'm doing nothing for you,' he said to me. 'I'm sending you back to where you came from', and I was sent to Hare Park Camp to Hut 35. 'A Mayo doctor **[109/82R]** comes in here,' said one of the lads to me, and when he did come in, who was it but Bertie O'Malley (I had once done medicine with him) from Westport and he cried when he saw me. He told me that there was a rumour that Morrin was to be replaced by Coffey and that he would get Coffey to look after me. When Coffey came he operated on my arm, straightaway, and he strengthened my arm as a result of his care. Coffey was very good to prisoners and he operated on them when he thought it was necessary. He was from Fethard and had been in the British navy, but he was praised so much by our prisoners that our papers got hold of it and the Staters threatened to reduce him in rank, but he told them to go to hell.[180] They shifted me to Hare Park where the Staters had begun to dig trenches around but inside the camp to neutralise the tunnels.

They took out Bob Barton. A Captain O'Connell from Kilkenny used to call Bob Barton 'O/C f—g Treaties'. Bob would get in a lot of stuff from home, and then he would share it with us, and he dug at the trench. Once they brought in detectives and soldiers to the camp, and they had a Red Cross Van outside. They took out eleven Wexford men, but a young lad Sammy refused to work … and even on the ground he refused.

179 Wellington Barracks is now Griffith College.
180 Fethard, Co. Tipperary.

The detectives … held their coats. An order was issued from the Camp Council to refuse the Staters to give men for the trench.[181] Then each hut was to decide itself whether it would work or not. The eleven Wexford men who refused to work sat down, and they wrote their last letters. Then the Staters opened all the huts, and the Camp Council gave the men orders to work under protest. Tom Hales **[109/82L]** of Cork was Camp O/C, and I was on the Camp Council. Paul … from Cork, a Battalion O/C, … Murphy from Wexford. If they had taken out Tom Hales' hut, they would have found that the men in it would refuse to work so they could have shot them for they were determined to refuse to dig.

Dr Brennan from Dun Laoghaire was in my hut, Jack Lynch from Moore's Bar in Cork. Love was in charge of the Staters first and then Guiney. When the Staters shouted 'Lights out', if the lights weren't put out, they fired through the hut. We protested the next day to the O/C Camp but nothing happened to prevent the Staters from firing, but at last the firing ceased. One day we saw the bould Michael McHugh going around to inspect the guard outside.[182] In my hut were Cork men.

---

181 Within each camp the anti-Treaty men appointed their own officer commanding as well as a camp council to run all their affairs in the camp, including deciding whether the men should work on labour projects assigned by the commanding officer of the prison camp.

182 Michael McHugh was former O/C of the West Mayo Brigade before Tom Derrig.

South Mayo

Tom Maguire

(UCDA 17b/100, pp. 146–57)[1]

Courtesy of Mary Maguire McMonagle

Thomas 'Tom' Maguire (1892–1993) was born in Cross, Ballinrobe, Co. Mayo. He joined the Irish Volunteers and became the first O/C, South Mayo Brigade in 1920. In May 1921 he led his men in the Tourmakeady engagement. Shortly after the Truce in August 1921 he was appointed O/C, 2nd Western Division, with the rank of commandant general. He took the anti-Treaty side and was captured in October 1922, just six months before his younger brother, Seán, was captured and executed. He was first elected a TD in June 1922 for Mayo South and Roscommon South and at the time of his death he was the last surviving member of that second Dáil Éireann. In 1925 Maguire married Annie Christina Feeney of Ballinrobe, sister of Pádraig Feeney. They lived in Cross, near Cong, and had five children. Maguire became an insurance broker.

---

1 The initial transcription and footnotes for this interview were done by Dominic Price. UCDA 17b/120, pp. 26–9 do not relate to Tom Maguire, but have been mistakenly attributed to him by O'Malley in his process of transcribing his notes to his second series of notebooks.

This interview took place in Cross in September 1951.

[1920–1921 PERIOD]

[146L] County Mayo was a Brigade area until September of 1920.[2] Joe MacBride was in charge up until then, but although there was an occasional Brigade meeting in Castlebar, I never attended.[3] They did nothing.

Then there were four Brigades. I was put in charge of South Mayo. Éamon Price came down to that meeting in Castlebar.[4] I agreed that I would have my own Adjutant who was from near Cross and that was agreed. Michael O'Brien, killed in Tourmakeady,[5] from Kildrum.[6] Quartermaster: Martin Hare, Kildrum. This Kildrum was a very good area.[7]

West Mayo: Tom Derrig in charge;[8] Quartermaster: Michael Kilroy.[9]

North Mayo: O/C: Tom Ruane, Senator and County Councillor in Ballina.[10]

V/C: Éamonn Gannon.[11]

Adjutant[12]

Quartermaster

East Mayo: O/C: Seán Corcoran, Kiltimagh, killed in April 1921.

---

2 Maguire's memory may not be correct here as many sources cite the decision to create the four brigades as having been taken in July 1920.

3 Joseph MacBride (1860–1938) of Westport.

4 Éamon or 'Bob' Price was a member of the general headquarters staff who organised brigade areas.

5 The ambush of the RIC patrol at Tourmakeady took place on 3 May 1921.

6 Kildrum lies between Headford and Tuam.

7 Maguire was probably referring to Kildrum as being a highly Republican area.

8 Tom Derrig of Westport. See biographical sketches.

9 Michael Kilroy of Newport. See his interview.

10 Tom Ruane of Ballina. See biographical sketches.

11 He became O/C, North Mayo Brigade in late 1921.

12 Tom Coen was adjutant at the time but not mentioned by Maguire.

V/C: Tommy Ruane.[13]

Adjutant: Maurice [Mullins].[14]

In Crossard, off Ballyhaunis, they were preparing for a meeting and they had left a house in Crossard. The men [were] ready to move on when they ran into a lorry of British soldiers who called on them to halt; and they fought. Maurice Mullins, Lurganboy, Ballyhaunis, was wounded and taken prisoner. Seán [Mullins] was killed. This was a big loss (Paddy Mullins was his brother) to County Mayo.

The only man in touch with General Headquarters that we ever met was Dick Walsh of Balla who was on the Executive.[15]

[146R] Claremorris was the strongest post in South Mayo for the British, but I don't know how many there were there. Also they used the old barracks in Ballinrobe. I found the people very good. There was a fine response to the police boycotts and in moving around I found the people very good when I was on the run. Tans and RIC from Galway often came in on us. They never did much damage but after Portroyal they shot up Ballinrobe.[16] After the Tourmakeady ambush they came in in a worse temper but they didn't do much damage.

Four battalions in our [East Mayo] Brigade: Cross, Ballinrobe, Claremorris, Balla.

We were very poorly armed, with shotguns taken up on raids and revolvers only. We got a few Mausers from General

13 Tommy Ruane of Kiltimagh became V/C of the East Mayo Brigade. He was dismissed from the IRA in September 1921 after being investigated by two GHQ officers. He went pro-Treaty and on 29 June 1922 a party of IRA men went to his home to arrest him for recruiting for the Free State army. Ruane resisted arrest and in the affray Willie Moran, O/C Bohola Company, was shot dead. Ruane was wounded and died on 5 July.
14 Possibly Maurice Mullins.
15 Balla (not Ball as in the original text) is pronounced as Ball.
16 The Portroyal ambush on the Ballinrobe–Castlebar road was on 7 March 1921. 'After' Portroyal, not 'at' Portroyal as in the original text.

Headquarters, about six, and I carried down from General Headquarters a few old Italian revolvers which were absolutely useless. We got two or three Lee-Enfields later on but we were unfortunate in missing six rifles in Cross at the RIC **[147L]** barracks there, where there were eight men. I proposed to Dick Walsh, before the Brigade was formed, to attack it, but Dick said that any plans for an attack would have first to be submitted to General Headquarters. I met Dick Mulcahy in Dublin and he approved of the plan, but he said if you do this now they'll make it hot for you and you won't be able to organise the Brigade; so do it some other way.[17] If we went as British Military and drove up after Mass when only two men were present, we could have done it. I met Dick ... but he didn't ...

There was a boy friendly with me and with the Police. He told me that they [RIC] were ready to leave Cross [Barracks] even though they were then sandbagging the barracks. I told Pat Dunleavy, then in Claremorris, now in Tuam. They wanted to do it at once then. I told the Claremorris men to come to Cross, and I'd show them the lie of the land. The teacher at Lough George wanted a frontal attack, but I wouldn't accept that as there would not be time. Two of them were to dress as British officers with a Tommy to drive them. Michael O'Brien met them, and they changed into uniform at Hugh Maguire's of Claremorris. Michael Hare was there also. Dunleavy lost his nerve for he got water from the RIC in the barracks, but he wouldn't draw his revolver. A Tan gave him the water.

We had several ambushes at which nothing occurred.

[147R] An attack on Cong Barracks, but we hadn't sufficient arms. We, one Sunday night, were to have rushed it when the garrison was low. Across from the barracks was an archway to Ryan's Yard. MacCarthy, an Excise man, told the sergeant

17 Richard Mulcahy was chief of staff of the Irish Volunteers and later the IRA until early 1922.

about our movements. So I rushed across to the door, but it was locked. I couldn't get in. As we had few revolvers, we held up the sergeant in the yard. (Evidently the sergeant came out to investigate and was held up.)

Dick Mulcahy hadn't much to say when I met him save that he wanted the place organised and put on a proper basis.

IRB. Dick Walsh took me in to it. (I was called up for debates on the Treaty.) I was elected a TD on May 24th 1921.[18] Conor Maguire and Coyne, now a District Justice, were up as candidates, but later on at a meeting some fellows came in and proposed me.[19] Coyne would not withdraw his name, but on a vote he was beaten.

[149R][20] Portroyal, Partry, March 7th, 1921.

Intelligence. It was not too good. We got certain information from Ballinrobe Post Office.[21] We got copies of the codes from the Post Office there. There was no tapping of the RIC in this area or no tapping of the military. We got information from General Headquarters about this. We knew they used to pass on a special message **[150L]** to Castlebar.[22]

Some IRA from Ballyglass Company, Balla Company, Srah Company.[23] There was a market day in Ballinrobe, and we were waiting for the military. We had not blocked the road and when we got word, we got in behind the stone wall for cover. It had been loopholed and there were thirteen men in line to pick off the driver and then the lorry would run into the main body of the ambush party further on. They got the driver alright and the car ran into the side of the road. They shouted out something

18 24 May, not 21 May as Maguire mentioned in the original text.
19 District Justice (written as D.J in the original text) Coyne (not Coyle as in the original text) sat in the Mayo area in the 1950s.
20 Pages 149R to 153R have been moved to here since they relate to the Tan War.
21 Post Office is written as P/O or P.O in the original text.
22 The 'they' probably refers to the RIC.
23 These three companies were part of the Ballinrobe Battalion. Srah, not Scragh as in the original text.

which I couldn't hear. Chatfield, in charge of Ballinrobe, and Craig, a lieutenant, was with him. They got out of the lorry, and they used it as cover. The Tommies stood by their officers, but the fellows up the road had not fired as yet. The soldiers ran up the road. Chatfield was hit in the knee. We got about ten rifles, but we didn't bother about the other three who ran up the road, three men and one officer.

Reprisal for the ambush. They killed a civilian in Srah, named Tully. They came out from Castlebar to search. The RIC shot this man dead in his own house. We had no casualties.

There were several attempted ambushes waiting and missing them. On Easter Monday there was a fair in Shrule. The British went in a lorry. At dawn we were there, and **[150R]** it got worse for it was cold, and there was no cover and the men were frozen stiff.

Tourmakeady [ambush, 3 May 1921.] Derrypark, a mountainous district beyond.

[RIC] Barracks evacuated: Cross

    Cong

    Shrule

    Ballyglass

    Kilmaine

    Partry

This [Partry Barracks] is a very strong house built in the Land War on the north-west side of Lough Mask. The RIC and Tans numbered about twelve men. That morning the mail came in to Tourmakeady. One letter we opened that morning was giving jib to a Tan for not sending money to his wife. 'How can I go out to my friends when I have no bleaten shoes?'[24] A party [of RIC]

---

24 Bleaten or bleeding is a slang word commonly used in Dublin.

went out regularly with pay and supplies from Ballinrobe.[25] The village **[151L]** itself was the best place for an ambush from the Ballinrobe side.[26] Srah was a very friendly area, and the villages around it were as friendly. On Sunday and Monday we stayed in S[rah] and on Tuesday we went from Srah along the road early in the morning. There was a boy in Ballinrobe who was watching the barracks, and he was to tell us when the escort left. Another lad left to tell us, but he was too late for they were there before he arrived. We were in position anyhow, waiting. In Stewart's Hotel an old man and his wife, RIC he was, and both were Protestants, and Dr Murphy was there also.[27] We got them all out, and we took out the people as well from the village houses and put a guard over them. They were only in there … when the policeman's wife wanted to raise the alarm.

We had three parties: (1) at Fair Green along the ditch; (2) in the village around Post Office, links in between the two; (3) at Drumbawn Gate.

We expected three lorries. The north party was to get the first lorry. I was in No. 2 party. Michael O'Brien was with No. 1. Patrick May, Ballinrobe, was in charge of No. 3. When the British reached No. 3, fire was to be opened on them, and the fire would have stopped the first lorry.

When the British reached No. 3, fire stopped the first lorry. **[151R]** Shots rang out; between (1) and (2) they stopped. I divided up my party, and I sent some men to Paddy … and linked up with O'Brien with my men.[28] The fellows in (1) and (3) had left their positions after they had fired a few shots. The first lorry then was out on the road and there was a river between us and Michael O'Brien's party and we couldn't get over it. One

25   Maguire's 'party' refers to a party of RIC.
26   Tourmakeady.
27   Stewart's Hotel in Tourmakeady. Protestants is shortened to 'Prots' in the original text.
28   Captain Paddy May of the South Mayo flying column.

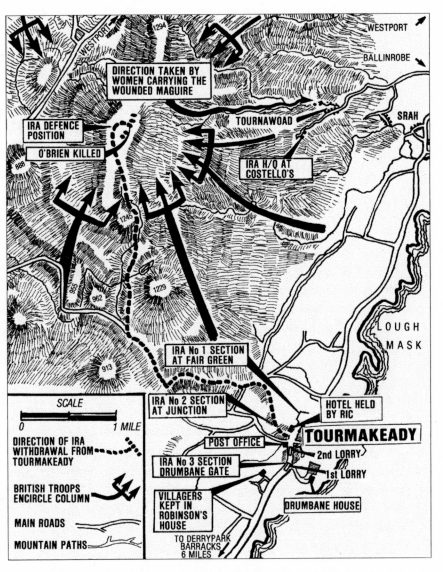

Plan of the Tourmakeady ambush, taken from Ernie O'Malley, *Raids and Rallies* (Mercier Press, 2011)

fellow with a rifle inflicted most casualties on the soldiers near No. 3, who were on the road.

We took their stuff, four rifles. It was I who fired the shots. We had no casualties there.

We went further for the hills. In Ballinrobe the British heard the shooting, and we hadn't blocked the roads. The British came quickly from Galway, Castlebar, Westport, Claremorris, Ballinrobe, and they completely surrounded us. We got in touch with them at 12 noon, and we fought, running, until we took cover, and we held them all day. They failed to dig **[152L]** us out. We had twenty-five men, for I had sent the local men home when the ambush was over. Then they concentrated on the Column with rifles and Lewis guns. Under cover a party of theirs came up to us under Lt Ibberson.[29] I was hit in the arm first by Lewis gun fire. Michael O'Brien came over to me to tie me up, but I felt no pain much nor did I feel weak. He ripped up my sleeve and bandaged the wound lightly around my arm, and I was lying over on my side when I saw a head coming up out of a ridge. I shouted to the lads. He shouted, 'Hands up boys.'[30] Mick picked up a rifle and aimed at him and he fired at him close by to us.[31] Mick fell across my two legs, and then one of our fellows got the officer with a charge of buck-shot. He turned and ran, and his men ran whilst our men opened up on them. He was very badly wounded in the legs and arms, so Dr Peter Daly of Ballinrobe, friendly to us, told us later. The Lieutenant was promoted Captain for his bravery.

They did not try any further assault on us, but they poured in lead on us all day until night time. Both of us in charge were then knocked out so we had to depend on the men. Then they sent up Very lights. Dr Murphy told me that reports were

29 Lt Geoffrey Ibberson, not Everson as in the original text.
30 Probably referring to Lt Ibberson.
31 Michael O'Brien.

coming in to Ballinrobe **[152R]** all that day. 'Rebels completely surrounded, waiting for dawn to capture them.' In the darkness the men carried me and left me in the first house they met with for I was very weak from loss of blood. This was a Tuesday and not until Saturday did I get outside the cordon for they had the area surrounded and were combing it, slowly. I had to be carried out by [a] girl a few times during these days to hide me.

Bourke was wounded but not seriously, and Pádraig Feeney, who had come from Ballinrobe, was captured with his message, but he escaped. The RIC came up with him again and they shot him dead. We could never find out what casualties they had on the hill in the open fight, but the local people say they saw two soldiers bringing a man down on the ground.

I was knocked up then until after the Truce. Dr O'Daly **[153L]** was friendly to us, Dr O'Brien of Balla looked after me afterwards, and Dr George Maguire, Claremorris, then P. J. Smith after the Truce.

The Column varied in strength. Usually it was twenty-five men. From early in March we camped out in the woods in felt-tarred shelters to keep out the rain, straw bed, with bed clothes given to us by the people.

A few weeks before the Truce I was back again for duty. The RIC evacuated several barracks (three): Kinuary, Derrypark on the Westport side, and some others I cannot recall.[32]

Influences of the priests and others. They tried to change the men. One Vice-Commandant of a battalion went into the priest. The shopkeepers and others, the solid men were trying to get our men away by offering them jobs as officers and as police officers.

Rifles: fifteen to sixteen in the Brigade. A good number of shotguns, but morale was very high.

---

32 Kinuary, not Kinnury as in the original text. Derrypark was another of the barracks.

[TRUCE PERIOD]

[147R] Michael O'Draingan (Thornton) was my senior in the IRB. He came to me in the hall of the Exchange Hotel, **[148L]** and he told me the Supreme Council decision before I had even taken off my coat there on arrival.[33] He was on the Connaught Council. I was in charge of a Circle then. He said that the Supreme Council thought the Treaty should be supported. I told him I thought I was a free agent myself, as I was representing the people, and also I regarded the pledges I had made to the established Republic as binding. I would do, I said, what I thought best with regard to the people I represented. He left me then.

At the private meeting of the Dáil there was no real bitterness.[34] The Treaty position was pressed but not bitterly. The Treaty had been debated. I had flu but I thought I could shake it off, but I was really run down from the lack of blood.[35] At night I was sick, drinking rum given me by lads who were anxious to cure me.

I didn't go home through the Christmas recess. Pádraic Ó Máille and others were very solicitous about my health. Dr Dalton (of Ballyhaunis) and others wrote, but I didn't reply to Dr Cleary who was in charge of Dalgan Park for we had arranged an ambush on Shrule Road and they received us very kindly. Canon Hannelly wrote to me. He said it was rumoured that I was going to vote against the Treaty and that I should abstain if I wasn't going to vote for it. I told him what I was going to do. In his reply he said that I was **[148R]** suffering from an erroneous

---

33 Micheál Ó Droighneain/Michael O'Draingan/Thornton (not O'Drenan as in the original text) was a schoolteacher in Furbo. His home and that of his father were badly damaged by British forces because of his involvement in the Republican movement. He was pro-Treaty.
34 Treaty debates, December 1921. Maguire was in the Dáil at the time.
35 Maguire had been wounded the previous May during the Tourmakeady ambush.

conscience. 'I have never touched politics as you know, but I have been asked by the Archbishop[36] to use all my influence with you, and I wouldn't write to you now save for that reason.'[37]

Before the Civil War broke out Dean Macken of Claremorris was sent to me by the bishop. He wanted me to withdraw. We had a very friendly conversation so I didn't want them to go away thinking I had no grounds for my belief. I talked for two hours.[38] 'I won't take your answer now,' he said, 'I'll come back in a week's time.' In the meantime we had moved from Brookhill House (Lambert's Place), near Claremorris, to Claremorris. I met the Dean again and [he] said, 'No preliminaries. What answer am I to take to the bishop?'

'Exactly what I told you a week ago,' I said.

He made for the door. 'I'm telling you I'm not going to be stopped by your men' (evidently they had held him up).

'They will stop you,' I said; so he left me in a terrible temper.

[149L] The Canon – Dalton of Ballinrobe – was very friendly to me. My elbow joint was very stiff on account of wounds. I stopped some weeks in Dublin in the Exchange Hotel. I had been told that two priests had been in to see me, Canon Dalton and the parish priest from Kilmaine.[39] They had been in to see me early during the Truce. They were very friendly. They wanted me to have a drink. Then they got abusive before we left barracks.[40]

Volunteers for the North. None of them picked in our area. There was a question of us swapping some arms, but there was nothing done by us as we didn't send any of ours away.

36 Dr Gilmartin, archbishop of Tuam.
37 Canon Hannelly's comment to Maguire.
38 O'Malley's original text has '2/6 hours' but it is probably not quite what he means. Even two hours would be a long time.
39 Parish priest is written as P.P in the original text.
40 Perhaps Maguire is referring to the priests visiting him in the Claremorris Barracks – the workhouse.

After the Truce Price came to see us, and he and I went around the area. I had been appointed Divisional O/C by Cathal Brugha.[41] There was a meeting of Divisional O/Cs in Dublin at which O'Duffy[42] and Collins were present.[43] Collins asked us if we were prepared to give a guarantee that we wouldn't use our arms against the Irish people and all of us agreed they would not.

Collins had a little tiff with me that night. I thought there was a catch in it. And I said we have never used our arms against the Irish people or we never will. 'What exactly do you mean Maguire?' asked Collins. 'I never,' I said, 'intend to use my arms against the Irish people for I have used my arms against their enemies, but I'm not going to tie myself down with regard to any action [149R] I may take in future.' This happened at the meeting. There was a full muster of both sides. This was the only meeting I ever attended at which Mick Collins was present. (This must have been in January 1922.)

Division. Adjutant O'Gorman, an Australian, [was] in the British Army once.[44] He had been a deserter from the British Army and had been around the South with the IRA. He had been appointed by General Headquarters. Later when I talked to Liam Lynch about him, he was amazed that he had been appointed Division Adjutant.[45] He was a devil to drink and would then come to me craving for forgiveness.

Quartermaster: Martin Coyne, Abbeyton, Co. Galway.[46] Now in USA.[47]

---

41 Maguire is referring to his appointment as officer commanding the 2nd Western Division in late summer 1921 when Cathal Brugha was still the Minister for Defence, and Richard Mulcahy was chief of staff of the IRA.
42 Eoin O'Duffy was assistant chief of staff at IRA GHQ.
43 Michael Collins was director of intelligence at IRA GHQ.
44 British Army is written as B.A. in the original text.
45 Liam Lynch at this time was O/C, 1st Southern Division of the IRA.
46 Coyne, not Kyne as in the original text.
47 The rest of page 149R and the pages up to part of page 153L have been moved

[153L] IRB. Weak in this area [Kinuary], but strong in Balla. Mairteen Condon, a Roscommon man came around during the Truce as organiser for the IRB.

When the Division was formed, most of the fellows were handpicked. Pat Dunleavy, Brigade O/C, North Galway, Second Western Division, deserted to the Free State.[48]

South Roscommon: Frank Simons, IRB, in charge of [the] Brigade.

[153R] Pat Madden of Roscommon IRB was with Simons and both went Free State. They believed that Mick Collins could do no wrong. They gave me a lot of trouble for I had to arrest and then release them for trying to organise in my area.

Second Western was my Division. It consisted of:

South Mayo [Brigade]. Tom Dole O/C, an RIC man's son, a teacher, a doctor now in Galway in Castle Street.
North Galway [Brigade].
South Roscommon [Brigade].
Roscommon [Brigade]. Gerald O'Connor, a decent fellow, who faded out. His appointment caused trouble as he had no pre-Truce service in action. The officer material here was damn bad.

Papers. *Western People* has the most circulation. It was bad during the Truce and it had a bad influence. Without the priests the Treaty would never have been put across. I was **[154L]** told by TDs that at Christmas the priests had got after them. During the Truce the priests dined them and wined them and made big fellows of them.

Cathal Brugha, I met late in the summer in Lalor's on the

earlier, since these relate to the Tan War.
48 By using the term deserted, Maguire is probably referring to Pat Dunleavy's siding with the Free State and leaving the Republican cause.

Quays.[49] He was convinced that nothing would come out of the negotiations. He mentioned to me his proposal that men from my area would go across to shoot up members of the British Government.

South Roscommon Brigade wasn't Free State. Matt Davis was alright.[50]

Dunleavy did a certain amount of damage in North Galway, but the men came back again, Republicans.[51] Practically all the executions the Free State carried out were from this area, excepting my brother, aged eighteen, and a man from Athlone.[52]

When I was in Athlone the sergeant in charge of police, Sergeant Farrell, gave a note to Dole with six names on it, and he was to change the six men to the Garrison Detention which had twelve cells.[53] All the men caught in arms after the Murder Bill were put in there.[54] Tom [Dole] came in to me in January 1923, and he showed me the list of six men who had been changed to different cells. Five men taken and put in one cell and that left one man, but the sixth man was not taken out, and I was the sixth man. When we received [154R] the list I knew it was for execution. Two months later my brother was captured on January 20th, 1922 on a Saturday. My brother was executed on the 11th April with the other five Galway men.[55]

---

49 Lower Ormond Quay, Dublin.
50 Matt Davis of Cloontymullan, Kilteevan, Co. Roscommon, helped found the Irish Volunteers in that county. He became O/C 3rd Battalion, South Roscommon, and quartermaster for the South Roscommon Brigade. O'Malley had stayed with him when helping to organise the Roscommon brigades in 1918. Only his company went anti-Treaty in South Roscommon.
51 Maguire possibly means that when the O/C of that brigade joined the Free State army, the Republicans were weakened and took some time to recover.
52 Seán Maguire was executed in Tuam.
53 PA Sergeant Farrell was formerly a sergeant major in the British Army. See Broddie Malone interview.
54 Free State Public Safety Act, passed on 18 October 1922.
55 Seán Maguire was executed along with Frank Cunnane, Michael Monaghan, Martin Moylan, John Newell and Séamus Ó Máille.

Conventions. At the first big convention there was a committee of fifteen nominated by the convention who were to select an Executive. Liam Lynch broke it up for he wanted Tom Crofts,[56] Florry O'Donoghue[57] and Liam Deasy[58] on it, and on that account I would not allow my name to go forward at the second convention. So Michael Kilroy went forward instead of me.[59] The first convention I thought a very representative one. Seán Hegarty would upset everything at the conventions.[60]

[CIVIL WAR PERIOD]

[155L] Tom Barry and the bishop of Cashel were trying to get a separate truce. I was in prison at the time, but the *Independent* had something on it about this affair. They sent us in the *Independent* whenever there was bad news on it.

No messenger was sent to me by Traynor at the start of the fighting.[61] I got a letter in script from someone via the underground stating 'offence is the best defence'. One trouble was that our army was being constantly undermined. If we held a council one night there might be a man who was on it with the Free State the next night. In the beginning our fellows would not kill the Staters.

My Division was a buffer between Brennan[62] and South

---

56 Tom Crofts was adjutant to Liam Lynch, and later O/C, 1st Southern Division.

57 Florence/Florrie/Florry O'Donoghue was on the IRA Executive and became adjutant general of the IRA on 9 April 1922, but when the fighting started in July he became neutral.

58 Liam Deasy (not Deacy as in the original text) succeeded Liam Lynch as O/C, 1st Southern Division, but on his arrest in February 1922 he called on his comrades to lay down their arms in the fight against the Free State.

59 No doubt Kilroy's going forward in place of Maguire may have been one of the many factors in their fractious relationship, as can be seen here and in Kilroy's interview.

60 Possibly Seán O'Hegarty of Cork No. 1 Brigade.

61 Oscar Traynor had been O/C Dublin No. 1 Brigade in the War of Independence and went anti-Treaty.

62 Commandant Michael Brennan of Clare had been O/C 1st Western Division

Roscommon which contained MacEoin's Fifth Column.[63] The Free State in South Roscommon tried to establish posts.[64] At first we did not realise that men could be so bitter against us. Mount Talbot, near Ballygar, was attacked, but was not taken by us. We had Simons and a few others (who were Free State) in Ballinrobe before the scrap started. Mitchell was sent down by MacEoin with an armoured car to release them, so we were prepared to meet them on a day fixed. Then I had to release them on an order given me by Liam Lynch. Before an Executive meeting in the Four Courts, I was ordered by Liam Lynch to release these men, and he called me in before the convention (?) **[155R]** (and) said I was reluctant to carry out his orders. I then resigned, and when the Free State attacked the Four Courts I had resigned. My area was sapped. In Kilmaine, in the parish priest's house, Sinnott and company were there organising, and O'Gorman reported it to me. He surrounded the house, and I went over to Kilmaine. Then I went in. I told them to clear out, and they did clear out.

Castlerea.[65] We had a garrison in Castlerea in a hostile district. With the first drive of the Free State some of these men were captured.

[Capture.] I was taken prisoner in October 10, 1922, and I was brought to Athlone. I was not personally ill-treated. The food and conditions there were very bad. It was overcrowded. There were stone floored cells without heat or light. Our food was sent in from the garrison. They brought porridge in in a bucket, then the[y] used the bucket for tea at once, and they **[156L]** were very dirty (the buckets). The detention barracks was inside in the barracks. In each of the twelve cells there

and went pro-Treaty.
63 Seán MacEoin, not MacKeown as in the original text.
64 Roscommon is abbreviated to Rosc in the original text.
65 Castlerea (not Castlereagh as in the original text), Co. Roscommon.

were three men in rooms round about. There were about fifty men there when I was there. I wasn't told I was to be brought before a Court, but I was taken out one day before a Court in a room where there were three fellows from the South Mayo Brigade who had gone over to the Free State. They began their proceedings. 'I don't recognise that you have got any authority to try me, and so I won't give any evidence.' There was no sentence promulgated, although that was the usual procedure at the time. The Court produced the evidence about my capture, but I did not cross-examine them.

Headford [Barracks, 8 April 1923]. There was a fight there. Christie Macken was in charge.[66] Following that fight they executed my brother and the Tuam lads as a reprisal.

MacEoin was decent to me and to the men, but before that Tony Lawlor annoyed our men.[67] Two of our men escaped. Then Crow's Nest(s) were put [erected] so that sentries could see our men. The man could see over the wall into the next yard.[68]

[Escape, 10 June.] We had plans for an escape. Athlone fellows came in amongst us. I thought we could get out through the wash house for Mick Mullins, now a doctor in Dublin, had cut a hole in the roof of the wash house, but it was found out before it was finished. Later, some Athlone lads **[156L]** were brought in as prisoners. They suggested that they would widen a hole from a brick in the wash house. They worked all day on a Sunday, and at 6 o'clock the hole was wide enough. We decided to go through it when the new guard came on. The fellow in the Crow's Nest could see but he was not watching. We could get from the hole into a house. Jimmy Martin from Berries in

---

66 Christie Macken (1899–1972) was adjutant, 4th Western Division, and later O/C, 2nd Western Division. See his interview in O'Malley, *The Men Will Talk to Me: Galway Interviews*, pp. 187–200.

67 Brigadier General Anthony Lawlor (not Lalor as in the original text). See biographical sketches.

68 A crow's nest is a raised military sentry post.

Athlone got to Pump Square by Artillery Square to where the British soldiers were accustomed to get out at night. There was an alarm there, but it had been cut to prevent the men getting out, but the barracks had wire hooked on to the barbed wire with a rope on the far side. Martin knew that the barracks could be sealed at this point. The next two men were caught, and they were recognised in the Pump Square.

We got ten miles from Athlone that night to Rockingham Demesne where there were good dug-outs. Pat Brennan was in charge of the Brigade there.[69] The 'Cease Fire' was **[157L]** on and that was very depressing for when I went in (to Gaol) there was a bit of fight left in the crowd, but the people after the Executions were beginning to distrust the Free State.[70] The lads brought out never recanted when they were sent before the firing squads.

Martin Coyne,[71] Quartermaster, now in the USA, he got an awful doing in Galway.[72] There was a sketch of him two weeks ago in the *Western People*.[73]

I saw no beatings in Athlone from the time I went in there but there were nice fellows outside of our cells at night pretending to shoot in.

Recruiting for Free State. They were easily bribed.

Spies. No spies were shot in our area during the Tan War.

Priests. Fealy was the Chaplain in Athlone. About three times in six or seven months there was Mass. They claimed there that they had no priests (so they could not serve us). One of these Masses was held on Christmas Day.

---

69 The anti-Treaty North Roscommon Brigade in 1923.
70 Referring to the ceasefire ordered by Frank Aiken, Republican chief of staff, as of 30 April 1923.
71 Martin Coyne, not Kyne as in the original text.
72 Probably referring to Galway Gaol where he was held.
73 Referring to a publication in the *Western People* just before the time of the interview in about 1951.

Paddy Mannion, who was a native of Dublin, was wounded, then deliberately killed. He came down to us after the attack on the Four Courts.

The Staters were inclined to shoot to kill at the start.

Sporting Mausers. We got them from Birr. They were very good.

[157R] A brother of the present Archbishop of Dublin, McQuaid was killed fighting against us in West Mayo in the Shramore district.[74] There were two good fellows of ours who were being followed, but they turned around and fired, and they saw the fellow fall on his face.

The evening I was brought in to Ballinrobe,[75] Fr Dalton came in to see me in Ballinrobe.[76] His brother had been killed on our side outside of Galway. He came in to Valkenburg Hotel to see me and he talked to the fellow in charge of me.[77] He said he was friendly to me and that he would do anything he could for me.

74 Maguire is mistaken here. Private McQuaid (not MacQuaid as in the original text), a medical orderly in the Free State army, was killed on 23 February 1923 at Shramore, north of Newport and not in Claremorris as in the original text. He was a brother of John Charles McQuaid (1895–1973), later archbishop of Dublin for many years.
75 The evening that Maguire was captured by the Free State army, 10 October 1922.
76 Probably Canon Dalton of Ballinrobe (not Fr Donlon as in the original text); see p. 149L above.
77 Valkenburg Hotel (not Valkenbergs as in the original text) in Ballinrobe.

NORTH MAYO

MATT KILCAWLEY

(UCDA 17b/137, pp. 57–71)[1]

Matthew 'Matt' Kilcawley (1900–1955) was born in Kilglass, near Enniscrone, Co. Sligo. His father was a farmer. He joined the Irish Volunteers and was company adjutant and later vice-commandant in the Enniscrone Company of the North Mayo Brigade. He participated in many of the activities of the local IRA flying column, including the attacks on Enniscrone Coast Guard Station,

Courtesy of Micky Kilcawley

Easky Barracks and Tuffy's shop in Culleens. He joined the anti-Treaty side. He was appointed O/C of the North Mayo Brigade but was captured after the April 1923 ceasefire and imprisoned in Ballina, Galway and Hare Park in the Curragh where he went on hunger strike. In 1933 he married Bridget McEvilly of Killala. They settled in Enniscrone and had six children. In 1934 he and his brother, Tom, started the Kilcawley Construction Company in Sligo.

This interview took place in Enniscrone in November 1951.

---

1   The initial transcription and footnotes for this interview were done by Dominic Price.

[1916–1921 PERIOD: NORTH MAYO BRIGADE]

[Attack on Enniscrone Coast Guard Station. 30 August 1920.][2] [57R] There were six Coast Guards and four Marines, and we were ready to rush the roof in case it failed. The military at Ballina had an outpost at Bunree Bridge. The first night that they put out the outpost, they began to search the people who were coming in from Enniscrone at 7 o'clock in the evening, and our attack was timed for half past 8. The Ballina lads had already brought out their guns for this was a half day in Ballina, and they held those who were returning from Enniscrone that evening. Perhaps they were aware that the lads had left the town and they were waiting to hold them up as they came back. Then there was a meeting held on the cliff road a few hundred yards away as to the advisability of carrying out the operation, fearing that information might have leaked out to the British in Ballina. About at least twelve of the active fellows had come out, and they were very active. There was a good tradition there and Paddy O'Connor was in charge of the operation. The Brigade O/C was ill, but it was he who had organised and planned it. Tom Ruane was ill on this night and the Brigade Adjutant took over instead of him.[3] He was a native of Ballynagarrigy, Westmeath and he had a drapery shop.[4]

My rank at the time was Company Adjutant of Enniscrone which was a very good Company. We had about fifty men who were active, roughly. Twenty-five of them have pensions and all of them were in use that night between cutting wires, knocking down telegraph poles and scouting.[5] Éamonn Gannon was

2 Enniscrone is now sometimes referred to as Inishcrone but the old spelling has been left; the town is located on the coast about eight miles north-east of Ballina. Kilcawley often refers to 'here' in his interview meaning Enniscrone and the reference has been changed to the town name accordingly.
3 Tom Ruane of Ballina. See biographical sketches.
4 Ballynagarrigy, not Ballinagary as in the original text.
5 A pension here refers to a pension granted by the Irish government to those people whose service during the War of Independence had been recognised by

Vice-O/C [of] the Brigade at that time, but he was not on this attack for he was too well known, and he was teaching. He ran the MacFerbis College here for MacFerbis's Castle was convenient to him. There was some grant from the Department of Education for the National Schoolteachers of the district. He compiled the information, but it was a daylight job.

Mrs Levimore was the Chief Boatman's wife here for the Coast [57L] Guards were in charge of the station. She got hysterical inside, and there was difficulty in getting her under control and that was impossible. She kicked up a row about her belongings and some of the lads salvaged them. She afterwards identified some of the parties and she swore information about local men.[6] Paddy O'Connor wore glasses and another fellow wore glasses also, Martin Mack Tobin, and she identified him as being on the attack, and that was her mistake. She swore against three others who were not there, but who were on outpost work. Martin Mack was released and another man, but others did sentences of eighteen months. This operation had already been considered by outside units of the East Mayo Brigade then. Jim Healy was the Battalion O/C in Swinford.[7]

Wires were cut at Scurmore on the way to Ballina, and there was no connection the other way.[8] This road was not much used but the straight road or the high road was much used. Ballina came under Castlebar (in the RIC administration?) and the RIC and the forces came on under Sligo. They did come in afterwards on several occasions from Castlebar when Sligo requisitioned them. The nearest RIC barracks was Easky and

the Irish Pensions Board.

6   To swear information would imply that she had informed to the RIC on the local IRA men.
7   Swinford, not Swineford as in the original text here and elsewhere. There is a townland on the outskirts of Swinford named Swineford, but reference is probably being made to the town itself.
8   'Wires' here refers to telephone wires. Scurmore is located near the coast about six miles from Ballina and two miles from Enniscrone.

that was [eight] miles away, but the other barracks which would have been nearer was Enniscrone RIC Barracks, but that had been vacated about six months previously. There was a District Inspector in Easky, and there were Tans and RIC. There would have been from twenty to thirty there. The RIC when there was a District Inspector were stronger, but military were then not [58L] near[er] than Castlebar.

It was the RIC who held the bridge, and there were at least forty of them there if not more. August 30th was the last Thursday in August. I think that there were military in from Castlebar on that occasion. The holiday season in Enniscrone was to mid-September and August was the busiest season. It is mostly people from Mayo and Sligo who came here. The long cars were fitted up to take from sixteen to eighteen people, and they were open.[9]

Donnegan of Swinford would run them in from Swinford. Previously the people used to bring their own straw mattresses with them and feather pillows to make their own 'shake downs' in the houses. Those people do come from Swinford, Ballaghaderreen, Gurteen, Tobbercurry and East Mayo.[10] Elderly people come yet and they stay in the country farmer's houses near the shore and they cook for themselves, buy their provisions: yet they do that. The cribs of the carts were the divisions of the sexes on the floor. They believed in drinking salt water in the morning and in the evening. And they would collect dillisk and carageen moss on the rocks; and they used to bring it home with them.

The operation was timed for 8.20 [p.m.], and one Company was mobilised at 7 o'clock. We entered [Enniscrone] with the people in threes and fours and some of the lads remained in doors in houses. People walked past the walls of the Coast

9   The long cars were horse-drawn cars for carrying visitors.
10 Tobbercurry, not Tubbercurry as in the original text.

Guard Station.[11] It is near the pier and there is a local house near the slip. The pier is a centre for gathering and for bathing also. The original plan was not changed, and at ten past eight on the cliff road, mid-way between the village and the pier, and at least 300 yards from it, the plan was to rush the Watch-House which was independent of the Coast Guard Station, and usually a Coast Guard was there on watch with a telescope. We came down the sea road, the cliff road, and we stopped near the boat house, and we checked up on the placing of the men. There were quite a number of visitors about [58R] at the time, at least a couple of hundred of them. Four men who were armed with revolvers jumped the wall and held up the two armed guards and got them, and then they pushed them in the front door of the station.

The arms of the garrison were on the first floor opposite the stairway over the entrance. When the two Coast Guards had been held up, twelve men jumped the wall and followed them in the door to get control of the arms room first. Another group of men went to the rear of the building and stood to guard the doors which opened on to the sea and the out offices, which were separated from the main building. They did duty there at night. There was a wall to the rear with these openings so a group of us entered there from the sea and had the windows under fire. Cocks of hay gave an ideal approach to the openings, under cover. I was with the group on the openings, and a brother of mine was on the rushing party. We carried the barrels down the leg of our pants, and/or you stuck it under the coat, and you walked stiff legged.

I have shot deer at night with a ball cartridge and a torch. A ball cartridge is deadly accurate up to seventy yards.[12] We had the

---

11 The coast guard station was sometimes referred to as C.G.S. in the original text.

12 A ball cartridge (abbreviated to cart. in the original text) refers to a cartridge

ball bearings of bicycles and scrap iron in our cartridges. The ball is effective no matter where it hits, and is over a half an inch in diameter, and we would run it in with candle grease. There were two Marines on this corridor but one of our fellows got panicky and started to fire. One of the Marines blazed all around him with a revolver. He did fire out at the fellows who were outside close to us before he was overpowered. They were shot at also, but no one was wounded. The rifles and the revolvers were taken out. They had revolvers on the ends of their beds, four revolvers there. On our way down to the station at *Tighes* corner, two Coast Guards pulled up, a Marine and a Coast [Guard] **[59L]** with supplies were captured and two more [Guards] were taken at Mahons, the nearest pub in the village as they were drinking. That disposed of [ten] plus four Marines. There were officers in the building then for us to disarm, six rifles and six revolvers.[13] The old rifles were much heavier than the Long Lee-Enfield. They took a .303 cartridge, and they were lovely rifles for sniping, and they were more accurate than the Short Lee-Enfield. At least six to eight revolvers, a big amount. They had bell-mouthed guns for signals and telescopes and binoculars, a big amount of .45 and .303 ammunition.[14] Very pistols also.[15] There was a good deal of gelignite there, for after the RIC vacated the barracks, the gelignite was kept there for County Council work and detonators and fuses as well. After clearing the arms out to my home place, one and a half miles away, we buried it. By the shore way you could come up under my home.

The other party then remained behind and burned the building with petrol and paraffin. These had been brought down that evening. Also there was an ... with ladders on the north

using a combination of ball shot.
13 O'Malley often used O² to refer to 'officers'.
14 Ammunition is shortened to amm. in the original text.
15 Very pistols were used by the British Army to fire a flare that could be seen for miles.

side of the station. With crow bars and sledges with a view to getting on to the roof on the north side if we didn't get in the front door. These tools had been hidden away the previous night and some of them were brought in that evening. The local people were one hundred per cent reliable. When the attack started a party moved in behind of a ditch and hid in under the wall which was five feet high. We came up towards the village then for the public didn't know except for the sudden shots. The furniture and stuff was taken out and their personal property was not destroyed. But any of the station stuff there was destroyed. We did not destroy either their boat or the boat house and into this latter they stored their personal belongings. The women, four or five of them, were very aggressive, the men were not. The building was completely destroyed **[59R]** and our fellows cleared away from it at 12 o'clock. All the lads from Ballina had to have their arms collected and dumped. They went back themselves in safety. (Between Ballysadare[16] and Skreen[17] was a hell of a Unionist centre and Dromore.[18] These were 'Protestant lands' for the Plantation was reasonably successful there.)

The British from Sligo raided here and they made six arrests. Seven days after, the Auxies, Tans and the RIC came in between 3 and 6 [o'clock] in the morning, and made six arrests, probably after the woman made the statements.[19]

Later, early in November there was some activity in the meantime, but in November a large force of Auxiliaries and Tans, at least six Crossley tenders, painted most of the house with skull and crossbones and slogans. One of the houses was a

---

16 Ballysadare, not Ballysodare as in the original text.
17 Skreen, not Screen as in the original text.
18 Dromore, not Drumore as in the original text.
19 The Auxiliary forces used to supplement the RIC were sometimes referred to as 'Auxies' or Auxiliaries.

shop, Sweeneys, which they associated with Terry MacSwiney.[20] They burned the town hall that day. This was a reprisal for the Coast Guard Station. They carried out a desperate raid on our house, and they looted everything: linen, pillow cases, and they arrested a brother of mine[21] in the house who was on Dromore West Board of Guardians, District Councillor: and also they found a copy of *An T-Óglach*.[22] They got a rope and slung him from the roof to get information, then they beat him up and they brought him with them to Sligo handcuffed. The first thing they did in the village was to raid our house, and they kept him a prisoner on the tender first. O'Meara, a sergeant from Easky, was a guide with them. My brother was the Battalion Quartermaster. He got eighteen months in Belfast Gaol.

[**Easky Barracks attack, April 1921.**] Another attack on Easky, eight miles north … a desperate hostile area. Quite a number of people from there were in the RIC, and it is practically one hundred per cent Catholic. It [Easky] was the District Inspector's headquarters. We could never get much information there. We had three or four lads there. Then [**60L**] the girls of the village used to go out on patrol with the RIC. And we had an ambush planned, and we weren't going to regard the girls.

We went right into this village in April. The Brigade ASU was organised [with] thirty [men], and thirty more as a support.[23] Easky is in our battalion area. We had about fifteen rifles in the ASU, the No. 2 Brigade ASU, but it operated in this battalion. Twelve [men] from this Company were in it and a

20 MacSwiney, not Mac Sweeney as in the original text. The inference is that the Tans associated Sweeneys with the Lord Mayor of Cork, Terence MacSwiney (1879–1920), who died on hunger strike in gaol while in office.
21 Tom Kilcawley.
22 *An t-Óglach* was the internal training and news pamphlet of the IRA and was edited by Piaras Béaslaí.
23 The Active Service Unit, or ASU as in the original text, was also known as a flying column.

few from Ballina and Bunnyconnellan.[24] The Companies in the [Enniscrone] Battalion were: Corbally,[25] Enniscrone, Easky,[26] Culleens,[27] Dromore West (about fourteen to fifteen RIC in 1921), and Curenbla.

The plan was to get the patrol which left the barracks and went out the Easky road at 10.30 every night. It was early April and a party went on to keep Dromore West Barracks under fire to prevent reinforcements coming in from it. We were mobilised at Culleens and we went in at 9 o'clock [p.m.]. It was dark then. We occupied a good position at the bridge and in the Protestant church grounds. The two sides were occupied at a right angle of the road to enfilade the patrol along [the road] from the barracks.[28] We were to allow the patrol to come [part way] and then both of our sides could fire on them then. Men were to move into [position opposite the barracks] to prevent reinforcements leaving the barracks when the firing started and then they were to move down from a point up here at [the Protestant church]. The patrol did not come out so the church party fired on the barracks for a couple of hours and [another] party went out and burned the Court House. We had decided that we would attack the patrol and the six girls. Two or three of them were sisters of the RIC men. Practically every night they came out.

Three IRA men early on left the village for life was impossible for them in [the] early stages. In 1918 it was very hostile. And it was hostile during the Truce, and in the Civil War they joined **[60R]** the Free State army. During the Truce they pelted

24 Bunnyconnellan, not Bunnyconlon or Bunniconlan as in the original text.
25 Corbally, not Corballa as in the original text. The names of these units were written completely in uppercase in the original text for the sake of clarity but have been put here in lower case.
26 Easky, not Easkey as in the original text.
27 Culleens, sometimes written as Cullens in the original text.
28 A diagram by O'Malley is not included here, and references to it in the text have been removed.

us with rotten eggs. The country round about it is very good.
There are a good deal of the ex-soldier crowd there. All through
these patches in the Civil War, Leaffoney (Orange) district lies
away near Nogher and the Anagalan district where there is a
Protestant area. The Catholics here are less to be trusted than
the Protestants. Strange it was the same in the Civil War, and
once you stood inside it you could look out for a raid in from
six to twelve hours afterwards. Company members in that area
never had a chance for an operation and they did more in those
hostile areas.

Culleens [1 July 1921]. This ASU was camped along the
Fublain Hill on the 1st of July.[29] The weather was good. We slept
on the ground on cart covers and on lorry covers under and over
us; and we took in grub and we cooked it ourselves. We were
there then five weeks up in the mountains. There were twenty-
five men. We did carry out some sniping round about, and we
would hit out for bigger forces and then we would retreat in
here. The British used the road between Bunnyconnellan and
Tobbercurry. We tried it twice, but they used it very little, did
the British. The next road was not passable for a tender by Easky
Lake. We moved into Dromore West, and we camped for two
nights in Gleneasky, a village, and near the village were our
camps. The local Company lads would carry these covers for
us. We did a good deal of training and we could have fairly
long route marches. Seamus Kilcullen was the O/C and I was
the Vice-O/C. Tom Loftus was our Adjutant-Quartermaster.
We were the three officers in charge. Ranks did not count very
much that time. We had about twelve rifles in that column, but
we had no hand grenades. We did try mines, but there was no
success. We had no electric detonators only fuses, and **[61L]** we
experimented on them. North Sligo sent us in Jack Brennan, Dr

---

29 There is a conflict in sources over the date of the ambush of the RIC patrol at
   Culleens. Kilcawley mentions 1 July here but others have mentioned 3 July.

Brennan and Martin Durcan, who was killed in the Civil War in Ballymoate.[30]

They [ASU] came in for this particular job. The idea was to ambush the RIC in Templeboy. First they were to rob the Post Office there, and by this means draw out the RIC from Dromore West. This was the first plan. I went against that plan for I was in at home from the column, and when I went back one night we were to move in on Templeboy which was rather a hostile country, and we were not familiar with it. I decided that we would rob Tuffy's in Culleens.[31] It was not in our battalion area. It was in Collooney Battalion and our men were not familiar with the ground.[32] Tuffy I knew and I knew what he'd do if he was robbed, but I did not know what would happen to a Post Office lady in Templeboy, but I felt that we could genuinely bluff Tuffy.

We moved in early into Culleens at dark, and we cooked our own breakfast in a small room near the ambush position. Then at 8 o'clock [a.m.] Jack Brennan and Tom Loftus disguised themselves as tinkers. We brought old [clothes] from Gleneasky with us, and they went into the shop. They robbed the money from Tuffy, and they acted the blackguard. I don't think they brought any of our men with them. They took £60 or £70 away with them.

Tuffy was not there, but his sister was. He had gone away to get scallops for there was a thatcher to thatch his house, and we watched for his return, and we saw him dump his scallops, and at 8.45 a.m. we saw him again whipping his horse. The house was in view from a few positions in which we had men. Before

30 Jack/John Brennan from Coonacool and Dr Martin Brennan (not related) who had finished his medical studies at University College Galway, where he had been O/C of the UCG Irish Volunteers unit while there.
31 Tuffy was in charge of the local post office.
32 Colloney is used throughout this interview instead of Cooloney, which was the spelling used in the original text.

daylight in the early morning at dawn we selected our positions, the best positions we could find. Then we retreated back so that we could have our sleep and our breakfast. Then when we saw Tuffy in a hurry we gave him time enough and we allowed at least [61R] an hour for the RIC to show up. This was on a main road and it was a very public road. We did not cut wires or anything either to excite or alert the RIC. At 10 [a.m.] we got into position, and the two lads went back and they returned the money that they had taken from Miss Tuffy. She went into hysterics when she saw them again. We occupied their house then and the garden and the yard of the house. Then we held the road as well for 400 yards on the west side for we knew that they would come in extended order, but the principal attack on them would have to be at the pub.[33]

The [ground rose] covering the fall of the road. There was [one] party behind a high garden wall, and there were a few men [nearby], and two men further back, and later I moved up [along the road]. We waited. We lay low and they came in as the Angelus rung, for we were then about to quit for Tuffy had not returned.[34] ... From [one position] we could see the road up and down, and we could cover the road from ... Dromore West for a half a mile of view.

They [RIC] were seen as they came in, and we all lay low, but they came in in very extended formation. The first two were 200 yards ahead and they were cycling and all of them were cycling. Then [62L] came the next two, and the next two, forty yards away, and the near two did not come in, 200 yards away. So the distance was as follows: 200 + 40 + 40 + 200 = 480 [yards]. When the first two of them reached Tuffy's, firing opened, but the last

33 O'Malley included a diagram of the ambush scene, which is not included here, and references in the text to locations on his map have been modified slightly.
34 Rung meaning the local usage for 'rang'.

two only came under fire at long range. The first two were taken prisoners, and they dropped into a shough along the road when they saw that the house was barricaded.[35] They dropped down before they were fired on. They replied to our fire and the firing continued and the other four were under fire. Two were badly wounded and two escaped across country. We hadn't a party on the other side; four of them got away across the road ... The first two fellows surrendered. We bandaged the wounded and we left them there. We had four rifles and two rifles from the other two who got away and their bikes. We got their six rifles and four revolvers. We had two prisoners. We were in open ground now. Whilst this scrap was on and the firing was highest, a motor car came through from Ballina. We let it go through, but one of the last fellows in the RIC jumped on the car at a stage near Dromore West and he got into Dromore West Barracks.

And at the same time who comes through but Tuffy with the horse and whip, and his handkerchief held as high as he could on the handle of his whip. Only then had he realised what had happened. The only thing that saved him from the RIC vengeance was his driving back through the fire. The RIC man who got into Dromore West got into Easky. Then Sligo and Easky sent out a cycling patrol and while we didn't delay yet the men had to get food, and we took three bottles of brandy and we gave the men a drink. Then we set off up the mountain road so that we could work back to our base at Goulaun.[36] When we were about a half a mile **[62R]** away from the ambush position, we were fired on from our west from a long distance away and we couldn't understand what was wrong. The military found that the Easky patrol had come up parallel to us and that they had fired on us. We replied to the fire and then we thought, 'How would we be able to surround them?' We then considered

---

35 A shough can be a ditch, like a ditch alongside the road.
36 Goulaun, not Gaalaun as in the original text.

it was only a delaying action on their part while they themselves were waiting for reinforcements to come up. We then retreated as hard as we could across country, and when we came to a bog road the bog was filled with people for the first three miles of it and they were cutting turf. We left the bog road then, and then we were on the open mountain. British reinforcements came tracking up this bog road. By this time we had dumped the captured RIC bicycles.

Four IRA lads who were cutting turf on the bog took up four shotguns. They opened fire on the military and on the RIC. The first four lorries were tenders containing Auxiliaries and RIC, and they were only a half a mile away from them; and we saw them.

We had the two RIC prisoners with us. One of them was King, who had led the RIC and the Auxiliaries on several previous raids and who knew most of us. When we were being fired on we asked what we could do with our prisoners. So we had a short Council of War and we decided to shoot them.[37] We gave them a short few seconds in which to say their prayers. King pleaded hard for mercy. He made all kinds of promises, and we would have ... liked to let the other RIC man go free. He was younger. He pleaded hard and he cried and again pleaded with us. The others would have heard the shots. They were not dead then. King could say 'Enniscrone'. They got up the parish priest, but by that time the two of them were dead.[38]

We were going parallel with the mountain for the Goulaun area [63L] and we were keeping close to the houses. We knew every foot of this area by this time. This group that were following us was now further reinforced from Sligo by six tenders more, and they had cut into the mountains to intercept us on our

---

37 RIC Constables Thomas Higgins and John King were shot on 1 July 1921, the day of the Culleens ambush.
38 Parish priest is written as PP in the original text.

retreat. They went up the Carns road to the end and they formed a party to [the] right flank of the party who were following us up the mountainside. We, however, had crossed that road before they had been able to come up. We intended to keep close to the mountainside and to avoid roads, and in Tawnagh an old man told us that six tenders had gone up the Bunnyconnellan road about three miles to our ...[39] We also heard that four tenders had come up from Corbally, and then it was reasonable to assume that they were trying to get in front of our line of retreat and that they had taken up positions above us at Rathhumish.[40] At the Sligo side of Rathhumish our fellows were very slow for the going was stiff. We had to wait so as to cover their retreat. They were about 200 yards behind us in an open bog, and they were exposed to the fire of the enemy, and we got into cover. Auxiliaries, RIC and the military from Castlebar had gone on to Bunnyconnellan to cut us off. They had moved quickly.

Then at right angles we went to the Sligo side of Rathhumish Wood while the British from Castlebar were on the Bunnyconnellan side of that wood. That day myself and another lad had our kit with us, and it contained a mug, plate and grub. I got down and I milked a cow, and I mixed the milk with water. We were played out by this time for we had been going hard. We had gone six miles upwards and the day was very hot, and we had been up the night before with little or no rest. We crossed then, right across the Bunnyconnellan road. We left the British reinforcements [63R] right behind on the mountain, and we went on until we were within a mile of Ballina that night. Half of us slept in Clunshoo and the other half slept in Ardvally for there was a dugout there. We had a good dugout or two in each Company area in centres of danger. There were two dugouts near to Ballina and two also in this Ardvally ground. [Jack] Connolly

---

39 Tawnagh, not Tawnalachta or Tawnalghta as in the original text.
40 Corbally, not Corballa as in the original text.

was captured. He dropped his gun, and he pretended to be a local farmer. The Castlebar military took him with them for a mile and then they dropped him again. He had got detached somehow and he had got lost.

Then we anticipated reprisals, and every night we were mobilised for the following week to wait for the enemy. We had about twelve or thirteen of us from this (Enniscrone) Company area in the column, and we stood to waiting for them. But nothing happened. There had been two [IRA] killed, and two wounded in the action and two RIC executed. Our first intention was to hold the RIC prisoners. They were RIC men, not Tans.[41] Our parish priest who had been brought up to the scene spoke of them [as] 'Gallant young Irishmen' who were brutally murdered, at Kilglass Chapel.

Priests in the area. A curate here was good. One parish priest was good also. Fr Tom Byrne[42] of Castleconor between Enniscrone and Bunnyconnellan.[43] He was exceptional (because he was friendly or was he exceptionally good?). Always in the Tan War we called in to his place for a feed and a bed.

[69R] Courts.[44] We held them rather openly. They raided to try to locate the Courts and maybe that was why they burned out the town hall for it was used for the holding there of Republican Courts. We kept our prisoners in vacant houses, but we moved them around from Company area to Company area. A couple of men were pulled for robbing, but they were deported from Ballina Quay.[45] There were disputes between neighbours. Police

---

41 The IRA GHQ had made a distinction in terms of standing instructions as normally only the Tans were to be executed.

42 Fr Thomas Byrne is referred to subsequently in the original text as Fr Beirne, but it is assumed this is the same person.

43 Castleconor (not Castleconnor as in the original text) is located halfway between Enniscrone and Ballina.

44 Pages 69R to 72L have been moved here to fit chronologically with the Tan War. Courts means Sinn Féin courts.

45 The text says exported, but presumably Kilcawley means deported.

had to collect dog licences. When there were such disputes the people were called out at night and they were warned that they had best stop their nonsense.

The two parties might be brought together. In case of trespass an agreement would be come to. The interest of everybody was concerned so that people in trouble would come to an understanding. Everybody was helpful, even the parties who were in dispute with each other. (I think they all realised the seriousness of the times that the men **[70L]** who protected Courts were taking a risk and that the less trouble they had the better would they be able to devote their time to army work.) One of the most surprising things was the reason why the older crowd gave way so thoroughly to the young fellows. (I expect their courage and directness influenced the aged. Ireland is not remarkable for courage in action or for morale, and when the youth were seen to face danger and difficulties and to make a gallant effort to solve problems, and to fight apathy, laziness in truth a previous generation was impressed.) They canvassed; they went around and they got money. Then they blossomed into an armed force. There was a great searching out process. The IRB faded out. The older Sinn Féiners and the priests with the pull, the politicians and the Irish Parliamentary Party type disappeared. They reappeared at the Treaty. They were allowed to reappear and they knew when to appear.

[Enniscrone Coast Guard Station attack.][46] This Coast Guard Station was built in about the year 1890.[47] Another Coast Guard Station had been evacuated in Pullheney between Enniscrone and Easky, and there was another near to Dromore West. *Pullnadivie* which had also been evacuated. The latter one

---

46 This is a repetition of the attack as told on 57B, but is a slightly different version so worth including.

47 O'Malley included two hand-drawn diagrams relating to the coast guard station attack in the original text and some accompanying text, all of which has been left out here.

had been destroyed at the end of 1920 but Pullheney was not destroyed until 1922. It had been sold to private people. There was a station also at *Derik* on towards Sligo. **[70R]**

August 30th 1920. Enniscrone Company carried it down and buried some ... and we put some in rabbit holes.[48] There were from five to sixteen fellows from Ballina who had guns with them. There was a tender on the Ardnaree Bridge in Ballina so that we had to dump their stuff as well.[49] The RIC were not there. (This, I expect, means in Enniscrone for they had left the place three weeks before this.) The whole Company in Enniscrone was mobilised for this operation and there were at least twelve of them picked for the Rushing Party. The wires had been cut but no roads had been blocked. ... was in charge of the raid and it was a difficult one. This Brigade had been formed at this time – Enniscrone was then a Company in the Ballina Battalion. Paddy O'Connor was the Battalion Adjutant. Corbally Battalion was being formed for it was the first Company in the Ballina Battalion before that.[50] The Brigade O/C was [Tom] Ruane. Stephen Fleming Flynn was the Battalion O/C of Ballina. He is now in Longford, and he was a damn good fellow. He lives in Blackrock. He is now retired and he travels for soap and jam in Drumshanbo.

There were four Marines and eight Coast Guards in this station. **[71L]** There were twelve rifles and eight revolvers, a good deal of ammunition and also a good lot of gelignite which was there for all purposes. The local lads who had to dump it put it in a wall not far from the station; and while they were handling it they thought it was 'Peggys Leg.'[51] Telescopes and all their equipment was buried on the outside by the lads. There was a

---

48 Probably referring to where some of the rifles were hidden.
49 Ardnaree, not Ard na Righ as in the original text.
50 Corbally, not Corbalagh as in the original text.
51 A Peggy's Leg referred to a sweet that children ate in those days that resembled in part a stick of gelignite.

big bonfire outside. After I had dumped the guns I came back to the flagstaff and the flag was set fire to (and the flagstaff). The hand grenades we captured were Mills Grenades. The captured arms and supplies were sent on to the Active Service Units in the North Mayo Brigade. This stuff went to No. 2 Column which had from two to three scraps.

At 8 o'clock there were two sentries on their beats near to the flagpost. They were not actually on a beat for they stood about near to an outpost building which was nearby. All the fittings were inside. There were always people about the station in the holiday season. We jumped across the road and we held them up and then we rushed them to the door. The arms room was inside. The main door was up a flight of stairs. A Marine fired out through a rear window at a party of us who had come to the rear of the building. He was surprised. One was wounded by a Coast Guard inside, but it was slight. The thing was well timed. There were two Marines taken prisoners up at the village and four of the Coast Guards who were on their way down from Enniscrone were also taken prisoners.

(Had the Marines, who were in the village, their revolvers with them?) They had. All the bedding and the furniture was to be burned, but some of them claimed material as their own personal property and they were allowed to remove it. Some of them brought their belongings down to the boat house then.

[71R] [Loughglynn: 19 April, 1921.][52] John Bergin was the O/C of the column. It began, the column, in 1921. I was on the column, and there were ten on it with eight rifles and two shotguns. The people were wonderful to us saving when we

---

52 The ambush at Loughglynn, Co. Roscommon (not Loughlynn as in the original text) was on 19 April 1921 (not 9 April as in the original text). Micky Kilcawley, son of Matt, does not believe that this section on Loughglynn refers to his father and thinks that there might have been another person present at the interview who spoke about this incident. He says that his father was never arrested during the Tan War.

were captured. This was on the 19th of April 1921. We were in Loughglynn and there were four of us there that day. The rest of us had gone home the previous day. We had rifles, but we were short of ammunition and we went into three ambush positions with [only] three rounds of ammunition. There was myself, Stephen MacDermot,[53] Tilly Ballingan,[54] Scally, Loughglynn. We were just in the house two hours at about 7 o'clock when military and Tans came in. They had the whole place surrounded. We were in MacDermots' of Aughaderry outside Loughglynn. We got away from them, and we got to McGlynn's house. He was shot in Ballinlough, and we ran into the military there and the Tans, and we got stuck into them. They got behind the back of an old ditch and we were 100 yards away, so we kept on firing away. Then a soldier came over the top, but he was wounded, and I got wounded in the foot and Scally got two bullets in the knee. He got away, ran in under an old gate and he lay down flat in a garden of stalks. They split the gate over his head, but he got out under it, and then he went on into this field of potatoes.

So when our ammunition was all gone they came in behind us from all sides. The Leicestershire Regiment they were.[55] I got an awful bad beating. They put down my teeth or some of them, and they beat me hard with rifles. When I was going up on a Crossley I was hit by a rifle between the two shoulders. A Tan split my nose with a revolver. There were three Crossleys of them, Tans and military. I was wounded, as was Scally in the knee. Revolver bullet. They handcuffed Bergin and me, but he wasn't wounded. They held a court-martial there and then, and then there was a Mr Dale, head of the RIC, with them.[56] Then

---

53 MacDermot, not McDermott as in the original text.
54 This name could be Ballingan or Ballantyre, both local names (not Bullingan as in the original text).
55 The 1st Battalion of the Royal Leicestershire Regiment was in Ireland for 1920–21.
56 Probably John H. W. L. Dale, RIC #55390.

they came back and they took the **[72L]** handcuffs from off me. They handcuffed MacDermot to Bergin, and they handed me over to the military and Tans, and I was marched away first. Bergin was left behind and MacD[ermot] with the RIC and the Tans and the military. From Castlerea they were all, both RIC and the Tans and the military.[57] After a half a mile through Loughglynn Wood I heard the shots ringing out and the officer said, 'Do you know what your so and so comrades are getting?' They had killed the two of them.[58]

We came in on Crossleys on … Ballaghaderreen … at Loughglynn school house. The Canon came along and he consulted the two men who were on the Crossley. So we were taken into the Workhouse in Castlerea, which acted as the barracks. There were roughly 300 there, the Lincolnshires.[59] Some of them were very bad. They had the Murder Gang picked out of them. The two dead men were left into the Workhouse, and I was kept there for the night. This officer in civvies came in and said, 'Why is this so and so alive? Why didn't you shoot him?' He was about thirty-five and he looked like a detective. Next day they brought me into Athlone where I was court-martialled, and I was placed into the Detention Cells. I got Penal Servitude for life. Athlone was all right. (He means no beating-up.) They put me in hospital for a week, and then I was put back to the cells again.

Jerry Davis and I were in the one cell in Athlone.[60] He was tried before me for firing at Black and Tans. Jerry was recognised when he came into Athlone. I was sent to the Joy with him. Jerry

---

57 Castlerea, not Castlereagh as in the original text.
58 Stephen MacDermot and John Bergin were shot in the woods of Loughglynn House on 19 April 1921.
59 The 1st and 3rd Battalions of the Royal Lincolnshire Regiment were in Ireland for 1918–21.
60 Jerry/Gerry Davis of Co. Westmeath. See O'Malley's interviews, UCDA P17b/96, 106, 117, 118, 137.

led the twelve who got out of the Joy, and Jerry took the lead from the Joy. Bergin's father bought timber in Mount Druid near Ballygar, and he joined the boys then. He had a bad lung.

[64L] [Spies.] There were no spies shot [64R] by us in the Tan War. We cleared out two or three from the area who were suspects. The first of them, early in the Tan War.[61] They left the countryside, but they never came back. They were people who came in from the outside. There was Daly from Crossmolina area who worked in a bar in Tuffy's shop. Eighteen months before she was caught, we gave her notice, and she left the area. She was suspected in connection with the wounded fellows in Kilmeena. Carrabinna was her native place. She disappeared then, and I don't know where she went afterwards. I know that she did come under suspicion over the wounded in Kilmeena, and she was supposed to have given something away about Crossmolina Barracks.

There was a ballad about the commandeering of a motor car in the Dromore West area.

Cartridges. Ball bearings and melted wax we used here. It was hard to keep the cardboard dry. When a shot was fired from such a refilled cartridge the wax would be held solid until it hit something and then the material would be spread in an awful gash. The Auxies themselves used cartridges, but they had brass cartridges. The half brass cartridge was there before 1914 but then it went out of use. We had a few automatic shotguns here. At Coolura the worst wound was from the blast of a shotgun charge.

Raids. In the arms raids on houses it was mostly small arms that we procured. *Kerqueth* of Bartra Island was raided on the mouth of the Moy.[62] He lived there, and he was a direct

---

61 'No. 1 of them' in the original text has been changed to 'the first of them'.
62 Kerqueth in the original text could have been Kirkwood as noted subsequently. Bartra Island just off Killala.

descendent of Kirkwood of Cromwell's army; a captain, I think. We got two good revolvers, a good .22 mm., and a good deal of ammunition with it; also a good deal of powder and heavy shot; .303 mm. ammunition, but no rifle, and a few shotguns. There was at least two hundredweight of powder and shot.[63] And there were cartridge fillers, etc. We raided **[65L]** the place by boat. His daughter was there. She was a crack shot, and his revolver was under the pillow in his bed. This raid was the first big shot they got. The RIC could not protect them then they realised. (Now [in 1951] people hostile to us have not respect for us, but at that time it was different. We were an unknown quantity and our strength was increased by imagination and by the element of revenge the imperialists judged to be stored up by the past.) They used to maintain contacts to strengthen their contacts and their influences. The Emergency Forces did harm. It put the parish priest back in the parish defence stuff. He was elevated, and so were the Unionists and the Jackeens, and they worked themselves up into positions that made our men feel they were trotting after them.[64] And that gave them power.

Ballina. There was a limited extraction of [Intelligence] information there. Battalion 5 Enniscrone; Ballina Battalion; Foxford [Battalion]: Jim Boyle, Willie Doherty; Crossmolina [Battalion]: Ned O'Boyle, Mulhearne; Ballycastle [Battalion];[65] Bangor [Battalion]; Belmullet [Battalion]: Jim Kilroy.[66] In Foxford John O'Donnell would know and Terence Doherty, who is a rate collector. In Cross there is Mulhearne, who has a fairly small shop. Ned O'Boyle who is near to the village was the best of them. Ballycastle: Paddy Burke has a shop … and he

---

63 Hundredweight is written as 'cwt' in the original text.
64 Jackeens is a slang name among Irish country people for Dubliners – not a term of endearment.
65 Ballycastle, not Ballycashel as in the original text.
66 This is a list of the local battalions, their headquarter locations and significant local leaders.

was a Councillor. Bangor: Mick Henry and Jim Kilroy. Ballina: Calleary and Ruane.[67]

There were a couple of shootings in Ballina for a patrol of RIC was shot up there. Armstrong of the RIC was killed and another was wounded.[68] Two Tans were fired on at Bridge Street and they were wounded. Most of the Ballina fellows were out in Clydagh in Ballycastle. It was not a good fight. The Column No. 1 Brigade ASU. They moved around into the village at night, and they were surrounded and ... by local RIC. One was killed and others were taken prisoners by fifteen RIC from Ballycastle. [65R] No. 1 Column had then about ten to twenty rifles and a few advantages.[69] Bartley Hegarty and Johnny Barrets were two ex-British soldiers. Bartley was the Brigade O/C, and Johnny was later in charge of Divisional Training for Kilroy.[70]

In Ballina there were Tans and Auxiliaries, and they marched the merchants through the town, and they forced them to carry Union Jacks. There was a Murder Gang in Ballina. They scoured the country. Ned Hannon ... in this village [Enniscrone] was badly beaten up. He was a quartermaster. They beat him with the butts of their guns, and they left him away from his home, and Seamus Kavanagh they also beat. They were both of them, County Councillors. Kavanagh was a Battalion Adjutant. They looked upon them both as Sinn Féiners. (The English as usual did not know the implication of a word, Sinn Féin. 'Sin Feghan' as they pronounced it meant someone whom they hated.) They came out from Ballina this day. Didn't they bring Dr Ferran's wife and family [66L] out and around the country.[71] In Ballycastle they did something. I think the Ferrans had a very

---

67 Calleary, not Collarey as in the original text.
68 RIC Sergeant Thomas R. Armstrong was fatally wounded on 21 July 1920.
69 It is not clear what Kilcawley meant here by 'advantages'.
70 A large section on the Truce has been moved from here to later, to put it in chronological sequence.
71 Dr Francis P. Ferran from Co. Fermanagh. See biographical sketches.

nasty time. It was at 12 or 1 in the night that they brought them around. They did not use hostages in this area. We have not a lot of troops passing through this area. A naval boat came in to the pier, and it took away the Coast Guards from Enniscrone.

IRB. No IRB here or very few of them. Early on there were IRB in Ballina, but not after 1918. They were an older type of man. The Fenians had been strong here and they were fairly well organised. The Land War was very active in the neighbourhood.

Boycott. The evicted parties were put in on the land and at night the land was dug and sown. They all mobilised and during the night they dug and sowed the land. And they fixed up temporary structures where the people had been evicted so that they and their children were protected. Then the landlords gave way afterwards.

[67R][72] **Tan War Round-Ups.** The British had done East Mayo, and they were coming in to … They had a few aeroplanes. About the 5th of July that was; but they did not come into this area, but they were about to come in from East Mayo. They had a plane in here which was scouting around on the 5th of July.

There was an attack on Foxford RIC Barracks, on May 23rd, 1921, so as to relieve the pressure on Kilroy. There was a round-up there in operation on the West Mayo Column. This was a sniping attack to draw off the troops.

There was an attack on the District Inspector White at Ballina **[68L]** on the Quay Road.[73] He was out with his wife on the 21st of May 1921. That night this lad who was about seventeen and another young lad, the principals in that shooting, went down scouting and the District Inspector swings around on the road. They had to open fire, and he got back into Ballina, and a patrol was sent out. The Bunree Bridge and the district

---

72 Parts of pages 67R–68R have been moved to here to follow chronological order.
73 Probably RIC District Inspector William Eugene White from Strokestown.

around it [were] surrounded by military from Castlebar. They surrounded Quinn's house when the British heard they were there. They were captured when they were getting away. Young Tommy Howley was wounded,[74] and he died afterwards of wounds. He was from Enniscrone.

[Bunnyconnellan.] There was an ambush in Bunnyconnellan and good lads from the upper end of the battalion were in it.[75] The British were expected to raid a dance there. Two tenders: they halted lorries and then they went along on foot. The advance party was not recognised, but the second party was identified. The RIC retreated across the country to Ballina, the RIC and others. There were twenty-four of them in all, and the others remained in the school. There was chaos for they were waiting for a tender, and only by their accent and talk and by the click of a rifle butt on the road did they recognise them. The ambushers weren't sure about [whether] these [were] RIC, and they didn't open fire for they thought that they might be civilians. There was a mix up as a result, and a few of the RIC [were] wounded and others remained in the town hall until the morning when they went back for reinforcements.

Bunnyconnellan. Foody was an RIC man who had been associated with the shooting of the Dwyers in the Ragg (in 1920 in [the] Mid-Tipperary Brigade). He was a native of Bunnyconnellan. He had been in the Ragg, and he was the guide to the Murder Gang that night there. He came back on holidays during the Truce, and he was shot.[76] We had a tiff with Mulcahy about this.[77] Four fellows had been arrested by the RIC [68R] and Mulcahy refused to take responsibility. It was being

---

74 The original text here mistakenly says killed.
75 Bunnyconnellan, not Bunnecoolan as in the original text.
76 Actually the shooting of Anthony Foody took place just before the Truce was implemented on 11 July 1921.
77 Richard Mulcahy was IRA chief of staff at the time and no militant activities were supposed to be undertaken once the Truce went into effect.

regarded as a family row, and some of the relatives of Foody had been arrested, and they were charged with the murder of Foody for the IRA were not suspected, and these cases had to be withdrawn. Tom Loftus, who was Captain of the Guard on Leinster House, would know about this. He did try to escape, Foody, and it was while escaping that he had been shot. They tied the corpse on to an ass, and they put the ass out on the main road for Ballina. The British military came out from Ballina, and they got him. The Truce was then only on a few days.[78]

Beckett's Mill Bridge. The RIC got information that there were arms in a dump. The RIC raided for it and they had the place surrounded, but our lads came to get the stuff and they opened fire on the RIC. They got into the Mill and they removed the stuff.[79]

Ballyvary Barracks was captured in the East Mayo Brigade [area].[80] It was taken by surprise by the Swinford men.

[TRUCE PERIOD]

[65R] [In] this mountain district during the Truce we restricted the manufacture of poteen and that was reasonably successful. We licenced two distillers in each parish. If any complaints came about whiskey they would be deprived of their licence. Treacle and sugar they used here. It was good poteen, and at one time in the Truce we had one distiller set up his counter on the road opposite to the local pub, and he sold his stuff to the general public. During the Tan War by the shore when the RIC went off poteen duty early in 1920, we had a lot of flax growing and a … made for each flax …[81] There is good land along the shore

---

78 Kilcawley's statement is not accurate as Foody was shot shortly before the Truce. A repeated sentence about the shooting of RIC Sergeant Armstrong has been omitted.
79 Kilcawley's statement might not be accurate on this point.
80 The Ballyvary Barracks attack was on 22 August 1920.
81 O'Malley was confused in his own notes here and placed a question mark after

here to Dromore West. The farms are small now – fifty per cent of the farmers or seventy-five per cent own twenty acres. Near the mountains there are commonages, and there is little tillage. The nearest creamery to us here in Enniscrone is Donard and Screen. The latter collects north up to here. It is an auxiliary to *Achonry*. The only burning here was the town hall.

[66L] The Division was established.[82] We took over Dromore West and Easky RIC Barracks, and we occupied both of them into the Civil War. The Provisional Government troops came in to Dromore West Workhouse from Sligo, and they occupied it.[83] Before the attack on the Four Courts, they withdrew on the request of the Free State. This area remained Republican. About four of the active lads, who were in the Volunteers, and not four from each Company, went into the Free State army, and from the Brigade only a Company Captain, Stephen Donnelly of Ballina, and a Battalion O/C, Hopkins of Crossmolina, Bangor['s] Neary, a Company Captain, and *Timoney*, a quartermaster. There was very little bitterness or soreness here. It was against Donnelly's will that he went Free State.

[Arms Swap.] There was no exchange of arms here, and no men had been picked for service in the North. We were then the North Mayo Brigade. There was the North-West Brigade in [66R] the Belmullet area which took in Achill, Belmullet and Bangor.[84] It had a new battalion. North Mayo had four of its original battalions.

---

a word since it did not make sense. The words omitted include 'naked(?). Flax changes from one to the other to wheat or potatoes'.

82 The 4th and other Western Divisions were established in August–September 1921.

83 Provisional Government is shortened to Prov. Govt in the original text.

84 Kilcawley mistakenly referred to the North East Brigade, when he probably meant the North-West Mayo Brigade covering the Achill–Belmullet area. There is no mention of this brigade elsewhere as it would have been a fifth brigade within the 4th Western Division, but perhaps it was created during the Civil War.

We had seventy-five men on active service. We had more staff. During the Truce the Mausers came in, and we got about twenty of them. About 150 of them then came into the Brigade. I found the double trigger good for sniping but not for active service or for continuous work. In this battalion we sent a unit into the Brigade in Ballina, and there was another here in the battalion. So I went out with this unit, and I operated in this battalion area from Foxford to Dromore West. There were between thirty-five to forty men with rifles. Then I was in the attack on Ballina. Most of the column was in it and some of the men from other Brigade units. I went back to Newport with thirty men [and on to] Belderg and Glenamoy.[85]

[CIVIL WAR]

[Ballina counter-attack, 12 September 1922.] The first battalion. The North Sligo sections were in an armoured car and five lorries of mine, and we swooped at 9 a.m. into Ballina, rushed their Free State positions.[86] The armoured car drove through the sentries. The positions they held were the Post Office, railway, the Workhouse, the Imperial Hotel, Hannigans, but there were others as well that we didn't know about.[87] Their Headquarters was in the Imperial Hotel. We rushed it before they opened fire on us, and they surrendered although they fired from the roof but not from the windows. Fifteen officers there. The Workhouse defended itself until we got the O/C to go up and surrender the post. All the others [at] Hannigans resisted. The front of the Post Office was blown in with a mine. 'The Ballinalee' opened fire, and we put in a mine under cover of the armoured car; then we blew the mine and we rushed the building. There was a huge quantity of stuff and over 150 rifles

---

85 Belderg, not Ballderig as in the original text.
86 Armoured car was written as a/car in the original text.
87 Hannigan, not Hennigan as in the original text.

there. Kilroy was in charge of that attack and Ruttledge, Ruane, and Seamus Kilcullen and Kilroy were then to take Crossmolina afterwards, but they did not go there.[88]

Then there was word that the Staters had mined the roads at Crossmolina, and we were afraid to go the roads. The [Staters] [67L] in Ballina had mined their place so as to get the armoured car in Ballina. The armoured car was afraid to go to Cross. We captured an armoured Lancia in Ballina and with the two of them, we were to go around by Belmullet and into Newport [on] the North Coast road Ballycastle–Glenamoy, but the armoured car began to sink and the Lancia broke down. A lathe for bombmaking had been recaptured by Kilroy from the Staters. The engine gave up and we left it. We had to send back 'the Ballinalee' to North Sligo. Having got it back, then Lawlor came through Ballina,[89] and he went out through the Gap, and there was a series of fighting with Carty's ASU and our ASU from Bunnyconnellan to Tobbercurry. Joe Ring was shot dead then before he reached the Gap with one column.[90] The Staters got through to Tobbercurry and there were two armoured cars, and they fought it out: 'the Big Fellow' and 'the Ballinalee'.[91] The Free State gunner was shot dead in the Ballinalee, and there was another wounded inside in it. Martin Brennan was operating a column there, and a damn good man he was.[92]

The Staters captured a good number of our lads. Twelve of our men were going out from Bunnyconnellan there, and they brought them through to Tobbercurry. They surrounded them for they had become detached from the rest of the men.

88 P. J. Ruttledge (not Routledge as in the original text) and Tom Ruane.
89 General Anthony Lawlor (not Lalor as in the original text), Free State army.
90 Joe Ring from Westport. See biographical sketches.
91 The two captured Free State armoured cars were nicknamed 'The Big Fellow' after Michael Collins and 'The Ballinalee' after the birthplace of General Seán MacEoin, who came from Ballinalee, Co. Longford.
92 Dr Martin Brennan of Sligo. See O'Malley interview with him, UCDA P17b/133.

All the priests were bitterly hostile. Fr Tom Brown, Catholic Curate Dromore West, at one stage came out with us and he remained out for a while.[93] He wouldn't read the Bishops' Pastoral but he went back again.[94] He always remained staunch. The contacts of the clergy are petty and they live in a glove. They became bashful for they live in themselves. They believe that familiarity breeds contempt (and that's a mistaken view for them to adopt). The [Bishops'] Pastoral had very little effect and the refusal of the sacraments had little effect on the men. Some priests did not carry out the regulations **[67R]** to refuse the sacraments. The Bishop was very hostile and a good many priests then had to be careful.

[Gaols.] They were nasty enough to their prisoners, the Staters. Lawlor protected these IO.[95] He made the prisoners clear the roads for mines, but he would not have them abused. Some of MacEoin's men came on here. A crowd came on from Kerry, a desperate crowd. They brought Nicholas Corcoran, a lad from Tipperary, a bank clerk, who came out with us in the Civil War, out to clear the Foxford side of the Ballina railway, and he was shot there on the railway; Kerry and Cork men they were. They were famous for their dirty stuff early in 1923. Joe Healy from Ballina was shot in Headford trying to escape, but he was trying, I think.

Flannery of Easky was shot dead in an attack on Gurteen Barracks, a Free State post. No one was executed from this Brigade area, but then there were not many in the Staters from this area. There was a good deal of local spite and jealousy worked up.

93 Catholic Curate was written as CC in the original text.
94 The bishops' pastoral letter was issued on 10 October 1922 to be read on Sunday 22 October in an effort to persuade people not to support the anti-Treaty Republicans.
95 Perhaps Kilcawley is suggesting that Tony Lawlor used his intelligence officers (IOs) to get information from the prisoners and protected them from any consequences.

Peace Moves. There was an organisation known as the Neutral IRA.[96] A branch was formed here and a representation was made to Kevin O'Higgins, but the local people who were in it had never been active ever in the IRA.[97]

[63R][98] After about the following Christmas of 1922 we went, Tom Ruane, Dr Rowland and I into this place [Father Tom Byrne's house].[99] I was feeling rotten and Dr Rowland told me to stay in bed. I had a good hot bath and a hot drink. Tom Ruane took my automatic and Rowland took my haversack for carrying first aid outfits. The next morning Fr Tom Byrne went out **[64L]** on stations and weren't the Free State all around and even in the yard, but they didn't come in to the house. Fr Tom came in for fear that I would be found for his Bishop, Naughton, was an Imperialist (somehow the British seemed to think that the Irish clergy were violently Republican).[100] The problem for him [Fr Tom] then was how would he get me out without the Free State being able to spot me. If he hid me in a loft over the stables, he would not be suspect[ed] by the Bishop even if I were captured there. So he hit on an idea. He put a bag of Indian Meal on my back, then I would dump the bag of meal and get up into the loft.[101] When I got out into the yard, the Free State fellows did not stop me. I went up into the loft and I hid myself in a pile of hay and from there I went up to the collar

---

96 In all the brigade areas there were men who would not get involved in fighting against their former comrades. The neutral IRA appealed to de Valera, Liam Lynch, William Cosgrave and Richard Mulcahy for a truce of one month, but their efforts were unsuccessful.

97 Kevin O'Higgins was Minister of Home Affairs in the Free State government and agreed to the execution policy adopted by the government.

98 Parts of pages from 63R to 64L have been moved here so they would be in better chronological order.

99 Dr Harry Rowland (not Roland as in the original text) was from Crossmolina. Probably February 1923.

100 Jacob Naughton, bishop of Killala for sixty years, 1911–71.

101 Indian meal was maize or corn used to feed cattle. The locals called it 'Injun Meal'.

ties of the roof. The Staters hit me with the muzzle of a rifle up through the collar ties. They suspected Fr Tom and hadn't they both Tom Ruane and the doctor prisoners outside. Dr Rowland had a Mills Bomb in my haversack and they kicked the hell out of him. He didn't know at all that there was a bomb in it, and he was sent on to Galway Gaol. Ruane, in two weeks, escaped from Galway Gaol.

Dr Rowland was from Crossmolina. He was a brilliant student and in the Tan War he was friendly, and he joined in with us when Ballina Barracks (at the beginning of the Civil War) was sending a unit to Collooney. And in June when the unit went, he went with them also. This was in February of 1923. They gave him a hell of a time when he was arrested and in Ballina, afterwards. Mitchell was from somewhere from Ballinalee area.[102] He was on a mobile column of Staters: but was it him who was in charge of it, or not?

[68R] Men were arrested by degrees. At the Cease Fire in this Brigade we had about sixty to seventy men under arms, and we had three columns in use. It wasn't hard for columns to operate, but we found it hard to make contact with the Staters. They didn't move out much. We were moving about within half a mile of Ballina quite openly, and they'd only come out in a small raid, to raid a house. They [Staters] carried out a raid at Rays in Corbally. They were fired on for half an hour; our lads wished to get before [i.e. out ahead of] them, and they opened fire on them as they were going to Ballina, but they ran like hell and they skipped back. We used dug outs. We could move about openly, and we could go to pubs [69L] openly at night if we wanted to. It was only after the Cease Fire that they came into the area. And even the dugouts which we had, they never discovered them. From Bunnyconnellan North we could move.

102 Mitchell was a Free State army officer from Ballinalee, Co. Longford.

From Tobbercurry North the Free State army never went into it.

I was out to get hold of Tom Carney so that we could combine the two Brigades to bring off an operation on a Foxford Free State post before the Cease Fire.[103] Liam Deasy's decision – this created suspicion and it had a slowing down effect.[104] That was the first we knew of an approach to a surrender. (Did something crop up in October or November previous?) It produced, and meant for us, suspense and uncertainty. It slowed down the keeping up of pressure, and it made for a slowing down of interest in further activities. The Staters held Ballina and strongly, at least 200 of them. Not until after the Cease Fire did they come in to here and to Dromore West. We had a terrible time then. And I was arrested in the following September.[105] The people remained staunch, but the people that were opposed to us, as in Easky and in other areas, got worse then.

I was brought to Ballina and to Galway which was good at this stage. Many of the restrictions had been taken off then, and it was being emptied. I came on to Hare Park in time for the hunger strike.[106] There was no tunnel in my time there. Kilroy got out of it during my period.[107] I think the hunger strike was not started from [an] order.[108] It was voluntary for anyone to take

---

103 Tom Carney of Swinford, O/C East Mayo Brigade. See his interview.
104 Kilcawley is mistaken here: it was Liam Deasy (not Seán Leacy as in the original text) who signed a statement calling for a ceasefire after his capture in January 1922 which was then broadcast by the Free State in February.
105 September 1923, five months after the IRA ceasefire.
106 The hunger strike started in Mountjoy Gaol on 13 October 1923 and then spread to other camps as a show of sympathy. It lasted forty-one days, until 23 November.
107 Kilroy, who was initially in Mountjoy and Kilmainham, was perhaps then moved to Hare Park.
108 The question had been raised as to whether an order to go on hunger strike had been issued by the IRA headquarters or whether the prisoners started it independently.

part in it, but it was moved by the Camp Council that a hunger strike was taking place in other camps. Bob Barton opposed it in its early stages and he didn't come off it very willingly. It lasted from fourteen to sixteen days.[109] I was walking about up to the very last. 'Burgoo' (porridge) we got when we came off, and it nearly killed us.[110] We were tied completely. **[69R]** Some of us got colic and terrific pains. There was a desperate hunger which lasted for a full fortnight. A small bit of Bengers and Bovril.[111] The first four days were the bad days until home was contacted, and when you ate some biscuits and Bovril and oxo cubes you were only getting hungrier. There was not much meat dished up for a while. Dr Comer (Jack) was a great godsend.[112] He was very good, indeed.

We had a still made in Hut 13,[113] and we used treacle. I and another fellow who knew all about it, we were considering it, but we had the treacle and the yeast. To make the brew, boil the hot water, put in the treacle, then put in the yeast to make it ferment. At least ten to fourteen days it takes. Then we would distil it. We had a worm of a type and a bit of copper piping. Mick Martin from Galway was an engineer. Our office is out on Strand Hill road, a quarter of a mile out; and I go in practically every day.

109 Whereas the strikers in Kilmainham, where Kilroy, O'Malley and others were, lasted forty-one days.
110 Burgoo is a gruel made from thick oats and mixed with molasses.
111 Bovril is a drink made from meat extract. Bengers Food was a nourishing drink similar to Bovril (not Boveril as in the original text).
112 Jack Comer from Galway was active in the Irish Volunteers while studying medicine at University College Galway. After his graduation he established a practice in Clonaslee, Co. Laois, in July 1921 and became medical officer in the 3rd Southern Division. He was anti-Treaty and was not captured until February 1923 when he was interned in Maryborough Gaol and later in Tintown and Hare Park internment camps in the Curragh until June 1924.
113 Kilcawley is referring to the Tintown Camp in the Curragh.

[72R][114]

The summer sun was sinking low behind the western sea.

The lark's loud song sung hard in praise but it brought no joy to me.

The one I loved is gone for ere he left the tyrants den.

He fought till death and then he left the woodlands of Loughglynn.

---

114 Kilcawley's interview finishes with this verse. He probably told O'Malley of this ballad when talking about the Loughglynn Tan War incident, but it was not about MacDermot or Bergin as they were killed in April and this ballad refers to 'summer sun'. The song 'Woodlands of Loughglynn' was later sung by the Wolfe Tones.

P. J. RUTTLEDGE

(UCDA P17b/90, pp. 57-62 and P17b/97, pp. 45-47, 53-54)[1]

Patrick Joseph 'P. J.' Ruttledge (1892–1952) was born in Ardagh, near Ballina, Co. Mayo. He went to school at St Muredach's College, Ballina, and St Enda's College, Dublin. Having finished his law studies at Trinity College in 1918, he qualified as a solicitor and returned to start a practice in Ballina. He joined the Irish Volunteers in 1918, was the IRB Centre for North Mayo, and became intelligence officer of the North Mayo Brigade and later the 4th Western Division in 1921. He was arrested in November 1920 and imprisoned in Galway Gaol. In June 1921, while in prison, he was elected TD for North-West Mayo. He was released after the Truce and voted against the Treaty. He became vice-commandant of the IRA Western Command in September 1922, was on the Army Council and was made Minister for Home Affairs in November. He took over as acting president of the Irish Republic when Éamon de Valera resigned in August 1923 just before he was arrested.[2] He was a founding member of Fianna Fáil in 1926 and a government minister from 1932 to 1941. He married Helena Roddy of Dublin in 1928 and they had four children. They lived in Ballina and Dublin.

Courtesy of Mrs Emer Ryan (née Ruttledge)

---

1   Initial transcription of this interview was done by Roderick Ryan, grandson of P. J. Ruttledge. Throughout the original text Ruttledge's name was misspelled as 'Rutledge', and it has been corrected here.
2   De Valera's letter of resignation in which he appoints P. J. Ruttledge as acting president was dated 11 August 1923. See Ernie O'Malley Papers, NLI MS 10973.

This interview took place in Dublin in the late 1940s.

[1916–1921 PERIOD]

[90/57] [I was] Intelligence Officer, North Mayo Brigade, arrested November 1920 until the Truce.[3] Released as a TD. Galway Gaol: all right as gaols go.

Got six rifles and six rifles in all through Fitzgerald, early in 1920.[4]

Eglinton Street Barracks, a notorious place for beating up people.[5] Walsh murdered; Quirke and Costello murdered also.

Murphy, Chairman of Board of Commissioners, Dublin, cleared out then being afraid.[6] Then Galway said they were disorganised at that time.

[90/58R] 1918 Elections. I met Collins who sent for me. 'If someone doesn't go for N. Mayo that damned fellow will get in.'

[TRUCE PERIOD]

[90/57] 1921. O'Duffy went round end of August or September to form Divisions, and I was Intelligence Officer of the 4th Western.[7]

Reorganisation of IRB. Division Centre for North Mayo: Dick Walsh, Tom Maguire, Michael Kilroy County Centre, Ruane not present as he was in gaol, Dennis Sherrin Quartermaster, P. A. (Pat) Calleary,[8] now an engineer, and myself at a

---

3 In the original text this was written as 'I.O., N. Mayo Bde.'
4 Probably Desmond Fitzgerald, who was on the general headquarters staff in Dublin.
5 Eglinton Street RIC Barracks in Galway city, where British troops were stationed, was burned on 7 July 1922 at the start of the Civil War.
6 Seamus Murphy, O/C Galway Brigade, who moved to Dublin in 1920. See also O'Malley, *The Men Will Talk to Me: Galway Interviews*, p. 35.
7 Eoin O'Duffy (1892–1944) was deputy chief of staff at the time and was helping to organise local brigades into divisions around the country, but this was more likely during August or September, not October/November as in the original text.
8 Calleary, not Cealleary as in the original text.

meeting to elect a District Centre.

(Who was present from General Headquarters?) Mac-Andrew from Erris also some kind of a Centre brought in to the Midlands. I think Michael Kilroy would know.[9]

[Post-Treaty discussions.] Met at train by Joe McDonagh and others who came to Exchange Hotel. He was very bitter. Madden left word for me to call at Barry's whenever I got in, but train got in at 1 [a.m.] and I didn't go to see O'Duffy.[10]

O'Duffy, Paddy Hogan, Pádraic Ó Máille and O'Dwyer,[11] I think, and Seán T. O'Kelly on Stephen's Green on one side. [90/58R] Four of us, Seán T. ... P. J. ... Nothing came of that. (After the Division, five a side [were] appointed.)

Discussion. Nothing then brought up about Document No. 2 but the meeting was friendly.[12] O'Duffy did mention the chairmanship of the University and O'Dwyer wanted de Valera put in.[13]

Moylan[14]	MacEoin[15]
Mellows	[O']Dwyer
P. J. Ruttledge	Pádraic Ó Máille
	Price?[16]

---

9   Ruttledge probably means Michael Kilroy not Seamus Kilroy, as in the original text.

10 John A. Madden from Ballycastle. See biographical sketches.

11 Probably Seamus Dwyer (1886–1922), also known as O'Dwyer, a Sinn Féin activist from Rathmines, Dublin, who was pro-Treaty. See Michael McKenna http://www.theirishstory.com/2013/09/02/who-was-seamus-dwyer/#. Uk04jSR1OHl (accessed 2013).

12 Document No. 2 had been proposed by Éamon de Valera in the Dáil Éireann debate as an alternative to the Treaty.

13 The university is University College Dublin. The word university was abbreviated to 'Univ' in the original text.

14 This column lists anti-Treaty representatives at the discussion, including Seán Moylan.

15 This column lists pro-Treaty representatives at the discussion. Seán MacEoin, not McKeown as in the original text.

16 Probably Éamon 'Bob' Price, then director of organisation on GHQ staff.

Collins [was] not on it. This was in the Mansion House. The end of it was that Lynch was convinced that his position would be enough and felt that he should be at least Chief of Staff.

Pact. I went to Tipperary to do some meeting. I found both sides observed the Pact. An effort was made for Independents to go up but the individual parties did not support them. Dublin, and Cork had Larry O'Neill and Labour had …

Figgis had a hell of a hold of A. Griffith.[17] Always in Baileys with Seán Milroy and Figgis, A. Griffith.[18]

(Christie in Vaughan's, what happened to him, the porter?)[19] Dickie Walsh used to meet Mick Collins very often and would know something. He has a very good memory.

[90/58L] Taking over of places for Belfast Boycott.

Fintan Murphy, was he a clerk through Fitzgerald?

[90/59] Convention. Four Courts on Sunday, at which I presided.[20] It lasted only a few minutes, rejected the Agreement about Lynch not being Chief of Staff. They wanted to have more control. I don't think Lynch was there as he was forbidden [entry at] the Gate [of Four Courts].[21]

Derrig, Madden and Tom Maguire and I stayed on in the Exchange Hotel.[22] On [the] night of the attack[23] I was doing work for Boss Croker.[24] I met Needham from US representing Croker, a lawyer at Shelbourne, 8.30 [p.m.] – 11 returned to

---

17 Arthur Griffith, vice-president of Sinn Féin.
18 Baileys' was a public house on Duke Street, Dublin.
19 Vaughan's Hotel was at Parnell Square, Dublin. Michael Collins frequently met people up from the country there.
20 This anti-Treaty IRA convention was held on Sunday 16 June 1922.
21 There came a time in the discussions in mid-June when Liam Lynch was not allowed back into the Four Courts as he was effectively dismissed and a new chief of staff, Joe McKelvey of Belfast, was appointed.
22 Tom Derrig and Dr John Madden.
23 Referring to the Free State army attack on the Republican-held Four Courts on Thursday 28 June 1922.
24 Richard Croker.

Exchange.[25] We heard a movement in the street, and D[errig] told us they were placing guns. Derrig wanted to get into Four Courts Hotel.[26] Shooting started. Derrig, Kilroy and I knew that Lynch was in Clarence. [I] met Lynch, Liam Deasy. Liam Lynch ordered people back to their Units.[27]

I was Director of Civil Administration in the Four Courts … Conor Maguire [was] to take over all the land and divide it up. They worked on this document. It was sent up to every Unit.

[CIVIL WAR]

We met Feehan.[28] We went into Barry's [Hotel] and that night it was decided to evacuate and take over [the] Gresham [Hotel]. Furlong [was] killed crossing Parnell Street. Feehan, Tom Maguire and Kilroy went back.

Moss Twomey [was] in the Gresham or Hammam [Hotel]. I remember Liam Lynch saying that everyone should go back to their Units. Twomey, Seán McCarthy to get back. We went out from Gresham to Wicklow by York Street. Jim Ryan, Brian O'Higgins [were] there. We waited there and went off.

[90/60] Derrig and I went on towards Blessington. Near Templeogue we saw Moss Twomey and Seán McCarthy coming out of a pub, and Derrig waited there, and we went on to Mallow. We weren't stopped anywhere. [We spent] a day in Mallow trying to go west, but Liam Lynch told me to stay. I went to Limerick with Liam Lynch.[29] We met O'Hannigan to

---

25 The Dublin hotels referred to here and following are the Shelbourne Hotel, Exchange Hotel, Clarence Hotel and Four (written as 'F' in the original text) Courts Hotel.

26 Derrig's name is written here and later as T. D.

27 Lynch's name is abbreviated here and later in the text to L/L.

28 Jack Feehan of Kilmeena was quartermaster of the 4th Western Division and anti-Treaty. See his interview in O'Malley, *The Men Will Talk to Me: Galway Interviews*, pp. 99–186.

29 Limerick is abbreviated to Limk in the original text.

arrange a truce.[30] Then he saw Brennan and Bishop in Ennis.[31] I waited outside in [a] car. We met with Seán Lehane on his way to Donegal, in Limerick.[32] I went on with Seán Lehane, met Tom Maguire in Ballinrobe, through to Ballina where I left him. Kilroy wanted to push on across the Shannon but there wasn't much stuff to do anything with.

Collooney.[33] Some of our men went to help Pilkington but a good number [were] captured there. Pilkington took 'The Ballinalee'[34] [and] had promised it for a Mayo operation.[35] Kilroy and I got to Millmount near Tobbercurry, but Carty wanted to attack Tobbercurry despite our wishes.[36] They brought in the armoured car but they didn't capture any part of the town. That night we brought 'The Ballinalee' but it stuck a few times. [We] left [it] in Glenreigh, outside Ballina. Next day we were told the Staters knew of the car being where it was and she [a girl] said she heard that two bridges near Ballina would be mined. They waited all night but we went in [the] next day. The Free State had the Post Office and [we wanted] a mine to be laid underneath the Post Office.[37] [The] Post Office [was] taken [by us]; the Moy Hotel, P. J.['s] office, Workhouse, the Railway Station; about 135 rifles [were] captured.

---

30 Probably Donnacha Ó Hannacháin or O'Hannigan (not Hannigan as in the original text).

31 Michael Brennan was appointed O/C, 1st Western Division, in August 1921 and went pro-Treaty.

32 Seán Lehane from Cork was on his way north to become O/C, 1st Northern Division of anti-Treaty forces.

33 Collooney, Co. Sligo (not Cooloney as in the original text), about fifteen miles south of Sligo town, was attacked by the Free State army on 15 July 1922.

34 'The Ballinalee' was an armoured car that was captured from the Free State forces. In the original text an armoured car is often referred to as 'a/c' or 'a/ car'.

35 Liam/Billy/William Pilkington of Sligo was O/C, 3rd Western Division in 1921. He was a member of the IRA Executive.

36 Frank Carty from Sligo. See biographical sketches.

37 Post office is abbreviated to P.O. in the original text.

That evening at dusk [Michael] Kilroy wanted a lathe at the Quay. Crossmolina people fired at us from Gorteens Hill. M[ichael went] to view the North Coast road [and took] the armoured car with him. [There was] an ambush **[90/61]** on North Coast road, outside Bunnyconnellan:[38] eleven of ours [were] caught, six Free Staters killed including Ring.[39] Tony Lawlor [was] wounded a few times.[40] [There was a] delay in laying the mine and the Free Staters got in on the flank for the mine was in the hand cart.

Devins and company met Staters in the mist wearing caps. Four [men] shot there, and two [shot] on the way into Sligo.

Two Free Staters [were] captured in an ambush, and when our fellows were captured they would have been shot only for a priest. Mulcahy used this afterwards.[41] Tony Lawlor [was] in charge then and would be responsible for the shooting.

Adamson of Athlone inquiry.[42] Price and Tom Hales and Seán McCarthy were on this. I cross-examined Tony Lawlor. I said, 'Do you know anything about discipline?'

'Yes,' he said. 'I was in two armies,' and I said, 'Were any of them by any chance the IRA?' He had this against me and was anxious to get me.

Knockmore, near Pontoon, bad even in 1918 election.[43]

Laidlawn, bad also even in 1918 election.

[97/45L] IRB. Centre IRB for Mayo. Kilroy, Centre for

---

38 Ruttledge is mistaken here as Bunnyconnellan (not Bunnaconlan as in the original text) is inland and not near the coast road.
39 Joe Ring from Westport.
40 General Anthony 'Tony' B. Lawlor was pro-Treaty and in charge of a major sweep by their Western Command.
41 Richard Mulcahy, former IRA chief of staff and then Free State Minister for Defence.
42 There was an inquiry in Athlone at to the killing on 24 April Brigadier General George Adamson of the Free State army.
43 'Bad' probably refers to the area not being supportive of the Republican cause.

West Mayo.[44] Tom Maguire, for South Mayo.[45] MacAndrew, Killtane, for Erris.

Harry Boland told me of the IRB after the Treaty meeting.

There was a proposed reorganisation of the IRB. A fellow from General Headquarters, whose name I forget, met me at the Central Hotel, Ballina. He was to extend and reorganise the IRB or rather he invited me to do it. He wanted me to reorganise the area, but I said I wasn't keen on doing that.

About September 1921 or October there was an IRB meeting in Ballinasloe which I did not attend as I was sick at the time, but Michael Kilroy would know about it.

(Paddy Ruttledge tried to reconstruct the Supreme Council for me: Mr Seán Ó Muirthile, Fionán Lynch (old IRB), Diarmuid O'Hegarty, Sceilig (old IRB), Collins, Gearóid O'Sullivan, Seán McGarry, Hobson (old IRB), Dinny Mc-Cullough (old IRB).)[46]

On Sunday, before matches in Croke Park, the IRB would meet in Dublin. The GAA was a great blind and an organisation which had a good deal to do with the IRB as under **[97/45R]** cover of a football match men could travel without suspicion and come together.

(Ruttledge[47] took part in the political conferences which both parties held before the Pact.[48] He could not remember who was on either side except:

---

44 Michael Kilroy of Newport. See his interview.
45 Tom Maguire of Cross. See his interview.
46 This paragraph appears to be in the words of Ernie O'Malley and thus has been put in parentheses to be consistent. The references are to Seán Ó Muirthile, not O'Muirth as in the original text; Fionán or Finian Lynch, not Finnian as in the original text; J. J. 'Sceilig' O'Kelly, often referred to as merely Sceilig, not to be confused with Seán T. O'Kelly; Michael Collins; and Bulmer Hobson.
47 This paragraph also appears to be by O'Malley and has been put in parentheses.
48 The Election Pact between Éamon de Valera and Michael Collins was signed on 20 May 1921, and the elections were held on 16 June 1921.

Ruttledge   Pádraic Ó Máille[49]

Liam Mellows[50]   MacEoin[51]

                   O'Dwyer of Rathmines.[52]

They met in the Mansion House, but nothing was really agreed on.)

I met Dev later. 'Will you try to get these army fellows, IRA, to arrive at some arrangement soon?' he said to me.

Liam Lynch[53] thought that whatever job he was offered on the composite staff, that if he got it, he would be able to control the army.[54] He was very persistent in this belief. As Inspector General he felt that he would have great control. In these arrangements, the Free Staters would grant us any position except Chief of Staff.

[97/46L] South Tipperary meeting.[55] This was an Executive Meeting. Dinny Lacy was killed about ten days afterwards.[56] I came up to Dublin with Liam Lynch.[57] We were surrounded in Myshall near Graiguenamanagh across the river on the south side.[58] We crossed the river. The houses were clean and a great contrast to the other side. I remember what you had said about it as you were going to clean it up once as Joe said it was a dreadful area.[59] Anyhow we drove to Myshall. The place

---

49 Pádraic Ó Máille, not O Maillie or O'Malley as sometimes in the original text.

50 Liam Mellows, not Mellowes as in the original text.

51 Probably Seán MacEoin, not McKeown as in the original text.

52 Seamus Dwyer (or O'Dwyer as in the original text) was from Rathmines.

53 Liam Lynch was then O/C, 1st Southern Division and in April 1922 became chief of staff of the anti-Treaty IRA Republicans.

54 Referring to the army that would be created by rejoining the pro-Treaty and anti-Treaty sections of the former united IRA.

55 The anti-Treaty executive committee met over 16–17 October 1922 in Tipperary. See minutes in Ernie O'Malley Papers, NLI MS 10973.

56 Dinny Lacy (not Lacey as in the original text) was O/C, 3rd Tipperary Brigade, flying column, IRA.

57 On Friday 3 November 1922, the evening before Ernie O'Malley was captured.

58 Myshall, Co. Carlow (not Meyshell as in the original text).

59 Ruttledge is referring to an earlier conversation with O'Malley and calling him 'you'.

was supposed to be surrounded by the Free State who had evidently taken the two of us for a column of IRA. After that we drove to Barry's of Hacketstown[60] in a pony and trap and left for Annamoe.[61] We couldn't see the road over the mountains. Sometimes we were on it, other times not. We half walked, half wandered.

The Vice-Commandant of Carlow said to Liam, 'What will you do if we're stopped?'

'I know what I'll say,' said Liam pulling his gun. Then they got to Bartons.[62] Miss Barton said, 'Half these fellows here, the employees, are Free State.'[63] She showed us where the dump was. The only Free Stater who knew of it was Éamon Fleming, and he wouldn't talk about it we felt. We found Murphy there.[64]

[97/46R] (The Deacon) who had been in the British Air Force. He had come out by car from Dublin, and he told us we were to be brought into Humphreys that evening.[65] D. L. Robinson and Erskine Childers were there. Childers said that he intended to go to Gogarty as his throat was sore, and when we protested Childers said that professional etiquette would be honoured by Gogarty.[66] Máire Comerford had also come out for us. Dev wanted to see Lynch and myself so we went into Dev's place in Mount Street, where we stayed the night. Next morning we heard about the attack on you in Humphreys'

---

60 Co. Carlow.
61 The home of Robert Barton and Erskine Childers was located in Annamoe, Co. Wicklow.
62 The home of Robert Barton in Annamoe.
63 Dulcilabel or Da Barton was a sister of Robert Barton.
64 Murphy could be Humphrey Murphy, who moved in those circles.
65 Mrs Ellen Humphreys of 36 Ailesbury Road, Donnybrook, Dublin, was the sister of The O'Rahilly, who died in Easter Week 1916. Ernie O'Malley managed his Northern and Eastern Division headquarters from her upstairs secret room and was wounded when arrested there on the morning of 4 November 1922.
66 Oliver St John Gogarty, a medical doctor and at the time a member of the Free State senate.

house.[67] We stayed with Mrs Keane in No. 16 Upper Mount Street.[68] There was a dump there for Dev. Once there had been a raid for Dev, but Fr Paddy Brown, who was there, got into bed, and the raid did not find out the hiding place. They got Seán Russell to make it at the top of the house in a maid's room. There were two maids' rooms. We used to sleep there, Donal O'Callaghan and I.[69]

I then stayed with Liam Lynch and Moss Twomey at Ballymun most of the time.[70] Barry[71] and Fr Duggan came to see us.[72] At first Barry did not press the point about surrender. It looked as if he had come up to satisfy some of the people [97/47L] in the south who wanted to surrender. The first time Duggan was not with him. The second time he was and so was Crofts.[73] Lynch was in a hell of a state for Miss O'Donnell showed the way to Barry. It was she who brought him there. She might be followed, Liam felt, for he didn't meet many people at that time. Barry had a gun strapped on his leg. He was sneering at us for being afraid. He had helped to take three posts in Kilkenny. Later we found out that he had a free pass from the Staters. That is why he could stay in the Hibernian and carry a gun.

---

67 Reference to O'Malley's capture on the morning of 4 November 1922.

68 Mrs Keane (shortened to Mrs K in the original text) kept a safe house at No. 16 Upper Mount Street, where Éamon de Valera often stayed. The original text referred to No. 11.

69 Donal (not Donald as in the original text) O'Callaghan was the deputy lord mayor of Cork to Terence MacSwiney in 1920. In 1923 he was a member of de Valera's Republican cabinet and was one of the people asked publicly to surrender by Liam Deasy on 29 January 1923 when Deasy was captured.

70 Ballymun, on the outskirts of Dublin, had become Liam Lynch's headquarters when he came to Dublin in November 1922.

71 Tom Barry, born in Co. Kerry, fought with the British Army in Mesopotamia in 1917 and came to live in Bandon. He commanded the 3rd Cork Brigade flying column and was anti-Treaty. He was captured and interned, but escaped.

72 Fr Thomas Duggan.

73 Tom Crofts was adjutant, 1st Southern Division, in August 1922, and its officer commanding in April 1923.

Tom Crofts told us the point of view of the Cork men who thought the game was up and who wanted to surrender, but he didn't press their point of view as did Barry. The officers in Cork according to Crofts had decided that they could not succeed. He himself felt he could not carry on any longer. Liam Lynch paid a lot of attention to Crofts.

Lynch had a hell of a lot of dependence on the West. 'We have the West to depend on,' he'd say. He was determined to carry on the fight.

I got flu when that last meeting was to have been held in **[97/47R]** the South. Dev went down to near Kilkenny. Derrig[74] had gone down a week previously on the death of Liam Lynch.[75] For the next meeting I was told to go on to Shipton.[76] Dev wanted to hold it [the meeting] in Dublin. Aiken was down there (in the South?).[77] It must have been General Headquarters and Seán Hyde wanted it held there, but Dev thought Dublin best as Prout had that southern area surrounded.[78] Dev got a note … a girl with a car and a driver. Finley, who had a taxi in Camden Street, used to drive Dev who was still in Mrs K[eane]'s.

I received the last letter that Liam Lynch wrote, sent to me (from) Raglan road, about who would be Adjutant General, and I was the first to occur to him, but he was killed a few days later.[79] Dev said to me, 'I don't agree with the meeting being held in the south, but the girl who meets you will get you through.' She was a nice girl – I can't remember her name (eventually it turned out

74 Tom Derrig from Westport. See biographical sketches.
75 Liam Lynch was killed on 10 April 1923.
76 Shipton, Co. Kilkenny, is south-west of Kilkenny town and near Callan on the Co. Tipperary border.
77 Frank Aiken, O/C, 4th Northern Division. He succeeded Liam Lynch as chief of staff in April 1923.
78 J. T. Prout was an American soldier who became a Free State army general.
79 Adjutant general is abbreviated to A/G in the original text. Derrig had been adjutant general when captured on 6 April 1923, and it appears from this comment that Lynch was considering having Ruttledge replace him.

to be Mae Tobin of Tincurry).[80] I stopped at Carneys outside of Kilkenny, he was then the County Registrar, for tea. I got a message later that night to go on four miles. I went on. I met a guide who took me there but the meeting was then over. I met Tom Ruane, O/C North Mayo.[81] (From my notes it may have also been Seán Dowling he met.) There was a **[97/53L]** dump at the end of the stables. (Evidently another meeting was held.) I was amazed at Barry. He was advocating a 'Cease Fire'. They couldn't carry on the fight, and it was thrown back to Dev to arrange terms. The army were now 'passing the buck' to the politicals. Tom Ruane was for keeping on the fight and Billy Pilkington. Pilkington had already met Dev and Frank Aiken at Ballymun.

Afterwards the Army Council was to arrange terms of surrender or cease fire. Pilkington's point of view was that there could be no surrender – that we couldn't have a 'cease fire' no matter what would be the result of the fight to us. He couldn't see that we had any right to surrender.

Ruane got away from Galway. They never had a real dose of the Free Staters in Sligo. That was why they were more optimistic there. Frank Carty shot five or six people, spies, without orders from General Headquarters. They were mostly ex-soldiers. Liam Lynch was very disturbed that he had not been notified. Ruane's area also shot a few spies.[82]

Executive. The huge majority was for pushing back the decision on to the Army Council, especially those men from **[97/53R]** the South as they felt their position was hopeless.

---

80 Mae Tobin was the daughter of Mrs Marion Tobin of Tincurry House, near Cahir, Co. Tipperary. Headquarters for O'Malley's 2nd Southern Division in early 1921 was close to her house until the house was destroyed by the RIC.

81 Tom Ruane, not Rowane as in the original text. See biographical sketches.

82 Ruttledge's comment of Ruane's area shooting spies is not consistent with the views expressed by Michael Kilroy and Broddie Malone that no spies were shot in their areas.

They specified no conditions at the time. Pilkington could not see how we could end the war even by 'Cease Fire'. Dev put up ceasefire. Then he said, 'We'll wait and see what will happen.'

Donal O'Callaghan (ESB Dun Laoghaire).[83] I found him an extremely rude bastard when I tried to get information, mainly because I knew his O'Sullivan relatives of West Cork and I tried to get him to talk about Luzio.[84] In all Ireland he was the rudest. He went out to see the Pope when de Valera was in gaol, himself and Con Murphy.[85] He told us when he came back that Luzio was in disgrace in Rome because when he reported back there he had stated that the Republicans were right. Borgoneira, I think, was Cardinal Secretary of State then, but they never got further than him.[86] The Pope wouldn't see them unless they were prepared to accept his laws as laid down by the Bishops. It was through Hales,[87] who had been Consul at Genoa, that they saw B[orgoneira].[88] Donal knew French. 'There was no one available,' the ecclesiastics said, 'who knew English.' So Con Murphy said: 'You are all pro-British – they have you on a string' (this place is festooned with pro-Britishers), to which the Cardinal Secretary said knowingly, 'We serve only God.'

It was said that some kind of a note came to the Free State about releasing prisoners or giving them decent treatment but it had no effect on them.

---

83 At the time of this interview Donal (not Donald as in the original text) O'Callaghan was working with the Electricity Supply Board or ESB.

84 Rt Rev Monsignor Salvatore Luzio, who had been a professor of canon law at Maynooth College, 1897–1910, had been appointed a special papal envoy to help initiate a peace settlement in Ireland.

85 Pope Benedict XV.

86 Cardinal Gasparri (not Borgoneira as in the text) was in fact Cardinal Secretary of State at the time.

87 Donal Hales (not Donald as used later in the original text) was the Irish consul in Genoa, Italy.

88 Borgoneira (not 'B' as in the original text) but referring to Gasparri.

[97/54L] Seán Hyde was at the last Executive Meeting. He would know about [O']Dwyer, once a TD, killed in Rathmines. He was said to be head of Free State Intelligence then. He had built up an Intelligence system and was in charge of it.

Micky Carolan, our Director of Intelligence, was supposed to get houses for people who were on the run, but as far as I can judge he never did anything about it.[89] I could not see that he was any good. I once met Micky during the Truce. He was then a traveller, in the West, but he was learning about himself – what he had done and what not.

Seán Goulding, O/C 'A' Company, works with Francis the tailor in Blessington Street, might verify about Noel Lemass.[90]

O'Keeffe, Company Adjutant, and I saw the gun in Wine-tavern Street. Twelve men [were] visible near the gun but I don't know what men were in the houses around.[91] I came back, and I said you could take the gun easily enough. This was on Thursday for I got back to York Street after reconnoitring.[92]

[90/61] Executive. Liam Lynch and I went to Dublin through Goatenbridge.[93] Bulreys of Hacketstown (Myshall in Carlow before this – surrounded him but the Free Staters thought there was a column and that more would come through and [were] waiting for reinforcements), across Michael Dwyer's, Military road to Annamoe (Éamon Fleming [was] the only one who knew of the Barton dump). The Deacon Murphy said a car would come at 8 p.m. next night. Childers and Robinson [were] there.[94] He wanted to be examined by Gogarty as Erskine

89 Anti-Treaty IRA director of intelligence (not D/I as in the original text).
90 Reference to the killing of Noel Lemass, a brother of Seán Lemass, in July 1923.
91 The gun could have been the artillery used by the Free State army to bombard the Four Courts.
92 Thursday 28 June 1922.
93 In south Co. Tipperary. This is a slightly different version of the story from 90/46L–R.
94 Erskine Childers and David L. Robinson.

Childers' throat was bad. Car came out to return to 16 Lower Mount Street to where Dev was.[95] Then you were shot up as they were to have gone to Humphreys'. Máire Comerford made the other arrangement.

[90/62R] Mount Street: Mrs Keane. Mrs Keane under [the] name of Williams or Cassidy of Brown Bread, one married to a man, Fitzgerald, in Ballymun. You couldn't get out.[96] Madge Clifford joined us there.[97] Liam Lynch and P. J. [were] there and often Tom Derrig.[98]

Ballymun House. Nan carried in/out dispatches. [I was] there until the meeting in the south, but I was laid up by the flu.

Barry, Tom Duggan[99] [and] Tom Crofts arrived up one night, but Liam Lynch said there was a debate in the South and they couldn't carry on.[100] Miss O'Donnell of Eccles Street came out with Fr Duggan.

Barry came out to see Lynch and he had a bloody machine gun tied on to his leg. 'We should walk out and not be afraid of anyone.' He was staying at the Hibernian Hotel. He was always very annoying to Liam Lynch stating he'd fight but no one else would fight. Dev went down South with Tom Derrig, John Dowling and Liam Lynch. Dev came back after Lynch's death.[101] I was told there was to be a meeting in the S[outh],

---

95 No. 16 Mount Street, not No. 11 as in the original text.

96 This comment probably refers to the fact that they were in effect confined to the Ballymun premises for security reasons and did not want to go outside in case they might be recognised. Visitors came to them there.

97 Madge Clifford of Kerry had been O'Malley's Cumann na mBan assistant and after his capture in November 1922 she worked for Liam Lynch and others. She later married Dr Jack Comer of Galway.

98 Presumably Ruttledge referred to himself here but O'Malley had written 'P. J.' in the original text.

99 Fr Thomas Duggan.

100 The debate referred to whether or not the Republicans should cease their activities against the Free State.

101 A meeting of the Army Council was held in Shipton and so the leaders went down 'South' to attend. References in the original text were made to 'T.D.' for Tom Derrig and 'L/L' for Liam Lynch, who was killed on 10 April 1923.

but said the meeting should be held in Dublin. Later heard of a girl who was coming up to escort us down. Free State soldiers [were] all over the place.

Shipton was the meeting place in a barn. ... (Barry, Frank Aiken, John Joe Rice, Crofts, Quirke, Ruttledge, Dowling, Derrig, Tom Ruane, O/C North Mayo.)[102] Meeting started again. It was left to the *first* to decide in conjunction with General Headquarters staff. Barry agreed to this. Barry's attitude was that he'd fight on but that no one else would. Crofts felt hopeless. In the West we weren't getting much trouble. Tom Ruane was definitely for carrying on, but he was the only one.

Saturday, I stayed there. I left on Sunday with Frank Aiken after Mass. We were held up fourteen or fifteen times **[90/62L]** on the way. P. J. in bad form as eighty of our fellows had escaped out of Newbridge the night before.[103]

A meeting held in Ballymun. Dev there, Frank Aiken, P. J. Ruttledge, Pilkington there.[104] His [Pilkington's] attitude was that we'd have to fight to the end. Meeting decided a 'Cease Fire' and a month given for the negotiations or a possibility of them.

I stayed on in Ballymun with F. Aiken.

[In] 12 Raglan Road, Tom Derrig [was] caught the day after he changed his place.[105]

15 August [1923]. [Dev to] go away on a Monday to stop this business of being on the run. He said I was to come in to take his place.[106] I got a note on Thursday from Dev that there

---

102 References are to Tom Barry, John Joe Rice of Kerry, Tom Crofts, Bill Quirke, P. J. Ruttledge, John Dowling, Tom Derrig and Tom Ruane (not Rohane as in the original text).

103 Newbridge internment camp associated with Newbridge Barracks, Co. Kildare.

104 References to Frank Aiken and P. J. Ruttledge were 'FA' and 'P. J.' in the original text.

105 Reference to Tom Derrig was 'Tom D.' in the original text. He was adjutant general when he was caught on 6 April 1923.

106 Referring to de Valera.

were a lot of things to be talked about. About an hour after I left, Ballymun was raided, 4 p.m. to 2 next day whilst Aiken was in the dump. Then I stayed on in Mount Street.

Headford shooting.[107] Four fellows picked out from a bunch who paraded, [including] Tom Maguire's brother. They were put in a lorry, brought to Headford and were executed when they arrived. There had been an ambush in Headford. Dick Walsh was then in Galway Gaol. Tried when you went in, but you didn't know when you'd be shot.[108] They were three to four months in gaol.

(Mrs O'Brien, 39 Blessington Street on Dick Bell.)

Waterford. Men marched in town to another ... gaol and they sang as they marched to death.

---

107 The Republicans attempted to capture Headford Barracks, then held by the Free State, and several Free State soldiers were killed. As a reprisal for the attack on 11 April 1923 the Free State army executed six Republicans in Tuam, including Tom Maguire's brother, Seán.

108 'Tried' meaning court-martialled.

EAST MAYO

JOHNNY GREALY[1]

(UCDA P17b/113, pp. 1–9)[2]

John 'Johnny' Grealy (1894–1979) was
born in Cloongawnah, Shanwall, Toureen,
Aghamore, just north of Ballyhaunis. He
joined the Irish Volunteers in 1914 and
later the IRB. He was employed by the
Department of Agriculture until he was
dismissed in 1919 while he was part of
the Crossard Company, 4th Battalion of
the East Mayo Brigade. He then went
'on the run' and participated in many
local actions in East Mayo during the Tan War including the
Enniscrone Coast Guard Station attack. He went anti-Treaty and
was in Dublin during the attack on the Four Courts. He returned
to Mayo but was captured in late 1922, interned in the Curragh
during the Civil War and released in March 1924. He married
May Healy from Belderg, Ballina. They had five children and in
later years lived in Donadea, Co. Kildare.

*Courtesy of
Seamus Grealy*

This interview probably took place in Co. Kildare in March
1950.

---

1   The family name is Grealy, not Greely or Griely as sometimes in the original
    text.
2   The initial transcription of this interview and some footnotes were done by
    Dominic Price.

[1914–1921 PERIOD]

[1aR][3] I joined the Irish Volunteers in 1914, and Dick Walsh took me in.[4] I went into Athenry the week after Liam Mellows took over the College.[5] A pig man, Cronin, turned state evidence against the lads from the College who went out with Liam Mellows, for there were three or four from the Agricultural College with him. Cronin, the informer, had to have police protection.

I was in the 4th Battalion of the East Mayo Brigade. Seán Corcoran was O/C [of] the Brigade. He was laying an ambush with me and himself and Maurice Mullins came to see me. There was an RIC man who rushed the shed where the lads were drilling in Ballyhaunis, and they arrested fifteen of the men. Seán put it to the meeting that this peeler should be shot. Joe Sheehy, Brigade Quartermaster, and Seán Corcoran came to me, and they asked if there was anyone to shoot him, and I said I would do it if I was given a gun.[6]

There was a Tan, who was an Intelligence Officer[7] in Ballyhaunis in 1921, and he was getting information from the geassers there.[8] 'If you can't get Slattery **[1bR]** get Stephens,' he said.[9] Kilkelly, who is now dead, came along with me.[10] We got the Tan, and poor Seán came over for we heard that Curley's

3   O'Malley numbered successive pages, 1a and 1, and these are marked here as **[1aR]** and **[1bR/L]**.

4   Richard 'Dick' Walsh of Balla. See biographical sketches.

5   Liam Mellows was sent by the GHQ of the Irish Volunteers from Dublin to organise and mobilise the Irish Volunteers in Co. Galway in 1916. The mobilisation centre chosen was the Agricultural College at Athenry. After the Rising Mellows hid out in North Clare before going to New York in October 1916.

6   Seán Corcoran was O/C, East Mayo Brigade.

7   Intelligence Officer is abbreviated to I/O in the original text.

8   'Geassers' is a local expression meaning men.

9   It seems likely that Grealy means Black and Tan Constable William H. Stephens here (not Stevenson as in the original text), as it was Stephens who was killed on 29 March 1920 by Grealy.

10 Jim Kilkelly.

house was to be burned, and we went to get rifles to defend it.[11] Seán and Maurice Mullins were supposed to call at this house, but when he was coming over Seán ran into a patrol of Tans. His revolver jammed at the first shot and he was shot dead, and Mullins, who was unarmed, was beaten almost to death. They beat him there and they threw him in on top of the dead Seán Corcoran in the turf house of the barracks.

Ballyhaunis RIC. One peeler there, Flynn, would give information. He sent word to me about the Tans who were raiding for me, and he asked me to save him if I could for he had a wife and a family and was near his pension. If they had got a guarantee from Collins[12] or from us that the [pension][13] would have been looked after, they would have given information. Paddy Mullins was Brigade O/C in 1921.[14]

In 1919 I was put on to a job at a dance. At that time I was working in Roscommon for the Department of Agriculture. I used to have to go to the RIC barracks to get maps of the farmers' holdings to find out what acreage they had under tillage, and I could give information then to Bill Doherty of the Department of Agriculture about arms there.[15] But the RIC copped on to me.

I used to come home on Sundays. There was a dance at the schoolhouse in Aghamore for the Gaelic League.[16] There was a family there that had three sons in the RIC, and the parents had refused to ask their sons to leave the Force.[17] One of them

11 Seán Corcoran, O/C, East Mayo Brigade, was killed on 1 April 1921.
12 Michael Collins.
13 The word pension has been added as many of the RIC were waiting their time within the RIC to keep their pensions. The IRA was not in a position to offer a pension replacement if they left the RIC.
14 Paddy Mullins, brother of Maurice Mullins, took over as O/C, East Mayo Brigade, after Seán Corcoran's death.
15 Possibly Liam O'Doherty.
16 Aghamore, not Aughamore as in the original text.
17 The RIC referred to their organisation as the 'Force'.

came home with another RIC man, and they went to Kilkelly, and after a few drinks he said that he'd go ankle deep in Sinn Féin blood. They went down to get a **[1bL]** girl from the Post Office to go to the dance with them as she was a sergeant's daughter.[18] The local Company had a meeting on, and Crossard Company was told of the RIC by the Intelligence Officer in Kilkelly.[19] They called me, and they asked me if I was used to a shotgun, and I said that I would want another chap with me so we brought the two guns, and we went to the dance.

After the first dance the RIC went down to the local pubs for the local girls wouldn't dance with them. We had shotguns in a field, and we waited for an hour, and I went to the pub, but they were in there drinking. I had a few drinks, but when I came up to the field the other lad had gone so …

Mulcrannan was the peeler who was to go ankle deep in Sinn Féin blood. He was the most badly wounded, and it is said that he afterwards joined the Tans. There was loose talk about this, and the RIC raided for me in several places, but I went back to my work. I got into a scrap with an RIC man in Ballyhaunis, a North of Ireland man. There was a dance for the Volunteers in the Town Hall. They were knocking at a door for drink in a house where there was a spy. The RIC came up and they struck me and I was arrested. I was to give a written apology to the District Inspector RIC for I struck the **[2R]** man who hit me, but I refused to give this apology so I lost my job.

There was spying going on in Ballyhaunis. We got a fellow from our village. The fellows fired on him, but only one bullet took effect. This was during the Truce. He came back, but they shot him and three sergeants who were wounded in St Bridget's

18 Post office is written as P.O. in the original text.
19 Company and Intelligence Officer are abbreviated to 'Co' and 'I/O' in the original text.

Hospital in Galway.[20] His father had been a bailiff, and my father had been the head of the Fenians and for this spy's father, Cassidy, the police made a barracks out of a stables to protect him. He was wounded one night, the son, and he was killed the next night.

I left the Department in 1919. The headquarters of the 4th Battalion was in Ballyhaunis. The RIC evacuated Knock and three or four other stations. Cloonbrook (?) where we had an ambush on the Tans out there. ... Kenny was wounded attacking soldiers on the road who were guarding lorries which had broken down. Ballyhaunis. RIC ... military. They would take over Moyletts' Hall for a weekend. Claremorris, the headquarters for the military, Kilkelly, Charlestown, Ballaghaderreen was well held.[21] Kiltimagh well held.

The police strength was withdrawn from outlying places and ... the RIC strength was added to in the towns.

Barracks: Crossard, Ballyhaunis, Loughboy, Aghamore, Coolgarra, Kilkelly, Brickeens,[22] Kiltimagh, Charlestown, Kilmovee, Lisacul,[23] Carracastle,[24] Ballaghaderreen.

We had no arms save shotguns. There were a couple of rifles but you couldn't be sure of them. We fired off **[2L]** ammunition from Seán Corcoran's rifles, but only an odd round went off. We had very few short arms. We had an ambush on a broken down military lorry. The soldiers went in to a hut about thirty

---

20 St Bridget's Hospital, not St Bride's as in the original text. Patrick Cassidy of Aghamore was in the hospital recovering from wounds of 6 March 1922 when he was shot again on 15 March along with three RIC men, two fatally (T. Gibbons of Westport and J. Gilmartin of Oughterard) and one seriously wounded (Constable P. McGloin of Cahergrove). Cassidy survived and returned home and was killed as described.

21 Ballaghaderreen is used throughout this interview instead of Ballahadreen or Ballaghadreen, the spellings used in the original text.

22 Brickeens is used throughout this interview instead of Bricins, the spelling used in the original text.

23 Lisacul, not Lisacill as in the original text.

24 Carracastle, not Carrickcastle as in the original text.

or forty of them, and we attacked the hut, and didn't lorry loads of soldiers, who had come on from Claremorris by chance, hear the firing and came on our way.[25] Kenny was coming out with five or six rifles in his arms when he was wounded by one of our fellows, and we lost the rifles. P. Kenny was in charge of that attack, but he was not good enough for he should have taken the hut. There must have been four or five soldiers wounded there. Also we held up a train near Brickeens which was carrying steel shutters for Westport, and we buried them in a bog.

There were a number of fellows who wanted to fight, but the officers stopped them from fighting.

Ballyhaunis was bad at this kind of thing. Once Ballyhaunis Barracks was attacked for three or four hours to keep troops away from other places when we were doing something.

Ballaghaderreen Barracks. There was a mine placed in a cart of hay by Eugene Kelly. The lads wheeled the cart down but it was in such a way that it wouldn't blow up the barracks, but even then the mine didn't go off.

[3R] Intelligence was not well organised here for very seldom did we get any tips in time to be of use to us.

Tans. When there was any harm done, they came down to my village. They came to Curley's house where there were two girls. They took out the two girls and they burned the house, in the night time. They surrounded the whole place with military and police. They rounded up the local people, the Scottish Borderers, and they made them walk in front.[26] Anderson, an officer in that Regiment, was a great scoundrel. But we could not see them coming. They had information that we would be in the bog, the six of us, myself and Paddy Boland, the Company O/C, Padraic Forkan, a Gaelic teacher, Austin Kenny and Jim

25 Hear makes more sense here than the 'heard' used in the original text.
26 The Scottish Borderers refers to the King's Own Scottish Borderers, a regiment of the British Army.

Kilkelly.[27] They wanted these six of us. We were in a neighbour's house where we used to stay when Paddy Mullins, the Brigadier, sent over bombs with me. The master sent word to us by a young lad, who came across the fields, and we had just time to get out. They, the soldiers, fired shots, and they went into the house again, and they bayoneted poor Paddy Boland who was an old son.[28] They bursted the bayonet in him and they almost cut his nose off with a bayonet also. Mick Coen, they found in his own house, and they cut off his private parts and pinned them on his breast, and they cut the flesh of his legs and arms. They cut off his ears and they left him out on the road. That dirty work was supposed to be the work of Anderson of the Scottish Borderers. They captured him in his own home outside of Ballyhaunis. They took him away from his house. That had a terrible effect on the people. A girl of the Waldrons in Ballyhaunis was supposed to have told Stephens, the Tan, when our fellows called …[29] I dropped the bomb that night, [3L] and the bomb didn't go off. I threw it into the … Kilkelly had a .22 and I had a .45. Stephens pulled his gun, but it didn't go off, and I shot Stephens. I stayed there waiting, but the Waldron girl did not come down until the man was dying.

There were two lads in Galway who were tied to a lorry which dragged them along the road until they died.[30] Then they sprinkled leaves and petrol on them and they set fire to them. This happened outside of our area.

They [RIC] were night and day in that area in Crossard townland, searching, for they must have had information.

---

27 Kilkelly, not Kilkenny as in the original text. This action happened around 27 May 1921.

28 Perhaps O'Malley intended to write 'only son'.

29 Although the text calls the man Stevenson, it was RIC Constable William H. Stephens who was killed on 29 March 1920 by Grealy.

30 Patrick and Henry Loughnane were killed in Drumharsna, Co. Galway. See O'Malley, *The Men Will Talk to Me: Galway Interviews*, pp. 285–93.

The houses of the Battalion O/C and the Vice-O/C were not touched. If poor Seán Corcoran hadn't been killed, East Mayo would have been a different area.

The people stiffened their resistance. There was a Fr Gurrey, a great man, who cautioned people at Mass on Sundays about loose talk in Aghamore parish. Fr Hugh Curley used to call there. He was a young priest and a good man. His two brothers were in the IRA. Canon McHugh was hostile but he didn't get his chance until later. My uncle used to send the column up to the hayshed and send up food to them there whenever they called.

The Battalion column started in 1921. It had a few shotguns and a few rifles. Paddy Mullins was nearly always with it. **[4R]** Each Battalion had a little column of its own, but there were not ten rifles in the Brigade area. I don't know who is to blame for the lack of rifles. Also one bullet out of ten wouldn't go off in these Kiltimagh rifles which were sent over after Seán Corcoran was killed.

There was only an odd IRB man here and there in East Mayo, about three in all: Joe Kelly of Ballaghaderreen and Liam Forde.[31] I think the latter was a Brigadier for a while.

Republican Courts were held in the area in my own parents' house in Aghamore, and we would enforce the decrees of the Sinn Féin Courts held in Ballyhaunis.

The King's Own Scottish Borderers.[32] Sheehy and I went into Claremorris to get Anderson for the military had a big camp there.[33] In Claremorris was Joe Brennan who collected the Dáil Éireann Loan.[34] He was alright, but he wouldn't fight.

31 Forde (not Ford as in the original text) of Lisacul, a staff officer of the 4th Battalion of the East Mayo Brigade.
32 King's Own Scottish Borderers is abbreviated to KOSB in the original text.
33 Anderson is the King's Own Scottish Borderers officer who had committed the atrocities on 1 April on Mick Coen, described above.
34 Dáil Éireann authorised the raising of a National Loan on 4 April 1919. The loan was for use in propagating the Irish case internationally and for national purposes generally.

The Dáil Loan did well in that area.

The capture of Enniscrone Coast Guard Station.[35] I was on the run, and I stayed in McKeown's house for he was the pilot, and he wasn't suspected. An Enniscrone lad asked me to come on this job so I took a revolver and as the crowd were gone Tomás Loftus from Ballina came down to capture it. I lined the Coast Guards against the wall and the local lads used hay to burn the station. We captured nine or ten rifles, shotguns and ammunition. Loftus, is now Captain of the Guard on Leinster House and he was in charge of the raid that night.

[TRUCE PERIOD]

After the Truce everyone was allowed in to the Sinn Féin Clubs, and it was by vote that members of the Sinn Féin Clubs accepted or rejected the Treaty. Only four Trucers came in in our Battalion, but in other Battalions a good number of them joined up the IRA.[36]

Sinn Féin Clubs. Over fifty per cent and under seventy-five per cent of the members were for the Treaty. [4L] Coming on towards the end of the Tan War the people had been strengthening themselves. The area didn't decrease in numbers, but no one wanted to give in. We had a few bombs, but not much good they were. I had a little black police bomb which I flung into the police in the hall ..., but it wasn't detonated.

[Priests.] During the Truce Canon McHugh in Ballyhaunis was playing away with the pro-British element there, and they were numerous. Fr Gurrey in Aghamore was a topper.[37]

---

35 The Enniscrone Coast Guard Station, located on the coast about eight miles from Ballina, was burned on 30 August–2 September 1920. See Kilcawley interview above for greater detail.

36 The term 'Trucers' referred to those lads who joined the IRA after the Truce had been declared in July 1921, and it was usually employed in a disparaging manner.

37 This perhaps should be Fr Gurrey, who was noted as being sympathetic, and not Fr McHugh as in the original text.

Our TDs. Dick Walsh,[38] Republican, Dr Ferran (Foxford),[39] Republican, Dr Crowley, Ballycastle, Republican,[40] P. J. Rut-tledge (Ballina).[41]

Training. Campbell, who had been in the British Army, and Brian MacNeill, who was our Divisional Adjutant,[42] were on training in the camp at Oldcastle near Swinford.[43] There were over 100 men at a time there for three weeks' courses. We had even Company camps.

We took Charlestown Barracks, where we got close on sixty rifles. Eugene Kelly and I and Dan Sheehy went the following day to capture arms at the station in Kiltimagh, and we had a waggon filled with arms uncoupled when the British got the tip, and they surrounded us, but we got away. We rushed it. **[5R]** There was one sergeant shot, a sergeant Mulvanny.

Split in the Brigade area. Ruane of Kiltimagh had a following.[44] Tommy Ruane was killed during the Truce by Republicans who went in to arrest him. That did great harm, and they said that he tried to pull a gun on the men who went in. He had a certain following in his area. Around Ballyhaunis P. Kenny went Free State and his brother, and the Vice-O/C, Dominick Byrne, but he didn't join the Free State army.[45] All the rest in our Battalion remained Republican.

Brigade O/C	Tom Carney.[46]
Vice O/C	Patrick Dunleavy.[47]

38 Dick Walsh of Balla was not a TD at this time as he was only elected in 1927.
39 Dr Francis P. Ferran of Fermanagh. See biographical sketches.
40 Dr John Crowley lived at Ballycastle, Co. Mayo. He was elected as a Sinn Féin TD four times from 1918 to 1923. He treated several injured IRA men and represented the movement at various inquests. He was anti-Treaty.
41 P. J. Ruttledge from Ballina. See the previous interview.
42 Brian MacNeill. See biographical sketches.
43 Oldcastle near Swinford, not Old Castle near Swineford as in the original text.
44 Not to be confused with Tom Ruane of Ballina.
45 Free State was abbreviated to 'F/S' in the original text.
46 See his interview.
47 Dunleavy, not Dunlevy as in the original text.

| Adjutant | Dr Jim Vesey, Ballaghaderreen. |
| Quartermaster | Joe Kelly. |

We were under orders for the North. Billy Pilkington was in the barracks in Boyle one evening when the Free State thought they would rush the place.[48] Billy held on and he sent out word to the Brigade to send in men who could be trusted. Brian MacNeill was also in the barracks at the time. Fallon or Lenihan were in that crowd and one of them fired point blank at Billy, but he left the Free State within three weeks. Billy said to him, 'Did you fire at me purposely?' 'I did,' he said, but Billy took him in again.

There was fighting there for a while in Boyle, and that was the first fighting in our area also in the Civil War.

I came up for the last Convention in the Four Courts with Peadar O'Donnell's crowd.[49] Peadar stayed with me in Boyle, then I came up with him on Sunday morning. We were in Whelan's Hotel and we had an idea that something would happen. There was to have been an attack on the British military in the Park,[50] but the politicians wouldn't hear [5L] of it.[51] Rory O'Connor proposed to do something, but the rest said it would be like a dictatorship to do what he had suggested. A military dictatorship was to be set up for a certain time in Ireland, and it was Rory they wanted to be dictator.[52]

---

48 Liam or Billy Pilkington of Sligo became O/C 3rd Western Division IRA in 1921.

49 This would be mid June 1922. Peadar O'Donnell from Donegal had lived in Achill in 1919. He held the rank of colonel commandant and was on the IRA Executive that occupied the Four Courts in Dublin. Later he was under sentence of death at Finner Camp, Donegal, but the ceasefire saved him.

50 British abbreviated to 'Br' in the original text.

51 Phoenix Park in Dublin.

52 Rory O'Connor was Minister for Defence in the 1919 Dáil, went anti-Treaty, and was the leader of the IRA Executive forces that took over the Four Courts building in Dublin on 13 April 1922. He had previously been director of engineering in GHQ. He was executed with Liam Mellows, Joe McKelvey

Swap of Arms.[53] Arms were taken from Boyle Barracks to be swapped. Our column was under orders for the North for a few months before the Civil War. We had transport and all ready there, but our progress to the North was cancelled. We had nine to fifteen Mausers in our column in the barracks in Boyle and we had some others in East Mayo. During a fight in Boyle I saw a lad in an armoured car wounded by a Mauser bullet, *Mac an Boola*.

Bank Raids. Charlie Kildea, the Division Quartermaster, on Pilkington's orders, had to give back money. During the Civil War I don't know how many times we arrested fellows, [released them] and took them prisoners again. If we had dealt severely with those fellas at first there would not have been so many of them joining up the Free State army.

[CIVIL WAR]

I was in Dublin when the [Four] Courts was attacked. Paddy Mullins was there also in Barry's.[54] We sent messages down to see if we would be accepted, and we were told that any of us who had arms would be accepted. [6R] After five hours I received word from the Courts that I was to go down to my area and start the fight at once. There were thirty-nine of us so we went down by train.

and Richard Barrett on 8 December 1922 as an act of reprisal by the Free State government for an IRA attack on 7 December which killed Seán Hales and wounded Pádraic Ó Máille, both TDs.

53 When the Northern Ireland government was created under the Government of Ireland Act in 1920, the nationalist community, which was mostly Catholic, came under attack from loyalist forces, official and unofficial. After several deputations were sent to the Free State government, Collins agreed to supply arms to them for their defence. As the Free State weapons had been supplied by the British Army, Collins could not send them to the north, as they would have been easily identified. To overcome this he agreed to swap weapons with the IRA, giving them the new rifles so the old ones could be sent north. After several attempts to swap weapons, the IRA withdrew from the scheme, owing to an amount of subterfuge on the Free State army side.

54 Barry's Hotel, where many Republicans stayed.

[Boyle.] I went on to Sligo to Billy Pilkington, and I gave him the message, so Billy told me to go back to Boyle and prepare the lads.

[1aR][55] The IRA oath was administered again in 1922 for we all took it in the barracks in Boyle, those who were on the column. *Lionann* [was] then O/C of the 3rd Western Division Active Service Unit in Boyle.[56] They were the pick of the Division, sixty of them, but some were from Tom Maguire's area, the Second Western [Division].[57] I came from Aghamore, Ballyhaunis. I think Dan Sheehy was Vice-O/C of the Divisional ASU. Sheehy was Republican all the time. I was IRB, but I don't think the others were.

Mick Dockery escaped out of Boyle Barracks in the Tan War when he was to have been executed.[58]

[6R] On the next night we tried to take the Workhouse there, where there were 100 Free Staters. Mick Dockery was in charge of them, but he got killed within the first five minutes, and after three days a priest asked for a truce; and we granted it provided that no reinforcements were brought in and no fresh positions occupied. They broke both of these undertakings. Ten lorry loads of troops came in, and they occupied fresh positions. There was a fight on then in Collooney.[59] We cleared out of Boyle for Seán MacEoin[60] came in with his eighteen pounder.[61]

---

55 The next six sentences have been moved from the first page (1aR) of this interview and are placed in chronological order as they deal with the start of the Civil War. This was on 1 July 1922, and Mick Dockery was shot on 2 July.

56 Active service unit abbreviated to ASU in the original text. ASUs were sometimes called flying columns.

57 Tom Maguire of Cross. See his interview.

58 The following line has been omitted so as not to confuse the reader. It is talking about the same incident as that described at the start of 6R: 'Mick was to have given [handed over to] us the barracks [Workhouse] in the Civil War, but he had drink taken and he was shot in the first five minutes.'

59 Collooney, not Cooloney as in the original text.

60 Seán MacEoin, not McKeown as in the original text.

61 Eighteen-pounder field artillery guns were loaned by the British government

Tom Carney was sent in to assist us.[62] I had been wounded. We had positions outside of Boyle, and we wouldn't allow the Free State to go in or come out. An armoured car attacked our position, but we held out until the following morning. Tom [Carney] took twenty to thirty of my column, and he was rushed before I was attacked, and all men captured. They were holding a house, but the Free State rushed the house. The officer in charge was shot dead and we were attacked at the same time. They got to the back of the house, but a few of them were killed and they withdrew. Dan Sheehy escaped. Tom Carney and I came on to Ballaghaderreen. We formed two Brigade columns. I had about forty men in one, and Dan Sheehy had about forty men in the other. He was in charge of Kiltimagh and Charlestown, and I was in charge around Ballaghaderreen.[63]

[**Swinford, 4 August 1922.**] We captured Swinford, and Tom Carney took the barracks there with eighty or ninety rifles in it, on a fair day.[64] The Staters fought until the barracks fell in on top [**6L**] of them. *MacPadon* was in charge of the Staters there. Then we went back again to our own areas. They sent in hundreds and hundreds of troops, nothing but rounds of them, and we were captured one by one. In the Tan War we used to sleep in dugouts, but the lads got broken down for they had only sticks on top, and as a result the lads got rheumatism and suffered a lot. Rockingham had a place into which you went in by boat for Billy Pilkington engineered all that.[65] All the

to the Free State government to attack the Four Courts buildings in June 1922. After the fall of Dublin these guns were brought about the country to help dislodge the IRA from various strongholds. Some were landed at Westport when the Free State army went there on 24 July 1922 and were used to attack Newport in November of that year.

62 See Tom Carney interview below.
63 In charge is abbreviated to i/c in the original text.
64 Swinford (not Swineford as in the original text) was captured on 4 August 1922.
65 Rockingham Castle, known locally as Cloontykilla Castle, was built in 1839

Divisional Staff were there, and the column as well. Afterwards, when all was over, it leaked out about this good hiding place, and the Staters found it.

They got me at home, after I had escaped a big round-up, in October or November 1922, and they took me to Ballyhaunis. They charged me with the shooting of Mick Dockery during the attack on Boyle.[66] Before the attack all our lads went to confession, and when we went up to attack in three rushing parties the Staters were out amongst the trees waiting for us. We were to have got in for we intended to starve them out, and we sent word to the North Roscommon Brigade. We had to shoot a bulldog who was under a car so that we could take the car. Fitzsimmons or Simons charged me, but I explained what had happened, and they said those shots were the ones that were supposed to have shot Dockery, and afterwards he never let the Staters abuse me.[67]

[7R] (This going to confession before an attack was often the signal for an attack, and word was often passed on about it.)

Dockery and a few other officers shot a deer in Rockingham and the Republican crowd began to beat him up. They came in for a drink, and I asked him if he would have a drink. But he said with a blow, 'a bottle of stout never bought me', so I brought him then to the Workhouse where the Free State were.

I was brought to Athlone, and the tunnel was made there by Christmas Eve. Conditions were very bad in Athlone which was the worst place I was in, for Mountjoy was a palace compared to Athlone. MacEoin's brother-in-law was the quartermaster there and between them they didn't give food or meat to prisoners. There were no grounds for the prisoners to exercise in and it was a filthy place. After the dinner prisoners went in to warm water

on the site of an older castle. It is situated on Lough Key on the Shannon River and was owned by Lord Stafford King Harman.

66 The IRA attack on the Boyle Workhouse where Dockery was killed.

67 Dockery, not Doherty as in the original text.

to make tea from … They'd use condensed milk tins instead of cups. MacEoin wouldn't allow the fellows back into the huts once they got out for exercise so they had to walk the compound even in the rain from 10 or 11 until the evening and then we were closed into the huts again.

Patch Mulrennan raised a window and went in to boil water one day.[68] Someone shouted at him that MacEoin and Tony Lawlor had come in.[69] Tony Lawlor fired as Patch was coming out the window. 'You missed,' said MacEoin.

'Well, I won't miss this time,' said Tony Lawlor, and he fired again and Patch died there and then.[70]

The Tunnel. The tunnel came out from a block of buildings and it was half made by the time I got in to Athlone. It went out to a canal. There was an Athlone man picked to lead out each group, and I had Curley from my place to lead our crowd out. The tunnel was [7L] propped, it had electric light and there were names on parts of the tunnel, on the turns. Charlie MacDonagh from Ballaghaderreen, who worked on coal mines in England, gave us great help. The last bit of the tunnel was named, 'The Run Home'. We had everything ready for an escape on Christmas Eve, but the night before the Staters came in, and we were all brought out the following night handcuffed together in twos and we were brought away by train. I found [Dan] Sheehy in the Joy before me.[71] There had been some hundreds of us in Athlone at the time. I was put in 'C' Wing in the Joy. Jim Gibbons was there and Matty Connolly, Dr Jim Vesey, Bill Shouldice, Peadar O'Donnell, Tom Loftus, and I were to get away in a tunnel. Seán MacEntee was brought in when I was there, and you couldn't recognise him for on a Sunday he was

68 Patrick 'Patch' Mulrennan, brother of Seamus.
69 Brigadier General Anthony 'Tony' Lawlor. See biographical sketches.
70 Grealy is not quite accurate as Mulrennan was wounded in the leg in October and died on 3 November from the resulting infection.
71 Mountjoy Gaol is often referred to as the 'Joy'.

brought to Mass and the new prisoners from the basement were put in certain seats, and we would be put up the chapel. Peadar kicked up a row about the beating MacEntee had got, and he sent word up to the priest.

We broke through the guard between the two lots of prisoners, and we took back with us a man who was under sentence of death.

A tunnel was being made from the padded cell. Tom Loftus came in to me and he asked if I would be fit enough to get **[8R]** away, and I said I would, but the next thing we heard of the tunnel was that it had been found. I think that it was only Dublin men who were to have got away in that tunnel. It was on the second landing where I met Tom Kitterick for he was in my Wing.[72] Himself and Paudeen could have some awful slanging matches.[73] Matty Connolly and Jim Gibbons and myself and a big tall man … were brought out at the time that an appeal appeared on the paper from Liam Deasy to surrender.[74] The daily papers for the first time were brought in to each Wing, but the O/C Wing gave instructions that the papers were not to be taken in. There was a fellow from my place who was reading the paper and he wasn't much and I went down to see him about it but he went down to see O'Keefe and Cosgrave, the Governor, and he gave my right name.[75]

I was court-martialled then. I had been called 'Morrissey' up to that for there were so many Grealys. He said if any more

---

72 Tom Kitterick from Westport. See biographical sketches.
73 Paudeen O'Keefe, former secretary of Sinn Féin, was deputy governor of Mountjoy.
74 Liam Deasy (not Deacy as in the original text) was captured on 18 January 1923 and sentenced to death. On 29 January he signed a brief statement, prepared by the Free State Army Council, in effect calling for the IRA to surrender. The Free State government delayed publishing this statement until 9 February.
75 Phil Cosgrave, a brother to William Cosgrave, was governor of Mountjoy, and when he died in 1923 he was replaced by Dermot MacManus.

soldiers are shot in your area, you'll be shot. This lad said that he'd do the speaking if we were questioned.

Hunt, the traitor, was sent into another wing. He was in charge of the party when Tommy Ruane was killed, but he didn't kill him. Sheehy pelted down a stool at him in the new wing and Hunt was knocked out. He was taken out then and we never heard of him afterwards.

In 1923 we were sent to the Curragh, and we were there until March 1924. The O/C told me to answer my name, and Jim Vesey took my place in my cell. That night they came in, and they beat up poor Jim Vesey and I think they thought it was myself who was in the cell.

[8L] There was a row on in the Joy so that parcels or papers were not allowed in to us, so that was why the Staters gave us the papers to read about Liam Deasy's surrender and appeal. I was in Tintown No. 2 where Christie Smith was. P. J. Ryan from Dublin was O/C there. There were 2,200 men there. Jack Comer was the doctor in that camp.[76] Seán Robbins, from Clare, Tommy Jordan, a medical student, helped Dr Comer, who was Medical Officer in the Hospital Hut.[77] Paddy Egan, a fine fellow from Offaly, was always around with Seán Robbins. Seán Twomey[78] was in there, a good scrapper and a Dublin man, and Joe Campbell, the poet, and a Seán a'Chóta.[79] Christie Byrne was O/C of the camp for a while.

---

76 Jack Comer from Galway was active in the Irish Volunteers while studying medicine at University College Galway. After his graduation he established a practice in Clonaslee, Co. Laois, in July 1921 and became medical officer in the 3rd Southern Division. He was anti-Treaty and was not captured until February 1923 when he was interned in Maryborough Gaol and later in Tintown and Hare Park internment camps in the Curragh until June 1924.
77 Medical officer is abbreviated to M/O in the original text.
78 Probably Twomey, not Toomey as in the original text.
79 Seán Ó Chaománaigh or Kavanagh from West Kerry was also known as Seán a'Chóta (not Seán a Hota as in the original text) or Seán of the coat, as he wore a petticoat.

I was in No. 12 Hut where Peter White was our O/C. Mick Rooney from the West, who had a partly bald head, was there and he was a nice fellow. I was in bed there nearly the whole time. I saw one fellow's hands twisted behind his back. Heavey, a little fellow from Galway, was beaten until the blood came out his ears, from Hut No. 2, and then Bunny came in and they beat him outside.[80] A topping lad he was, and Mick Stack of Kerry never entered a Church later. He wouldn't take up a pick and shovel. They used a bayonet on [9R] Heavey.[81] They had to send him to hospital. Bunny Lynham was from Dunboyne. He became a Captain and he was there when the prisoners were beaten up. McCormack, a Commandant, a tough fellow from Kilcock with a sallow face, was there at the digging of the trench also. But that resistance didn't last long, and they never got Heavey to dig after that. McCormack rounded us up in the compound, and there he was swinging his Parabellum in his hand. 'You'll get me for this I suppose when you get out of here.'

When they were searching for a tunnel they put us out in the compound. Then they scattered everything around in our huts. They smashed our little boiling tin cans and they threw the tea around and splashed water around as well. They fired over our heads when we were out in the open, with machine guns, and we were herded there until the night time when they allowed us to go back into the huts. Afterwards the PAs would come into the huts and put our tin cans which had tea in them flying round the place with their sticks.[82] There was a PA there who was always drunk, and you'd see him jumping from bed to bed in the hut with a revolver in his hand. Dan Sheehy got a uniform coat and only for that he'd have been done in for

---

80 Bunny Lynham.
81 This Heavey from Galway is not the same as Tommy Heavey from Westport whose interview is above.
82 PA refers to póilíní airm or Military Police used by the Free State in prisons.

the Ruanes of Kiltimagh and the Sheehys never pulled at home and they were death on one another. (This explains a good deal of Irish history – the bickering of the chiefs, their taking sides with the English and their various allegiances determined by their local enmities.) Bergin, the PA, gave Sheehy this uniform coat and Sheehy walked out before Bergin had made a count, so he must have had everything carefully planned.[83] Bergin told Paddy Mullins that he was going to be done in. [9L] Sheehy got back to his own area then, but Bergin was foully murdered by the Staters as he had feared.

When I was captured McGarry gave me away, and he was from my own place. I took of[f] my apron I went out into the lane outside. Barney Flannigan, a boots in a hotel in Ballyhaunis, straight away put a bullet up the spout. 'What did you shoot Mick Dockery for,' he shouted, but the officer took the rifle from him. 'If ever I came out of prison,' I said to [Flannigan] 'and if it's to the North Pole I have to go, I'll get you.'

Bill Shouldice would send in good food if he could and he'd always allow us milk (from the hospital hut?).

Benbulbin.[84] There had been a round-up there. Brian MacNeill used to go in the armoured car but the roads were blocked and he blew it up and made for the hills. There were Staters in trench coats on the mountain, and they showed their butts to the officers who were with MacNeill, who made towards them, but 100 yards away MacNeill saw that he had made a mistake, and then fire was opened on them. Benson's body was in a bog hole and they put a flag on his feet. The Cumann na mBan searched Benbulbin that night, but they could find only

83 Joseph Bergin from Camross, Co. Laois, was a member of the Free State army's Military Police. He was suspected of spying for the Republicans and was arrested, tortured and killed by a unit attached to the Free State's intelligence department on 15 December 1923.

84 Benbulbin is the mountain overlooking Sligo town where Brian MacNeill was killed on 20 September.

three bodies, but a week later a shepherd was looking for his sheep and his dog scratched at the flag.[85] He raised it up and there was Benson. There was a rumour that Eoin MacNeill said to the soldiers who were leaving Dublin for the round-up in the West, 'If you come across my son, don't spare him.'

---

85 Cumann na mBan is abbreviated to C na mBan in the original text.

TOM CARNEY

(UCDA P17b/109, pp. 29–30, 41–53)[1]

Thomas 'Tom' Carney (1891–1971) was born in Kiltimagh. He joined the RIC in 1914 and worked in Co. Tipperary for five years before resigning and joining the IRA in 1920. He then returned to Kiltimagh and joined the Kiltimagh Company, 3rd Battalion of the East Mayo Brigade, but as he was a former RIC man some people were suspicious of him. He was also a member of the East Mayo flying column. He went anti-Treaty, became adjutant and later intelligence officer of the East Mayo Brigade, was captured in August 1922 during the Civil War, but later escaped. In 1926 he married Evelyn Groarke, a member of Cumann na mBan and a teacher, from Swinford. They had one son and lived in Swinford until 1955, after which they moved to Dublin and then to California.

*Courtesy of
Dr Pádraig Carney*

This interview was conducted in Swinford in 1950.[2]

[1914–1921 PERIOD]

[29R] I joined the RIC depot 1st October 1914. Then Sergeant Mulhearne, from between Pontoon and Ballina, my

---

1 The initial transcription of this interview and some footnotes were done by Dominic Price.
2 The original text of this interview refers to Swineford, but this has been changed to Swinford throughout. There is a small Swineford village on the outskirts of Swinford, but reference was probably meant to the larger town. Also, Ballaghaderreen has replaced variations including Ballaghadreen, Ballaghadereen.

schoolteacher, had a special interest in me for I had served my monitorship under his first cousin.[3] There were a couple of companies of recruits then in [training in] the Phoenix Park. We were trained in the use of revolver and rifle, and we practised with both these weapons. (Also, I expect with the bayonet.) We had a special rifle range of our own, and we used military barracks going right to them from the depot. We did six months training. We swore an oath that we would give allegiance to His Majesty King George, his heirs and successors, and also that we would not belong to any Secret Society except the Society of Freemasons, and I think that later this society was removed from the oath.[4] I had been three years as a monitor in Lisduff National School, a mile from Kiltimagh.

[RIC work, 1915–1920: Co. Tipperary.] My first station was Dovea in Mid-Tipperary, and it included Annfield and the Ragg.[5] It was about March 1915 when I got there. We ploughed and harrowed with the people when there was a threshing. Half the porter was held over for the dance that night. This was unofficial. In Dovea a Captain Trait lived a half a mile from us. He had a couple of sisters and the barracks at Dovea had been originally built to protect him. You patrolled with a senior constable or with the sergeant until you got to know the people. When I was in Dovea the local hurlers kept their hurleys in the barracks and the[y] played in [29L] a field in front of us and they also played football. If I were the barracks orderly I would be out to play hurley with the lads while a sedate countryman would be left in the barracks to look after the rifles for me. Mick

3   In the national school system an outstanding student was often asked to stay on as a monitor for several years to help the schoolteacher run the small school.
4   Many of the officer class of the RIC were members, and this undoubtedly helped their chances of promotion. Catholic members of the RIC shunned Freemasonry.
5   Dovea is a small village halfway between Borrisoleigh and Thurles, Co. Tipperary.

Small's people had a pub in the Ragg and Mick Whelan lived near the church.

A duty list was made out by the sergeant, and, as a result of the duty list you paraded, and as a barrack orderly you slept in the dayroom and you recorded in a diary the activities of the garrison during the day. The barracks orderly was out of bed at 8 a.m. and his bed was removed. The sergeant would parade the men at 9 [a.m.] with or without equipment, and you went through drill on the barracks' yard. But if the sergeant was easy going there was no parade, or you fell in on the dayroom floor. You were supposed to have a half an hour of school or police duties or on acts of punishment and in this you were responsible to the sergeant.

Our first sergeant was a Mick Donoghue, and our force was a sergeant and three men. The sergeant was usually a married man and if he was fond of porter the ... helped. The sergeant on a [30R] slip of paper wrote up the duties for the day. The nominal duty was for six hours. Patrolling three times each day, and if you didn't get on with your sergeant he would make you go out at 12 midnight and inspect you then at the end of your beat. The idea was to support authority at all cost. There was a three-hour day and a three-hour night patrol which meant going to the Ragg Village, strolling up and down, or when things were quiet sitting at the fire and drinking. The District Inspector would arrange that patrols for adjacent barracks would meet half-way. Then there were 'Rising Patrols,' which increased later on, between 12 midnight and daylight. The District Inspector's office had to be notified of the hours so that he could inspect them suddenly and the hours at which patrols met the patrols from the adjoining barracks.

The RIC had dug in themselves well in in Mid-Tipp. There was no poteen made in that area. In winter we often played at cards for cocks and hens until daylight in the morning. You could have all the rabbits and all the timber you wanted. The pay was small. After 1916 we attended a Mills Bomb course under William Harding Wilson, the District Inspector in Templemore, which was I think also the headquarters of the Munster Fusiliers.[6] I was then in his district but later on I went in under District Inspector Hunt.[7] Not a dog barked in our area in 1916, which was described in our propaganda as looters and robbers and Countess Markievicz who was a prostitute or led them.

The standard of education was low amongst **[30L]** the sergeants. After from five to six years in 'The Force', a civil service examination was held in Dublin, and you were brought to Dublin for police duties and drill, and if you passed, you would get promotion. Before you sat for the exam the local District Inspector had to recommend you as being physically and mentally suitable.

District Inspector Wilson was killed when he was coming from the barracks to his home.[8] He had a Miss Moynahan and George M. a garage man in Templemore, who accompanied him on day and night inspections. He was a ranker and a Free Mason and independent in his mind.[9] The Protestants in 'The Force' were independent, the Catholics were more subservient. The same thing applied down the ranks to the Protestant constable.

There were two of us in the Station one day, and I was Mess Man or orderly, and there was a shopkeeper on the road to Borrisoleigh, who drove a car for him, so we went off. While

6   RIC District Inspector William Harding Wilson (1864–1920) was killed on 16 August 1920 in Templemore, Co. Tipperary.
7   RIC District Inspector Michael Hunt (1873–1919) was killed on 23 June 1919 in Thurles, Co. Tipperary.
8   Charles Wilson was killed on 15 June 1920.
9   The term ranker might refer to an officer who rose through the ranks from the lowest level.

we were away, the District Inspector, Charles Wilson, a humpy, cranky, *asthmatic* Englishman drove up but all he found was the barrack servant.[10] John Collins, a Cork man with a pug nose, was there waiting twenty minutes when we got back. **[41R]** We at once made up a story that a girl was driving along in a pony and trap, and the pony ran away, turned upside down and that we went out to help. We gave her name as a Protestant girl in the locality, whom we told at once, but Hunt came and measured the ground, and I felt sure that he did not believe us.

There was land trouble in the Rosheen Barracks area, below Drumbane village. Patsy Ryan's pub was at Drumbane Cross. A police hut had been established in a derelict house, and this man who lived near Carens, …Tom Dwyer, bought the land, and a boycott was begun, and I was sent to Rosheen under Wallace to supplement the garrison.[11] His house was protected day and night for his milk was spilt and his harness cut on its way to the village.[12] You had to guard him to Mass and his family carried arms.

Wallace, in plain clothes, brought me to an aeridheacht, and the two of us were instructed by Hunt.[13] I got on all right with him. He had no children and he had plenty of money but he was itching for promotion. Nothing happened. Darrell Figgis, Seán Milroy were there, and also Seamus Malone was in the area at the time. Malone was doing a strong line with Breed Walsh in Drumbane parish where he was a teacher.[14] Coming home we were within a quarter mile of Drumbane. We saw two fellows, and they made some move and went for the ditch. Wallace fired

10 District inspector, not county inspector as in the original text.
11 RIC Sergeant Peter Wallace.
12 The house of Tom Dwyer.
13 Aeridheacht (not aireadacht as in the original text) was a gathering to celebrate Irish language and culture.
14 The following text has been omitted: 'She'd put a special shoulder on her, and she had a set on Wallace.'

his revolver at them, and I argued with him about this though he didn't hit either of them. Then Hunt, who had been told by Wallace, I expect, about me, came **[41L]** out, and I was moved to Littleton. John Joe Hogan was arrested in Maher's of Annefield by Wallace. Hogan was armed that day, and he had plenty of time in which to get away. It is the first house on the right above Annefield Bridge as you get to Rosheen.

Littleton [Barracks, Co. Tipperary.] We never made a raid for a political prisoner. It was some one of the Ryans, Jacky, I think, who was fired on by Wallace that day. I was doing a line with a first cousin of Jerry Ryan, Mary Leamy. There was a sergeant, Patrick O'Flaherty, Admiral Togo we called him, for he wore a beard. Togo was a great old character. He hated the Protestants and the Orangemen, and he used to crease his trousers both inside and outside. Himself and the parish priest were the two lords of the parish. He had a terrible set on Jerry Ryan's mother who was a six footer, named Johanna Leamy. Togo was a Dillionite.[15] He had a great disrespect for the Protestant Minister, and we were doing duty at his house. He was very vain as regards his hand writing. He never cycled but always walked for he didn't approve of bicycles, and he was hated by the men for he always paraded them spick and span, and he kept to all regulations. Also he was very proud of being an O'Flaherty, and he knew their history.

[42R] Some Belfast RIC came down in full kit during the time Martial Law was imposed.[16] They were nearly all Catholics. There were a few rebels such as James Ryan, now a

---

15 John Dillon succeeded John Redmond as leader of the Irish Parliament Party in March 1918. He was first elected for East Mayo in 1885. The party supported the constitutional approach of the Home Rule Act rather than the revolutionary approach, but was decimated by Sinn Féin in the December 1918 general elections.

16 Martial law was imposed in Munster and some other parts of Ireland in 1919 after the Knocklong ambush.

Super. Most of them had long service. The Tans came later. They were middle-class English, a few, and they were perfect for they wouldn't stay unless they had their women, their porter and the pictures to go to. But the lower class who were in the Tans were the world's worst. They were sergeants and sergeant majors. They wouldn't impress you much physically or in any other way, but they were hated especially by the Catholic sergeants. Some of the instructors did instruct us if the sergeant asked them to. There was a special crowd of British Ordnance men who cut holes in walls for loopholes and who put sand bags into position. Also they put up barbed wire. Our barracks now had steel shutters around us, in Dovea, Rosheen and Littleton.

We patrolled the area heavily. Enright was with me in Rosheen.[17] He was a quiet Limerick man, and he was shot through the heart in the Knocklong rescue. Togo, who maybe couldn't stand the new order, resigned, and went on pension and he was replaced by two army majors who held the rank of sergeant. They had joined the British Army and had been promoted, and now they came back as constables until they were promoted. To induce the RIC in the 1914–18 War to join the British Army, you were given the rank of sergeant as soon as you did join up. All these RIC came back with at least the rank of Captain for the offer of sergeant used as a bait made a lot of them fall **[42L]** for it, but those who did come back were all crocked, either by reason of wounds, or of malaria.

The Northern Protestant was bad and a lousy type corrupted in the British Army by drink and by women. James Igoe was a Roscommon man, and a decent man.[18] Igoe from Foxford, as

17 RIC Constable Michael Enright was killed at Knocklong, Co. Tipperary, 13 May 1919.
18 This family name is often spelled as Igoe (not Igo as in the original text). This man is not to be confused with RIC Sergeant Eugene Igoe from North Mayo, the leader of the Igoe Gang, who identified rural Volunteers when they arrived in Dublin from the country and 'took care of them'.

James Jones an ex-Major, and he scarcely ever spoke. He was fond of the ladies in Littleton and a sneak. There was a fellow, Grehane, a bad article he was, on duty when the barracks was taken. He was a half shell-shocked ex-officer. I fell out badly with him. This Igoe, the ex-soldier, also suffered a bit from malaria and was interested in barmaids.

James Rocket of Kilkenny and I resigned the same night, and we went in to Hayes Hotel. Hunt was replaced by John Golden, a ranker from Galway, a porter man who had a large family and had been promoted from the detective side. He drank heavily. He came out the day after our resignation, and he pointed out how shocking it was to have these blackguards in the Force and how he had no confidence in them.

We were supposed to report to Dublin to Dáil Éireann, when we resigned, to Fionán Lynch for there was a [43R] special employment bureau which was to have got suitable employment for us when we resigned.[19] John M. Heaneen, an RIC man stationed in Dovea was shot … officer in Dublin. There was an incident in Lar Fanning's bar in Dovea. There was an O'Brien from Silvermines there and H[eaneen] and … came in to the bar and H[eaneen] was shot dead and another (wounded or killed?). That started my headache. There was a pub, Dwyers at Balladuff, near the Ragg and five miles from Thurles. Probably the RIC raided Dwyers for they shot Tom Dwyer, and they shot him dead. There were three sons, Mick, Éamon and Tom, there and they were friends of mine. Mick was to be ordained.

Hunt, the District Inspector, had a clerk, Cahill, a daily communicant, who they said was very bad. He was made a sergeant, and Jackson from Ballina was very bad they said also. On the public street of Thurles we were interviewed by Jerry Ryan. In Thurles at that time the RIC had to commandeer all

19 Fionán Lynch, not Fionann as in the original text.

the goods they wanted (for no one would sell them food or drink or material – at least no one was supposed to sell them necessaries). On patrol if we went in for a drink the publican refused to serve us and at Two Mile Borris and at the Horse and Jockey pubs the patrol had to go inside the counter, draw the pints and go to the till for their change. A patrol in a Lancia car came to where we were in Thurles, surrounded us and searched us and Jerry Ryan as well. They took my wallet which had all my money in it, but I [43L] appealed to one of the sergeants there, and they gave it back to me. Then I went back home but I found it difficult on account of being so long in the RIC.[20]

[IRA work 1920–1921: East Mayo.][21] [52L] AOH. Dillon's party was strong in East Mayo but Dillon was beaten here by de Valera in 1918.[22]

Intelligence. The RIC were supposed to have perfect Intelligence here in the Tan War.[23] This woman was teaching in Meelick.[24] Jimmy Henry, the Battalion O/C was arrested, and the Vice-Commandant was [53L] made O/C then, and G[realy] was V/C.[25]

All the teachers had to get permits to use their bicycles to school, and she[26] went down to see McGarry for a permit, and he couldn't give it to her as her brother had got a big appointment in the IRA.[27] He had been made Vice-Commandant.

There was no column in this area in the Tan War. The British rounded up all the inhabitants of a town. They lined them up

---

20 Carney's home was in East Mayo.
21 The next four paragraphs were at the end of the original Carney interview but have been inserted here to allow the interview to follow in a better chronological order.
22 John Dillon, MP, had held this seat since 1885.
23 Carney is relating here some events that took place during the Tan War.
24 Meelick is a townland near Swinford.
25 Possibly Johnny Grealy of Aghamore, near Ballyhaunis. See his interview.
26 The teacher is not identified.
27 McGarry was an RIC District Inspector.

and got them to sing 'God Save the King', or they brought them to a stream and they made them double across it under machine-gun fire, or put them lined up near a bridge and said the last across is for it, then fired over their heads. This attitude antagonised the civilian Britishers. Once in Kiltimagh this happened and the soldiers came from Claremorris and brought some people back there as prisoners, but Fr Dennis O'Hara went to complain to the Officer Commanding Troops, and I think he got them released. And as a result of his complaints the Auxies from Claremorris carried out a raid on the parish priest's house a night afterwards. He got away in his night attire into the garden. This was done by officers in the garrison.

[43L] East Mayo Brigade had started off on a high note after 1917, but a split developed among the brigade staff owing to the Vice-Brigadier, Tom Ruane, commandeering petrol at the Railway Station.[28] He had some row with the Quartermaster over it and the split was never healed. Both sides went on the run with a greater hatred of each other than they had of the Tans. There was an official and an unofficial crowd on the run and nothing happened in the brigade as a result. I offered my services to them. Seán Corcoran, the Brigadier, who was on the official side, was killed in April of 1921.[29] Éamonn Corbett from Galway who was a big empty name was no good. I often wondered how he got the name when I discussed the use of arms with him.

I went home, and I worked on the land, but there was no boycott of the RIC here. The Tans walked out with the best-

---

28 The East Mayo Brigade was formed in 1920. Tommy Ruane was from Main Street, Kiltimagh, where the family owned a shop. He became a controversial character in the brigade and later joined the Free State army. He was fatally wounded in an affray with William Moran, O/C, Bohola Company, IRA, who had come to arrest him for recruiting for the Free State army.

29 Seán Corcoran, O/C, East Mayo Brigade IRA, was killed in an affray with the British Army on 1 April 1921 at Crossard, Ballyhaunis.

looking girls from the village of Kiltimagh. There was a sinister parish priest there, a Rev. Dennis O'Hara, who was a **[44R]** member of the Congested District Board and who entertained Chief Secretaries and others from the CDB.[30] He was a Dillonite. He was a personal friend of the Brigadier (the British one?). Joseph Sheehy, who was a brother of 'Dynamite' Dan, was a law clerk, was the Quartermaster but then was adjutant.[31] He worked for the O'Connors who were [an] ex-British Army crowd there. The District Inspector, who was a Catholic, McGarry, would know all the history of the faction.[32]

Scanlon from Sligo was Battalion Commandant.[33] He was a promoted Fianna lad who served in the Tan War and in the Civil War. I became a member of the local Company, and it was Kiltimagh in the 3rd Battalion Kiltimagh.[34] Joe Kelly, Ballaghaderreen, about sixteen miles from here, would know most of this area in the Tan War.[35] Séan Corcoran ran into an ambush of RIC, and was killed. There were burnings in Ballaghaderreen after a Jim Hunt, a brother of District Inspector Hunt, who had also been killed[36] … Beyond Tibohine, after an ambush, one of the first places sacked was Flannery's, and it was

30 The Congested District Board, or CDB as in the original text, was set up in the aftermath of the introduction of the Land Acts in order to redistribute the estates to the local people.

31 Joe and Dan Sheehy were officers in the Kiltimagh IRA Company who were involved in local controversies and charged with neglect and misappropriation of property, leading to a court-martial. The Kiltimagh IRA Company was stood down as a result of various complaints, mostly relating to breaches of discipline.

32 McGarry, not MacGarry as in the original text.

33 Tom Scanlon of Ballina was a ranking officer in the Sligo Brigade. See his O'Malley interview, UCDA P17b/133, 136.

34 Carney is mistaken here, as the 3rd Battalion was Kiltimagh and not Swinford as in the original text.

35 Ballaghaderreen (not Ballinsaloe as in the original text) as stated three lines below.

36 An incomplete sentence in the original text following this has been omitted here.

burned to the ground.[37] Joe Kelly of Ballaghaderreen had shot two policemen early on.

Raids. Here were a good deal of raids, but there was no IRA provocation. Let sleeping dogs lie was the attitude. I suggested several things that might be done but I was only a private then. As a result of the split in the Brigade I was between the devil and the deep blue sea and beside there was no recommendation forwarded from the Mid-Tipp men to say that I was alright.[38]

[TRUCE PERIOD]

[44L] When the Treaty came, the unofficial crowd were ninety per cent Treatyite in our Battalion.[39] Corbett had no status either.[40] Bob Price at the reorganisation came down from GHQ.[41] This was some time around Christmas and then I was Director of Intelligence for the brigade. MacNeill came down to form a brigade meeting and Connell came here.[42] Before they came I was Director of Intelligence for the brigade. I was then in the Camp to help them in their training in the Battalion and in the Company Camps.

East Mayo. The majority of the IRA were Republican.[43] The hostility was due to people in the faction trying to resurrect

37 Tibohine, not Teebohen as in the original text.
38 Mid-Tipp refers to the Mid-Tipperary Brigade, where Carney had previously served in the RIC.
39 Ninety per cent, not nine per cent as in the original text. It is likely that O'Malley left out the '0' in transcribing his notes, and a few lines later it is recorded that 'the majority of people accepted the Treaty'.
40 Éamonn Corbett, from neighbouring South Galway Brigade, was an IRA officer 'on the run'. He was of great assistance to Brigadier Seán Corcoran when the Kiltimagh dispute was brewing.
41 Éamon Price, also known as Bob Price, was director of organisation at IRA GHQ and acted as a 'troubleshooter' when disputes arose in the brigades.
42 Eoin MacNeill was one of the founders and first chief of staff of the Irish Volunteers in 1913. He was responsible for countermanding the 1916 orders for the Volunteers to rise on Easter Sunday. He was pro-Treaty. His son, Brian, was anti-Treaty and was killed by the Free State troops in Sligo.
43 For Carney being Republican probably meant being anti-Treaty.

their fighting record. The majority of people accepted the Treaty, and the priests were ninety-eight per cent against us. Dr Ferran from Foxford was our TD,[44] and Billy Pilkington was the Divisional O/C.[45] Brian MacNeill was his adjutant. Bob Price's recommendation was that both Ruane and Sheehy be dismissed at once from the Kiltimagh area, but both of them had dug themselves in and they had caused a good deal of trouble. The IRA in the area, backed by others, had robbed the Charlestown Bank of £5,000, the night that [Seán] Corcoran was killed.[46] They included an Irish teacher, Peadar Dignan, who is living in here now. They [45R] were on the run in the poteen area, for Carracastle and Charlestown were poteen areas/districts. Some said that the bank was raided so that arms could be bought with them, but the spoils were divided (and they didn't go for arms), and the local Battalion O/C [Paddy] Cassidy got some of it.[47] Paddy Fitzpatrick, Brigade Quartermaster, got a bit also.

The bank was robbed in February 1922 during the Truce by an unofficial crowd, some of whom had taken part in the first bank raid. I was Brigade Adjutant at the time, and Sheehy was the Brigade Police Officer and after a week we pulled in seven or eight men and we brought them before the local Republican Court and we put them in Sligo Gaol. While they were there they made statements about the first raid. So we set out, and we pulled the Battalion O/C and the ex-Brigade Adjutant, Flatley, from here, and a remarkable thing is that when they were here,

44 Dr Francis P. Ferran from Fermanagh. See biographical sketches.
45 William/Liam 'Billy' Pilkington was O/C, Sligo Brigade, in 1920 and was later O/C, 3rd Western Division in 1921, and went anti-Treaty in that command.
46 Sean Corcoran, O/C East Mayo Brigade, was killed on 1 April 1921, but the bank raid was on 3 April.
47 Cassidy was a staff officer in the Carracastle Battalion. He went to Dublin following the setting up of the Free State and joined the notorious Criminal Investigation Department or CID at Oriel House. Another companion, McDonnell, from the same locality was with him but they both left the CID in August 1922 and joined the Free State army.

we sent a Battalion staff car over to Charlestown for a District Justice to remand the prisoners.[48] This District Justice was Jack Foy; and McGeevin and a lad made a statement by God that these, also, had got some money too. Mc[Geevin] was a brother-in-law of the then Imperial Bishop, Pat Morris Roe, the worst Bishop in Ireland, he was. We phoned Scanlon who brought the prisoners to Sligo. We got most of the money in bags of meal, and there (like as in a pirate store) in the corner of the field, twelve steps up and twelve steps down, lift a sod and there was buried a couple of hundred pounds from the second raid.

Limerick. We went the time you were in charge of Limerick.[49] We had thirty men and Scanlon from Sligo, and we were in the Shannon Rowing Club.

Most of that **[45L]** money taken in the second raid was recovered. The local Bank made us a grant of £500 for our good police duty. Paddy Cassidy, the Commandant, joined Oriel House. He had £80 in a canister, and if we left him the money he'd leave for the USA, but we didn't want to expose him so he went to Dublin where he joined the CID. Peadar McMahon was down here on a tour of inspection, attended a brigade meeting and he offered me a rank in the new Police Force. I was then the Brigade Adjutant, and, I think, it was an Inspectorship or a Superintendent he wanted to make me. The O/C Brigade was Liam Forde, and he was no good.[50] He was a first cousin of Dr Madden and teaches in Lisacul.[51] The Vice-Commandant was Moffatt from that area who had a fairly good record.[52] The Assistant Brigade Adjutant, James Vesey, a medical

---

48 District justice is abbreviated to D. J. in the original text.
49 The 'you' refers to Ernie O'Malley who in early March 1922 put out a call for anti-Treaty Republicans to assist him in the recapture of Limerick city after Michael Brennan had taken over barracks from the departing British troops.
50 Forde, not Ford as in the original text.
51 Dr John A. Madden from Ballycastle. See biographical sketches.
52 Michael Moffatt or Moffitt, not Moffet as in the original text.

student from Dublin ... with a Dublin fighting record, [is] now a medical officer in Carrick-on-Shannon.[53] He came down here as his health was bad. Forde was a real fire and water man. He was hanging around his own house in the Civil War, then Liam Forde was arrested, but came out after six months and went back to teach his school.[54] There were 400 men in the brigade during [46R] hostilities but 1700 men at the end of the Truce.

Sligo Meeting. The Division occupied places in Sligo town, and Pilkington was in charge there. Forty men went in from this brigade.

[**Swinford Barracks, 17 January 1922.**] There was a hasty brigade meeting in Swinford before the British cleared out, which I didn't know of. They met in the workhouse, and the[y] said they'd have to do something. In the town were the King's Own Scottish Borderers – Highlanders, with Captain Grant in charge of the Company.[55] This raid that was planned was supposed to have come from the IRB section of the brigade. They all met in the workhouse, and I was there. The town hall was scouted as the British were ready to leave, and Joe Kelly came in from Ballaghaderreen with Alfie [Kelly] who had a special Italian dagger.[56] He was to stick up the sentry with this knife. Ex-prisoners scouted the place, and it was thought by the IRA in the town that it was not possible to take it. Charlestown said that the RIC barracks, which held between Tans [and] RIC thirty [men] and two sergeants, could be easily taken. This plan was abandoned. The Tans did a bit of drinking. I, with Eugene Kelly, the Brigade Engineer, was put in charge of the raid.[57] He was a step-brother of Mick Kelly who was accidentally killed in

53 James Vesey, not Veesey as in the original text.
54 Probably Liam Forde, not Larry Ford as in the original text.
55 King's Own Scottish Borderers is abbreviated to K.O.S.B. in the original text. The Highlanders were the Argyle & Sutherland Highlanders.
56 Alfred 'Alfie' Kelly was Joe Kelly's brother.
57 Eugene Kelly, not O'Kelly as in the original text.

Boyle Barracks by Mick McLoughlin, Brigade Quartermaster, who was himself killed by gangsters in the USA.[58] We had over thirty men and a few revolvers, and we packed the transport this side of Charlestown. We lined up the men, and it was snowing, and we marched up to the local town hall. The Scouts were not there at all. The RIC at 10 o'clock [p.m.] appeared to be gathered around a table inside, so I thought it might be roll call. We heard that two Tans who were down the town were drunk so [46L] that meant that they were missing so we walked in disarmed the sergeant, and the RIC handed over the rifles and revolvers.

Ballyhaunis. Grealy and Paddy Mullins were there.[59] Paddy Mullins succeeded Corcoran as Brigade O/C. He was then a medical student. He was married to Seamus ... wife's sister, a big hefty lady she was. P. Kennedy, who was wounded in the Tan War, was Battalion Commandant from that area, and he went Free State. Paddy Mullins was no good here due to drink in the Tan War. Maurice Mullins was Brigade Adjutant under Corcoran and was badly beaten (for he was captured the day Corcoran was killed).[60] He is dead now, and he was teaching in Howth.

Carty was all out for Pilkington's blood, and it led to Pilkington's court martial on Carty's complaint.[61] There was never very friendly feeling between the two of them for Carty felt that he should have been Division O/C. (Carty gave a complete history of the brigade and the Pension Board have it now.) James Groarke, Bridge Street, Swinford is in the Labour Exchange there. The Sligo meeting of fighters was proclaimed by Pilkington, and we went in to hold the place, but we didn't hold it. It was [47R] mentioned that General O'Connell came

58 Carney is mistaken here as it was Eugene Kelly that was killed in Boyle Barracks.
59 Probably Johnny Grealy. See his interview.
60 Seán Corcoran was killed on 1 April 1920.
61 Frank Carty from Sligo. See biographical sketches.

in marching with his guns strapped on his legs.[62] Pilkington was later exonerated. One of our lads was killed. There was a Division Unit recruited from the Division. Grealy and Sheehy were in charge of it. The unit was supposed to hold Boyle Barracks and to be ready for any emergency. There was some shooting at the disbanded RIC. One of them, a Sergeant Dowd was wounded[63] and his wife was wounded and died as a result. They had six children, and we were on a garrison in the workhouse. This IRB section came in and they didn't notify me. They weren't all disbanded, the RIC. I think 'Dynamite Dan' Sheehy and [Joe] Sheehy were IRB, and Grealy,[64] and he should know about these shootings.[65] Mrs Seamus Malone's only brother, Paddy Walsh, wandered into this area on account of his relationship with the Mullins, and he was appointed to look after the Special (Signalling) Services. There were two RIC shot in Brolly, Cranna and Butler-Larnis, Cranna half drunken in his bed. Most of the people who took part in unofficial shootings were no damn good in the Civil War, and it made things very difficult for me and for others. This Dowd's son is now a detective sergeant in Dublin in the CID and took part in shootings on the IRA in the last Emergency.[66]

There were RIC in Swinford. Tans in the town hall. RIC in Kiltimagh, Kilbagh, Ballaghaderreen.[67] Auxies were in Tobbercurry. It was from Tobbercurry they were said to have come that time they killed Fr Griffin.[68] They evacuated the following RIC

---

62 Commandant General J. J. 'Ginger' O'Connell was then assistant chief of staff, Free State army.
63 O'Malley corrected 'killed' to wounded in his original text. Dowd is sometimes O'Dowd in the text.
64 Johnny Grealy. See his interview.
65 Referring to Joe Sheehy.
66 Reference to the Emergency, the Irish name for the Second World War.
67 Ballaghaderreen, not Ballydereen as in the original text.
68 Fr Michael Griffin of Barna, Co. Galway, had been invited to the USA to give evidence of the atrocities committed by the crown forces in Ireland. However,

posts: Bohola, Ballyvary, Kilkelly **[47L]** Kilmovee. The district headquarters of the RIC for this area was Claremorris. There was a Catholic, Major Ballards, in charge of Claremorris Military in the Tan War.

[CIVIL WAR]

We held Swinford Workhouse and RIC barracks and the RIC barracks in Ballyhaunis. I attended the last Convention in Dublin, and when we were coming home, it was expected that hostilities would commence at once.[69] Grealy would know what happened at Boyle. There was a lot of shooting by the divisional unit of RIC who had been disbanded and were in Boyle, and Pilkington went up there a few times, but he didn't know how to locate the men who had shot the policemen to control it. In April some … were here on inspection. MacNeill, the Division Adjutant, had by that [time] been home a few times, and his views had been watered down as a result.[70]

When the Four Courts was attacked everything was in chaos here. Kilroy came on here the night of the Four Courts, a Division meeting was held in Sligo, and I was in there later for we were the last brigade into that meeting.[71] Carty was fighting on his own for destruction at once, but Brian MacNeill was discussing his idea that all available men and arms should **[48R]** march at once on the North. Most of the Divisional Officers were in favour of this plan. Then we turned the tide back to work in our own province. We had met Kilroy and Maguire,[72] and they had decided on an immediate opposition to the Free

he was taken from his house and killed on 13 November 1920 and his body was buried in a bog. General Crozier of the Auxiliaries investigated this death and found that his own men were guilty.

69 The last IRA convention was held in June 1922 and voted against the Treaty.
70 Brian MacNeill. See biographical sketches.
71 Michael Kilroy of Newport. See his interview.
72 Tom Maguire of Cross. See his interview.

State in Connaught.[73] Carty was very grateful to us for our stand. Fighting at the time was actually going on in Boyle. I left this area, and I went with twelve men to Carty's column. He had eighty men or more. His column was based in Tobbercurry. We went on to attack Collooney, and we burned them out there, about twenty or so we got there.[74] We captured a few lorries in Collooney. Carty had read a lot about guerrilla warfare but he took no chances. He was particular about dress and about his personal appearance. I think it was Carty who discovered that their spies were communicating with the garrison in Moylough, two married farmers with large families.[75] Carty brought them out, blindfolded them and went in [to the town] for a priest. Then he shot the two of them. The Civil War was on for a month at the time. Dr Martin Brennan lives in Banna, Toorlestraun or Aclare is his dispensary but near Aclare – Banna, about seventeen miles from Castlebar.[76] At some divisional meeting either Carty or … proposed that in the event of any execution of men from this area we would have twelve selected men shot in each brigade [area] in rotation, but no man from the Division was executed.

[**Boyle attack, 1 July 1922.**] Pilkington came out and he said that the position in Boyle was getting worse, so I was sent in there. There was a flying column from West Mayo under Broddie Malone outside Boyle,[77] and a column from the 2nd Western, Tom [48L] Maguire's area under Ferguson (dead) near Boyle. Apparently, the divisional unit had attacked the Free State barracks and had killed Dockery, the Free State officer in

---

73 O'Malley wrote opposite in the original text and this has been changed to opposition.
74 Collooney, not Cooloney as in the original text.
75 Moylough (not Moylock as in the original text) is near Tobbercurry, Co. Sligo.
76 Dr Martin Brennan from Gurteen was the O/C, Irish Volunteers at University College Galway. He was later active in Sligo and Mayo engagements and was O/C of his local battalion. He lived in Banna, Co. Sligo.
77 James 'Broddie' Malone from Westport. See his interview.

charge.[78] The attack on the [workhouse] barracks failed, and this unit left Boyle and had formed a kind of a column.[79] I was sent to see if anything could be done, or to get them back [here]. We came back then to this area, and we took to the hills.

The Free State were in the old RIC barracks in Swinford. There was a brigade muster in Brabegan Park near the town. The Ballaghaderreen crowd [men] were addicted to drink and hard to deal with. We told off different parties for the attack. We occupied Cockle's house, the parson's in front and the house adjoining it and small houses at the rear. They had in the barracks ten prisoners, civilians and active men, Tommy Campbell was a good fellow. He is now registrar in Co. Wicklow. We drove in their sentries and we found there were fifteen prisoners whom they had taken the night before. In Irish she [a girl] … talked to Campbell and told him about the attack. So we had a brain wave.[80] We arrested fifteen of the richest pro-Treaty shopkeepers in Swinford, all well-conditioned men, and we got the … of them, and we put a white flag on top of a hay fork. He was shouting 'flag of truce' at the top of his voice **[49R]** in the middle of the street at dawn. Our ultimatum was that in the event of a barracks attack, we would shoot every member of the garrison if the prisoners were shot. And he [Campbell] came back to say that the Free State would release the prisoners if we withdrew from the town. We sent back word to release the prisoners within ten minutes. They agreed and we paraded them. Then we sent the Brigade Engineer for mines so that we could open an attack. After about a few hours we smashed the slates for though we had mines, we didn't blow them. And then the roof went on fire. Two of our fellows were shot dead, and

78 Mick Dockery. Grealy refers to this incident as the workhouse that was used as a barracks.
79 O'Malley included 'is' before unit in the original text, but it has been omitted.
80 Carney refers to a 'she' who is not identified.

a lot of their fellows were wounded. There were forty-five of a garrison, and we got fifty rifles. MacPartland from MacEoin's crowd was in charge. He had two columns of ninety men under arms there. I saw Joe Kelly of Ballaghaderreen, but we were both arrested by Jim Hunt and brought to Sligo Gaol. There was no way out but he was a type that would take all sorts of chances.

Before Swinford we had a few scraps. Word came at 3 o'clock at night to Vesey and I from Charlestown that the Free State were occupying it, 120 [men]. Five of us went over just at daylight. The local Battalion O/C was there, and when we were coming around the turn, we saw forty men – three lorries, and we were in front of the town hall. There were eight staff officers in front. Paddy Walsh and I rushed to meet them. They fired on us so I got down on the road channel and opened up. The officer turned the car and left me behind, and the men, thirty of them fully armed, surrendered.

Sligo [Gaol]. Tady McGivern, an officer of Jim Hunt's Battalion from Gurteen. There were over seventy there, mostly from **[49L]** the 3rd Western [Division], and from Donegal. We had a famous ex-British army man from Ballymote, a tinker by trade and a great handball player.[81] Joe Kelly in charge of prisoners, but every day at dinner we got good knives, and Joe was a good man out of gaol.[82] The gaol was a horse shoe of two storeys with a big corridor on the outside and cell[s] off it.[83] Joe opened all the cell blocks in twenty minutes, and we stole knives each day and hacked them into hacksaws for the prison bars. There was a flat bar across the centre set in lead and two square bars downwards set in stone and in lead. These went through the centre bar. You could get on to the corridor

---

81 Ballymote, Co. Sligo.
82 The i/c in the original text has been changed to 'in charge'.
83 O'Malley included a diagram of a horseshoe-shaped building arrangement in the original text which is not included here.

leading to the yard from the barred windows. After three weeks
we decided to test the bars. The first bar came out but the second
bar would not. We had rope ladders which we had made from
blankets and sticks tied in so as to make rungs which we had
kept hidden in mattresses in our cells. We tried this other bar
but there was nothing doing until 4 a.m. I smashed a four inch
baulk of timber by trying to smash the bar, but I could not move
it. We went back to our cells to wait for the next [night] **[50R]**
but at 5.30 next morning, we were pulled out of our cells for
Longford. Twelve [men] were left behind, but we went on. I
feigned sickness, but I had to go. The twelve who had been left
behind got out of the place in two or three days.

[Longford escape, November 1922.] We found seventy-
two men there already when we reached Longford. It was an
old British barracks, and we were put in a store department.
About the end of October this was.[84] We had a Council. Thomas
MacEvilly was O/C, the chief vocational officer in Sligo.[85] He
was hard but he was delicate. He had a committee of twelve,
and we drafted a proposal to escape which was turned down by
the Council. We got fourteen volunteers to escape. There was a
running door back and front.[86] There were four sentries and a
guard room twenty feet away under a sergeant who had twelve
men. The guard room was bounding the barracks.[87] There were
thirty-three sergeants in the sergeants' quarters, and the barracks
contained a huge garrison. One of them, Dignan from Leitrim,
was friendly, and he agreed to … the running door opposite to
the guard room. So we detailed our men in stockinged feet for
he undid the running door opposite to the guard room. We got
out two each of us, sprang on the sentries on duty. It was a dirty,

84 1922.
85 Thomas MacEvilly was originally from Castlebar and was the senior person in
    the Sligo vocation school. His brother, Seamus/Jim, was killed in Kilmeena.
86 O'Malley included a diagram in the original text that is not included here.
87 'Bounding' in the original text might refer to bordering.

cold, misty night. And there was an awful difficulty in hitting one of them with his own rifle. We got the four of them without us letting them make a whimper, and we gagged them.

The night before I was the last to go to bed. I was at the end of the room when I saw three drunken fellows in uniform come in. Seán MacEoin and Seamus Farrelly, a big stout Colonel Commandant, [50L] and the fellow in charge of the Swinford attack. They walked down. MacEoin was threatening the prisoners with revolvers in their backs and bombs and they said what they wouldn't do to the prisoners if they tried to escape. Mac[Eoin] was very drunk and he said, 'Hello, you don't know me now. Do you remember the man in charge?' But it passed off for he didn't do anything.

We went to the guard room. The soldiers were all around the fire, and the rifles were in the corner, so I put my hand across the rifles, and we got them all under control, and we had to bind and gag them and throw them out the window, nine of them.[88] And one soldier actually came down with the night rations so we took him in and the rations as well. We stacked up the beds to get on to the high wall. All the prisoners were going over[89] like flies and I was shouting where was Dignan, but he was tied up with the others.[90] We had to go back and unloosen him, and we were just on top of the wall when the machine guns opened up.

When the prisoners dropped down the[y] found some of the garrison courting their women under the walls. It was 10.30 p.m. MacEvilly [51R] with Brennan, Battalion O/C from Gurteen. The night was dark. It was the usual November night so as we were going out the Western side we went on across a

---

88 They gagged the soldiers and threw the rifles out.
89 The wall to escape.
90 The Free State soldier from Leitrim who had been sympathetic to the prisoners.

kind of a stream, in which we went waist deep. We had four Lee-Enfields and 1,000 rounds so we set off across this field under machine-gun fire. We walked until daylight and we got a cake from a countrywoman who was minding bonhams.[91] We should be, we thought, by daylight about thirty miles from Longford. At daylight we looked around, and we went into this cow house on left, and at half past 9 [a.m.], we told him that we had escaped.[92] But we found that we were only four and a half miles from Longford.

Evidently the right boot takes a longer stride than the left, so we were brought in a circle. There was a pig fair on in Longford so we sent him in for whiskey for Brennan had money. The Staters came within half a mile of us searching. The man told us of a Miss McKeown, who was an awful Republican in Drumlish, and at nightfall he led us to her house. She made beautiful tea for us and she played cards. She was engaged to a fellow in Aughavas, the other side of Drumlish, so we went over there and we knocked up this man.[93] He told us that Fr Ryan was a native of Arigna. His father had been a manager of the Arigna Mines and his brother was attacked by the staff of the Leitrim Brigade. The priest set out to drive to Arigna through Manorhamilton. 'But if I'm held up what you will do?' he asked. 'Let ye blaze like hell,' he said. So that was his solution for the situation. He brought us to his father's [51L] house in Arigna and we walked back to Ballaghaderreen.

Fr Ryan had a housekeeper who got into trouble.[94] The local story was that he asked his brother to assume responsibility for the child, and the brother refused. She was to leave the mining home, and a gentleman called for her, took her and the baby

---

91 Bonhams (not bonnows as in the original text) were small pigs.
92 A farmer they had met.
93 Aughavas (not Aughoras as in the original text) is near Mohill, Co. Leitrim.
94 An expression making reference to a young girl who had become pregnant out of wedlock.

out. The baby was left on a doorstep. The local Guards arrested both of them.

There was a Dr Muldoon, a local dispensary doctor and a prominent Republican and Fr Ryan approached him for he wanted him to perform an illegal operation on the girl, but he refused.[95] Muldoon was shot dead in his own house. Fr Ryan was sent out to the Australian Mission.

Ballaghaderreen. Joe Kelly was out for he had escaped three weeks before us. He occupied positions with the South Sligo Brigade waiting for Staters, but nothing came of it. There was an ambush at Glore Bridge, one mile from Kiltimagh.[96] The Free State left ... to go to Kiltimagh for a funeral, about sixty of them, and we were to get them on the road back. There was a school between the position, and we wanted to let the children home from school and as we **[52R]** were going in to the school, fire was opened on the lorries. There was a river in the centre (of the position?), and we were to cross and let them come into the Bridge. I was badly wounded in the lung so I handed over my equipment to the lad in charge. The Staters brought on artillery from Claremorris and they shelled away. I was brought in on an ass and cart to a farmer's house, but the grating of my ribs made me lose a good deal of blood. Dr Lyons was pro-Treaty and was our Brigade Medical Officer once.[97] He was from Kilkelly. 'It's a twenty to one chance,' he said. The local Catholic Curate Fr Leonard came out to see me and very nice he was.[98] They brought me to Clarke within a mile of Ballaghaderreen to a house where the son and daughters were doctors and another daughter was a nurse. I was in the basement. After Glore [Bridge] it was reported that I had been killed. After two weeks

---

95 The illegal operation would likely be an abortion.
96 The Glore River is a tributary of the Moy River.
97 Medical Officer is abbreviated to M/O in the original text.
98 Catholic Curate is abbreviated to C.C. in the original text.

I was brought to Archdeacon O'Hara of Kilmore, to his house, and a terrible reptile he was. The housekeeper was friendly and I was put to bed there. After five weeks, when I was able to move, I had nothing to put on me but she gave me one of the Archdeacon's trousers. All the generals stayed there afterwards, but the Archdeacon never knew I was there, and afterwards as the place was safe, it was used as a port of call for strangers.[99] Maggie Collins, a Limerick girl, was the priest's housekeeper. She was really the acting parish priest,[100] and everyone was afraid of her. I was wounded in January 1923 and I did not get up until March.

[52L] The Free State used to send cycling patrols daily from Swinford to Charlestown for raiding purposes so we arranged with the South Sligo men for a combined ambush. We waited for a day and they [Free State] didn't come in to the position, but they caught up with the Sligo men as they were on their way home, and they shot them red-handed.

Swinford. They were very bad to prisoners there later on as the Kiltimagh crowd were in charge, and the local officers were bad. This was pure brutality.

Murder of MacNeill.[101] There was a Free State round-up, personally conducted by MacEoin. All the back of MacNeill's head was blown away which would show that he ran for it. Benson was found at the bottom of a ravine after a few days had passed by, and he had several bayonet wounds in him. (Tom Scanlon from Ballina, now a Ford agent, formerly a Sligo Commandant, calls here on a Saturday.)[102]

---

99 'Generals' possibly meaning Free State army generals, thus creating an appearance of safety for the Republicans who could be cared for by the housekeeper.

100 Parish Priest is abbreviated to P.P. in the original text.

101 Brian MacNeill was killed on Benbulbin in September 1922 by Free State army troops.

102 For O'Malley's interview with Tom Scanlon see UCDA P17b/133, 136.

Short Biographical Sketches of Men Referenced in Footnotes

Joe Baker (1900–1988) was from Omagh, Co. Tyrone, where he joined the IRA. He came to Westport in 1920 to work in the jewellery trade for Harry Kelly of Bridge Street and soon joined the IRA's Westport Company and its ASU when it was started. He was anti-Treaty and was leading the last fighting column when he was captured at Shramore in March 1923. He was sentenced to death while in Galway Gaol but was not executed.

Frank Carty (1897–1942) from Tobbercurry, Co. Sligo, was O/C of the South Sligo Brigade. He escaped from Sligo Prison in June 1920 and from Derry Prison in February 1921. He was anti-Treaty.

Thomas 'Tom' Derrig (1897–1956) came from the Republican enclave on High Street, Westport. He was the main mover in bringing Na Fianna Éireann to Westport in 1913. In University College Galway he was a founder of the Irish Volunteers, after which he became a teacher in Ballina Vocational School in 1919. He was O/C of the West Mayo Brigade after Michael McHugh's arrest in 1920, but was arrested himself in August 1920 and interned in the Curragh. He was elected a TD in 1921. Released in December 1921, he was anti-Treaty and a member of the IRA Executive, while active in Dublin and the east. In July 1922 he became adjutant to Ernie O'Malley and later adjutant general. Captured in April 1923, he was shot in the eye while trying to escape and then jailed in Mountjoy and the Curragh until released.

Dr Francis P. Ferran from Co. Fermanagh was the local dispensary doctor in Foxford. He was O/C of the 4th Battalion, North Mayo Brigade. He was elected a Sinn Féin TD for Sligo and East Mayo in the 2nd and 3rd Dáils. He was interned in 1921 and again in 1922 by the Free State. He died in the Curragh internment camp in 1923.

Tom Kitterick (1899–1977) came from High Street, Westport, which was a Republican enclave. At thirteen he was a member of the Westport Fianna Éireann, founded by Tom Derrig. He worked in Charles Hughes' drapery store in the town. In 1920 he collected £400 for an arms fund in the town. He was sent to GHQ to get arms and was so successful that he was soon making regular trips to Dublin to get arms. His organisational skills were so good that Michael Kilroy promoted him to quartermaster for the West Mayo Brigade. After the Truce, Kitterick was ordered to the GHQ in Beggar's Bush Barracks in Dublin as assistant quartermaster general. He left there after the attack on the Four Courts and went anti-Treaty. After a term of internment he returned to Westport, often being harassed by the police. Kitterick is sometimes spelled as Ketterick in the sources, but the family gravestone uses the Kitterick form.

Brigadier General Anthony 'Tony' Lawlor served under General Seán MacEoin's Western Command in the Free State army, based in Athlone. His reported retort to MacEoin after he had shot but failed to kill the prisoner Patrick Mulrennan was that he would get him next time. However, Mulrennan died of his wound soon after. This story was corroborated when the IRA intercepted a letter by Lawlor to his mother boasting of how good a shot he was and it was published in *Éire*, in January 1923. Mulcahy Papers, UCDA P7/B/87.

Brian MacNeill was a son of Eoin MacNeill, a Free State minister. He went against the family position when he chose to oppose the Treaty and stay in the IRA. GHQ asked him to help reorganise the Sligo brigades. On 20 September 1922 he, with Brigadier Seamus Devins and four others, was killed at Benbulbin Mountain, Co. Sligo.

Dr John A. Madden (1896–1954) from Belderg Beg, Ballycastle, attended medical school at University College Galway where he joined the UCG IRA Company. Having gained his medical qualifications in Liverpool, he became an assistant surgeon at Castlebar Hospital in 1920. Soon after he became medical officer to the West Mayo Brigade ASU and went on the run full time. He took part in all the major engagements with the ASU. He was anti-Treaty and was captured and interned until the general release in 1924.

Ned Moane (1890–1973) was a farmer from Carrobaun, Westport. He was a long-standing member of the IRB and was interned in 1916 and again in 1918 during the 'German Plot' scare. Michael Kilroy appointed him vice-O/C of the West Mayo Brigade and its ASU, where he was the oldest member. He took part in most of the ASU activities. He was anti-Treaty and led a column in the Louisburgh Battalion area during the Civil War until he was captured.

Joe Ring was from Drummindoo, outside Westport on the Castlebar road. His father, who was from Kilkenny, joined the RIC, married a Westport woman and retired to Westport. Ring organised the Derrygorman Company in the IRA's Westport Battalion and eventually he became O/C of the battalion as well as being in the ASU. During the Truce Ring was influenced by Michael Staines, also the son of an RIC man, and decided to go pro-Treaty. He was asked by Staines to be the assistant commissioner of An Garda Síochána which was formed in February 1922. Ring left the gardaí when there was a mutiny at their Newbridge headquarters, and joined the Free State army as a brigadier general. He led the seaborne assault on Westport on 24 July 1922 which was to link up with Seán MacEoin's Western Command based at Athlone. He died in an ambush at Bunnyconnellan on 14 September 1922.

Tom Ruane from Ballina was O/C of the Ballina Company, IRA, and in 1920 became O/C of the new North Mayo Brigade which became No. 2 Brigade of the 4th Western Division in 1921. When captured he was interned at Ballykinlar until December 1921. He was anti-Treaty. He should not be confused with Tommy Ruane of Kiltimagh, who was pro-Treaty.

Richard 'Dick' Walsh (1888–1957) from Balla was the most prominent IRB person in Mayo post-1916. He was IRB Mayo County Centre. He made many daring visits to England to purchase arms for the IRA. He was the Irish Volunteers' organiser for Mayo, 1916–19, adjutant to Joseph MacBride, the Connaught representative on the Irish Volunteers executive, 1917–21, and inspection officer for the IRA, 1920–21. He was adjutant to the Mayo Brigade, 1918–20. Walsh persuaded GHQ to send Peadar McMahon to Mayo to organise the companies. He was anti-Treaty, and was captured and interned during the Civil War. O'Malley did not interview him.

BIBLIOGRAPHY

PRIMARY SOURCES

National Archives, Bureau of Military History: statements referring to men involved in actions in Mayo as well as individual statements by Patrick Cannon, WS 830, Michael Kilroy, WS 1162, and Ned Moane, WS 896

National Archives, Census 1901, 1911

UCD Archives, Ernie O'Malley Military Notebooks, P17b

PUBLISHED SOURCES

Buckley, Captain Donal, *The Battle of Tourmakeady, fact or fiction: a study of the IRA ambush and its aftermath* (Nonsuch Publishing, Dublin, 2008)

Herlihy, Jim, *Royal Irish Constabulary Officers* (Four Courts Press, Dublin, 2005)

Hopkinson, Michael, *Green against Green: the Irish Civil War* (Gill & Macmillan, Dublin, 1988)

Hopkinson, Michael, *The Irish War of Independence* (Gill & Macmillan, Dublin, 2004)

Macardle, Dorothy, *The Irish Republic* (The Irish Press, Dublin, 1951)

MacEoin, Uinseann, *Survivors* (Argenta Publications, Dublin, 1980)

Meehan, Rosa, *The Story of Mayo* (Mayo County Council, Castlebar, 2003)

Ó Brádaigh, Ruairí, *Dílseacht. The Story of Comdt General Tom Maguire and the Second (All-Ireland) Dáil* (Irish Freedom Press, Dublin, 1997)

Ó Gadhra, Nollaig, *Civil War in Connaught, 1922–1923* (Mercier Press, Cork, 1999)

O'Farrell, Padraic, *Who's Who in the Irish War of Independence, 1916–1921* (Mercier Press, Cork, 1980)

O'Hara, Bernard (ed.), *Mayo: Aspects of its Heritage* (Archaeological, Historical and Folklore Society, Galway, 1982)

O'Malley, Cormac K. H. & Anne Dolan (eds), *'No Surrender Here': The Civil War Papers of Ernie O'Malley* (Lilliput Press, Dublin, 2007)

O'Malley, Ernie, *Raids and Rallies* (Mercier Press, Cork, 2011)

O'Malley, Ernie, *The Singing Flame* (Mercier Press, Cork, 2012)

O'Malley, Ernie, *The Men Will Talk to Me: Kerry Interviews*, edited by Cormac K. H. O'Malley & Tim Horgan (Mercier Press, Cork, 2012)

O'Malley, Ernie, *The Men Will Talk to Me: Galway Interviews*, edited by Cormac K. H. O'Malley & Cormac Ó Comhraí (Mercier Press, Cork, 2013)

O'Malley, Ernie, *On Another Man's Wound* (Mercier Press, Cork, 2013)

Price, Dominic, *The Flame and the Candle: War in Mayo 1919–1924* (Collins Press, Cork, 2012)

Reddiough, James, *Michael Kilroy: a life 1884–1962* (booklet, 34 pages, 2008)

Thorne, Kathleen Hegarty, *They Put the Flag a Flyin': The Roscommon Volunteers, 1916–1923* (General Organization, Eugene, Oregon, 2007)

Younger, Calton, *Ireland's Civil War* (Taplinger, New York, 1969)

JOURNALS

Cathair na Mart, Journal of the Westport Historical Society, many articles from 1999 (Vol. 19) to 2012 (Vol. 30) by Aidan Clarke, Jarlath Duffy, Vincent Keane, Anthony J. Jordan, Seán Ó hOgáin and others

Back the Road, Newport Historical Society, Vol. 1, No. 2. Sammon, Willie, 'War of Independence and Civil War'

INDEX

1st Northern Division 65, 269
1st Southern Division 198, 220, 223, 272, 274
1st Western Division 23, 64, 141, 196, 223, 269
2nd Southern Division 13, 64, 141, 276
2nd Western Division 23, 62, 64, 116, 197, 208, 220, 221, 225, 294, 321
3rd Southern Division 262, 299
3rd Western Division 23, 64, 67, 269, 292, 294, 315, 318, 323
4th Northern Division 196, 275
4th Western Division 18, 23, 27, 35, 61, 62, 71, 96, 113, 118, 120, 139, 194, 225, 255, 264, 265, 268, 332

A

Aasleagh 97
Abbeyton 220
Achill 37, 127, 141, 255, 292
Aclare 321
Adamson, George 24, 270
Adderley, Albert 39
Aghamore 23, 26, 282, 284, 286, 289, 290, 294, 311
Aiken, Frank 27, 117, 161, 226, 275, 276, 280, 281
Aille 77, 86, 104, 105, 109
Aillemore 106
Ainsworth, Tom 180
American Alliance 167
Ancient Order of Hibernians (AOH) 167, 311

Anglo-Irish Treaty 13, 16, 23, 24, 62, 116, 140, 144, 164, 165, 194, 212, 218, 221, 244, 264, 266, 271, 290, 314, 331
Annamoe 273, 278
Arbour Hill 70, 160
Ardagh 264
Arderry 103
Ardnacrusha 64
Ardnaree 27, 245
Ardvally 242
Armstrong, Thomas R. 20, 251, 254
Athlone 24–27, 66, 68, 69, 73, 90–92, 94, 111–113, 142–144, 146, 148, 197, 199–203, 205, 222, 224–226, 248, 270, 296, 297, 330, 332
Aughagower 40, 53, 77, 86, 89, 90, 96, 97, 100, 102, 105, 107, 115, 119, 120, 123, 125, 162, 167, 173, 188, 192
Auxiliaries 60, 72, 89, 90, 139, 191, 193, 234, 241, 242, 249, 251, 312, 319, 320
Auxiliary Fire Brigades 30

B

Baker, Joe 27, 57, 101, 107, 108, 122, 127, 131, 134, 174, 179, 180, 192, 193, 196, 329
Balgriffin 118
Balla 36–38, 45, 59, 62, 63, 107, 114, 145, 170, 210, 212, 217, 221, 283, 291, 332
Balladuff 310

Ballaghaderreen 22, 25, 26, 69, 148, 203, 204, 231, 248, 286, 287, 289, 292, 295, 297, 303, 313, 314, 317, 319, 322, 323, 326, 327

Ballards, Major 320

Ballina, Co. Clare 64

Ballina, Co. Mayo 20–25, 27, 37, 66–68, 86, 113, 115, 119, 121, 142, 161, 162, 209, 228–230, 234, 236, 240, 242, 243, 245, 250–258, 260, 261, 264, 269, 271, 282, 290, 291, 303, 310, 313, 328, 329, 332

Ballinacarriga 77, 82, 89, 90, 121, 193

Ballinalee 66, 257, 260

'Ballinalee, The' 25, 65, 66, 194, 256, 257, 269

Ballinamore 152, 180, 192

Ballinasloe 271

Ballindine 22, 168

Ballingan, Tilly 247

Ballinrobe 21, 24, 77, 107, 162, 175, 176, 178, 191, 192, 208, 210, 212–214, 216, 217, 219, 224, 227, 269

Ballintleva 128

Ballintubber Abbey 170

Ballycarran 23

Ballycastle 43, 67, 107, 124, 161, 250, 251, 257, 266, 291, 316, 331

Ballycroy 38, 59, 67, 161

Ballygar 152, 224, 249

Ballyhaunis 19–21, 23, 25, 147, 210, 218, 282–291, 294, 296, 301, 311, 312, 318, 320

Ballyheane 26, 75, 90, 92

Ballyknockan 154

Ballymun 274, 276, 279–281

Ballysadare 234

Ballyvary 20, 38, 75, 254, 320

Bangor 162, 250, 251, 255

Banna 321

Barna 115, 319

Barrets, Johnny 251

Barrett, Johnny 141

Barrett, Richard 26, 293

Barry, Tom 30, 197, 223, 274, 276, 279, 280

Bartley, Gerald 57, 114, 115

Barton, Robert (Bob) 206, 262, 273

Beckett, Harry 22, 43, 129

Beckett's Mill 20, 254

Beggar's Bush Barracks 110, 140, 194, 330

Belderg 25, 68, 256, 282, 331

Bellacorick Barracks 19

Bellavary 138, 142

Belmullet 20, 23, 38, 54, 250, 255, 257

Benson, Dominick 143, 144, 199, 200, 202, 301, 328

Bergin, John 21, 246–249, 263

Bergin, Joseph 301

Berry, Johnny 100, 180

'Big Fellow, the' 257

Big (High) Wall ambush 22, 41, 76, 77, 98, 99, 126, 127, 172

Birreen 49, 50

Black and Tans 21, 32, 39, 41, 43, 44, 46, 52–54, 58, 60, 69, 72, 75, 76, 80, 81, 83, 91, 100–102, 122, 135, 137, 139, 140, 164, 169, 170, 177, 178, 182–184, 187, 188, 210, 211, 213, 231, 234, 235, 243, 247, 248, 251, 283–288, 309, 312, 317–319

Blackrock 153, 245
Black Watch, the 106
Blaney, Patrick 196
Blessington 153, 154, 206, 268
Blythe, Sydney 23, 182
Bofin, Ned 71
Bofin, Paul 64, 65, 71
Bohaun 103
Bohea 138, 176
Bohola 19, 24, 59, 107, 145, 203,
    210, 312, 320
Boland, Harry 22, 271
Boland, Paddy 23, 287, 288
Boras 89
Border Regiment 20, 75
Bourke, Joe 68
Bourke, Pat 23
Boyle 24, 111, 292–294, 296,
    318–322
Boyle, Jim 250
Brackloon 98, 121
Bradley, John 119
Breaffy 59, 147, 166, 180
Brehony, Dominick 144
Brehony, Harry 142, 201
Brennan, Jack 237, 238
Brennan, Jim 91
Brennan, Joe 289
Brennan, John 91
Brennan, Martin 194, 238, 257,
    321, 325, 326
Brennan, Michael 23, 24, 64, 141,
    196, 223, 269, 316
Brennan, Pat 226
Brickeens 286, 287
Brown, Fr Paddy 274
Brown, Fr Tom 258
Browne, James 23, 182, 184
Browne, Jim 22, 45, 46, 53, 77, 79,
    85, 91, 93, 128

Browne, Fr Maurice 154
Brugha, Cathal 197, 220, 221
Buckley, Johnny 160
Buckoogh 48, 49, 52, 53, 56, 89
Bunnyconnellan 21, 23, 25, 236,
    237, 242, 243, 253, 257, 260,
    270, 332
Burke, Frank 143
Burke, John 115
Burke, Martin 112
Burke, Michael 70
Burke, P. 26
Burke, Paddy 250
Burke, Tom 156
Butler, Francis J. 22, 77–79, 128
Byrne, Charlie 141, 195, 196
Byrne, Christie 299
Byrne, Dominick 291
Byrne, Fr Tom 162, 243, 259, 260

C

Cahir 66, 276
Calleary, Pat A. 251, 265
Campbell, Joe 299
Campbell, Tommy 322
Cannon, John 22, 129
Cannon, Paddy 25, 27, 48, 73, 74,
    79, 83, 90, 93, 129, 144, 146,
    148, 201, 203
Capermacloughlin 171
Carnaclay 56, 100, 139, 176
Carney, Broddie 123
Carney, Frank 40, 123
Carney, James 40
Carney, Tom 25–27, 261, 291,
    295, 303, 311, 313, 314, 318,
    322
Carolan, Micky 278
Carracastle 286, 315
Carrick 109

Carrickaneady 35, 51

Carrowbawn 54, 118, 120

Carrowkennedy 19, 21, 23, 33, 40,
41, 51, 53–58, 72, 73, 86, 88,
97, 103–109, 120, 122, 125,
130, 132, 133, 135, 136, 138,
161, 162, 172–174, 177, 179,
181, 186, 188, 190

Carty, Frank 22, 24, 66, 67, 110,
198, 199, 257, 269, 276, 318,
320, 321, 329

Casey, Frank 160

Cassidy, Patrick (Paddy) 286, 315,
316

Castlebar 13, 20, 21, 24, 25, 37, 41,
43, 45, 59, 62, 63, 65, 66, 72–77,
81, 83–85, 89, 90, 96, 98–100,
109–111, 119, 120, 122–124,
126, 128, 137, 139–142, 147,
164, 171, 172, 174, 176, 177,
179, 180, 185, 190, 191, 195,
196, 198, 199, 209, 210, 212,
213, 216, 230, 231, 242, 243,
253, 321, 324, 331

Castlecarra 27

Castleconor 243

Castlerea 62, 224, 248

Chambers, James 75

Chambers, Liam Willy 50

Chambers, Mrs 48

Charlestown 21, 24, 286, 291,
295, 315–318, 323, 328

Childers, Erskine 273, 278

Civil War 14–16, 24, 29, 30, 36,
40, 59, 64, 90, 92, 111, 117,
120, 121, 142, 157, 175, 198,
219, 223, 236–238, 255, 256,
258, 260, 265, 268, 282, 292–
294, 303, 313, 317, 319–321,
331, 332

Claddy 40, 54, 86, 125, 126, 130,
136, 173, 174, 184, 186, 188

Claremorris 24–26, 35, 112, 113,
118, 146, 203–205, 210, 211,
216, 217, 219, 227, 286, 287,
289, 312, 320, 327

Clew Bay 15, 39, 59, 138

Clifden 26, 57, 65, 66, 69,
114–116

Clifford, Madge 279

Clogher 21, 59, 78, 124, 125, 128,
172

Clooneed 162

Cloongee House 20

Cloonkeen 76, 172

Cloonskill 40, 96, 107, 120, 124,
189

Cloonsonvagh 107

Cloontumper 19

Clydagh 23, 251

Coen, Mick 21, 288, 289

Coen, Tom 209

Colbert, Con 33

Coleman, Patrick 20

Collins, John/Johnny/Seán 22, 45,
81, 82, 100, 129, 307

Collins, Maggie 328

Collins, Michael 24, 25, 63, 64, 141,
145, 146, 194–196, 220, 221,
257, 265, 267, 271, 284, 293

Collins, Tom 43

Collooney 24, 25, 198–200, 238,
260, 269, 294, 321

Comer, Jack 262, 279, 299

Comerford, Máire 273, 279

Condon, Mairteen 221

Cong 208, 211, 213

Congested District Board 90, 313

Connaught Rangers 34

Conneely, Paul 115, 116

Connelly, John 115
Connemara 27, 62, 65, 110, 115, 180
Connolly, Louis 200
Connolly, Matty 70, 297, 298
Connolly, Seán/John/Jack 15, 45–47, 50–52, 56, 57, 83, 180, 181, 242
Conroy, Fr 44, 162, 165, 168, 179
Coolgarra 286
Coolnabinna 106
Coonacool 238
Coosan 203
Corbally 236, 242, 245, 260
Corbett, Éamonn 198, 312, 314
Corbett, Joseph 115
Corcoran, Nicholas 27, 258
Corcoran, Seán 19–21, 172, 209, 283, 284, 286, 289, 312–315, 318
Cordarragh 176, 188, 189, 191, 192
Corissins 143, 144
Cork 25, 64, 157, 158, 160, 197, 207, 223, 235, 258, 267, 269, 274, 275, 277, 307
Corrig 100, 128, 172, 175
Corveagh 96, 97, 102, 103
Cosgrave, Phil 298
Cosgrave, William 259, 298
Costello, Michael 176
Coughlan, John 21, 103, 125, 161, 173
Coughlan, Paddy 70
Courtney, Freda 164
Coyle, Harry 63
Coyne, District Justice 212
Coyne, Martin 220, 226
Coyne, Stephen 27
Creegan, Francis 23, 58, 122, 134,

135, 181–184, 188
Cregganbaun 106
Croagh Patrick 39, 97, 121, 122, 171, 172, 188
Crofts, Tom 223, 274, 275, 279, 280
Croker, Richard 267
Cross 61, 76, 208–211, 213, 250, 257, 271, 294, 320
Crossard 21, 210, 282, 285, 286, 288, 312
Crossmolina 36, 46, 48, 86, 137, 141, 249, 250, 255, 257, 259, 260, 270
Crowley, Dr John 19, 22, 291
Cruise, R. F. 45
Crumlin 106, 137
Cryan, Battie 25, 27, 106, 121, 131, 151, 152, 180, 191, 192
Cuilmore 32, 35, 39, 108, 125
Cullane 126
Culleen 171
Culleens 20, 23, 39, 228, 236–238, 241
Cumann na mBan 30, 33, 279, 301–303
Cummins, Tom 44, 78–80
Cunnane, Frank 27, 162, 222
Curley, Hugh 289
Curragh, the 27, 73, 91, 113, 118, 147, 149, 152, 167, 206, 228, 262, 282, 299, 329, 330
Curtain, Captain 111
Cushin 100, 101, 124
Cushlough 96, 97, 104, 108, 109, 119, 125, 135, 136, 161, 165, 166, 173

D

Dáil Éireann 24, 29, 32, 33, 168,

208, 218, 266, 289, 290, 292, 310, 330
Dale, John H. W. L. 247
Dalton, Canon 162, 219, 227
Dalton, Dr 218
Daly, Dr Peter 216
Davis, Jerry 150, 248
Davis, Matt 222
Dawson, Martin 171
Deasy, Liam 26, 223, 261, 268, 274, 298, 299
Deasy, Private 25
Delahunty, Gus 58, 88, 182
Derrig, Tom 20, 22, 27, 37–39, 121, 140, 156, 164, 165, 207, 209, 267, 268, 275, 279, 280, 329, 330
Derrinbohan 106
Derrycraff 98, 126, 175, 176, 190, 192
Derrygorman 111, 119, 139, 167, 194, 331
Derryherbert 96, 103
Derrykillew 97, 103
Derryloughan 35, 82
Derrymaher 109
Derrymartin 89, 106
Derrymore 108
Derryulra 108
de Valera, Éamon 19, 163, 259, 264, 266, 271–277, 279, 280, 311
Devins, Seamus 22, 65, 66, 270, 331
Dignan, Peadar 315
Dillon, John 308, 311
Dockery, Mick 24, 294, 296, 301, 321, 322
Doherty, Bill 284
Doherty, John 23, 182, 184

Doherty, Josie 128
Doherty, Terence 250
Doherty, Willie 250
Dole, Tom 221, 222
Donegal 91, 140, 151, 170, 269, 292, 323
Donnellan, Peter 119, 120, 132, 137
Donnelly, Éamon 156
Donnelly, Jimmy 148
Donnelly, Peter 25
Donnelly, Stephen 255
Donoghue, Mick 305
Doogue, Pierce 20
Dovea 304, 309, 310
Dowling, John/Seán 276, 279, 280
Dowling, Thomas 23, 182
Doyle, Joe 92
Drangan 170
Driminahaha 19, 75
Dromore 234–240, 244, 249, 255, 256, 258, 261
Drumbane 307
Drumboe Castle 151
Drummin 23, 40, 59, 86, 89, 97, 103, 105, 108, 119, 122, 124, 125, 127, 129–131, 173, 174, 185, 188
Drummindoo 167, 331
Drumshanbo 245
Dublin 13, 14, 24, 26, 27, 30, 31, 33, 34, 36, 38, 40, 43–45, 61, 63, 69, 70, 85, 93, 100, 110, 113, 118, 121, 123, 126, 129, 140, 147, 153, 154, 156, 160, 161, 164, 167, 168, 170, 189, 194, 196, 197, 204, 206, 211, 213, 219, 220, 222, 223, 225, 227, 264–268, 271–275, 278,

280, 282, 283, 292, 293, 295, 298, 299, 302, 303, 306, 309, 310, 315–317, 319, 320, 329, 330

Dublin Fusiliers 34

Duffy, Broddie 196

Duffy, Jim 124

Duffy, Johnny 40, 57, 58, 87, 88, 102, 106, 120, 122, 130, 131, 171, 180, 183, 190–192

Duffy, Paddy 26, 27, 40, 41, 89, 96, 99, 102, 115, 116, 120, 122, 131, 134, 135, 138–141, 180, 188, 189, 195, 196

Duffy, Pat 171

Duggan, Fr Thomas 274, 279

Duggan, Tim 115

Dunboyne 300

Duncan, Joe 194

Dundalk 38, 118, 150, 168

Dundrum 38

Dun Laoghaire 207, 277

Dunleavy, Patrick 211, 221, 222, 291

Durcan, Martin 238

Durless 39, 59, 89, 103, 104, 106, 122, 129, 185, 186, 188

Durras 89

Dwyer, Michael 155, 278

Dwyer, Tom 307, 310

Dyra, Michael 46, 50

E

Easky 21, 228, 230, 231, 235–237, 240, 244, 255, 258, 261

Easter Rising 13, 29, 31, 163, 167, 273, 283, 314

East Mayo Brigade 20, 107, 209, 210, 230, 254, 261, 282–284, 289, 303, 312, 315

Egan, Paddy 299

Ennis 269

Enniscrone 20, 22, 23, 228–231, 236, 241, 243–246, 250–253, 255, 282, 290

Enright, Éamon 66

Errew 107

Erriff 108, 109, 130, 188

Erris 54, 58, 161, 266, 271

F

Fahey, Matty 115

Fairgreen, the 45, 168, 169, 177, 178, 188

Farrell, Anthony 23

Farrell, Tony 161

Farrelly, Seamus 325

Feehan, Jack 27, 65, 71, 115, 196, 268

Feeney, Annie Christina 208

Feeney, Pádraig 22, 208, 217

Fenian Rising, 1867 36

Fennelly, Joe 204

Ferran, Dr Francis P. 22, 146, 251, 291, 315, 330

Fianna Fáil 36, 42, 69, 73, 163, 264

Figgis, Darrell 267, 307

Fitzgerald, Desmond 265, 267

Fitzpatrick, Paddy 315

Flaherty, Jim/Jimmy 87, 88, 110, 124, 136, 180, 182, 183, 187, 188

Flaherty, Mally 110

Flannigan, Barney 301

Flatley, Fr John 105

Fleming, Éamon 273, 278

Flynn, Stephen Fleming 245

Foody, Anthony 23, 253, 254

Forde, Liam 289, 316, 317

Forkan, Padraic 287
Forrigle 177
Four Courts 13, 24, 34, 63, 91, 167, 198, 224, 227, 255, 267, 268, 278, 282, 292, 293, 295, 320, 330
Fox, Seamus 143, 144, 202, 203
Foxford 20, 22, 49, 89, 250, 252, 256, 258, 261, 291, 309, 315, 330
Foy, Jack 316
Fran, James 148
French, William 23, 122, 182–184, 188
Fuge, Thomas Hugh Hare 39
Furgill 122, 136

G

Gallagher, Johnny 126
Galway 34, 41, 42, 54, 61, 62, 72, 96, 113, 115–117, 139, 158, 162, 164, 167, 168, 175, 193, 194, 210, 216, 220–222, 226–228, 238, 261, 262, 265, 276, 279, 283, 286, 288, 299, 300, 310, 312, 314, 319, 321, 329, 331
Galway Gaol 27, 41, 112–116, 174, 226, 260, 264, 265, 281, 329
Gannon, Éamonn 23, 209, 229
Gargan, John 115
Gavan, Charlie 27, 41, 105, 111, 113–115, 120, 121, 165, 168
Gavan, Dan 107
Geraghty, Martin 165
Gibbons, Broddie 64
Gibbons, Jim 297, 298
Gibbons, Fr John 140, 195
Gibbons, John Dick 120, 175, 178

Gibbons, Johnny/Seán 27, 40, 48, 61, 82, 83, 86, 99, 111, 113, 115, 116, 120, 121, 138, 139, 170, 171, 179, 180
Gibbons, T. 286
Gilmartin, Dr T. P. 20, 140, 219
Gilmartin, J. 286
Gilmore, George 158
Glenamoy 25, 58, 68, 256, 257
Glenasmole 154
Glendalough 153, 155
Gleneasky 237, 238
Glenesk 23
Glenhest 25, 89, 118, 142
Glenisland 41, 51, 75, 85
Glenlara 48, 50, 52, 83, 84, 106
Glenlossera 67
Glenmask 90
Glenummera 106
Glosh 97, 123
Gloshpatrick 21, 39, 97
Gogarty, Oliver St John 273, 278
Golden, John 310
Gormanstown Camp 93
Goulaun 240, 241
Goulding, Seán 278
Grace, James 206
Grace, Paddy 90
Grealy, Johnny 26, 282, 283, 288, 297, 311, 318–320, 322
Greenaun's 89, 90
Green, Max 58
Griffin, Fr Michael 319
Griffith, Arthur 267
Groarke, Evelyn 303
Groarke, James 318
Gullin, Charles 116
Gurrey, Fr 290
Gurteen 231, 258, 321, 323, 325

H

Hales, Donal 277
Hales, Seán 293
Hales, Tom 207, 270
Hanlon, Head Constable 121, 136, 181, 182, 184, 185, 187, 190
Hannelly, Canon 218, 219
Hannon, Ned 251
Haran, Ned 127, 169, 178
Hare, Martin 197, 209
Hare, Michael 211
Hare Park 91–93, 147, 206, 228, 261, 262, 299
Harney, Andy 59, 109, 119
Harney, Tom 198
Hastings, Darby 131, 135
Hastings, John 125
Hastings, Tim 99, 175, 177
Hawkshaw, Myles 120
Headford 27, 162, 209, 225, 258, 281
Healy, Jim 230
Healy, Joe 27, 258
Healy, May 282
Healy, Ned 169
Heaneen, John M. 310
Heavey, Tommy 25, 73, 107, 118–120, 126, 128, 129, 136, 148, 156, 180, 181, 202, 203, 300
Hegarty, Bartley 23, 251
Hegarty, Edward 25
Hegarty, Paddy 19, 69, 92, 93
Hegarty, Peter 69
Hegarty, Seán 223
Henry, Jim 180
Henry, Jimmy 311
Henry, Mick 251

Herwood, John 115
Heuston, Seán 33
Higgins, John 27
Higgins, Paddy 196
Higgins, Thomas 23, 241
Hoban, Thomas 120
Hobson, Bulmer 271
Hogan, John Joe 308
Hogan, Ladeen 139, 180, 194
Hogan, Paddy 266
Hopkins, Thomas 22
Horgan, Tim 170
Horridge, Major 153
Houlihan, Larry 70
Howley, James 22
Howley, Tommy 253
Hughes, Charlie 106, 120, 127, 129, 178, 192, 195, 330
Hughes, Gus 91, 93
Hughes, Michael 81–83
Hughes, Tom 112
Humphreys, Ellen 273, 279
Hunt, Jim 313, 323
Hunt, Michael 306–308, 310, 313
Hurley, Fr 79
Hyde, Seán 275, 278

I

Ibberson, Geoffrey 22, 216
Igoe, James 309, 310
Inishbee 59
Irish Citizen Army 30
Irish Parliamentary Party 31, 167, 244
Irish Republican Brotherhood (IRB) 15, 48, 61, 83, 111, 153, 163, 165, 193, 212, 218, 221, 244, 252, 264, 265, 270, 271, 282, 289, 294, 317, 319, 331, 332

Islandeady 22, 26, 41, 43, 44, 53, 73–77, 86, 89, 90, 98, 100, 111, 121, 123, 124, 126, 128, 165, 172, 176, 186, 192

J

Jones, James 310
Jordan, Jack 142
Jordan, Paddy 22, 43–45, 74, 75, 81, 82, 85, 98, 129
Jordan, Tommy 299
Joyce, Red Pat 122, 129, 185, 188
Joyce, Rick 87–89, 137, 180
Joyce, Stephen 112

K

Kane, Jack 193, 194
Kane, Jim 51
Kane, Jimmy 46
Kane, John 51
Kane, Nelly Malone 178
Kane, Owney 38
Kavanagh, Seamus 251
Keane, Jack/James/John 56, 103, 131, 135, 139
Keane, Michael 55, 57
Kelly, Alfie 317
Kelly, Eugene 287, 291, 317, 318
Kelly, Jim 44, 80, 83, 128
Kelly, Joe 289, 292, 313, 314, 317, 323, 327
Kelly, Mick 317
Kelly, Paddy 91, 92, 93
Kelly, Paddy/P. J. 119, 180, 181, 197
Kenny, Austin 287
Kenny, P. 287, 291
Keogh Barracks 93
Keogh, Jack 71, 148
Kerry 34, 148, 258, 274, 279, 280, 299

Kilawullaun 107, 109
Kilbagh 319
Kilcawley, Matt 21, 28, 228, 229, 237, 243, 246, 251, 254, 255, 258, 261–263, 290
Kilcawley, Micky 246
Kilcawley, Tom 228, 235
Kilcock 300
Kilcommon 161
Kilcoona 162
Kilcoyne, John F. 111
Kilcullen 91, 152
Kilcullen, Seamus 237, 257
Kildea, Charlie 293
Kildea, Jimmy 176
Kildrum 209
Kilfaul 20
Kilkelly 25, 203, 285, 286, 320, 327
Kilkelly, Jim 283, 288
Kilkenny 206, 274–276, 310, 331
Killala 228, 249, 259
Killeen 89
Killilea, Mark 129, 158, 159
Kilmaine 213, 219, 224
Kilmainham 71, 118, 160, 261, 262
Kilmeena 22, 33, 36, 41–46, 49, 51, 53, 56, 70, 73, 74, 77–80, 82, 85, 87, 98–100, 103, 120, 127–129, 162, 165, 167, 174, 176, 249, 268, 324
Kilmilkin 54, 111
Kilmovee 21, 22, 286, 320
Kilroy, Ann 'Nan' Leonard 36, 46, 51
Kilroy, Jim 250, 251
Kilroy, John 27
Kilroy, Michael 20, 23, 26, 33, 35–40, 42, 46, 60–62, 69,

72, 77–81, 83–88, 97–101,
103, 107, 110, 111, 121–125,
127–130, 132, 134–142, 160,
161, 170–174, 179–181, 184,
186, 187, 195, 209, 223, 251,
252, 257, 261, 262, 265, 266,
268–271, 276, 320, 330, 331
Kiltarsaghaun 105
Kilteevan 91, 222
Kiltimagh 24–26, 198, 209, 210,
286, 289, 291, 295, 301, 303,
304, 312–315, 319, 327, 328,
332
King George V Military Hospital
43, 44, 85
King, Constable John 23, 241
King, John 115
King's Own Scottish Borderers
287–289, 317
King, Thomas 170
Kinuary 89, 105, 217, 221
Kinvara 66
Kitterick, Tom 38, 48, 52, 53,
55, 60, 74, 80, 83, 86, 101,
120, 121, 126, 127, 131, 132,
135, 138, 139, 156, 158, 160,
165, 168, 170, 174, 183–185,
187–190, 194, 195, 298, 330
Knappagh 138, 176, 189, 190

L

Lackan 153, 161
Lackderg 109
Lacy, Dinny 272
Lahardane 152
Lahardaun 92, 106, 193
Lally, Sergeant 25
Lally, Thomas 22, 41, 76, 127, 173
Lambert, Bull 177
Lambert, Butch 80, 123, 177, 180

Lambert, Paddy 178
Langan, Tom 194
Lanmore 107, 173, 176, 180
Lawlor, Anthony/Tony 25, 69,
147, 148, 200, 225, 257, 258,
270, 297, 330
Leamy, Mary 308
Lecanvey 123, 170, 171
Leenane 21, 41, 53–55, 87, 96, 98,
111, 116, 130, 131, 138, 164,
167, 168, 173, 174, 178, 181,
185, 186, 188–191
Lehane, Seán 64, 269
Leitrim 106, 120, 152, 192, 324,
325, 326
Lemass, Noel 278
Lemass, Seán 159, 278
Leonard, Fr 327
Leonard, Jack 55, 106, 193
Letter 43, 44, 74, 86
Lettermaglinskin 108
Lever, Charles 204
Limerick 24, 64, 119, 141, 196,
268, 269, 309, 316, 328
Lisacul 69, 148, 286, 289, 316
Liscarney 111, 138
Lisduff 304
Local Defence Force 30
Local Security Force 30
Loftus, Tomás/Tom 23, 237, 238,
254, 290, 297
Longford 15, 26, 66, 145, 197,
245, 257, 260, 324, 326
Loughboy 286
Lough Corrib 116, 117
Lough Furnace 42, 89
Loughglynn 21, 144, 246–248,
263
Lough Mask 37, 116, 117, 213
Loughnane, Henry 288

Loughnane, Patrick 288
Louisburgh 37, 39, 54, 59, 86, 87,
  89, 97, 109, 116, 119, 122, 171,
  197, 198, 331
Lydon, Tom 188, 189
Lynch, Diarmuid 61
Lynch, Fionán 271, 310
Lynch, Jack 207
Lynch, Liam 27, 66, 117, 220,
  223, 224, 259, 267, 268,
  272–276, 278, 279
Lynham, Bunny 300
Lyons, Dr 327
Lyons, Ned 38, 39

M

Maam 116
MacBride, John 19, 22, 31, 118,
  156, 164
MacBride, Joseph/Joe 105, 156,
  164, 165, 209, 332
MacBride, Seán 156–161
MacCarthy, Seán 64
MacDermot, Stephen 21, 247,
  248, 263
MacDiarmada, Seán 36
MacDonagh, Charlie 297
MacDonagh, John/Jack 48, 83,
  86, 87, 123, 131, 134
MacDonald, Canon 55, 80, 81
MacDonald, Jack 85
MacEntee, Seán 297
MacEoin, Seán 66, 69, 147, 197,
  200, 204, 205, 224, 225, 257,
  258, 266, 272, 294, 297, 323,
  325, 328, 330, 332
MacEvilly, Seamus/Jim 22, 43, 44,
  80, 82, 98, 99, 128, 324
MacEvilly, Thomas 43, 324, 325
MacHugh, Fr 162

Macken, Christie 26, 116, 194,
  197, 225
Macken, Dean 219
MacMahon, Seán 167
MacManus, Dermot 158, 159,
  298
MacNeill, Brian 26, 144, 194, 291,
  292, 301, 315, 320, 328, 331
MacNeill, Eoin 302, 314, 331
MacNulty, James 22
MacNulty, Michael 66
MacSwiney, Terence 235, 274
Madden, John A. 20, 43, 44, 46,
  47, 49, 50, 52, 55, 60, 66, 68,
  75, 78, 79, 81–84, 86, 97, 124,
  131, 138, 177, 180, 181, 183,
  266, 267, 316, 331
Madden, Pat 161, 162, 221
Maguire, Conor 69, 212, 268
Maguire, DI 119, 120
Maguire, George 217
Maguire, Hugh 211
Maguire, Joseph 22, 104, 129
Maguire, Seamus 144, 201, 203
Maguire, Seán 27, 162, 208, 222,
  281
Maguire, Tom 20, 22–24, 26, 27,
  42, 61, 62, 64, 65, 98, 111, 117,
  162, 176, 190, 194, 197, 208,
  209, 212, 214, 218–223, 227,
  265, 267–269, 271, 281, 294,
  320, 321
Máille, Peter 40
Malahide 153
Mallon, Tommy 148
Malone, Broddie 25, 27, 40, 41,
  55, 57, 86, 97, 99–101, 118,
  120, 122, 124–128, 131, 134,
  136, 141, 142, 144, 145, 163,
  164, 172, 174, 176–180, 182–

184, 187, 189, 194, 201–203, 205, 222, 276, 321
Malone, Martin 97
Malone, Michael 127, 168, 177, 179
Malone, Seamus 307, 319
Malone, Tom Johnny 178
Malone, Willie 59, 100, 108, 126, 135, 141, 142, 166, 180, 195
Mannion, Paddy 227
Markievicz, Countess 164, 306
Markree Castle 26, 110, 111, 198, 199
Martin, Jimmy 225, 226
Martin, Mick 262
May, Patrick 214
McCabe, Alec 22, 61, 141, 195, 196
McCarthy, Seán 64, 268, 270
McCorley, Felix 154–156
McCorley, Roger 159
McCormack, Dan 26, 27
McCullough, Dinny 271
McDevitt, Joe 142
McDonagh, Joe 266
McDonnell, Petie Joe 27, 61, 68, 69, 110, 158, 180
McEvilly, Bridget 228
McGarry, District Inspector 311, 313
McGarry, Seán 271
McGing, Paddy Nancy 102
McGivern, Tady 323
McGloin, P. 286
McGlynn, Bassy 194
McGovern, Larry 180
McGovern, Sergeant 24
McHugh, Canon 289, 290
McHugh, Michael 196, 207, 329
McKelvey, Joe 26, 267, 292

McKeown, Kit 145, 203
McLoughlin, Mick 318
McMahon, Anita 141
McMahon, Peadar 316, 332
McQuaid, Private 27, 227
Meenaghan, Dr 167, 168
Mellett, Michael 112
Mellows, Barney 158
Mellows, Liam 26, 33, 63, 167, 266, 272, 283, 292
Milling, John C. 19, 41
Mill Street 40, 41, 120, 123, 142, 175, 178
Milroy, Seán 267, 307
Mitchell, Comdt 26
Moane, Ned 20, 36, 39, 40, 54, 60, 96, 100, 103, 111, 118, 119, 121, 122, 124, 125, 128, 132, 139, 163, 165, 166, 168, 170, 171, 176, 177, 179–181, 183, 190, 331
Moffatt, Michael 316
Molloy, Broddy 163, 176, 177, 180, 181
Molloy, DI 169
Molloy, Frank 168
Molloy, John 167
Moloney, Con 71
Monaghan, Michael 27, 162, 222
Mooney, M. 19
Moran, Dr 62
Moran, James/Jim 45–47, 50, 51, 56, 57, 77, 79, 82, 99, 128, 180
Moran, Pat 36
Moran, William 24, 210, 312
Mountjoy Gaol 13, 69–71, 91, 94, 118, 147, 148, 156–158, 205, 248, 249, 261, 296–299, 329
Moylan, Martin 27, 162, 222
Moylan, Seán 266

Muckanagh 85, 86
Mularky, Jack 50
Mulcahy, Richard 69, 211, 212, 220, 253, 259, 270
Muldoon, Dr 327
Mulholland, Francis 104
Mullingar 143, 144
Mullins, Maurice 21, 210, 283, 284, 318
Mullins, Mick 111, 117, 225
Mullins, Paddy 172, 210, 284, 288, 289, 293, 301, 318
Mullins, Seán 210
Mullins, Tom 91–93, 147, 148, 151
Mulloy, Paddy 22, 43, 129
Mulrennan, James 21
Mulrennan, Patrick 'Patch' 26, 69, 147, 148, 297, 330
Mulrennan, Seamus 26, 297
Munnelly, Jack 37, 38
Munro, James 22, 49, 52, 53, 104
Munster Fusiliers 34, 75, 306
Murphy, Con 277
Murphy, Fintan 38, 267
Murphy, Humphrey 273
Murphy, Seamus 265
Murrisk 119, 121, 123
Myna 42
Myshall 272, 278

N

Naas 93, 154, 156, 159
Na Fianna Éireann 30, 33, 34, 40, 41, 142, 163–165, 313, 329, 330
Naughton, Jacob 259
Naughton, Martin/Maurteen 100, 122, 139, 259
Naughton, Paddy 122, 139

Navin, Tom 165
Nealon, Tom 23
Nephin 23, 59, 86
Newell, John 27, 162, 222
Newport 22, 25–27, 35, 36, 38–40, 42, 47–49, 51–53, 55, 56, 61, 62, 67–69, 74, 77–80, 83, 84, 86, 89, 90, 97–101, 106, 119, 121, 125, 128, 129, 142, 172, 174–176, 179, 209, 227, 256, 257, 271, 295, 320
Nogher 237
Nolan, Thomas/Tommy 22, 43, 45, 129
North Mayo Brigade 20, 23, 61, 62, 110, 209, 228, 229, 246, 255, 264, 265, 276, 280, 330, 332
North Roscommon Brigade 226, 296
North-West Mayo Brigade 161, 255, 264

O

Oakes, Herbert 21
O'Beirne, Frank 142, 144, 194, 199–203
O'Boyle, Frank 22, 76, 127
O'Boyle, Ned 250
O'Boyle, Neill 'Plunkett' 118, 153–155
O'Brien, Michael 22, 209, 211, 214, 216
O'Brien, Tom 165
O'Brien, William 105
O'Callaghan, Donal 274, 277
O'Connell, J. J. 'Ginger' 318, 319
O'Connell, Thomas 129
O'Connor, Art 156, 160
O'Connor, Gerald 221

O'Connor, Paddy 229, 230, 245
O'Connor, Rory 26, 292
O'Doherty, Louis 205, 206
O'Donnell, John 250
O'Donnell, Peadar 90, 91, 94, 148–151, 153, 292, 297
O'Donnell, Thomas 22, 82, 129
O'Donoghue, Diarmuid 68
O'Donoghue, Florence 223
O'Draingan, Michael 218
O'Duffy, Eoin 61, 62, 140, 194, 220, 265, 266
O'Dwyer, Seamus 266, 272
Offaly 147, 299
O'Flaherty, Patrick 308
O'Flynn, John 43, 44, 78, 79, 179
O'Gorman, Adjutant 194, 220, 224
O'Hanlon, Mick 148, 150
O'Hara, Archdeacon 328
O'Hara, Fr Dennis 312, 313
O'Hara, Fr Michael 162, 198
O'Hegarty, Diarmuid 271
O'Hegarty, Seán 197, 223
O'Higgins, Brian 34, 268
O'Higgins, Kevin 205, 259
O'Keefe, Paudeen 157, 298
O'Kelly, Sceilig 271
O'Kelly, Seán T. 266, 271
Ó Máille, Pádraic 54, 218, 266, 272, 293
Ó Máille, Séamus/O'Malley, James 27, 71, 72, 115, 162, 222
O'Malley, Bertie 206
O'Malley, Brigie 102
O'Malley, Paddy 22, 43–45, 49, 82, 129
O'Malley, Patrick 65
O'Malley, Peter 54

O'Malley, Thomas 22, 41, 76, 127, 173
Ó Muirthile, Seán 271
O'Neill, Larry 267
O'Regan, Christoper P. 21
O'Reilly, Ownie 178
O'Reilly, Steven 178
O'Reilly, Willie 178
O'Rourke, Dan 22, 144, 203
O'Sullivan, Gearóid 271
O'Toole, Broddy 86
Oughterard 71, 115, 162, 164, 286
Owenwee 41, 60, 86, 90, 107, 119, 122, 127, 128, 172, 189, 190, 191
Ox Mountains 25, 66, 67

P

Packington, Colonel 139
Partry 20, 60, 212, 213
Partry Mountains 42, 60
Phoenix Park 292, 304
Pidgeon, Johnny 93
Pierce, John 22, 43, 45, 82, 100, 129
Pilkington, William (Billy/Liam) 23, 64–66, 71, 269, 276, 277, 280, 292–295, 315, 317–321
Portacloy 37
Power, William 21
Prendergast, Jeffrey 142
Price, Éamon/Bob 209, 220, 266, 270, 314, 315

Q

Quinn, Tom 62
Quirke, Bill 280

R

Rarrigal 106

Rathhumish 242

Rathmines 266, 272, 278

Red Bridge 59, 101, 127, 174, 185

Red Cross 30, 204, 206

Regan, Constable 20

Regan, John 21

Reidy, Tommy 70, 146, 148, 151

Reilly, Broddie 165

Reilly, Ownie 165

Reilly, Stephen 169

Reilly, Willie 127

Rice, John Joe 280

Ring, Joe 24, 25, 39–41, 54, 56–59, 61, 63, 97, 99, 101, 111, 120–128, 132, 135–139, 142, 163, 165, 166, 172–174, 180, 183, 184, 187–195, 200, 257, 270, 331, 332

Ring, Martin 161

Robbins, Seán 299

Robinson, D. L. 156, 157, 160, 273, 278

Rocket, James 310

Rockingham Castle 295, 296

Roddy, Helena 264

Roe, Pat Morris 316

Rooney, Mick 300

Roscommon 16, 22, 62, 91, 121, 144, 203, 204, 208, 221, 222, 224, 226, 246, 284, 296, 309

Rosmuck 116

Rossow Bridge 78

Rowland, Harry 106, 259, 260

Ruane, Tom (Ballina) 19, 20, 27, 37, 67, 113, 115, 116, 209, 229, 245, 251, 257, 259, 260, 265, 276, 280, 291, 332

Ruane, Tommy (Kiltimagh) 24, 210, 291, 299, 301, 312, 315, 332

Rushe, Jim 60, 146

Russell, Seán 274

Ruttledge, P. J. 20, 22, 154, 257, 264, 266, 269–272, 275, 276, 279, 280, 291

Ryan, Fr 326, 327

Ryan, James 308

Ryan, Jerry 308, 310, 311

Ryan, Jim 148, 268

Ryan, Patsy 307

Ryan, P. J. 299

S

Salthill 115

Sammon, Bridget 104, 105

Sammon, Dan 170

Scahill, Peter 104

Scanlon, Dan 180

Scanlon, Seán 92–94, 150

Scanlon, Tom 313, 316, 328

Scurmore 230

Sears, William 19, 22

Shanbally 106

Sheeaune 77, 139

Sheeaune Hill 74

Sheeffry 108, 138

Sheeffry Bridge 87

Sheehy, Dan 291, 294, 295, 297, 299, 300, 313, 319

Sheehy, Joseph/Joe 283, 289, 313, 315, 319

Sherrin, Dennis 265

Shouldice, Bill 297, 301

Shraheen 176, 191, 192

Shramore 27, 50, 68, 174, 176, 227, 329

Simmons, Comdt 24

Simons, Frank 204, 221, 224

Sinn Féin 19, 20, 22, 27–30, 34, 36, 42, 61, 114, 141, 178,

243, 244, 251, 266, 267, 285, 289–291, 298, 308, 330

Skerdagh 22, 45, 46, 48–53, 82, 83, 85, 86, 89, 91, 100, 101, 104, 106, 128, 129, 141

Skreen 234

Sligo 16, 22, 24–26, 43, 61, 65–67, 92, 94, 106, 110, 141, 143, 144, 150, 162, 191, 194, 196, 198, 201, 202, 228, 230, 231, 234, 235, 237, 240–242, 245, 255–257, 269, 270, 276, 292, 294, 301, 313–318, 320, 321, 323, 324, 327–331

Sligo, Lord 104, 120, 129

Smith, Christie 299

Smith, P. J. 217

South Mayo Brigade 20, 21, 62, 145, 208, 209, 214, 221, 225

South Roscommon Brigade 62, 91, 221, 222

Spiddal 116

Srah 212–214

Sraheen 103, 109, 126

Stack, Mick 300

Staines, Michael 139, 193, 331, 332

Staunton, John 170

Staunton, John Patrick 22, 43, 44, 82, 87, 128

Staunton, Michael 75

Staunton, Michael 'Bully' 123, 130

Stephens, William H. 21, 283, 288

Stevenson, Edward J. 23, 54, 58, 59, 119, 120, 122, 132, 186

Sweeney, Maurice 164

Sweetman, Malachi 160

Swift, James/Jimmy 51, 81–83, 129

Swinford 20, 23–25, 162, 230, 231, 254, 261, 291, 295, 303, 311, 313, 317–320, 322, 323, 325, 328

T

Tallaghbawn 119, 128

Taylor, Luke 25

Teevenacroaghy 122, 170, 171

Teevinish 107

Templeboy 238

Templemore 306

Templeogue 268

Thurles 304, 306, 310, 311

Tibohine 313

Tiernaur 32, 36, 43, 50, 83

Tintown 73, 91, 94, 118, 148, 149, 151, 159, 262, 299

Tipperary 27, 64, 66, 115, 170, 206, 253, 258, 267, 272, 275, 278, 303–306, 308, 309, 314

Tobbercurry 66, 194, 198, 231, 237, 257, 261, 269, 319, 321, 329

Tobin, Mae 276

Tobin, Martin Mack 230

Togher, Captain 27

Tonlegee 96, 102, 107, 190, 192

Toorlestraun 321

Tourmakeady 21, 33, 41, 42, 59, 88, 89, 98, 116, 117, 126, 175, 176, 190, 208–210, 213–215, 218

Traynor, Oscar 223

Treaty 314, 315, 320

Truce 13, 15, 23, 33, 38, 40, 61, 65, 74, 83, 90, 109, 110, 116, 139, 170, 193, 197, 198, 208, 217–221, 236, 251, 253, 254, 256, 264, 265, 278, 285, 290, 291, 314, 315, 317, 330, 331

Tuam 20, 26, 27, 72, 140, 162,
   209, 211, 219, 222, 225, 281
Tuffy's Post Office 23, 228,
   238–240, 249
Tunney, James 161
Tunney, Mick 105
Tunney, Pat 161
Tunney, Tom 98, 175, 176, 190
Turlough 75, 138
Twomey, Moss 268, 274
Twomey, Seán 299

U

Ulster Volunteers 29

V

Valleymount 118, 153–155
Vesey, James/Jim 25, 292, 297,
   299, 316, 317, 323

W

Wales 118, 146
Wallace, Peter 307, 308
Walsh, Agnes 114, 116
Walsh, Joe 88, 100, 108, 126, 139,
   142, 166, 180, 194
Walsh, Michael 114
Walsh, Paddy 319, 323
Walsh, Richard 'Dick' 36, 38, 62,
   63, 111–115, 210–212, 265,
   267, 281, 283, 291, 332
Walsh, Seán 20

Walshe, John 115
Western Command FSA 66, 197,
   270, 330, 332
Western Command IRA 36, 66,
   264
West Mayo Brigade 20, 34, 35,
   37, 40, 62, 72, 73, 106, 110,
   118–120, 123, 194, 207, 209,
   252, 329–331
Westport 19, 21–25, 27, 31, 34,
   37–45, 48, 52–56, 58, 59, 61,
   62, 66, 67, 73, 74, 76–80, 83,
   86–88, 90, 96–101, 104–106,
   110–112, 115, 116, 118–129,
   131, 134–140, 142, 151, 152,
   156, 161, 163–165, 167–179,
   181, 182, 184–188, 190,
   192–196, 198, 206, 209, 216,
   217, 257, 270, 275, 286, 287,
   295, 298, 300, 321, 329–332
Westport Battalion 96, 97, 119–
   121, 123, 163, 172, 176, 331
Wexford 118, 155, 206, 207
Whelan, Mick 305
White, Paddy 159
White, Peter 300
White, William Eugene 22, 252
Wicklow 69, 118, 152–155, 268,
   273, 322
Wilson, Charles 306, 307
Wilson, William Harding 306
Wynne, Micky 140